THE FALL AND RISE OF

CAPTAIN ATOM

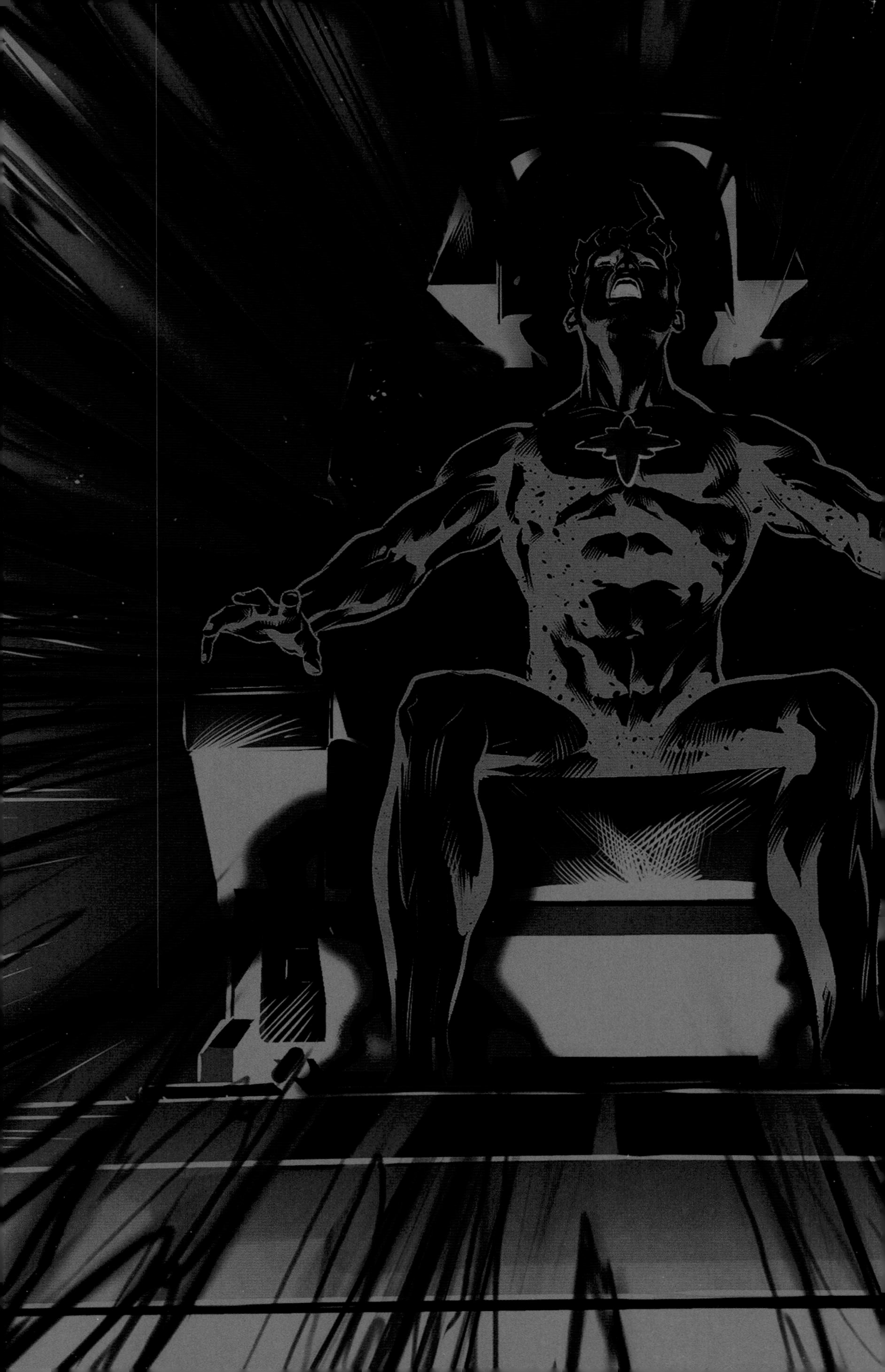

THE FALL AND RISE OF
CAPTAIN ATOM

CARY BATES   GREG WEISMAN WRITERS
WILL CONRAD ARTIST
IVAN NUNES COLORIST
SAIDA TEMOFONTE LETTERER
GABRIEL HARDMAN JORDAN BOYD COLLECTION COVER ARTISTS

KRISTY QUINN Editor – Original Series
JEB WOODARD Group Editor – Collected Editions
PAUL SANTOS Editor – Collected Edition
STEVE COOK Design Director – Books
LOUIS PRANDI Publication Design

BOB HARRAS Senior VP – Editor-in-Chief, DC Comics
PAT McCALLUM Executive Editor, DC Comics

DIANE NELSON President
DAN DiDIO Publisher
JIM LEE Publisher
GEOFF JOHNS President & Chief Creative Officer
AMIT DESAI Executive VP – Business & Marketing Strategy,
Direct to Consumer & Global Franchise Management
SAM ADES Senior VP & General Manager, Digital Services
BOBBIE CHASE VP & Executive Editor, Young Reader & Talent Development
MARK CHIARELLO Senior VP – Art, Design & Collected Editions
JOHN CUNNINGHAM Senior VP – Sales & Trade Marketing
ANNE DePIES Senior VP – Business Strategy, Finance & Administration
DON FALLETTI VP – Manufacturing Operations
LAWRENCE GANEM VP – Editorial Administration & Talent Relations
ALISON GILL Senior VP – Manufacturing & Operations
HANK KANALZ Senior VP – Editorial Strategy & Administration
JAY KOGAN VP – Legal Affairs
JACK MAHAN VP – Business Affairs
NICK J. NAPOLITANO VP – Manufacturing Administration
EDDIE SCANNELL VP – Consumer Marketing
COURTNEY SIMMONS Senior VP – Publicity & Communications
JIM (SKI) SOKOLOWSKI VP – Comic Book Specialty Sales & Trade Marketing
NANCY SPEARS VP – Mass, Book, Digital Sales & Trade Marketing
MICHELE R. WELLS VP – Content Strategy

CAPTAIN ATOM: THE FALL AND RISE OF CAPTAIN ATOM

DC Comics, 2900 West Alameda Ave., Burbank, CA 91505
Printed by Solisco Printers, Scott, QC, Canada. 12/1/17. First Printing.
ISBN: 978-1-4012-7417-7

Library of Congress Cataloging-in-Publication Data is available.

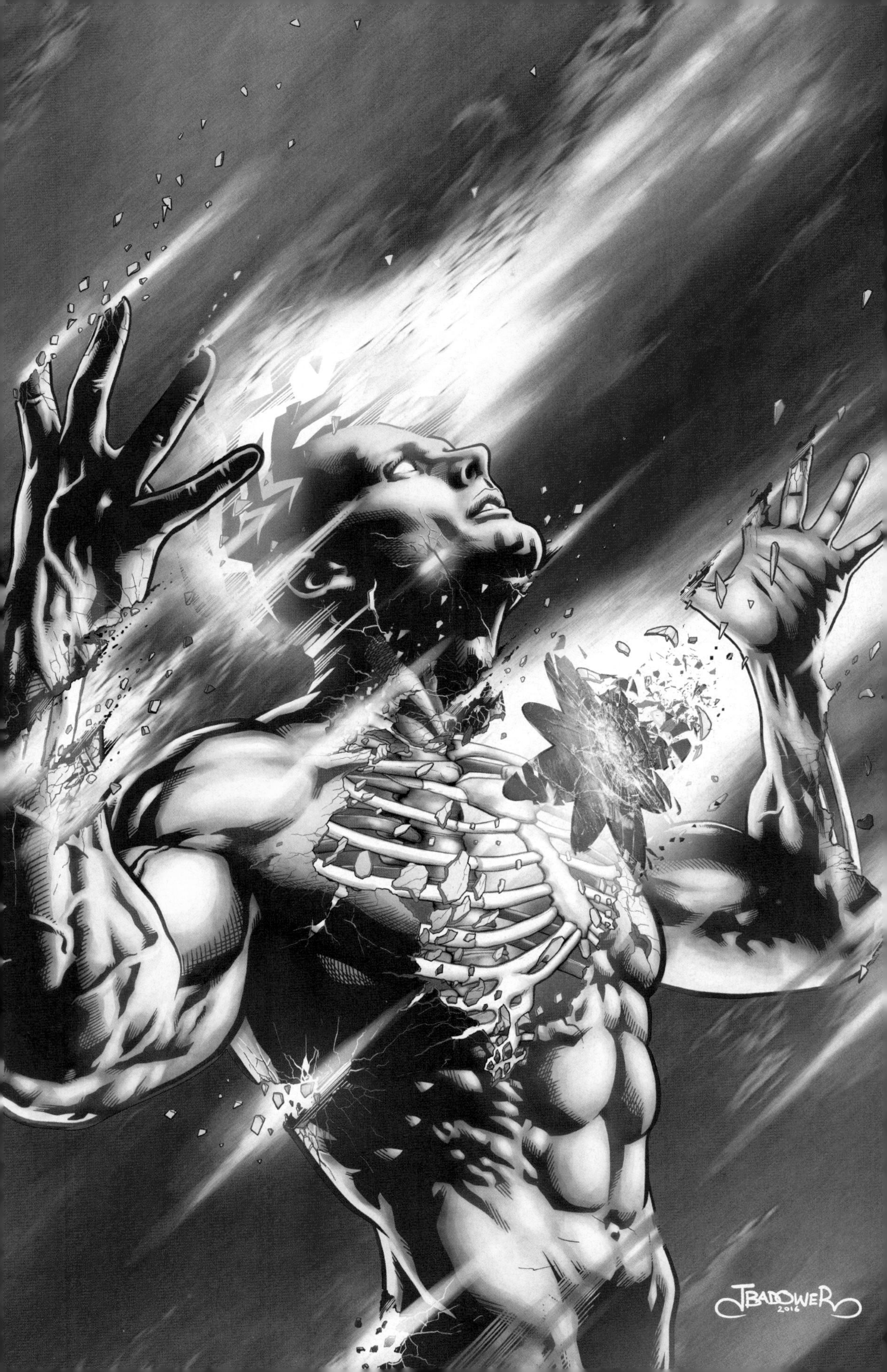
JBADOWER
2016

JASON BADOWER Cover Artist

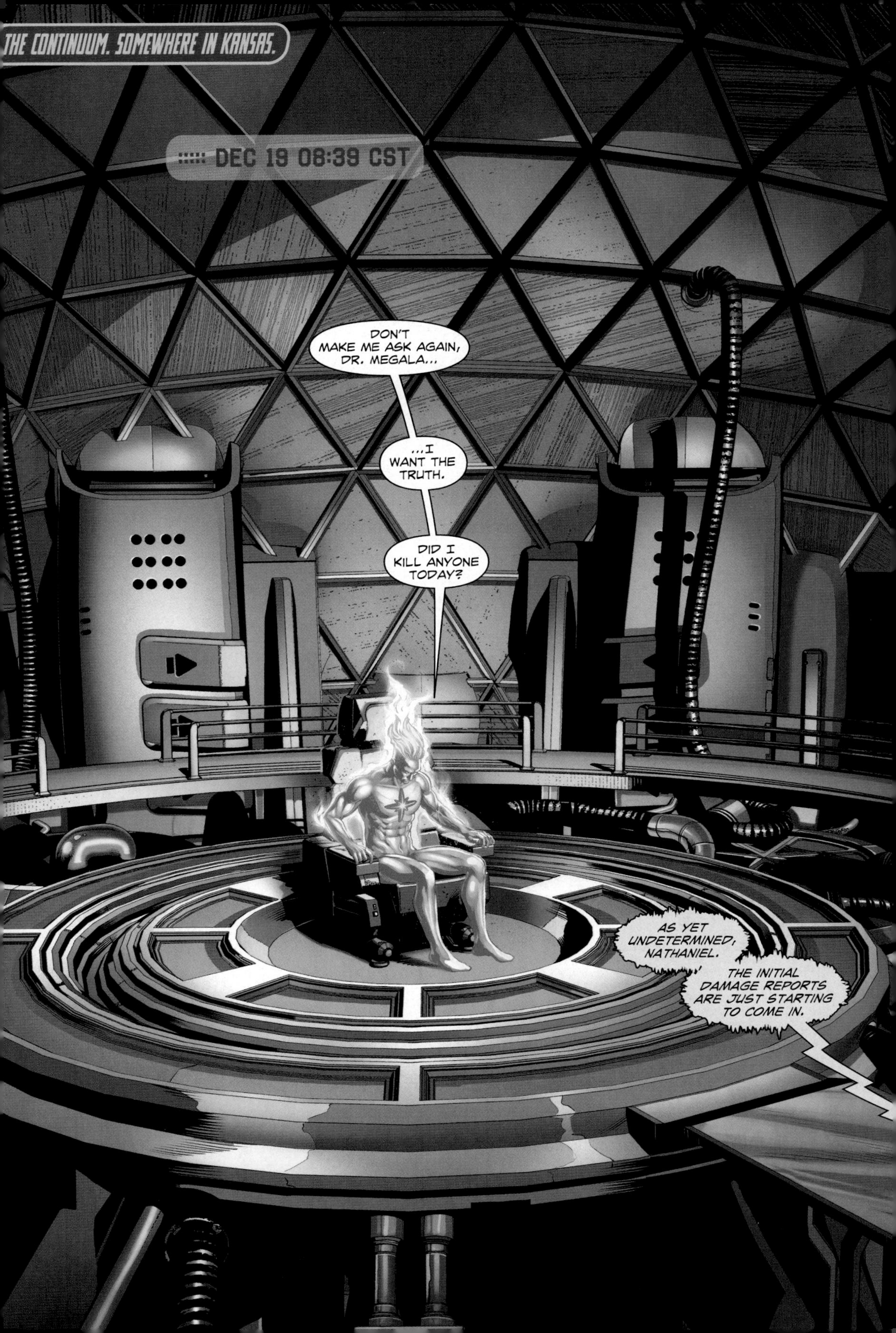

THE CONTINUUM. SOMEWHERE IN KANSAS.
DEC 19 08:39 CST
DON'T MAKE ME ASK AGAIN, DR. MEGALA...
...I WANT THE TRUTH.
DID I KILL ANYONE TODAY?
AS YET UNDETERMINED, NATHANIEL.
THE INITIAL DAMAGE REPORTS ARE JUST STARTING TO COME IN.

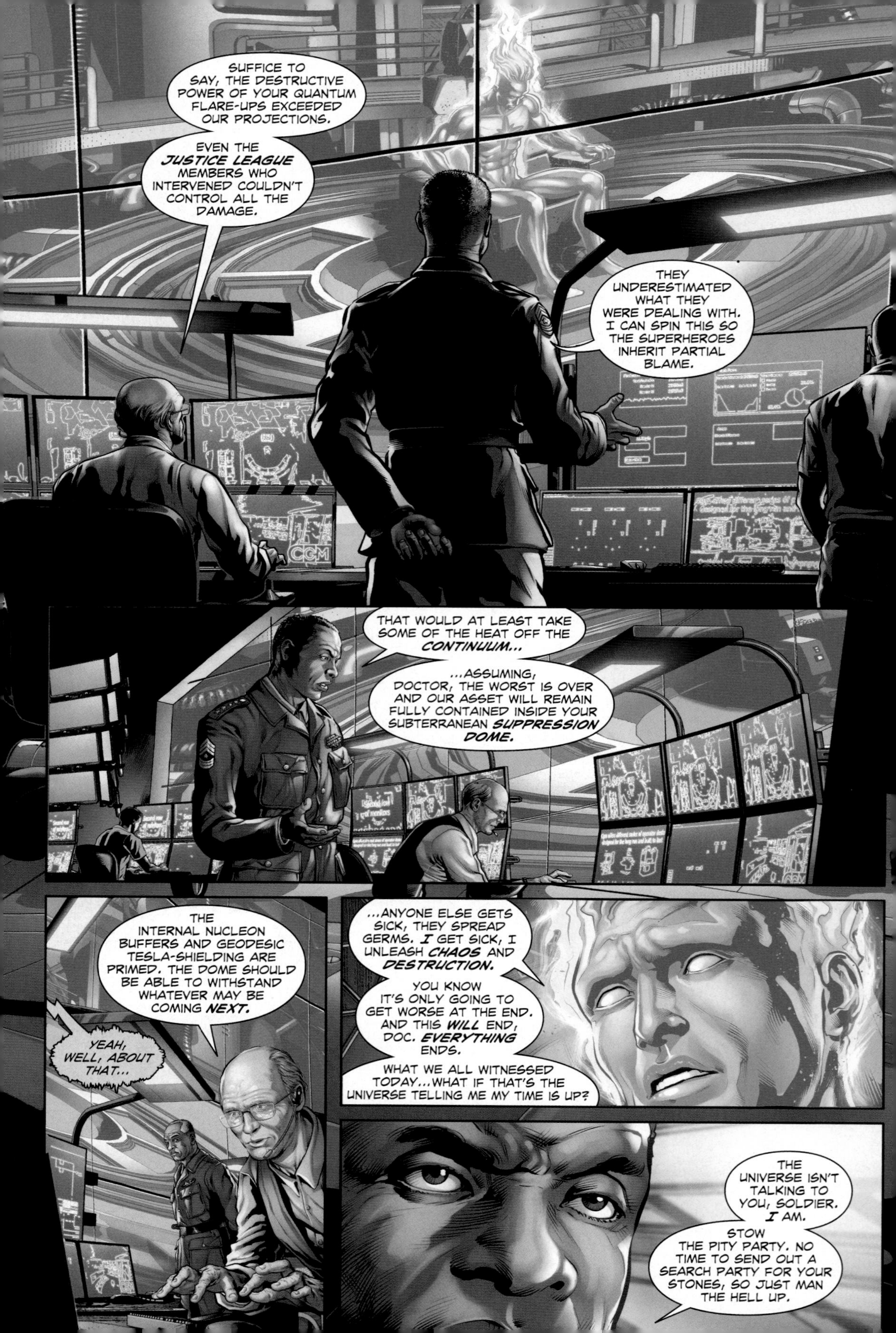
SUFFICE TO SAY, THE DESTRUCTIVE POWER OF YOUR QUANTUM FLARE-UPS EXCEEDED OUR PROJECTIONS.
EVEN THE JUSTICE LEAGUE MEMBERS WHO INTERVENED COULDN'T CONTROL ALL THE DAMAGE.
THEY UNDERESTIMATED WHAT THEY WERE DEALING WITH. I CAN SPIN THIS SO THE SUPERHEROES INHERIT PARTIAL BLAME.
THAT WOULD AT LEAST TAKE SOME OF THE HEAT OFF THE CONTINUUM...
...ASSUMING, DOCTOR, THE WORST IS OVER AND OUR ASSET WILL REMAIN FULLY CONTAINED INSIDE YOUR SUBTERRANEAN SUPPRESSION DOME.
THE INTERNAL NUCLEON BUFFERS AND GEODESIC TESLA-SHIELDING ARE PRIMED. THE DOME SHOULD BE ABLE TO WITHSTAND WHATEVER MAY BE COMING NEXT.
YEAH, WELL, ABOUT THAT...
...ANYONE ELSE GETS SICK, THEY SPREAD GERMS. I GET SICK, I UNLEASH CHAOS AND DESTRUCTION.
YOU KNOW IT'S ONLY GOING TO GET WORSE AT THE END. AND THIS WILL END, DOC. EVERYTHING ENDS.
WHAT WE ALL WITNESSED TODAY...WHAT IF THAT'S THE UNIVERSE TELLING ME MY TIME IS UP?
THE UNIVERSE ISN'T TALKING TO YOU, SOLDIER. I AM.
STOW THE PITY PARTY. NO TIME TO SEND OUT A SEARCH PARTY FOR YOUR STONES, SO JUST MAN THE HELL UP.

LET'S FACE IT. EVER SINCE MY ACCIDENT IN THE QUANTUM FIELD, I STOPPED BEING NATHANIEL ADAM.

CAPTAIN ATOM-- THAT'S JUST BEEN A CODENAME FOR AN ATOMIC FREAK SHOW.

A DISASTER WAITING TO HAPPEN.

I THOUGHT I COULD HOLD ONTO MY LAST SHREDS OF HUMANITY...BUT YOU KNEW BETTER, DOC. YOU KNEW SOONER OR LATER A DAY LIKE THIS WOULD COME...

A NUCLEAR MELTDOWN--*THAT*, I HAVE PROTOCOLS FOR. BUT A MELTDOWN LIKE THIS IS OUTSIDE MY WHEELHOUSE.

GIVEN THE TRAUMA OF TODAY'S EVENTS, IT MIGHT BE SOME FORM OF ACCELERATED PTSD.

...AND YET, NO MATTER HOW HOPELESS OR HOW BAD THINGS GOT, YOU WERE THERE FOR ME, DOC. YOU ALWAYS HAD MY BACK.

YOU, I AM GOING TO MISS.

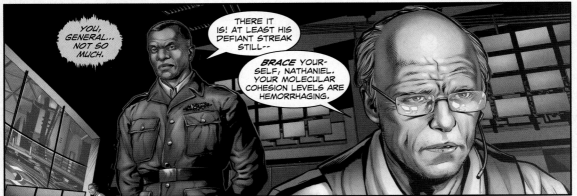

YOU, GENERAL... NOT SO MUCH.

THERE IT IS! AT LEAST HIS DEFIANT STREAK STILL--

BRACE YOUR-SELF, NATHANIEL. YOUR MOLECULAR COHESION LEVELS ARE HEMORRHAGING.

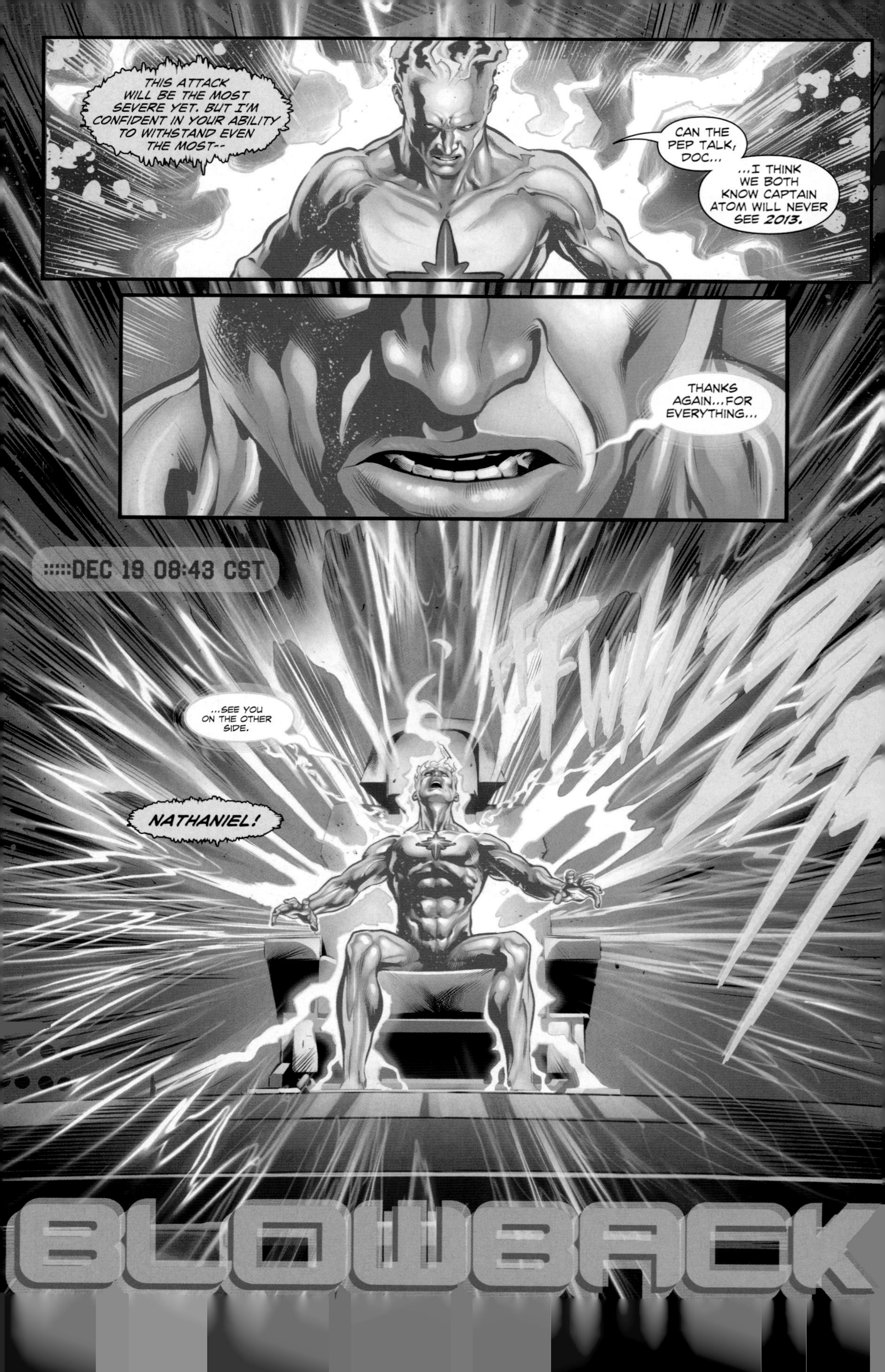
THIS ATTACK WILL BE THE MOST SEVERE YET. BUT I'M CONFIDENT IN YOUR ABILITY TO WITHSTAND EVEN THE MOST--
CAN THE PEP TALK, DOC...
...I THINK WE BOTH KNOW CAPTAIN ATOM WILL NEVER SEE 2013.
THANKS AGAIN...FOR EVERYTHING...
DEC 19 08:43 CST
FFWUZ
...SEE YOU ON THE OTHER SIDE.
NATHANIEL!
BLOWBACK

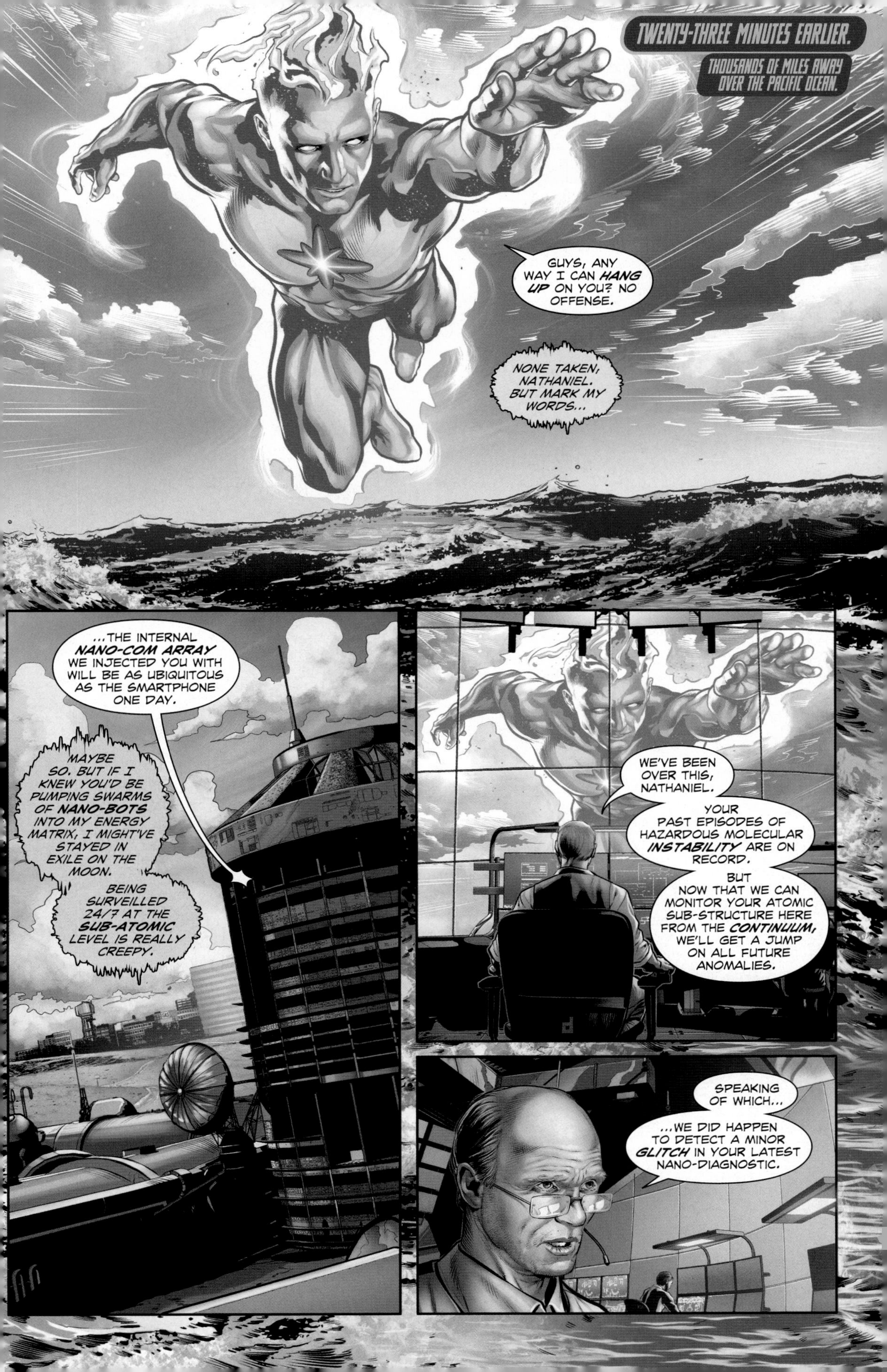
TWENTY-THREE MINUTES EARLIER.
THOUSANDS OF MILES AWAY OVER THE PACIFIC OCEAN.
GUYS, ANY WAY I CAN HANG UP ON YOU? NO OFFENSE.
NONE TAKEN, NATHANIEL. BUT MARK MY WORDS...
...THE INTERNAL NANO-COM ARRAY WE INJECTED YOU WITH WILL BE AS UBIQUITOUS AS THE SMARTPHONE ONE DAY.
MAYBE SO. BUT IF I KNEW YOU'D BE PUMPING SWARMS OF NANO-BOTS INTO MY ENERGY MATRIX, I MIGHT'VE STAYED IN EXILE ON THE MOON.
BEING SURVEILLED 24/7 AT THE SUB-ATOMIC LEVEL IS REALLY CREEPY.
WE'VE BEEN OVER THIS, NATHANIEL.
YOUR PAST EPISODES OF HAZARDOUS MOLECULAR INSTABILITY ARE ON RECORD.
BUT NOW THAT WE CAN MONITOR YOUR ATOMIC SUB-STRUCTURE HERE FROM THE CONTINUUM, WE'LL GET A JUMP ON ALL FUTURE ANOMALIES.
SPEAKING OF WHICH...
...WE DID HAPPEN TO DETECT A MINOR GLITCH IN YOUR LATEST NANO-DIAGNOSTIC.

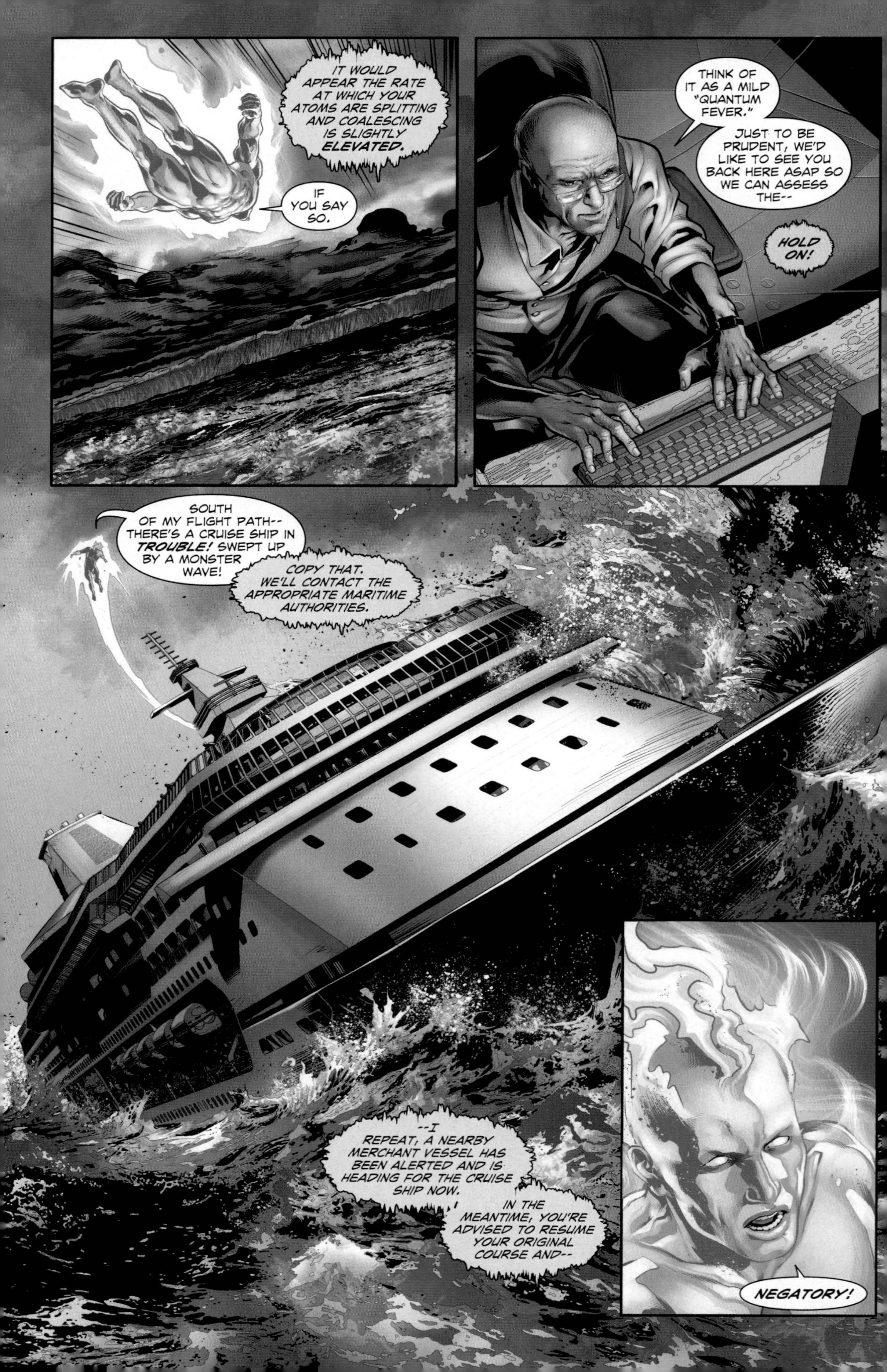
IT WOULD APPEAR THE RATE AT WHICH YOUR ATOMS ARE SPLITTING AND COALESCING IS SLIGHTLY ELEVATED.
IF YOU SAY SO.
THINK OF IT AS A MILD "QUANTUM FEVER."
JUST TO BE PRUDENT, WE'D LIKE TO SEE YOU BACK HERE ASAP SO WE CAN ASSESS THE--
HOLD ON!
SOUTH OF MY FLIGHT PATH--THERE'S A CRUISE SHIP IN TROUBLE! SWEPT UP BY A MONSTER WAVE!
COPY THAT. WE'LL CONTACT THE APPROPRIATE MARITIME AUTHORITIES.
--I REPEAT, A NEARBY MERCHANT VESSEL HAS BEEN ALERTED AND IS HEADING FOR THE CRUISE SHIP NOW.
IN THE MEANTIME, YOU'RE ADVISED TO RESUME YOUR ORIGINAL COURSE AND--
NEGATORY!

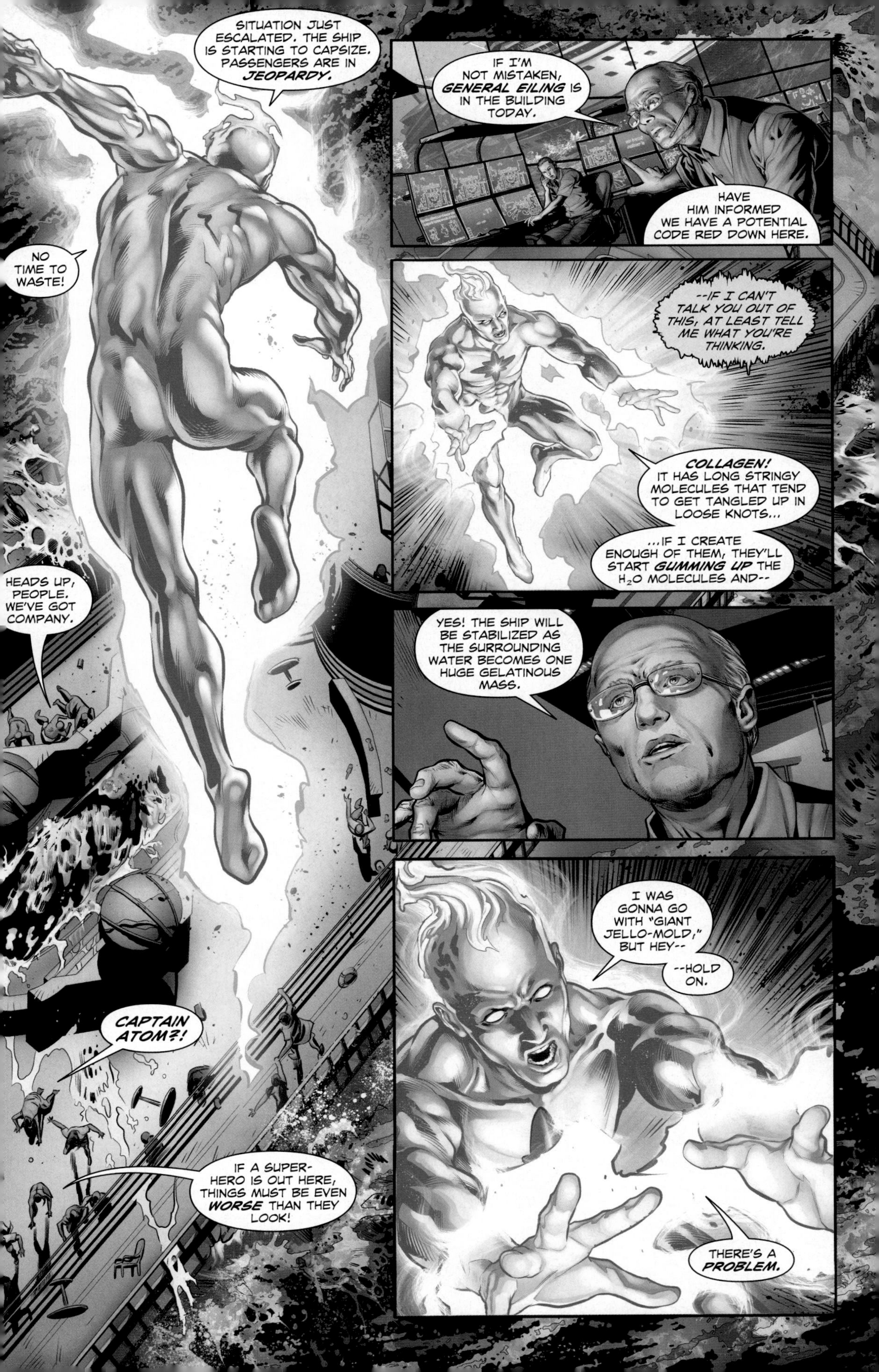
SITUATION JUST ESCALATED. THE SHIP IS STARTING TO CAPSIZE. PASSENGERS ARE IN JEOPARDY.
NO TIME TO WASTE!
IF I'M NOT MISTAKEN, GENERAL EILING IS IN THE BUILDING TODAY.
HAVE HIM INFORMED WE HAVE A POTENTIAL CODE RED DOWN HERE.
--IF I CAN'T TALK YOU OUT OF THIS, AT LEAST TELL ME WHAT YOU'RE THINKING.
COLLAGEN! IT HAS LONG STRINGY MOLECULES THAT TEND TO GET TANGLED UP IN LOOSE KNOTS...
...IF I CREATE ENOUGH OF THEM, THEY'LL START GUMMING UP THE H_2O MOLECULES AND--
HEADS UP, PEOPLE. WE'VE GOT COMPANY.
YES! THE SHIP WILL BE STABILIZED AS THE SURROUNDING WATER BECOMES ONE HUGE GELATINOUS MASS.
CAPTAIN ATOM?!
I WAS GONNA GO WITH "GIANT JELLO-MOLD," BUT HEY--
--HOLD ON.
IF A SUPER-HERO IS OUT HERE, THINGS MUST BE EVEN WORSE THAN THEY LOOK!
THERE'S A PROBLEM.

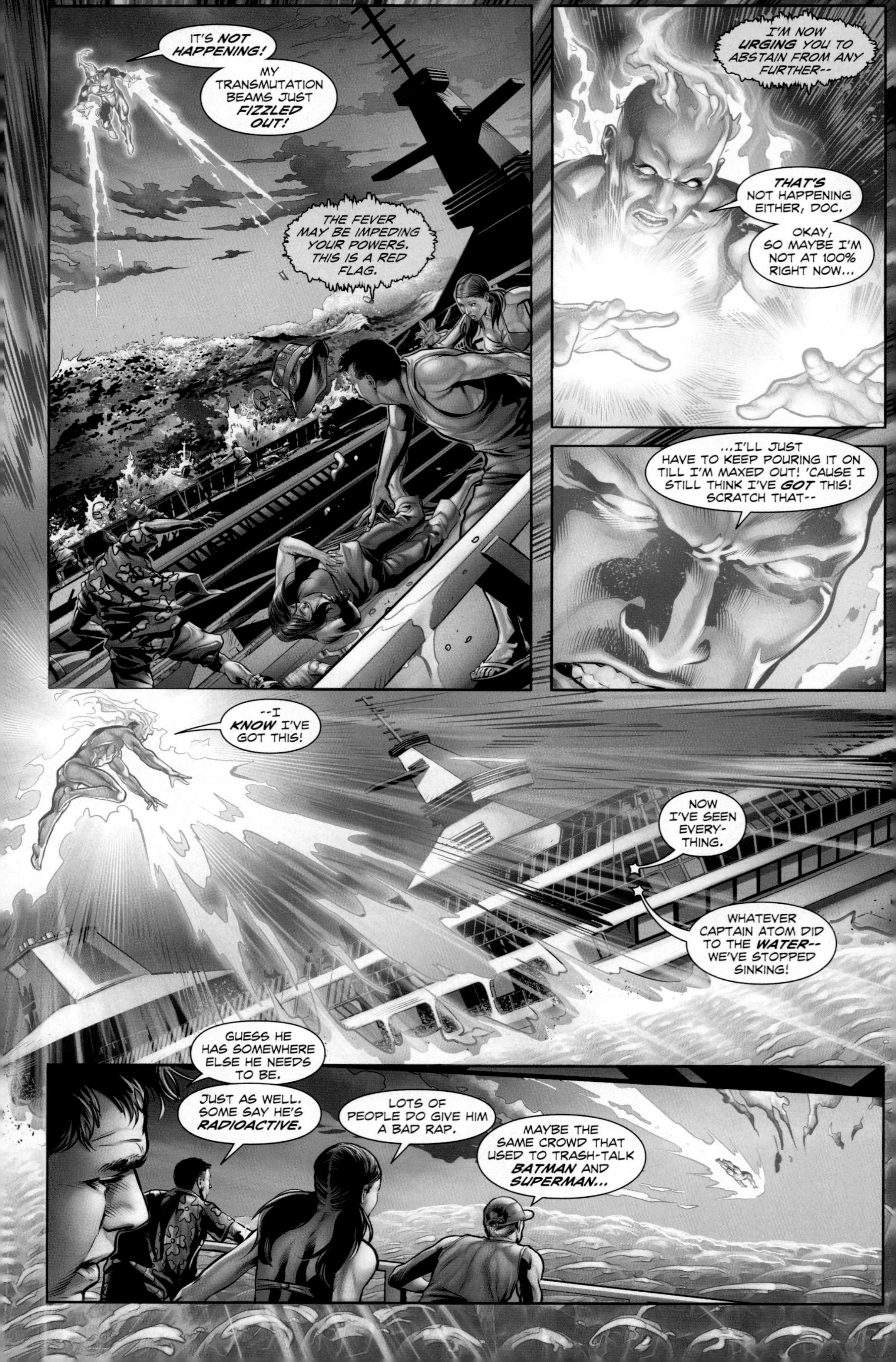
IT'S NOT HAPPENING!
MY TRANSMUTATION BEAMS JUST FIZZLED OUT!
THE FEVER MAY BE IMPEDING YOUR POWERS. THIS IS A RED FLAG.
I'M NOW URGING YOU TO ABSTAIN FROM ANY FURTHER--
THAT'S NOT HAPPENING EITHER, DOC.
OKAY, SO MAYBE I'M NOT AT 100% RIGHT NOW...
...I'LL JUST HAVE TO KEEP POURING IT ON TILL I'M MAXED OUT! 'CAUSE I STILL THINK I'VE GOT THIS! SCRATCH THAT--
--I KNOW I'VE GOT THIS!
NOW I'VE SEEN EVERY-THING.
WHATEVER CAPTAIN ATOM DID TO THE WATER-- WE'VE STOPPED SINKING!
GUESS HE HAS SOMEWHERE ELSE HE NEEDS TO BE.
JUST AS WELL. SOME SAY HE'S RADIOACTIVE.
LOTS OF PEOPLE DO GIVE HIM A BAD RAP.
MAYBE THE SAME CROWD THAT USED TO TRASH-TALK BATMAN AND SUPERMAN...

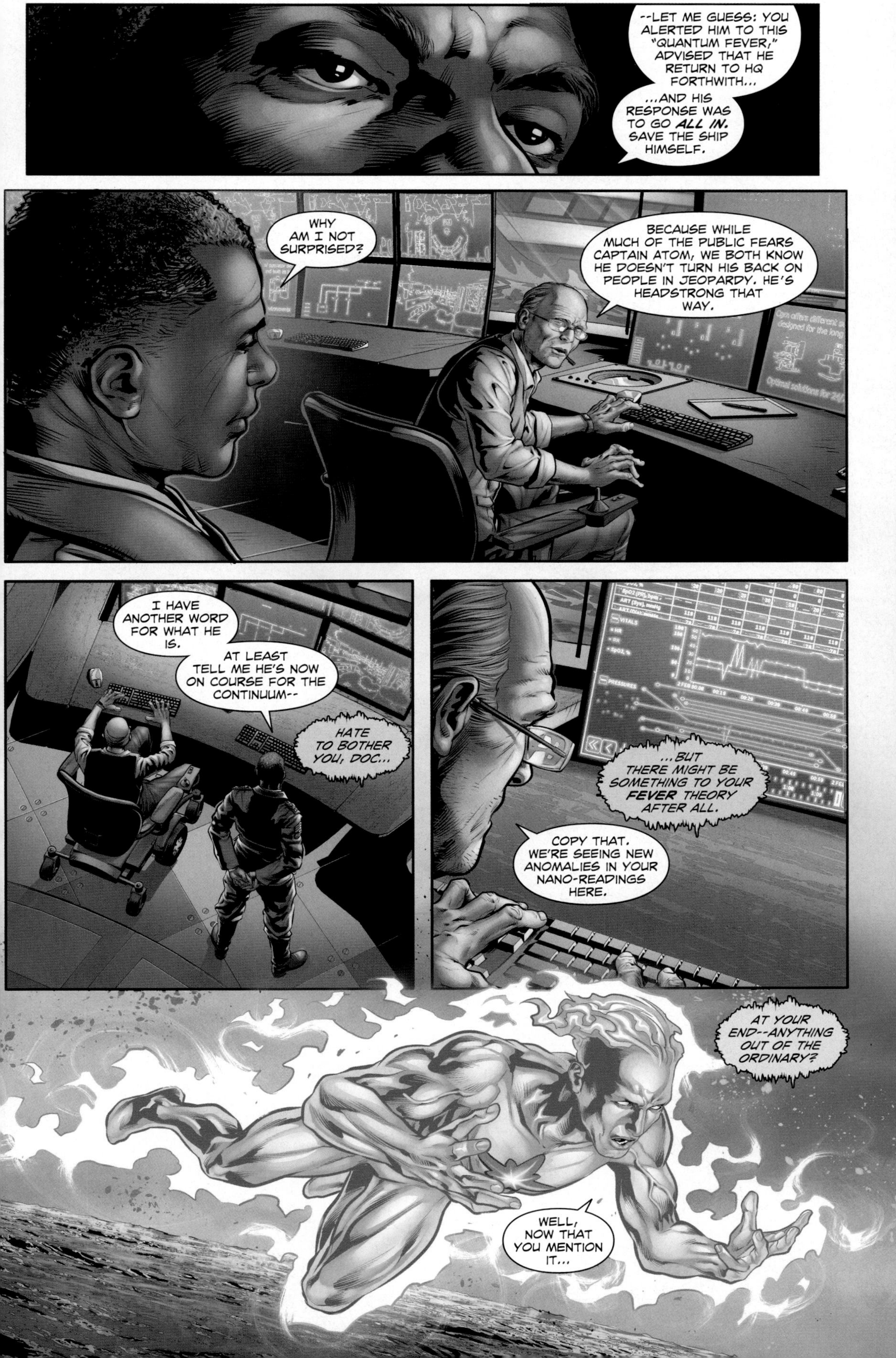

--LET ME GUESS: YOU ALERTED HIM TO THIS "QUANTUM FEVER," ADVISED THAT HE RETURN TO HQ FORTHWITH...
...AND HIS RESPONSE WAS TO GO ALL IN. SAVE THE SHIP HIMSELF.
WHY AM I NOT SURPRISED?
BECAUSE WHILE MUCH OF THE PUBLIC FEARS CAPTAIN ATOM, WE BOTH KNOW HE DOESN'T TURN HIS BACK ON PEOPLE IN JEOPARDY. HE'S HEADSTRONG THAT WAY.
I HAVE ANOTHER WORD FOR WHAT HE IS.
AT LEAST TELL ME HE'S NOW ON COURSE FOR THE CONTINUUM--
HATE TO BOTHER YOU, DOC...
...BUT THERE MIGHT BE SOMETHING TO YOUR FEVER THEORY AFTER ALL.
COPY THAT. WE'RE SEEING NEW ANOMALIES IN YOUR NANO-READINGS HERE.
AT YOUR END--ANYTHING OUT OF THE ORDINARY?
WELL, NOW THAT YOU MENTION IT...

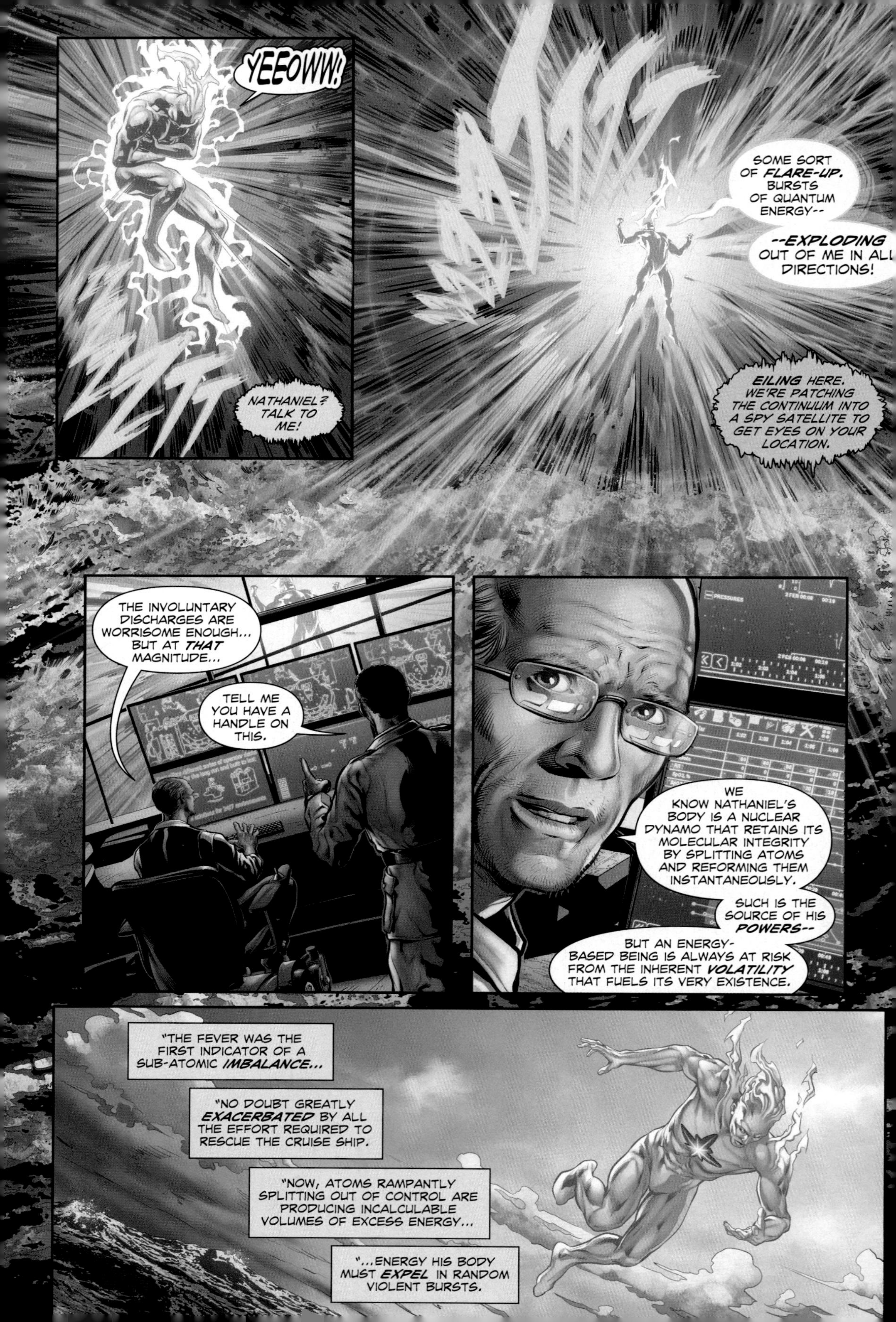
YEEOWW!
NATHANIEL? TALK TO ME!
SOME SORT OF FLARE-UP. BURSTS OF QUANTUM ENERGY--
--EXPLODING OUT OF ME IN ALL DIRECTIONS!
EILING HERE. WE'RE PATCHING THE CONTINUUM INTO A SPY SATELLITE TO GET EYES ON YOUR LOCATION.
THE INVOLUNTARY DISCHARGES ARE WORRISOME ENOUGH... BUT AT THAT MAGNITUDE...
TELL ME YOU HAVE A HANDLE ON THIS.
WE KNOW NATHANIEL'S BODY IS A NUCLEAR DYNAMO THAT RETAINS ITS MOLECULAR INTEGRITY BY SPLITTING ATOMS AND REFORMING THEM INSTANTANEOUSLY.
SUCH IS THE SOURCE OF HIS POWERS--
BUT AN ENERGY-BASED BEING IS ALWAYS AT RISK FROM THE INHERENT VOLATILITY THAT FUELS ITS VERY EXISTENCE.
"THE FEVER WAS THE FIRST INDICATOR OF A SUB-ATOMIC IMBALANCE...
"NO DOUBT GREATLY EXACERBATED BY ALL THE EFFORT REQUIRED TO RESCUE THE CRUISE SHIP.
"NOW, ATOMS RAMPANTLY SPLITTING OUT OF CONTROL ARE PRODUCING INCALCULABLE VOLUMES OF EXCESS ENERGY...
"...ENERGY HIS BODY MUST EXPEL IN RANDOM VIOLENT BURSTS.

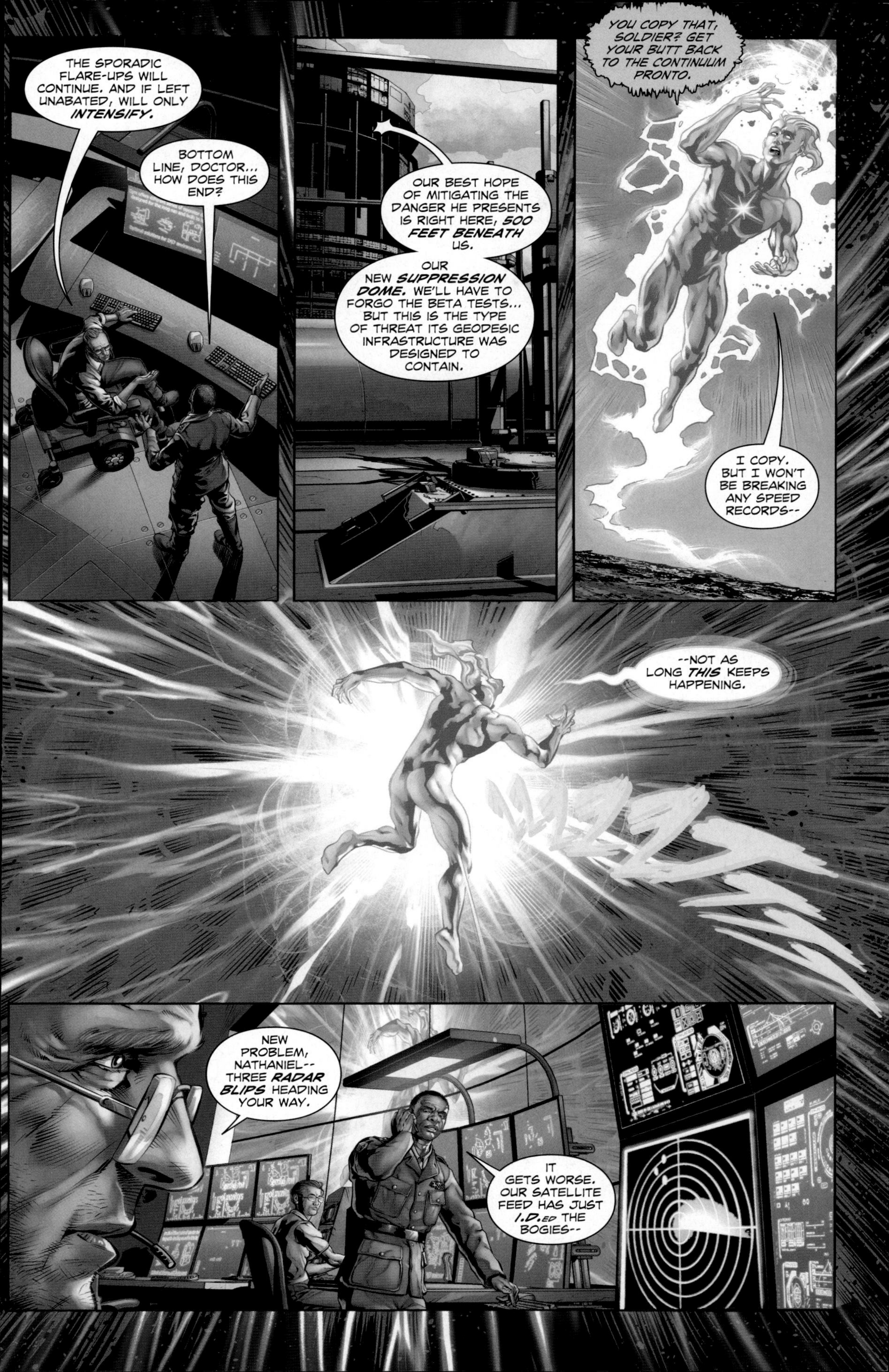
THE SPORADIC FLARE-UPS WILL CONTINUE. AND IF LEFT UNABATED, WILL ONLY INTENSIFY.
BOTTOM LINE, DOCTOR... HOW DOES THIS END?
OUR BEST HOPE OF MITIGATING THE DANGER HE PRESENTS IS RIGHT HERE, 500 FEET BENEATH US.
OUR NEW SUPPRESSION DOME. WE'LL HAVE TO FORGO THE BETA TESTS... BUT THIS IS THE TYPE OF THREAT ITS GEODESIC INFRASTRUCTURE WAS DESIGNED TO CONTAIN.
YOU COPY THAT, SOLDIER? GET YOUR BUTT BACK TO THE CONTINUUM PRONTO.
I COPY. BUT I WON'T BE BREAKING ANY SPEED RECORDS--
--NOT AS LONG THIS KEEPS HAPPENING.
NEW PROBLEM, NATHANIEL-- THREE RADAR BLIPS HEADING YOUR WAY.
IT GETS WORSE. OUR SATELLITE FEED HAS JUST I.D.ED THE BOGIES--

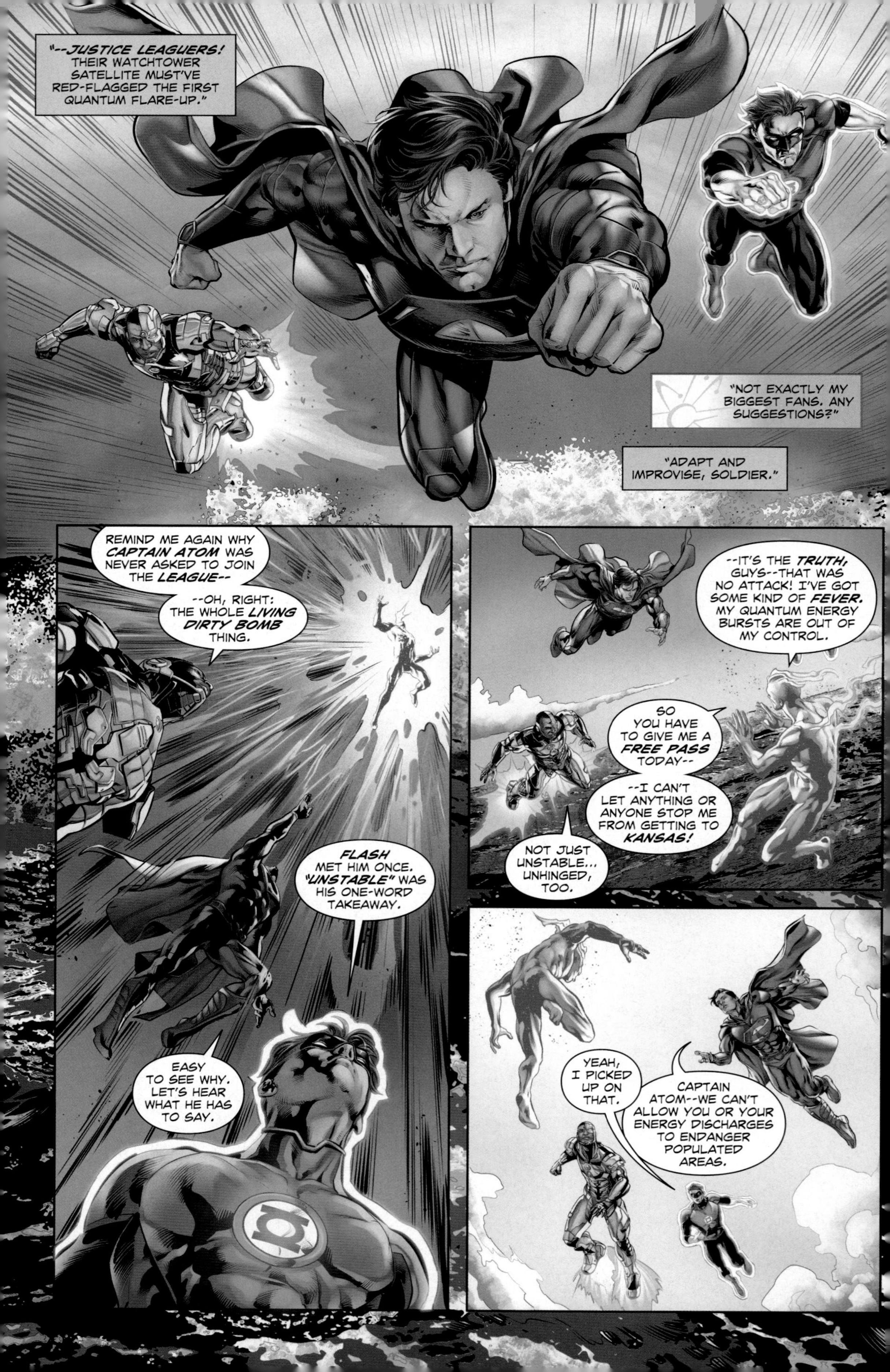
"--JUSTICE LEAGUERS! THEIR WATCHTOWER SATELLITE MUST'VE RED-FLAGGED THE FIRST QUANTUM FLARE-UP."
"NOT EXACTLY MY BIGGEST FANS. ANY SUGGESTIONS?"
"ADAPT AND IMPROVISE, SOLDIER."
REMIND ME AGAIN WHY CAPTAIN ATOM WAS NEVER ASKED TO JOIN THE LEAGUE--
--OH, RIGHT: THE WHOLE LIVING DIRTY BOMB THING.
FLASH MET HIM ONCE. "UNSTABLE" WAS HIS ONE-WORD TAKEAWAY.
EASY TO SEE WHY. LET'S HEAR WHAT HE HAS TO SAY.
--IT'S THE TRUTH, GUYS--THAT WAS NO ATTACK! I'VE GOT SOME KIND OF FEVER. MY QUANTUM ENERGY BURSTS ARE OUT OF MY CONTROL.
SO YOU HAVE TO GIVE ME A FREE PASS TODAY--
--I CAN'T LET ANYTHING OR ANYONE STOP ME FROM GETTING TO KANSAS!
NOT JUST UNSTABLE... UNHINGED, TOO.
CAPTAIN ATOM--WE CAN'T ALLOW YOU OR YOUR ENERGY DISCHARGES TO ENDANGER POPULATED AREAS.
YEAH, I PICKED UP ON THAT.

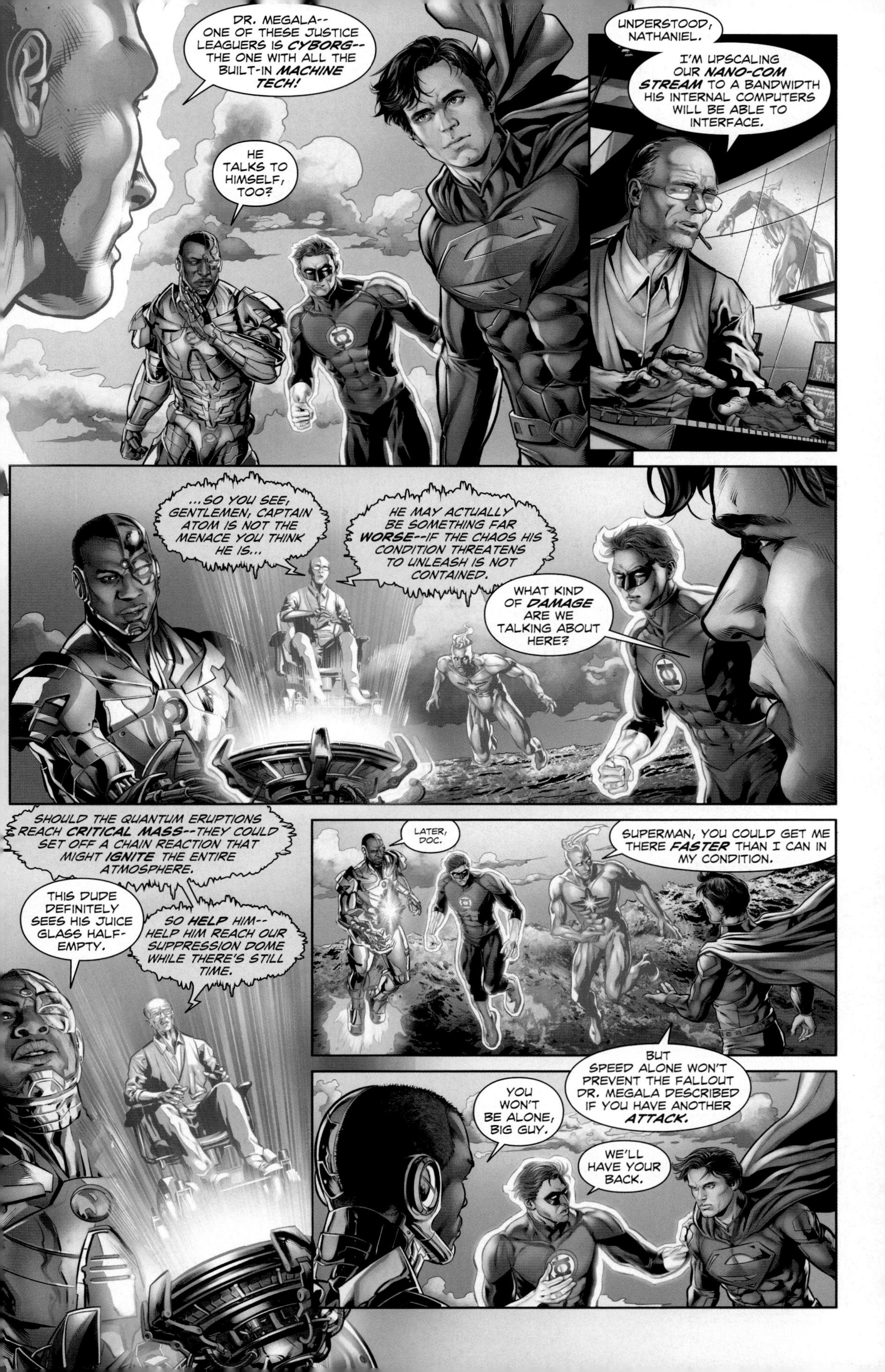
DR. MEGALA-- ONE OF THESE JUSTICE LEAGUERS IS CYBORG-- THE ONE WITH ALL THE BUILT-IN MACHINE TECH!
HE TALKS TO HIMSELF, TOO?
UNDERSTOOD, NATHANIEL.
I'M UPSCALING OUR NANO-COM STREAM TO A BANDWIDTH HIS INTERNAL COMPUTERS WILL BE ABLE TO INTERFACE.
...SO YOU SEE, GENTLEMEN, CAPTAIN ATOM IS NOT THE MENACE YOU THINK HE IS...
HE MAY ACTUALLY BE SOMETHING FAR WORSE--IF THE CHAOS HIS CONDITION THREATENS TO UNLEASH IS NOT CONTAINED.
WHAT KIND OF DAMAGE ARE WE TALKING ABOUT HERE?
SHOULD THE QUANTUM ERUPTIONS REACH CRITICAL MASS--THEY COULD SET OFF A CHAIN REACTION THAT MIGHT IGNITE THE ENTIRE ATMOSPHERE.
THIS DUDE DEFINITELY SEES HIS JUICE GLASS HALF-EMPTY.
SO HELP HIM-- HELP HIM REACH OUR SUPPRESSION DOME WHILE THERE'S STILL TIME.
LATER, DOC.
SUPERMAN, YOU COULD GET ME THERE FASTER THAN I CAN IN MY CONDITION.
BUT SPEED ALONE WON'T PREVENT THE FALLOUT DR. MEGALA DESCRIBED IF YOU HAVE ANOTHER ATTACK.
YOU WON'T BE ALONE, BIG GUY.
WE'LL HAVE YOUR BACK.

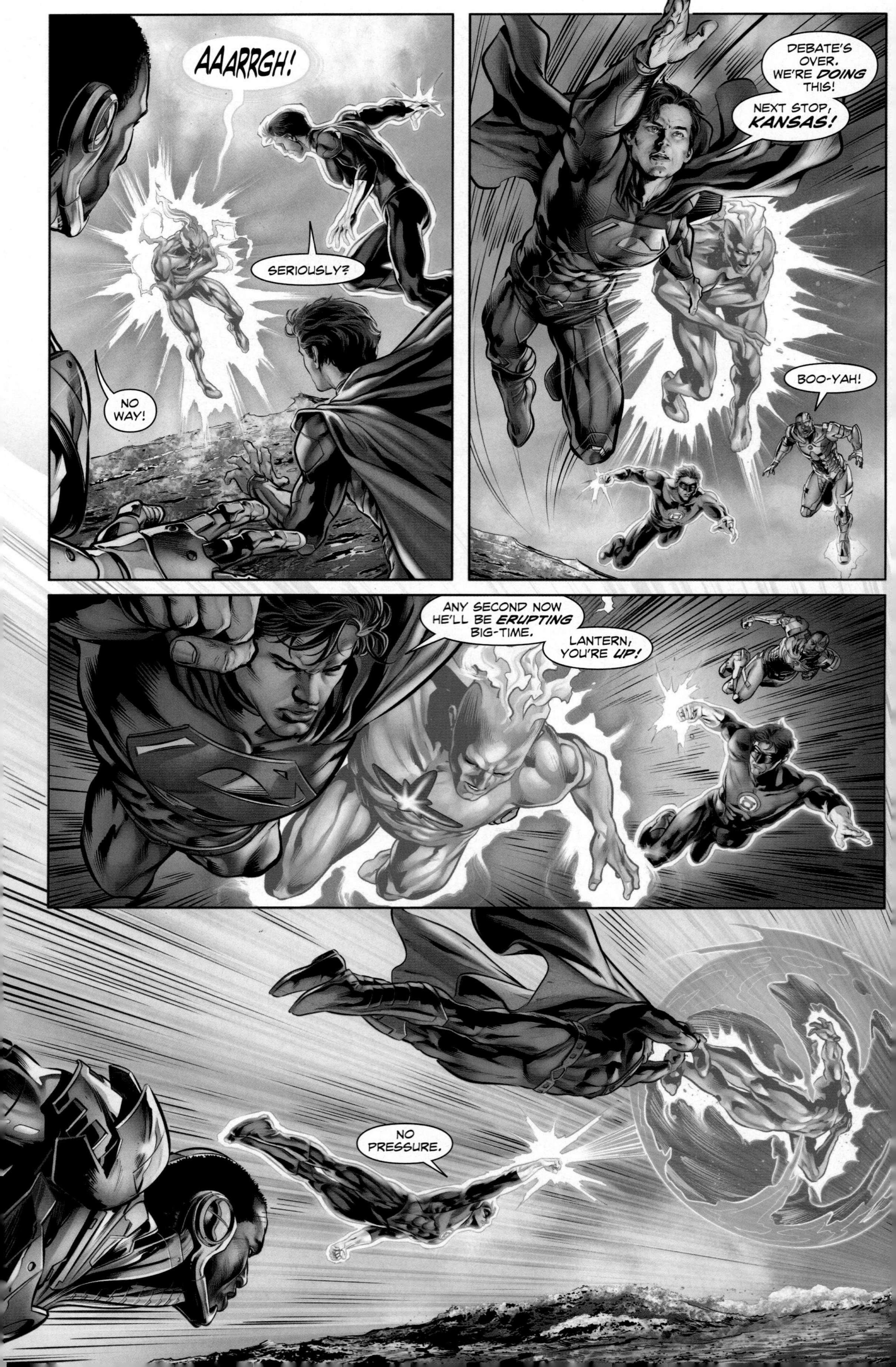
AAARRGH!
SERIOUSLY?
NO WAY!
DEBATE'S OVER. WE'RE DOING THIS!
NEXT STOP, KANSAS!
BOO-YAH!
ANY SECOND NOW HE'LL BE ERUPTING BIG-TIME.
LANTERN, YOU'RE UP!
NO PRESSURE.

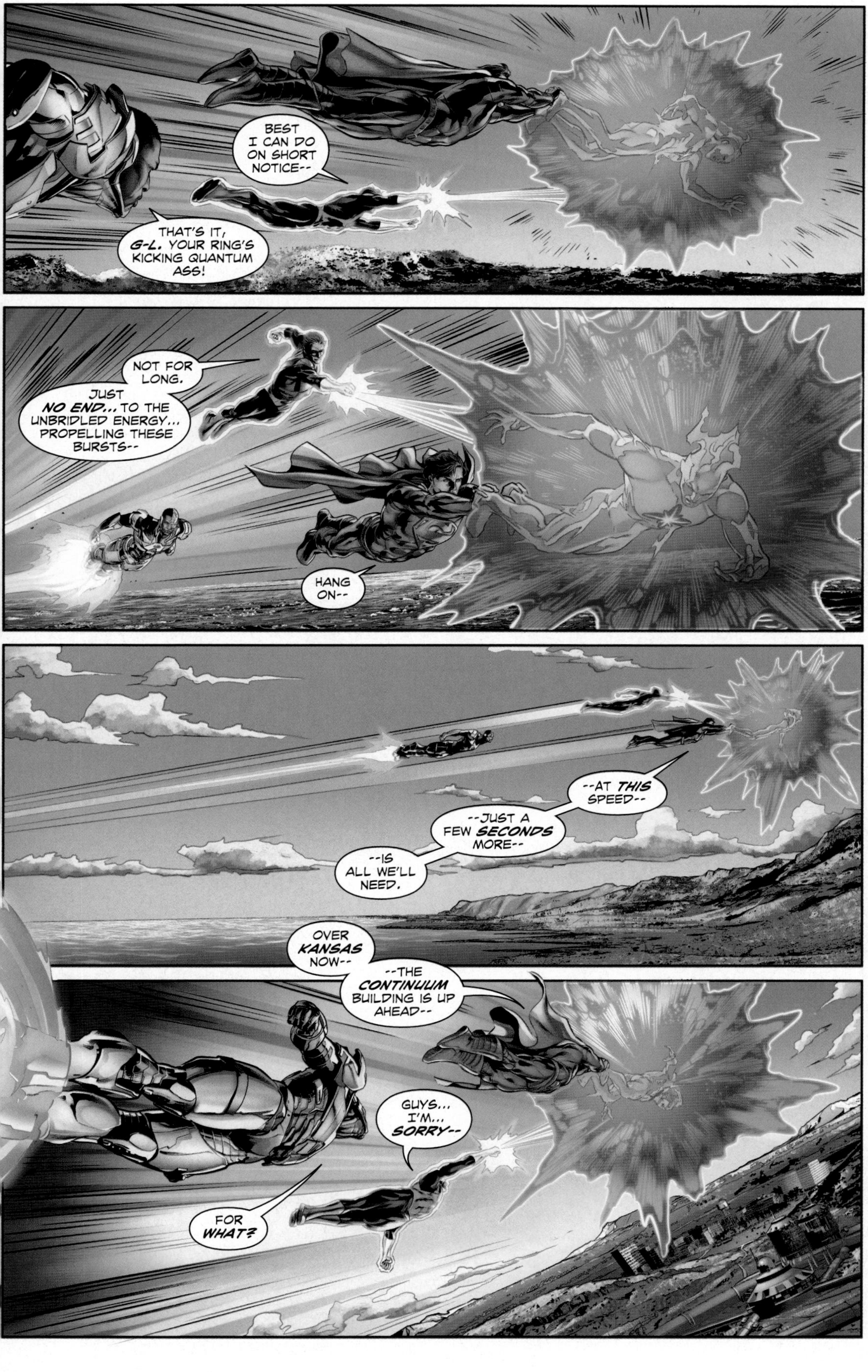
BEST I CAN DO ON SHORT NOTICE--
THAT'S IT, G-L. YOUR RING'S KICKING QUANTUM ASS!
NOT FOR LONG.
JUST NO END... TO THE UNBRIDLED ENERGY... PROPELLING THESE BURSTS--
HANG ON--
--AT THIS SPEED--
--JUST A FEW SECONDS MORE--
--IS ALL WE'LL NEED.
OVER KANSAS NOW--
--THE CONTINUUM BUILDING IS UP AHEAD--
GUYS... I'M... SORRY--
FOR WHAT?

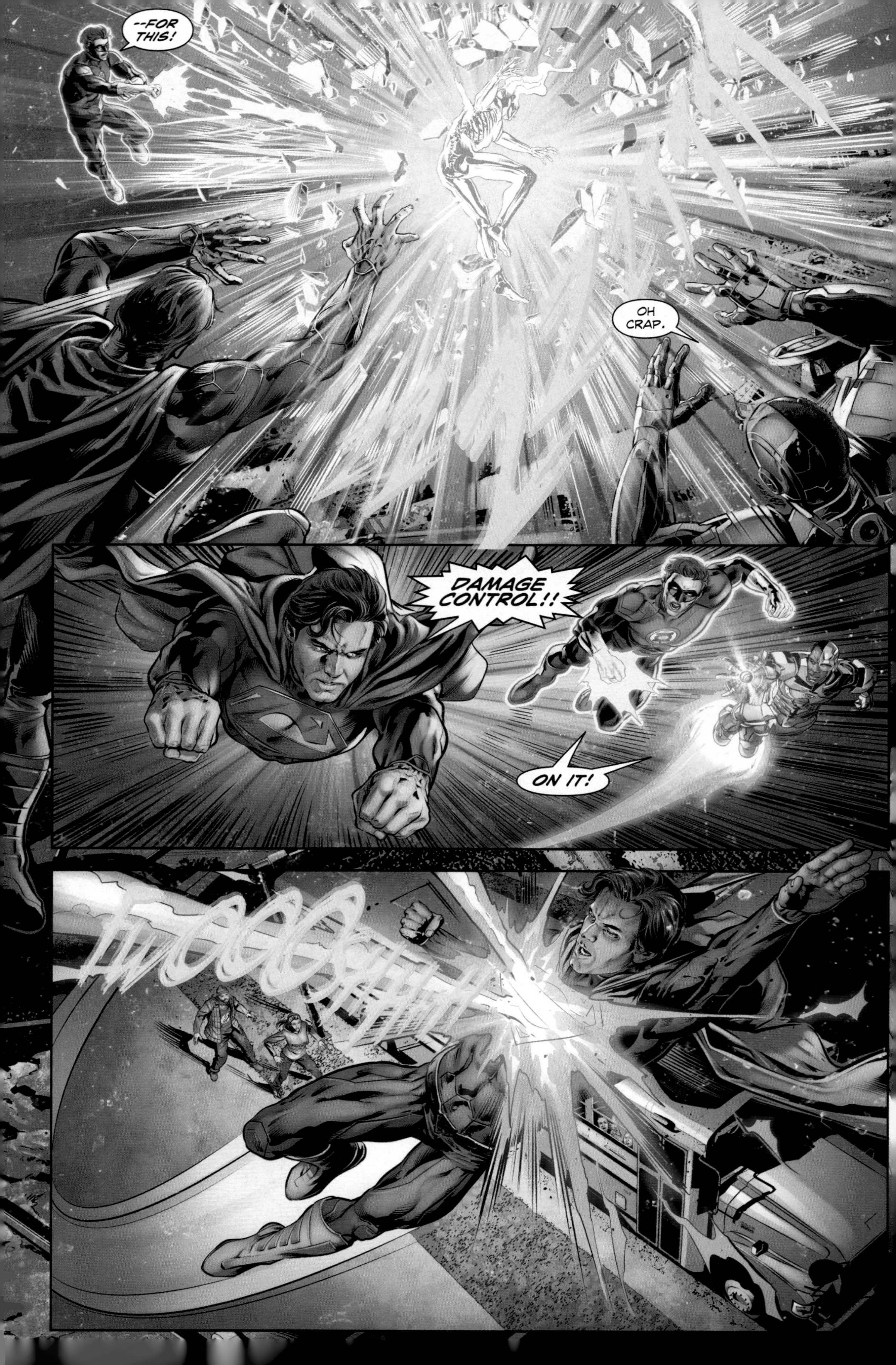
--FOR THIS!
OH CRAP.
DAMAGE CONTROL!!
ON IT!

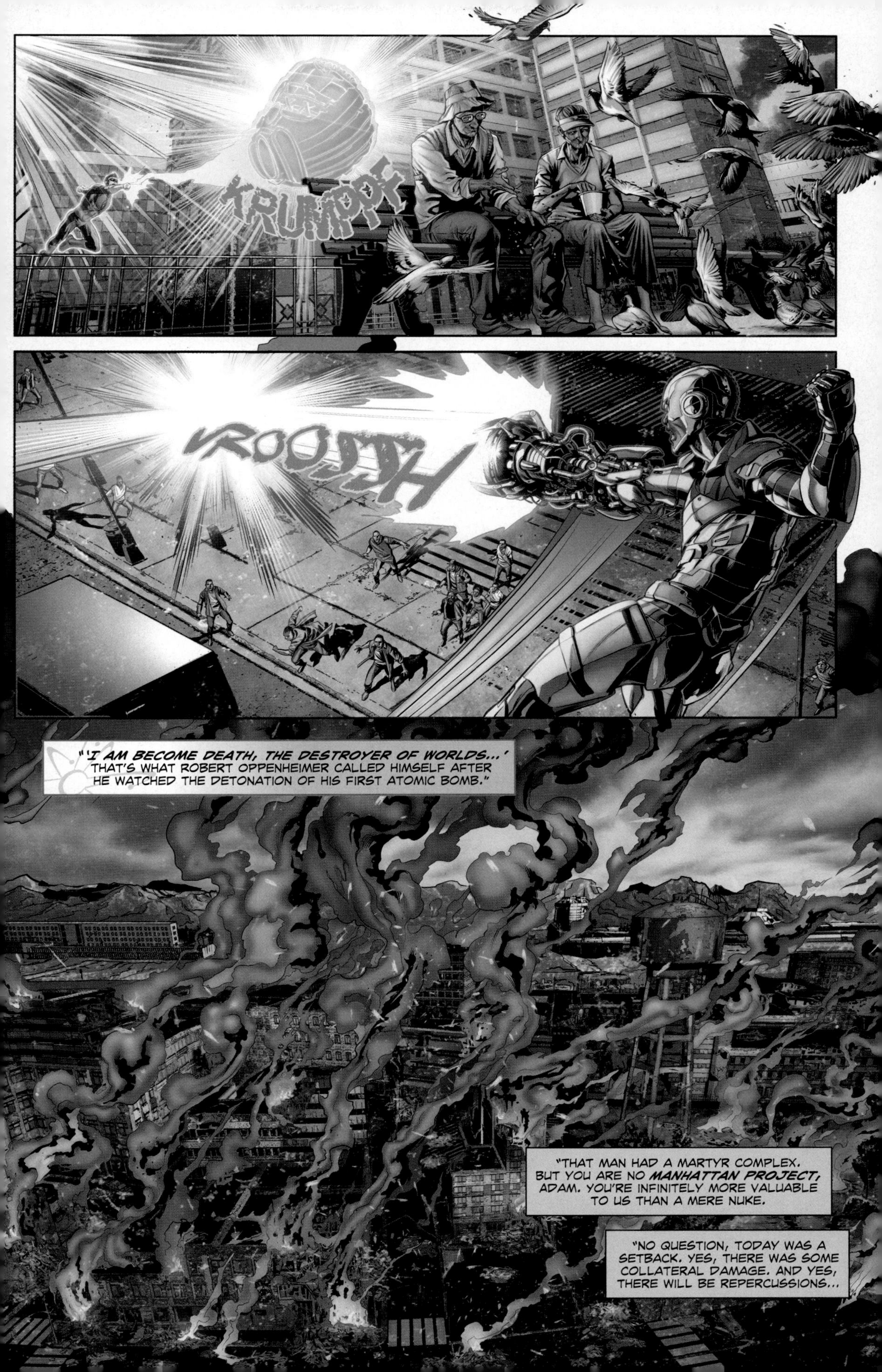
KRUMPF
VROOSH
"'I AM BECOME DEATH, THE DESTROYER OF WORLDS...' THAT'S WHAT ROBERT OPPENHEIMER CALLED HIMSELF AFTER HE WATCHED THE DETONATION OF HIS FIRST ATOMIC BOMB."
"THAT MAN HAD A MARTYR COMPLEX. BUT YOU ARE NO MANHATTAN PROJECT, ADAM. YOU'RE INFINITELY MORE VALUABLE TO US THAN A MERE NUKE.
"NO QUESTION, TODAY WAS A SETBACK. YES, THERE WAS SOME COLLATERAL DAMAGE. AND YES, THERE WILL BE REPERCUSSIONS...

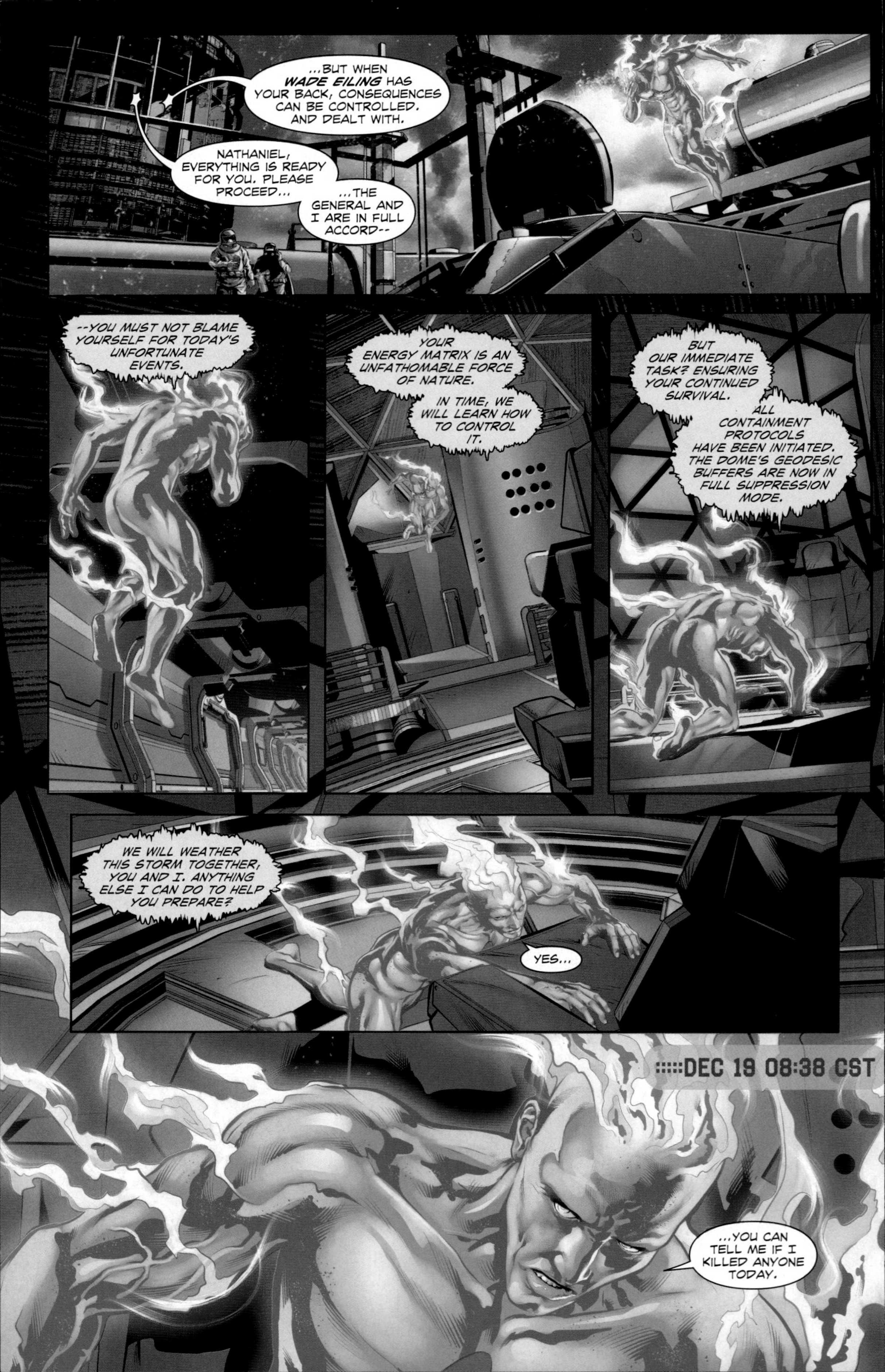
...BUT WHEN WADE EILING HAS YOUR BACK, CONSEQUENCES CAN BE CONTROLLED. AND DEALT WITH.
NATHANIEL, EVERYTHING IS READY FOR YOU. PLEASE PROCEED...
...THE GENERAL AND I ARE IN FULL ACCORD--
--YOU MUST NOT BLAME YOURSELF FOR TODAY'S UNFORTUNATE EVENTS.
YOUR ENERGY MATRIX IS AN UNFATHOMABLE FORCE OF NATURE.
IN TIME, WE WILL LEARN HOW TO CONTROL IT.
BUT OUR IMMEDIATE TASK? ENSURING YOUR CONTINUED SURVIVAL.
ALL CONTAINMENT PROTOCOLS HAVE BEEN INITIATED. THE DOME'S GEODESIC BUFFERS ARE NOW IN FULL SUPPRESSION MODE.
WE WILL WEATHER THIS STORM TOGETHER, YOU AND I. ANYTHING ELSE I CAN DO TO HELP YOU PREPARE?
YES...
DEC 19 08:38 CST
...YOU CAN TELL ME IF I KILLED ANYONE TODAY.

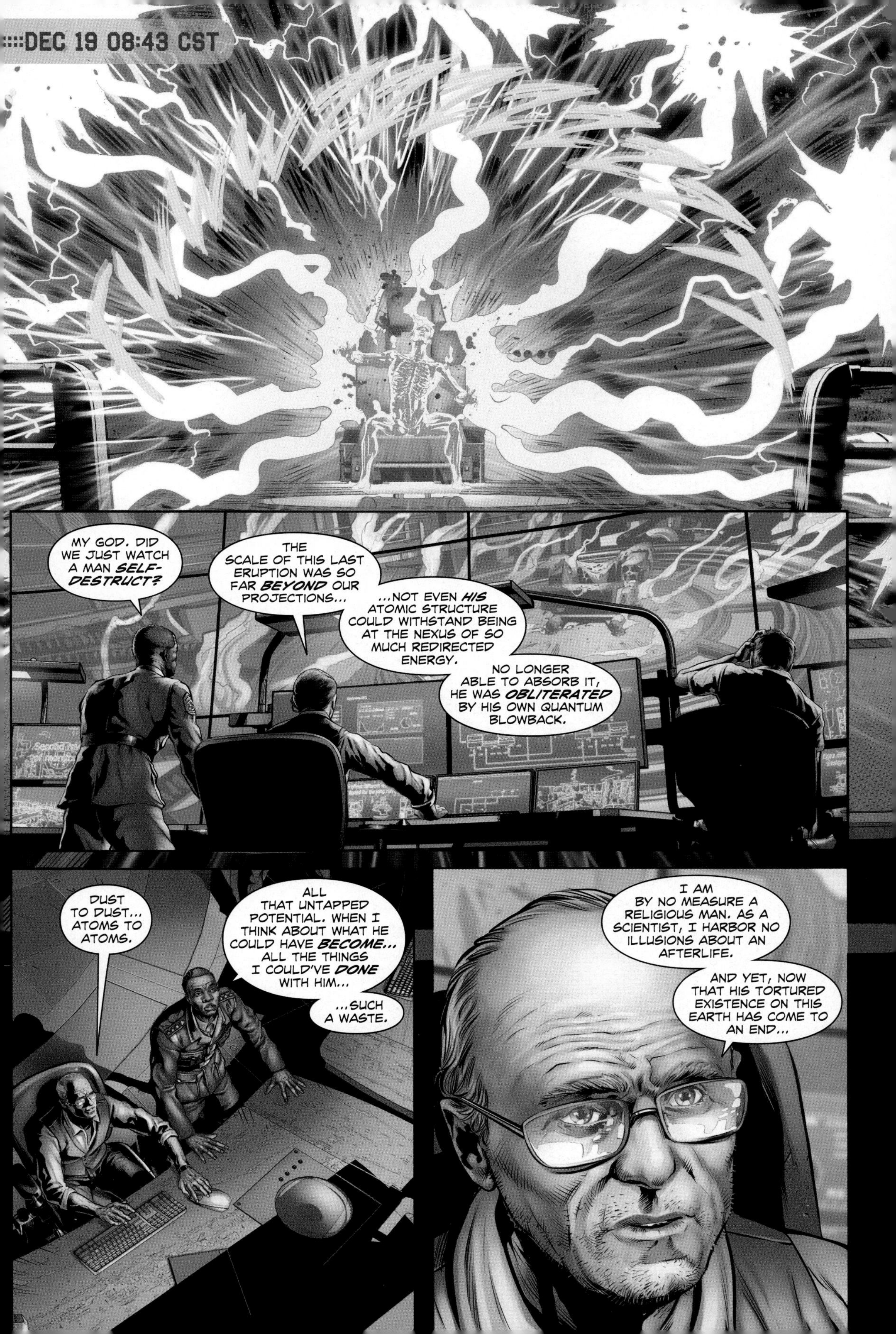

DEC 19 08:43 CST
MY GOD. DID WE JUST WATCH A MAN SELF-DESTRUCT?
THE SCALE OF THIS LAST ERUPTION WAS SO FAR BEYOND OUR PROJECTIONS...
...NOT EVEN HIS ATOMIC STRUCTURE COULD WITHSTAND BEING AT THE NEXUS OF SO MUCH REDIRECTED ENERGY.
NO LONGER ABLE TO ABSORB IT, HE WAS OBLITERATED BY HIS OWN QUANTUM BLOWBACK.
DUST TO DUST... ATOMS TO ATOMS.
ALL THAT UNTAPPED POTENTIAL. WHEN I THINK ABOUT WHAT HE COULD HAVE BECOME... ALL THE THINGS I COULD'VE DONE WITH HIM...
...SUCH A WASTE.
I AM BY NO MEASURE A RELIGIOUS MAN. AS A SCIENTIST, I HARBOR NO ILLUSIONS ABOUT AN AFTERLIFE.
AND YET, NOW THAT HIS TORTURED EXISTENCE ON THIS EARTH HAS COME TO AN END...

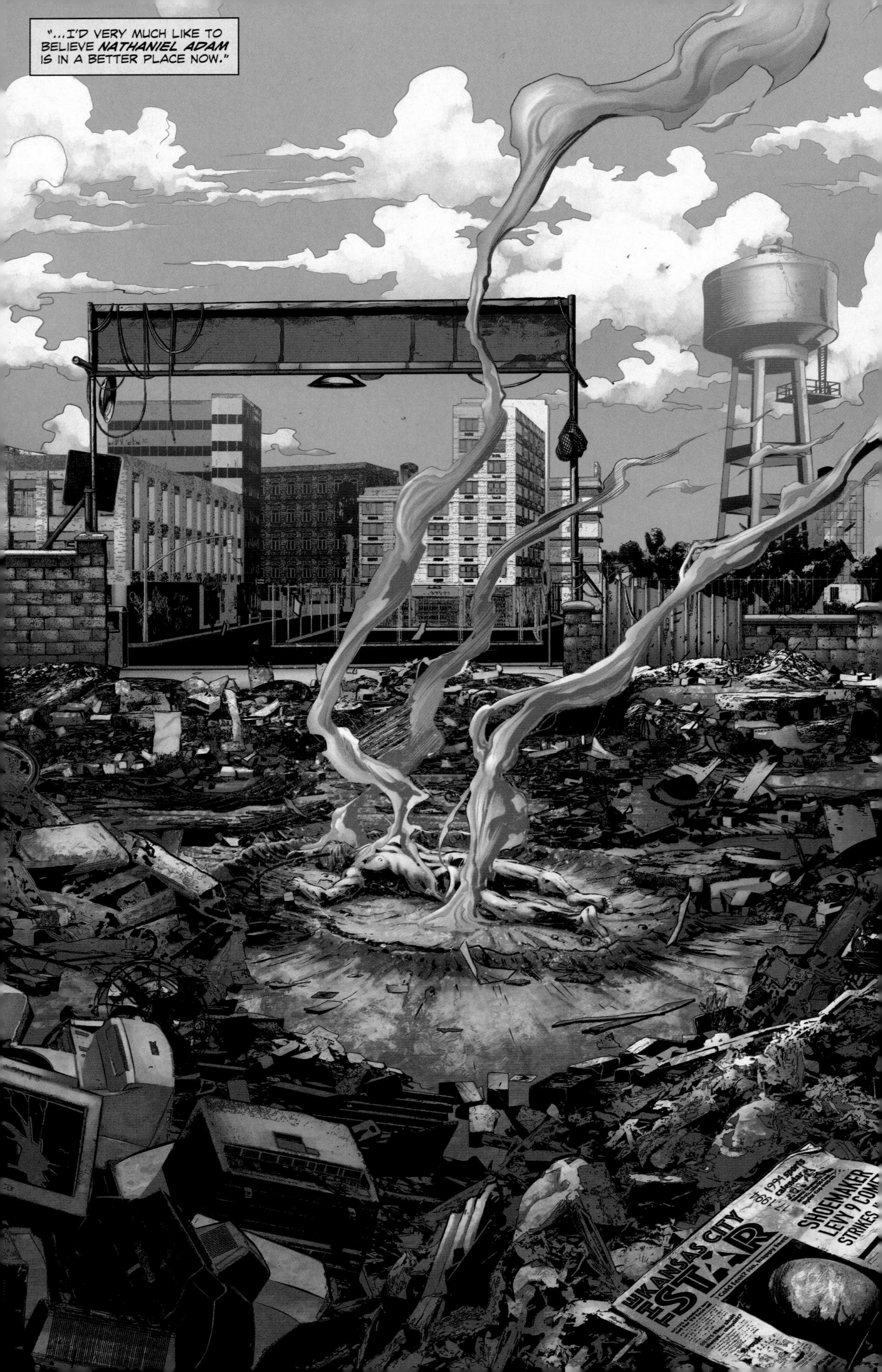
"...I'D VERY MUCH LIKE TO BELIEVE NATHANIEL ADAM IS IN A BETTER PLACE NOW."
KANSAS CITY
STAR
SHOEMAKER
STRIKES

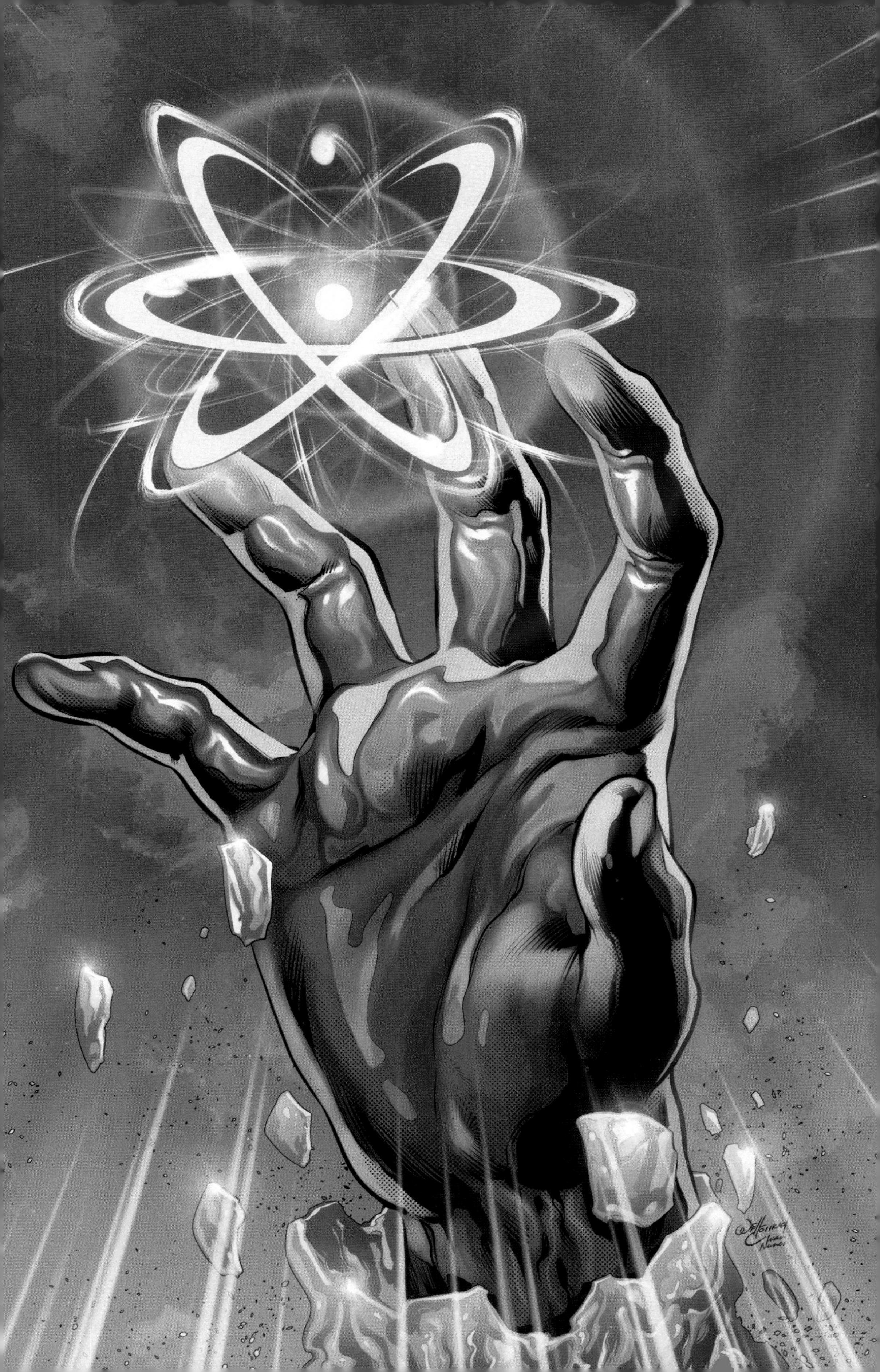

WILL CONRAD   IVAN NUNES   Cover Artists

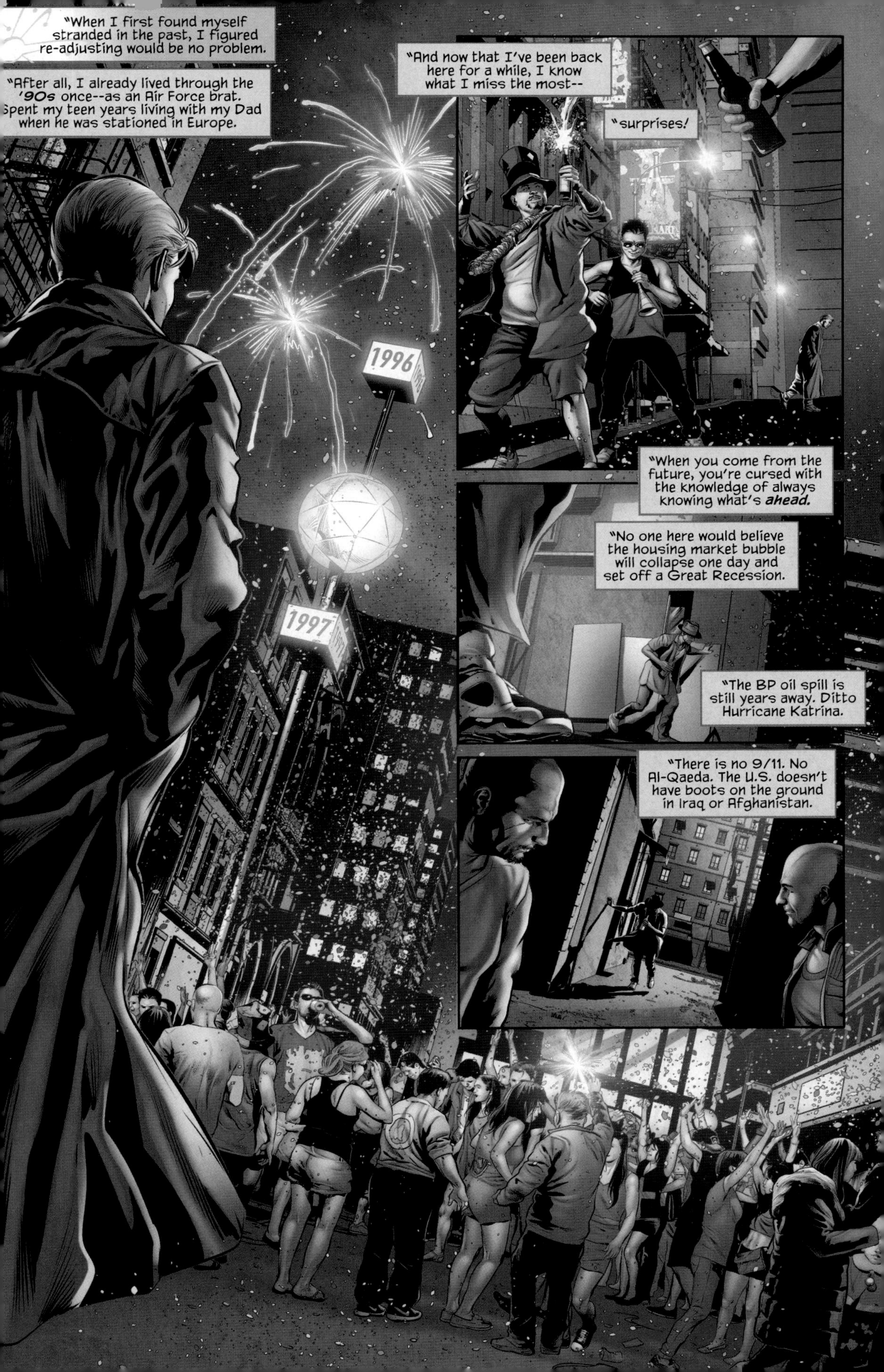
"When I first found myself stranded in the past, I figured re-adjusting would be no problem.
"After all, I already lived through the '90s once--as an Air Force brat. Spent my teen years living with my Dad when he was stationed in Europe.
1996
1997
"And now that I've been back here for a while, I know what I miss the most--
"surprises!
"When you come from the future, you're cursed with the knowledge of always knowing what's ahead.
"No one here would believe the housing market bubble will collapse one day and set off a Great Recession.
"The BP oil spill is still years away. Ditto Hurricane Katrina.
"There is no 9/11. No Al-Qaeda. The U.S. doesn't have boots on the ground in Iraq or Afghanistan.

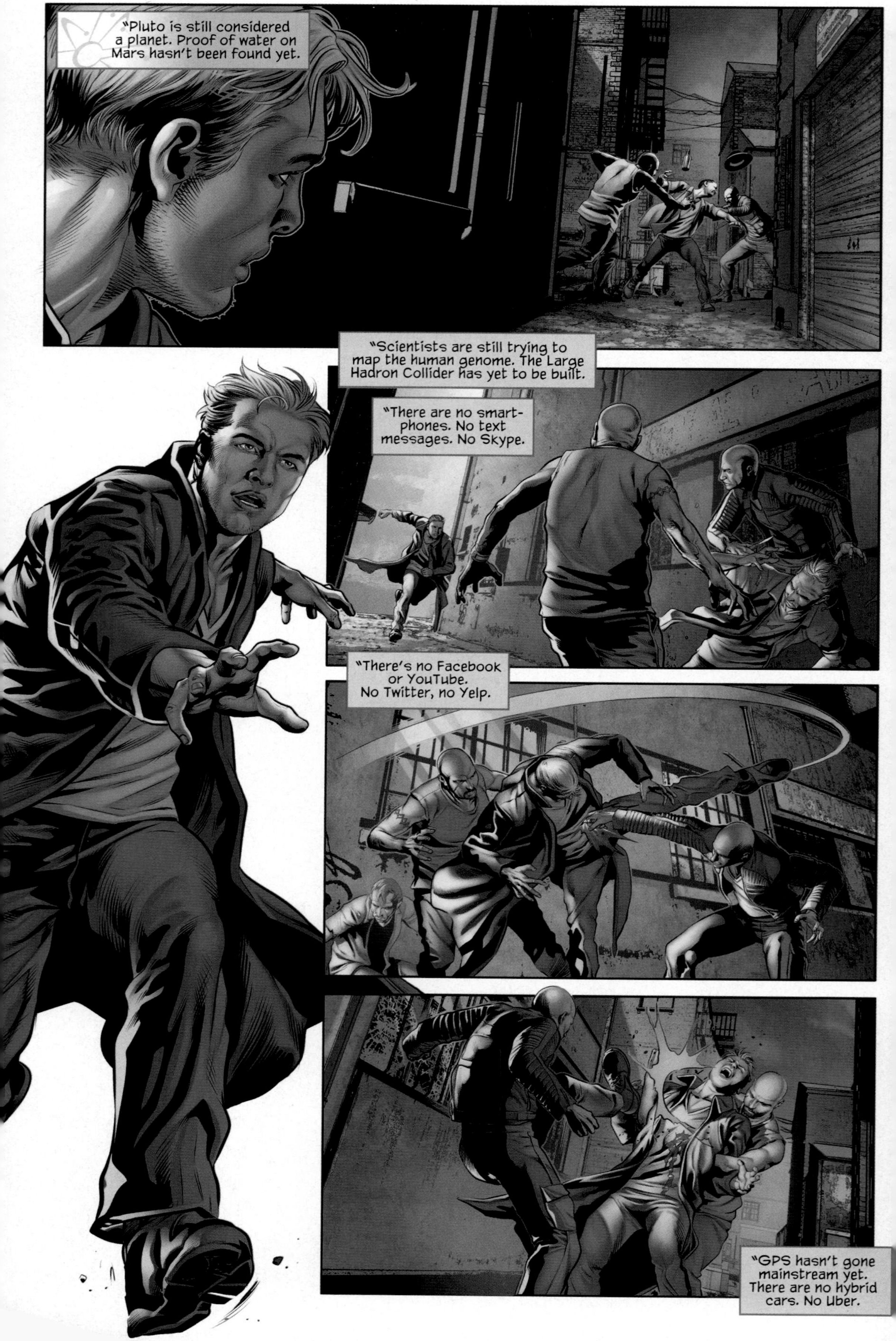
"Pluto is still considered a planet. Proof of water on Mars hasn't been found yet.
"Scientists are still trying to map the human genome. The Large Hadron Collider has yet to be built.
"There are no smart-phones. No text messages. No Skype.
"There's no Facebook or YouTube. No Twitter, no Yelp.
"GPS hasn't gone mainstream yet. There are no hybrid cars. No Uber.

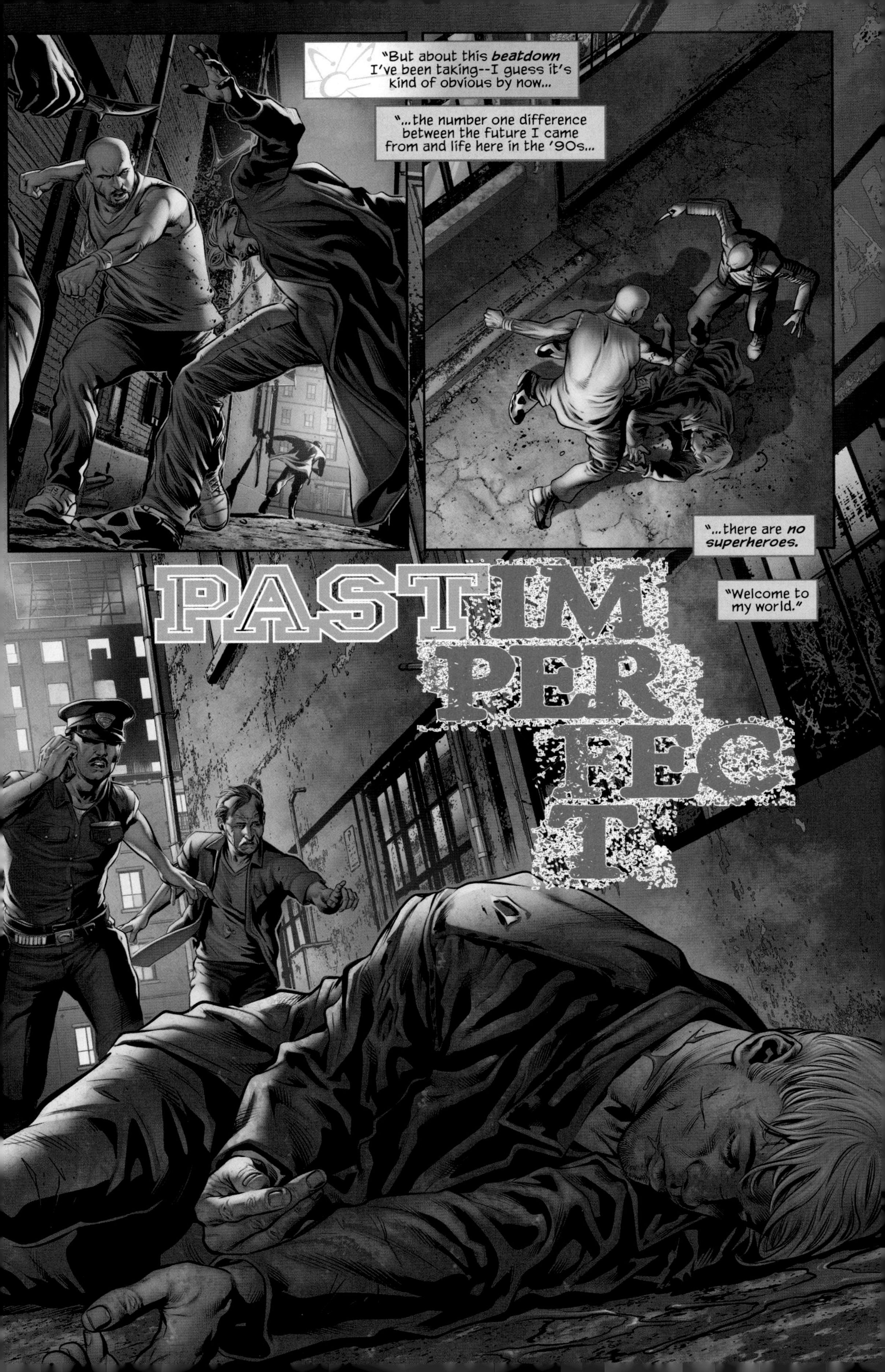
"But about this *beatdown* I've been taking--I guess it's kind of obvious by now...
"...the number one difference between the future I came from and life here in the '90s...
"...there are *no superheroes.*
PAST IMPERFECT
"Welcome to my world."

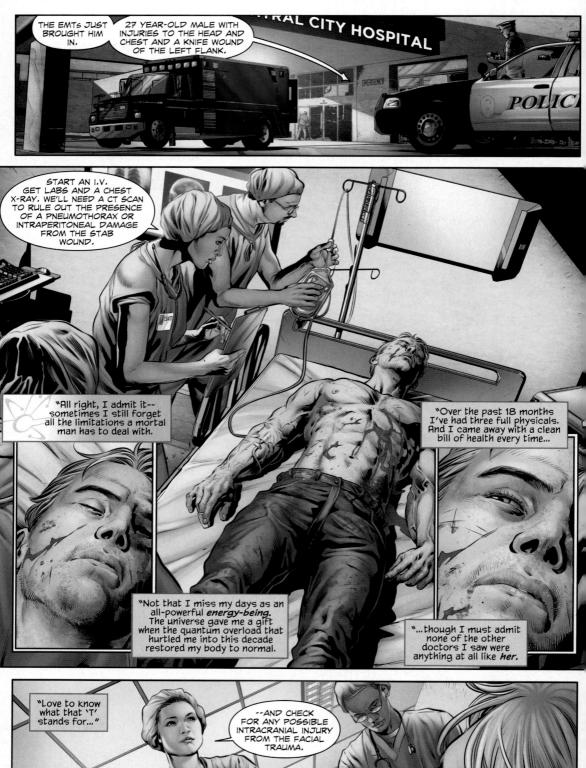

THE EMTs JUST BROUGHT HIM IN.

27 YEAR-OLD MALE WITH INJURIES TO THE HEAD AND CHEST AND A KNIFE WOUND OF THE LEFT FLANK.

CENTRAL CITY HOSPITAL

EMERGENCY

POLICE

START AN I.V. GET LABS AND A CHEST X-RAY. WE'LL NEED A CT SCAN TO RULE OUT THE PRESENCE OF A PNEUMOTHORAX OR INTRAPERITONEAL DAMAGE FROM THE STAB WOUND.

"All right, I admit it-- sometimes I still forget all the limitations a mortal man has to deal with.

"Over the past 18 months I've had three full physicals. And I came away with a clean bill of health every time...

"Not that I miss my days as an all-powerful *energy-being*. The universe gave me a gift when the quantum overload that hurtled me into this decade restored my body to normal.

"...though I must admit none of the other doctors I saw were anything at all like *her.*

"Love to know what that 'T' stands for..."

--AND CHECK FOR ANY POSSIBLE INTRACRANIAL INJURY FROM THE FACIAL TRAUMA.

T SATO

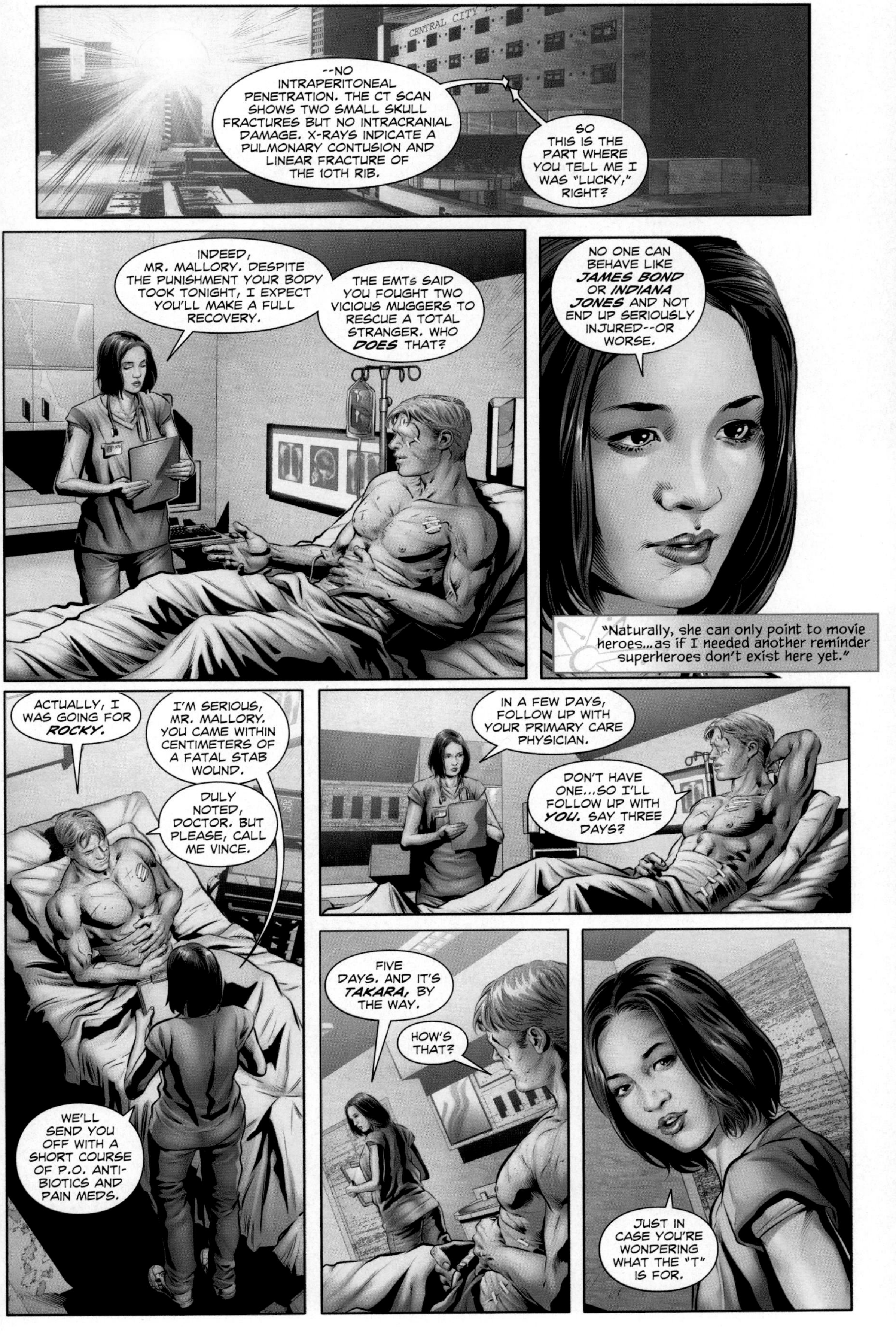
CENTRAL CITY
--NO INTRAPERITONEAL PENETRATION. THE CT SCAN SHOWS TWO SMALL SKULL FRACTURES BUT NO INTRACRANIAL DAMAGE. X-RAYS INDICATE A PULMONARY CONTUSION AND LINEAR FRACTURE OF THE 10TH RIB.
SO THIS IS THE PART WHERE YOU TELL ME I WAS "LUCKY," RIGHT?
INDEED, MR. MALLORY. DESPITE THE PUNISHMENT YOUR BODY TOOK TONIGHT, I EXPECT YOU'LL MAKE A FULL RECOVERY.
THE EMTs SAID YOU FOUGHT TWO VICIOUS MUGGERS TO RESCUE A TOTAL STRANGER. WHO DOES THAT?
NO ONE CAN BEHAVE LIKE JAMES BOND OR INDIANA JONES AND NOT END UP SERIOUSLY INJURED--OR WORSE.
"Naturally, she can only point to movie heroes...as if I needed another reminder superheroes don't exist here yet."
ACTUALLY, I WAS GOING FOR ROCKY.
I'M SERIOUS, MR. MALLORY. YOU CAME WITHIN CENTIMETERS OF A FATAL STAB WOUND.
DULY NOTED, DOCTOR. BUT PLEASE, CALL ME VINCE.
WE'LL SEND YOU OFF WITH A SHORT COURSE OF P.O. ANTI-BIOTICS AND PAIN MEDS.
IN A FEW DAYS, FOLLOW UP WITH YOUR PRIMARY CARE PHYSICIAN.
DON'T HAVE ONE...SO I'LL FOLLOW UP WITH YOU. SAY THREE DAYS?
FIVE DAYS. AND IT'S TAKARA, BY THE WAY.
HOW'S THAT?
JUST IN CASE YOU'RE WONDERING WHAT THE "T" IS FOR.

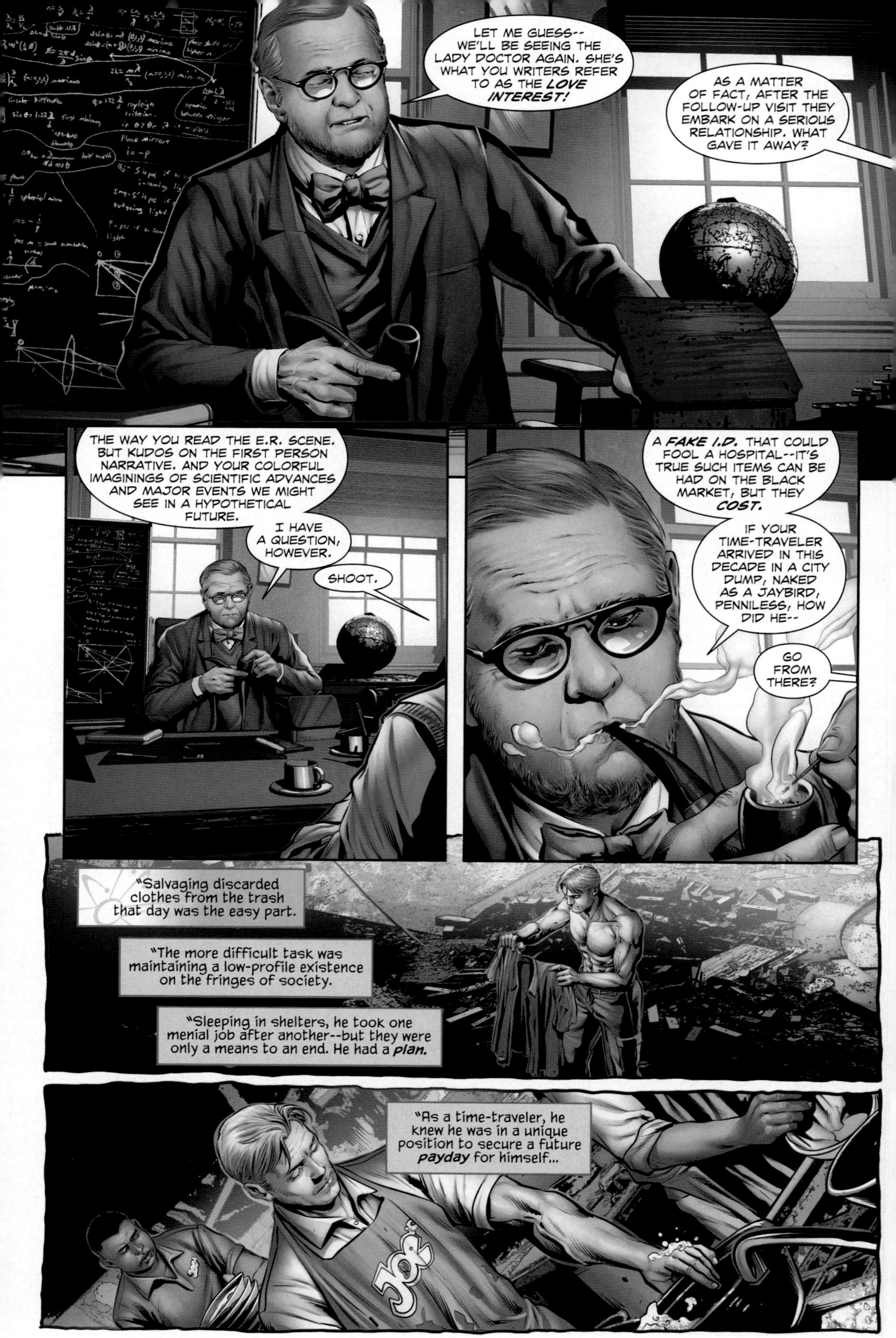
LET ME GUESS-- WE'LL BE SEEING THE LADY DOCTOR AGAIN. SHE'S WHAT YOU WRITERS REFER TO AS THE LOVE INTEREST!
AS A MATTER OF FACT, AFTER THE FOLLOW-UP VISIT THEY EMBARK ON A SERIOUS RELATIONSHIP. WHAT GAVE IT AWAY?
THE WAY YOU READ THE E.R. SCENE. BUT KUDOS ON THE FIRST PERSON NARRATIVE. AND YOUR COLORFUL IMAGININGS OF SCIENTIFIC ADVANCES AND MAJOR EVENTS WE MIGHT SEE IN A HYPOTHETICAL FUTURE.
I HAVE A QUESTION, HOWEVER.
SHOOT.
A FAKE I.D. THAT COULD FOOL A HOSPITAL--IT'S TRUE SUCH ITEMS CAN BE HAD ON THE BLACK MARKET, BUT THEY COST.
IF YOUR TIME-TRAVELER ARRIVED IN THIS DECADE IN A CITY DUMP, NAKED AS A JAYBIRD, PENNILESS, HOW DID HE--
GO FROM THERE?
"Salvaging discarded clothes from the trash that day was the easy part.
"The more difficult task was maintaining a low-profile existence on the fringes of society.
"Sleeping in shelters, he took one menial job after another--but they were only a means to an end. He had a plan.
"As a time-traveler, he knew he was in a unique position to secure a future payday for himself...

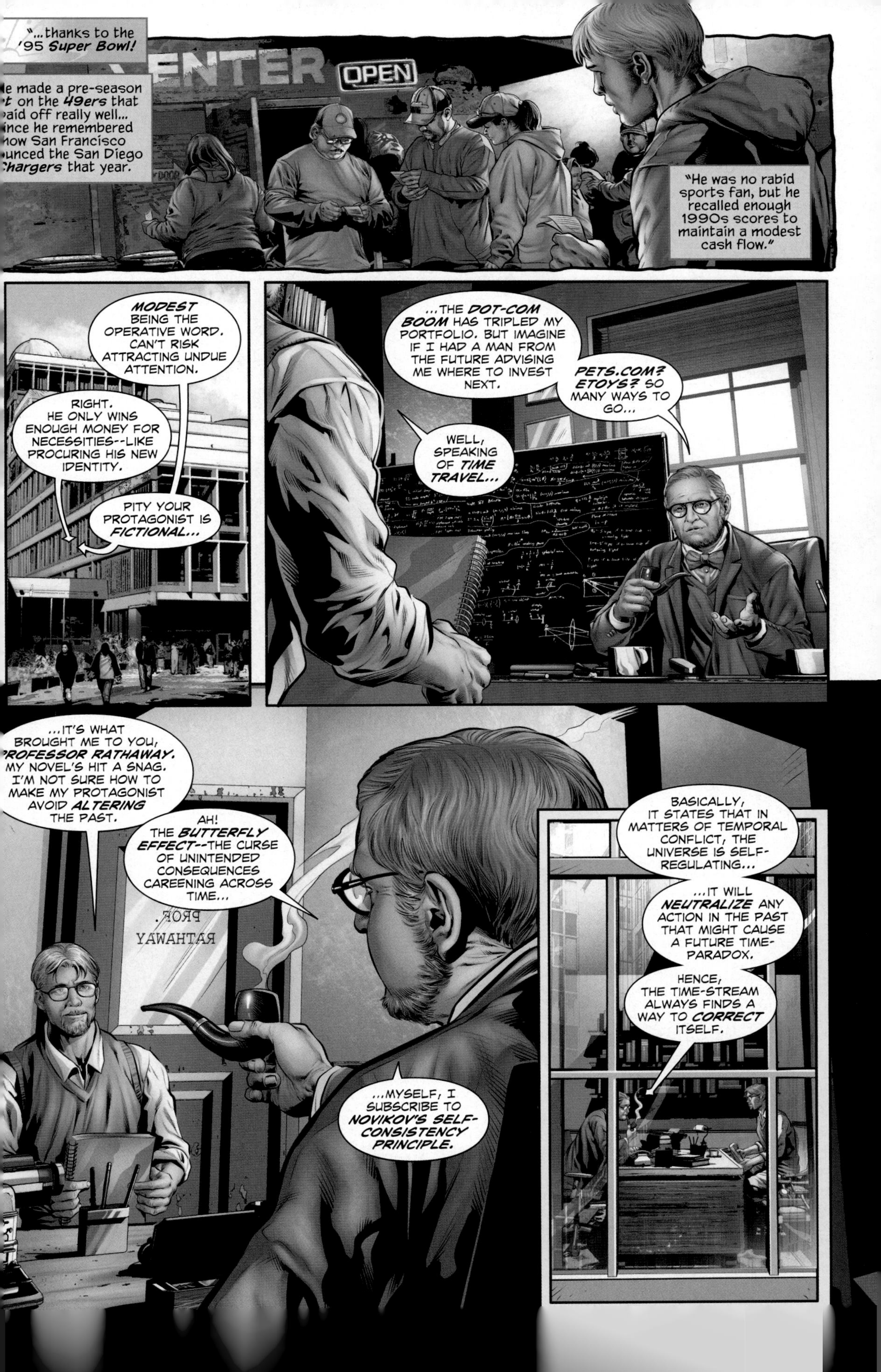
"...thanks to the '95 Super Bowl!
e made a pre-season t on the 49ers that aid off really well... ince he remembered how San Francisco unced the San Diego Chargers that year.
ENTER
OPEN
"He was no rabid sports fan, but he recalled enough 1990s scores to maintain a modest cash flow."
MODEST BEING THE OPERATIVE WORD. CAN'T RISK ATTRACTING UNDUE ATTENTION.
RIGHT. HE ONLY WINS ENOUGH MONEY FOR NECESSITIES--LIKE PROCURING HIS NEW IDENTITY.
PITY YOUR PROTAGONIST IS FICTIONAL...
...THE DOT-COM BOOM HAS TRIPLED MY PORTFOLIO. BUT IMAGINE IF I HAD A MAN FROM THE FUTURE ADVISING ME WHERE TO INVEST NEXT.
PETS.COM? ETOYS? SO MANY WAYS TO GO...
WELL, SPEAKING OF TIME TRAVEL...
...IT'S WHAT BROUGHT ME TO YOU, PROFESSOR RATHAWAY. MY NOVEL'S HIT A SNAG. I'M NOT SURE HOW TO MAKE MY PROTAGONIST AVOID ALTERING THE PAST.
AH! THE BUTTERFLY EFFECT--THE CURSE OF UNINTENDED CONSEQUENCES CAREENING ACROSS TIME...
...MYSELF, I SUBSCRIBE TO NOVIKOV'S SELF-CONSISTENCY PRINCIPLE.
BASICALLY, IT STATES THAT IN MATTERS OF TEMPORAL CONFLICT, THE UNIVERSE IS SELF-REGULATING...
...IT WILL NEUTRALIZE ANY ACTION IN THE PAST THAT MIGHT CAUSE A FUTURE TIME-PARADOX.
HENCE, THE TIME-STREAM ALWAYS FINDS A WAY TO CORRECT ITSELF.

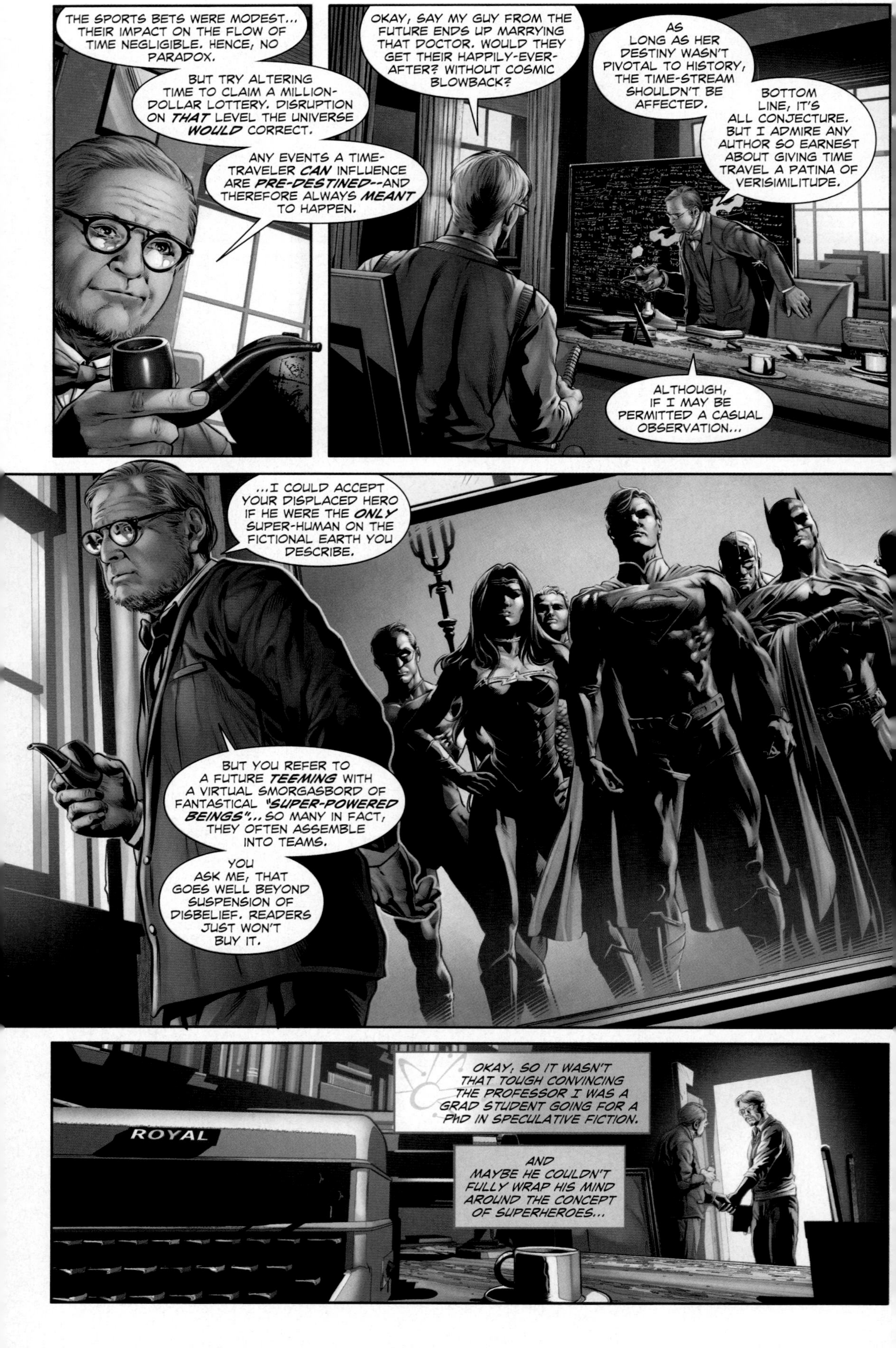
THE SPORTS BETS WERE MODEST... THEIR IMPACT ON THE FLOW OF TIME NEGLIGIBLE. HENCE, NO PARADOX.
BUT TRY ALTERING TIME TO CLAIM A MILLION-DOLLAR LOTTERY. DISRUPTION ON *THAT* LEVEL THE UNIVERSE *WOULD* CORRECT.
ANY EVENTS A TIME-TRAVELER *CAN* INFLUENCE ARE *PRE-DESTINED*--AND THEREFORE ALWAYS *MEANT* TO HAPPEN.
OKAY, SAY MY GUY FROM THE FUTURE ENDS UP MARRYING THAT DOCTOR. WOULD THEY GET THEIR HAPPILY-EVER-AFTER? WITHOUT COSMIC BLOWBACK?
AS LONG AS HER DESTINY WASN'T PIVOTAL TO HISTORY, THE TIME-STREAM SHOULDN'T BE AFFECTED.
BOTTOM LINE, IT'S ALL CONJECTURE. BUT I ADMIRE ANY AUTHOR SO EARNEST ABOUT GIVING TIME TRAVEL A PATINA OF VERISIMILITUDE.
ALTHOUGH, IF I MAY BE PERMITTED A CASUAL OBSERVATION...
...I COULD ACCEPT YOUR DISPLACED HERO IF HE WERE THE *ONLY* SUPER-HUMAN ON THE FICTIONAL EARTH YOU DESCRIBE.
BUT YOU REFER TO A FUTURE *TEEMING* WITH A VIRTUAL SMORGASBORD OF FANTASTICAL *"SUPER-POWERED BEINGS"*... SO MANY IN FACT, THEY OFTEN ASSEMBLE INTO TEAMS.
YOU ASK ME, THAT GOES WELL BEYOND SUSPENSION OF DISBELIEF. READERS JUST WON'T BUY IT.
ROYAL
OKAY, SO IT WASN'T THAT TOUGH CONVINCING THE PROFESSOR I WAS A GRAD STUDENT GOING FOR A PhD IN SPECULATIVE FICTION.
AND MAYBE HE COULDN'T FULLY WRAP HIS MIND AROUND THE CONCEPT OF SUPERHEROES...

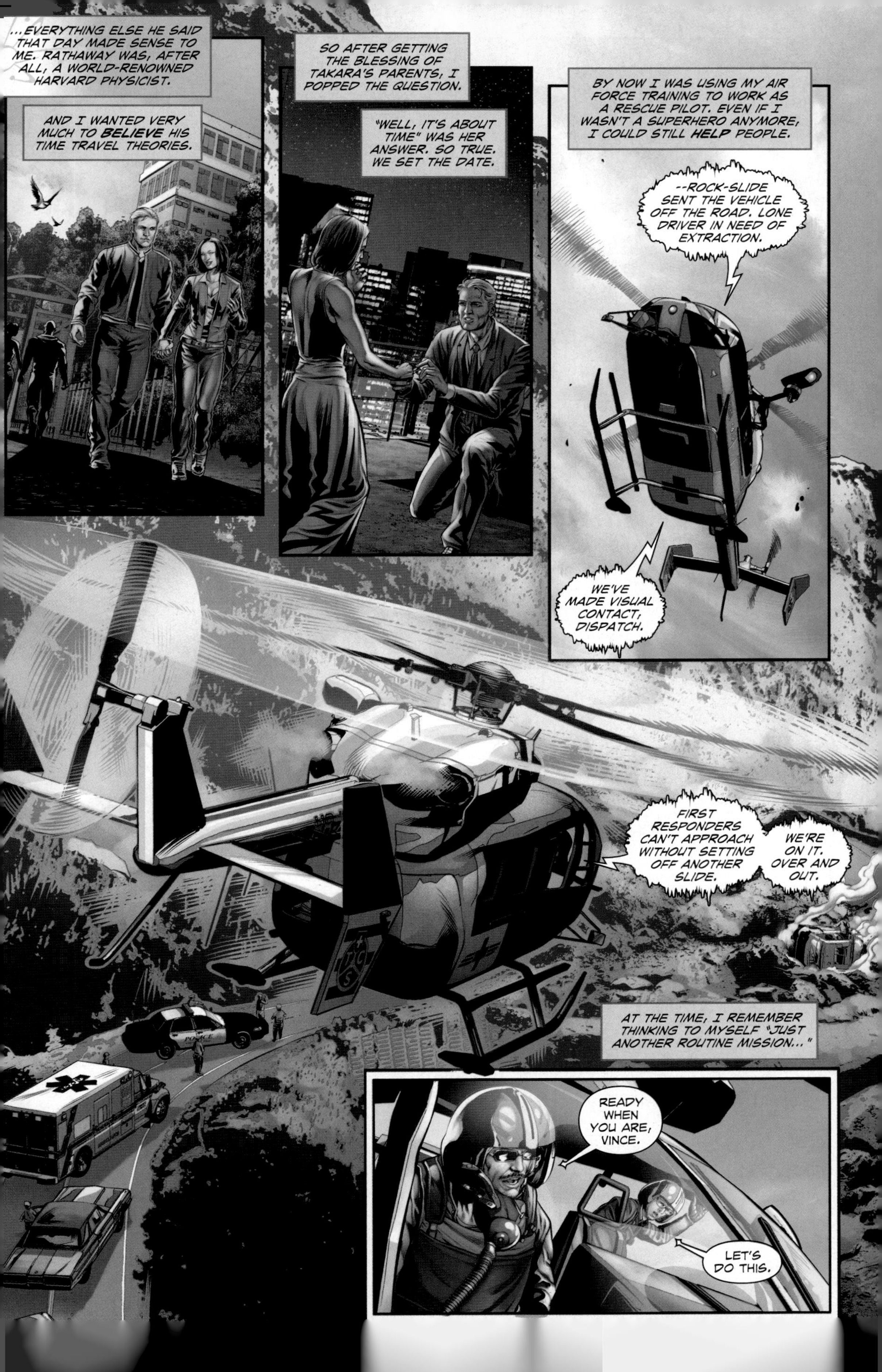
...EVERYTHING ELSE HE SAID THAT DAY MADE SENSE TO ME. RATHAWAY WAS, AFTER ALL, A WORLD-RENOWNED HARVARD PHYSICIST.
AND I WANTED VERY MUCH TO BELIEVE HIS TIME TRAVEL THEORIES.
SO AFTER GETTING THE BLESSING OF TAKARA'S PARENTS, I POPPED THE QUESTION.
"WELL, IT'S ABOUT TIME" WAS HER ANSWER. SO TRUE. WE SET THE DATE.
BY NOW I WAS USING MY AIR FORCE TRAINING TO WORK AS A RESCUE PILOT. EVEN IF I WASN'T A SUPERHERO ANYMORE, I COULD STILL HELP PEOPLE.
--ROCK-SLIDE SENT THE VEHICLE OFF THE ROAD. LONE DRIVER IN NEED OF EXTRACTION.
WE'VE MADE VISUAL CONTACT, DISPATCH.
FIRST RESPONDERS CAN'T APPROACH WITHOUT SETTING OFF ANOTHER SLIDE.
WE'RE ON IT. OVER AND OUT.
AT THE TIME, I REMEMBER THINKING TO MYSELF "JUST ANOTHER ROUTINE MISSION..."
READY WHEN YOU ARE, VINCE.
LET'S DO THIS.

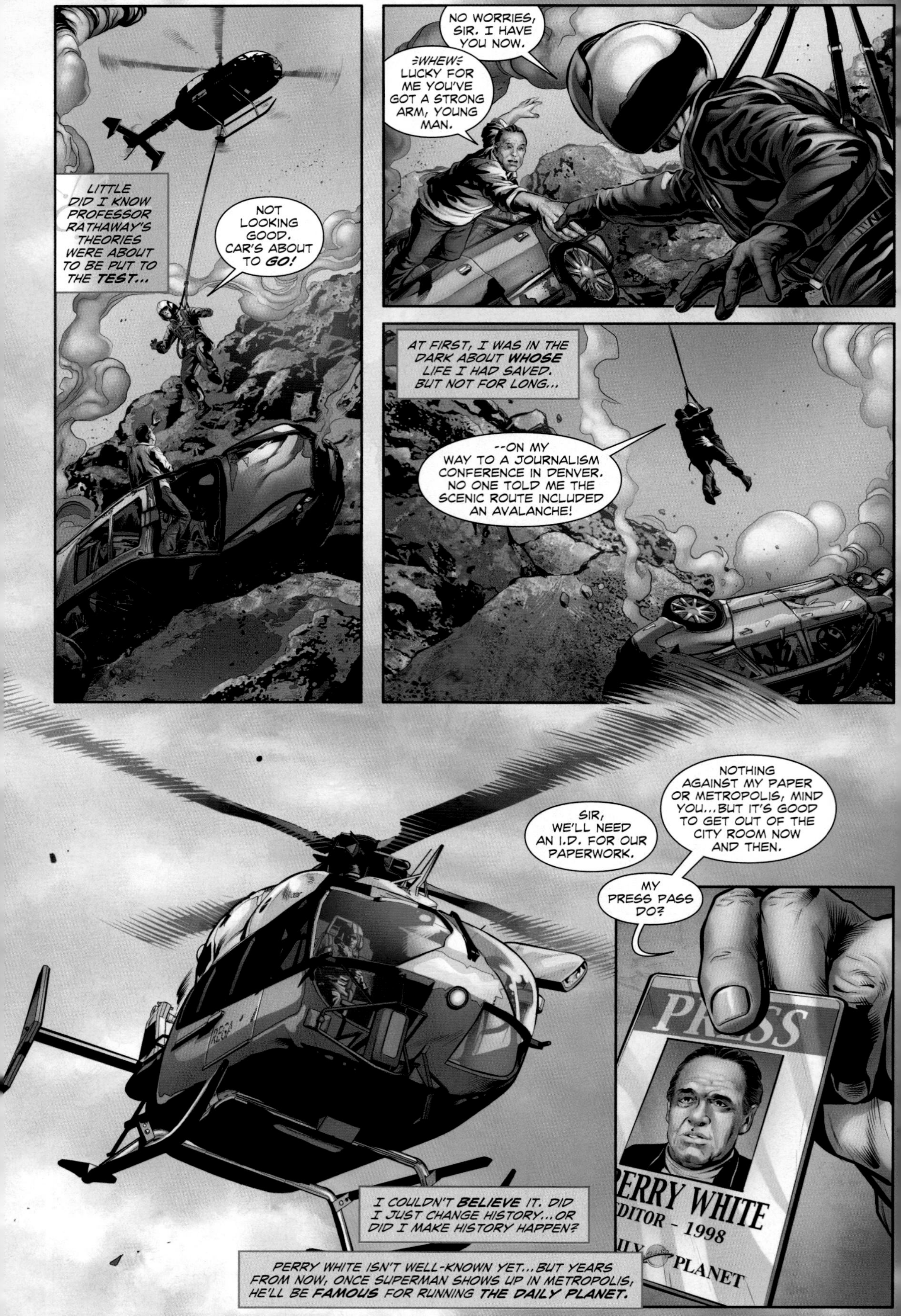
LITTLE DID I KNOW PROFESSOR RATHAWAY'S THEORIES WERE ABOUT TO BE PUT TO THE TEST...
NOT LOOKING GOOD. CAR'S ABOUT TO GO!
NO WORRIES, SIR. I HAVE YOU NOW.
=WHEW= LUCKY FOR ME YOU'VE GOT A STRONG ARM, YOUNG MAN.
AT FIRST, I WAS IN THE DARK ABOUT WHOSE LIFE I HAD SAVED. BUT NOT FOR LONG...
--ON MY WAY TO A JOURNALISM CONFERENCE IN DENVER. NO ONE TOLD ME THE SCENIC ROUTE INCLUDED AN AVALANCHE!
SIR, WE'LL NEED AN I.D. FOR OUR PAPERWORK.
NOTHING AGAINST MY PAPER OR METROPOLIS, MIND YOU...BUT IT'S GOOD TO GET OUT OF THE CITY ROOM NOW AND THEN.
MY PRESS PASS DO?
PRESS
ERRY WHITE
EDITOR - 1998
ILY PLANET
I COULDN'T BELIEVE IT. DID I JUST CHANGE HISTORY...OR DID I MAKE HISTORY HAPPEN?
PERRY WHITE ISN'T WELL-KNOWN YET...BUT YEARS FROM NOW, ONCE SUPERMAN SHOWS UP IN METROPOLIS, HE'LL BE FAMOUS FOR RUNNING THE DAILY PLANET.

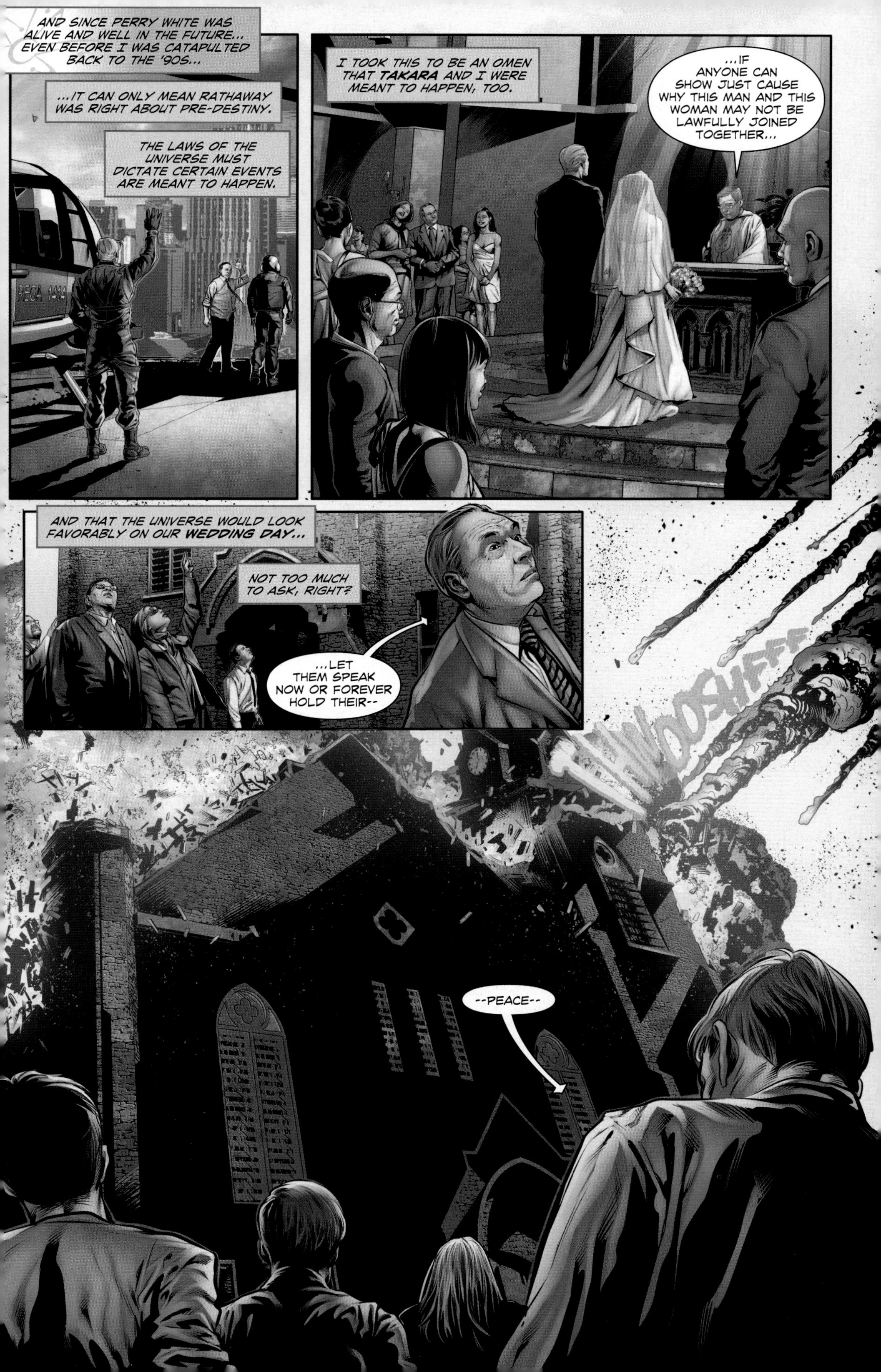
AND SINCE PERRY WHITE WAS ALIVE AND WELL IN THE FUTURE... EVEN BEFORE I WAS CATAPULTED BACK TO THE '90S...
...IT CAN ONLY MEAN RATHAWAY WAS RIGHT ABOUT PRE-DESTINY.
THE LAWS OF THE UNIVERSE MUST DICTATE CERTAIN EVENTS ARE MEANT TO HAPPEN.
REGA 1414
I TOOK THIS TO BE AN OMEN THAT TAKARA AND I WERE MEANT TO HAPPEN, TOO.
...IF ANYONE CAN SHOW JUST CAUSE WHY THIS MAN AND THIS WOMAN MAY NOT BE LAWFULLY JOINED TOGETHER...
AND THAT THE UNIVERSE WOULD LOOK FAVORABLY ON OUR WEDDING DAY...
NOT TOO MUCH TO ASK, RIGHT?
...LET THEM SPEAK NOW OR FOREVER HOLD THEIR--
WOOSHFFF
--PEACE--

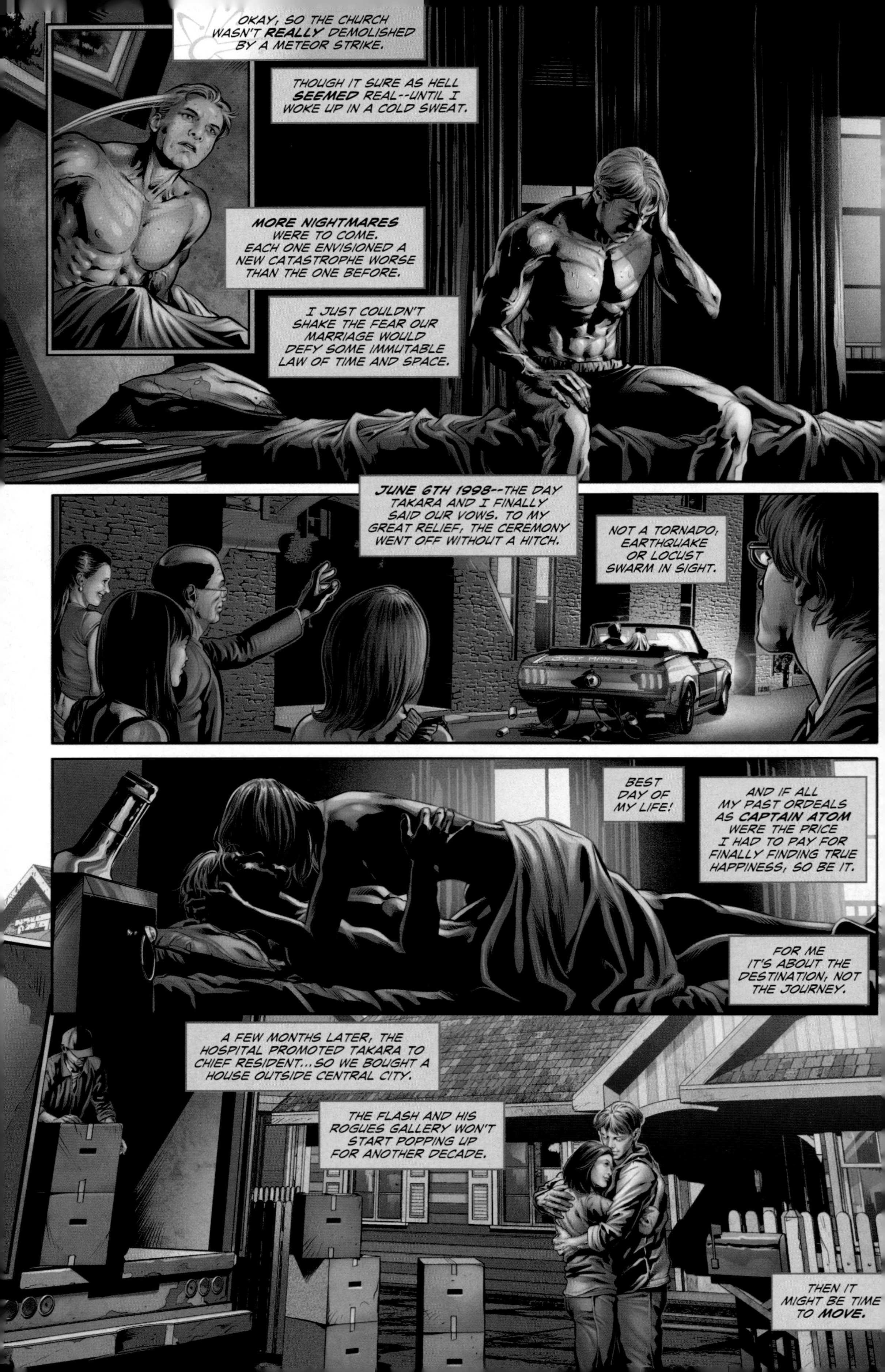
OKAY, SO THE CHURCH WASN'T REALLY DEMOLISHED BY A METEOR STRIKE.
THOUGH IT SURE AS HELL SEEMED REAL--UNTIL I WOKE UP IN A COLD SWEAT.
MORE NIGHTMARES WERE TO COME. EACH ONE ENVISIONED A NEW CATASTROPHE WORSE THAN THE ONE BEFORE.
I JUST COULDN'T SHAKE THE FEAR OUR MARRIAGE WOULD DEFY SOME IMMUTABLE LAW OF TIME AND SPACE.
JUNE 6TH 1998--THE DAY TAKARA AND I FINALLY SAID OUR VOWS. TO MY GREAT RELIEF, THE CEREMONY WENT OFF WITHOUT A HITCH.
NOT A TORNADO, EARTHQUAKE OR LOCUST SWARM IN SIGHT.
JUST MARRIED
BEST DAY OF MY LIFE!
AND IF ALL MY PAST ORDEALS AS CAPTAIN ATOM WERE THE PRICE I HAD TO PAY FOR FINALLY FINDING TRUE HAPPINESS, SO BE IT.
FOR ME IT'S ABOUT THE DESTINATION, NOT THE JOURNEY.
A FEW MONTHS LATER, THE HOSPITAL PROMOTED TAKARA TO CHIEF RESIDENT...SO WE BOUGHT A HOUSE OUTSIDE CENTRAL CITY.
THE FLASH AND HIS ROGUES GALLERY WON'T START POPPING UP FOR ANOTHER DECADE.
THEN IT MIGHT BE TIME TO MOVE.

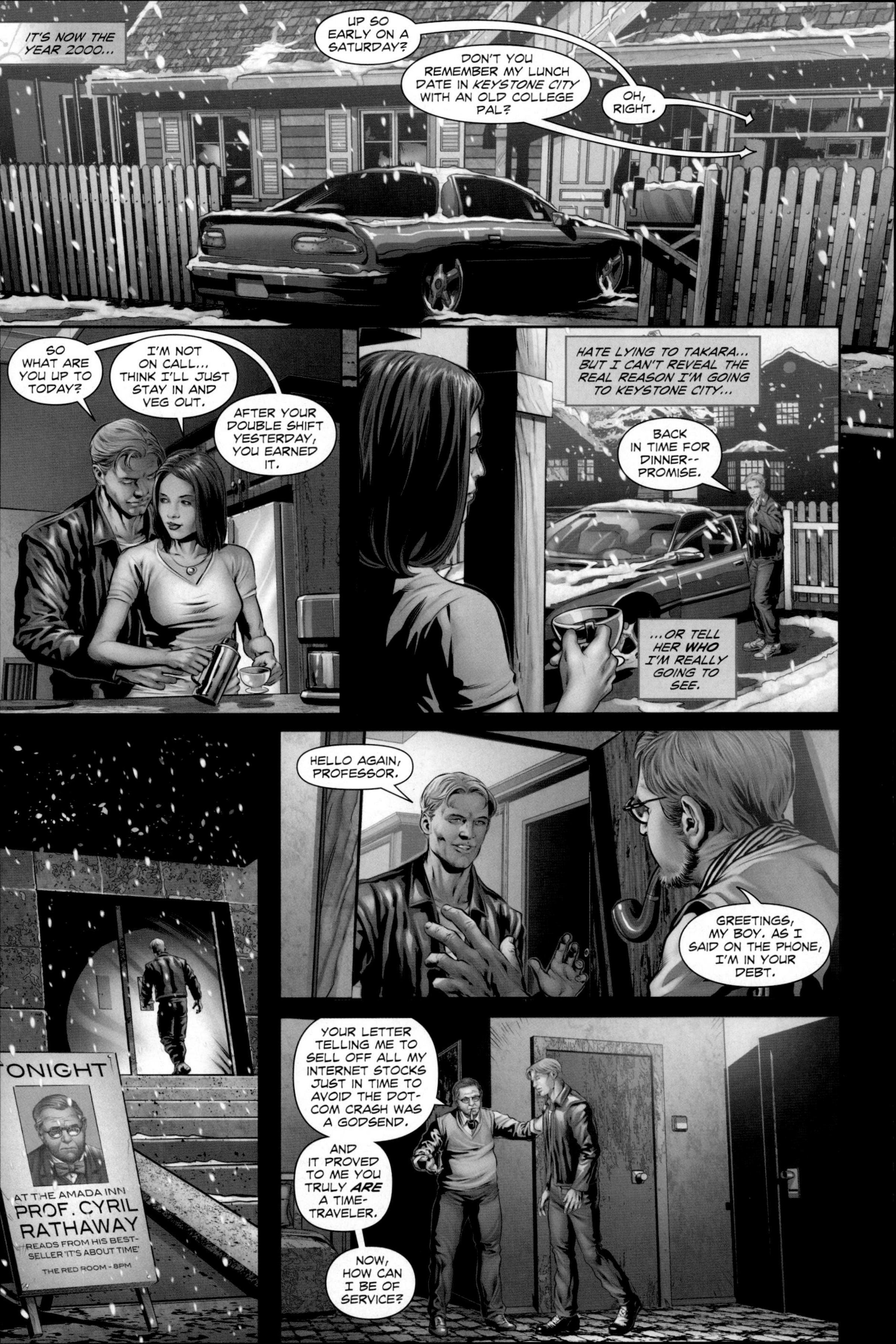
IT'S NOW THE YEAR 2000...
UP SO EARLY ON A SATURDAY?
DON'T YOU REMEMBER MY LUNCH DATE IN *KEYSTONE CITY* WITH AN OLD COLLEGE PAL?
OH, RIGHT.
SO WHAT ARE YOU UP TO TODAY?
I'M NOT ON CALL... THINK I'LL JUST STAY IN AND VEG OUT.
AFTER YOUR DOUBLE SHIFT YESTERDAY, YOU EARNED IT.
HATE LYING TO TAKARA... BUT I CAN'T REVEAL THE REAL REASON I'M GOING TO KEYSTONE CITY...
BACK IN TIME FOR DINNER--PROMISE.
...OR TELL HER **WHO** I'M REALLY GOING TO SEE.
TONIGHT
AT THE AMADA INN
PROF. CYRIL RATHAWAY
READS FROM HIS BEST-SELLER 'IT'S ABOUT TIME'
THE RED ROOM - 8PM
HELLO AGAIN, PROFESSOR.
GREETINGS, MY BOY. AS I SAID ON THE PHONE, I'M IN YOUR DEBT.
YOUR LETTER TELLING ME TO SELL OFF ALL MY INTERNET STOCKS JUST IN TIME TO AVOID THE DOT-COM CRASH WAS A GODSEND.
AND IT PROVED TO ME YOU TRULY ***ARE*** A TIME-TRAVELER.
NOW, HOW CAN I BE OF SERVICE?

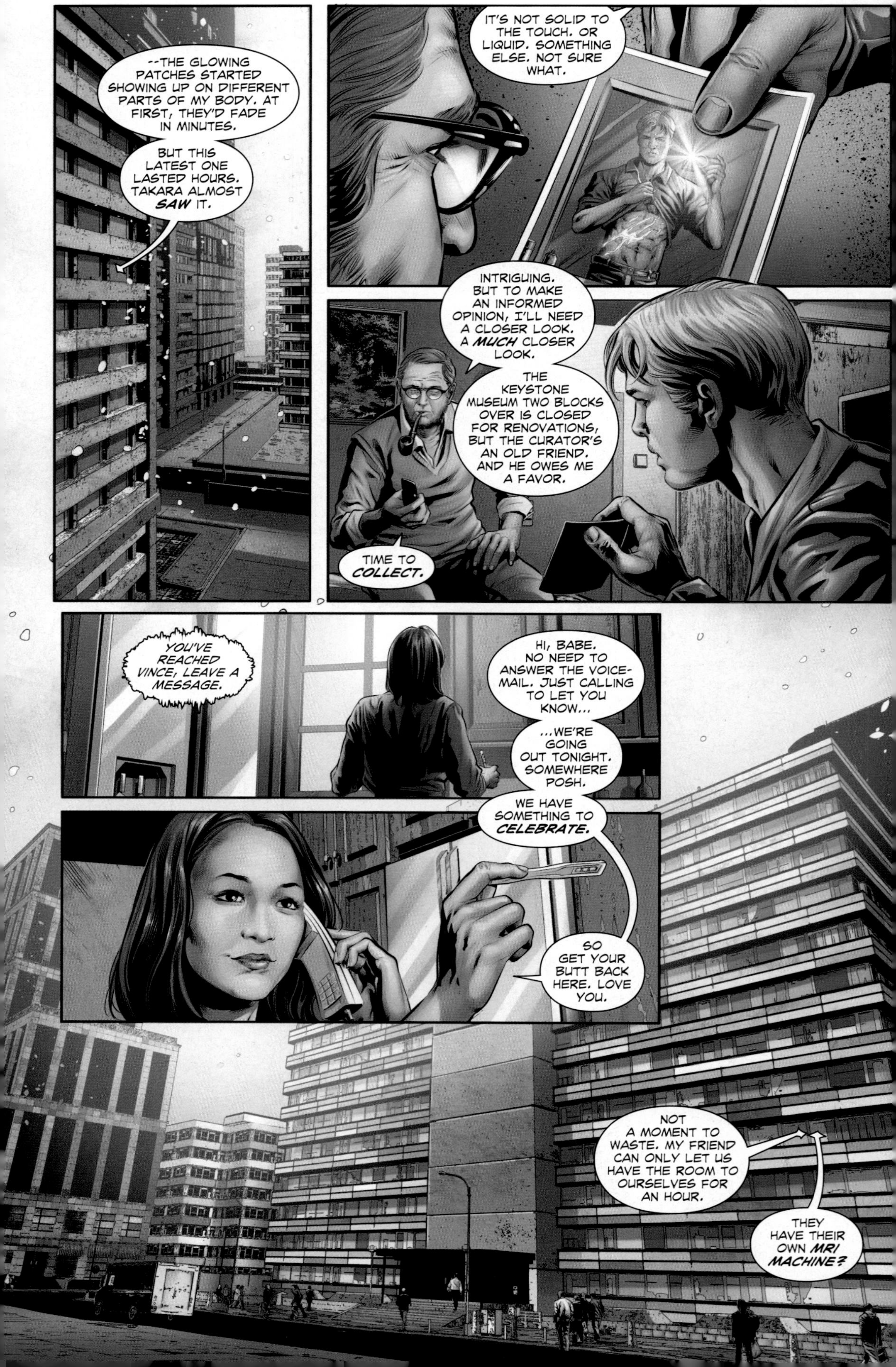
--THE GLOWING PATCHES STARTED SHOWING UP ON DIFFERENT PARTS OF MY BODY. AT FIRST, THEY'D FADE IN MINUTES.
BUT THIS LATEST ONE LASTED HOURS. TAKARA ALMOST SAW IT.
IT'S NOT SOLID TO THE TOUCH. OR LIQUID. SOMETHING ELSE. NOT SURE WHAT.
INTRIGUING. BUT TO MAKE AN INFORMED OPINION, I'LL NEED A CLOSER LOOK. A MUCH CLOSER LOOK.
THE KEYSTONE MUSEUM TWO BLOCKS OVER IS CLOSED FOR RENOVATIONS, BUT THE CURATOR'S AN OLD FRIEND. AND HE OWES ME A FAVOR.
TIME TO COLLECT.
YOU'VE REACHED VINCE; LEAVE A MESSAGE.
HI, BABE. NO NEED TO ANSWER THE VOICE-MAIL. JUST CALLING TO LET YOU KNOW...
...WE'RE GOING OUT TONIGHT. SOMEWHERE POSH.
WE HAVE SOMETHING TO CELEBRATE.
SO GET YOUR BUTT BACK HERE. LOVE YOU.
NOT A MOMENT TO WASTE. MY FRIEND CAN ONLY LET US HAVE THE ROOM TO OURSELVES FOR AN HOUR.
THEY HAVE THEIR OWN MRI MACHINE?

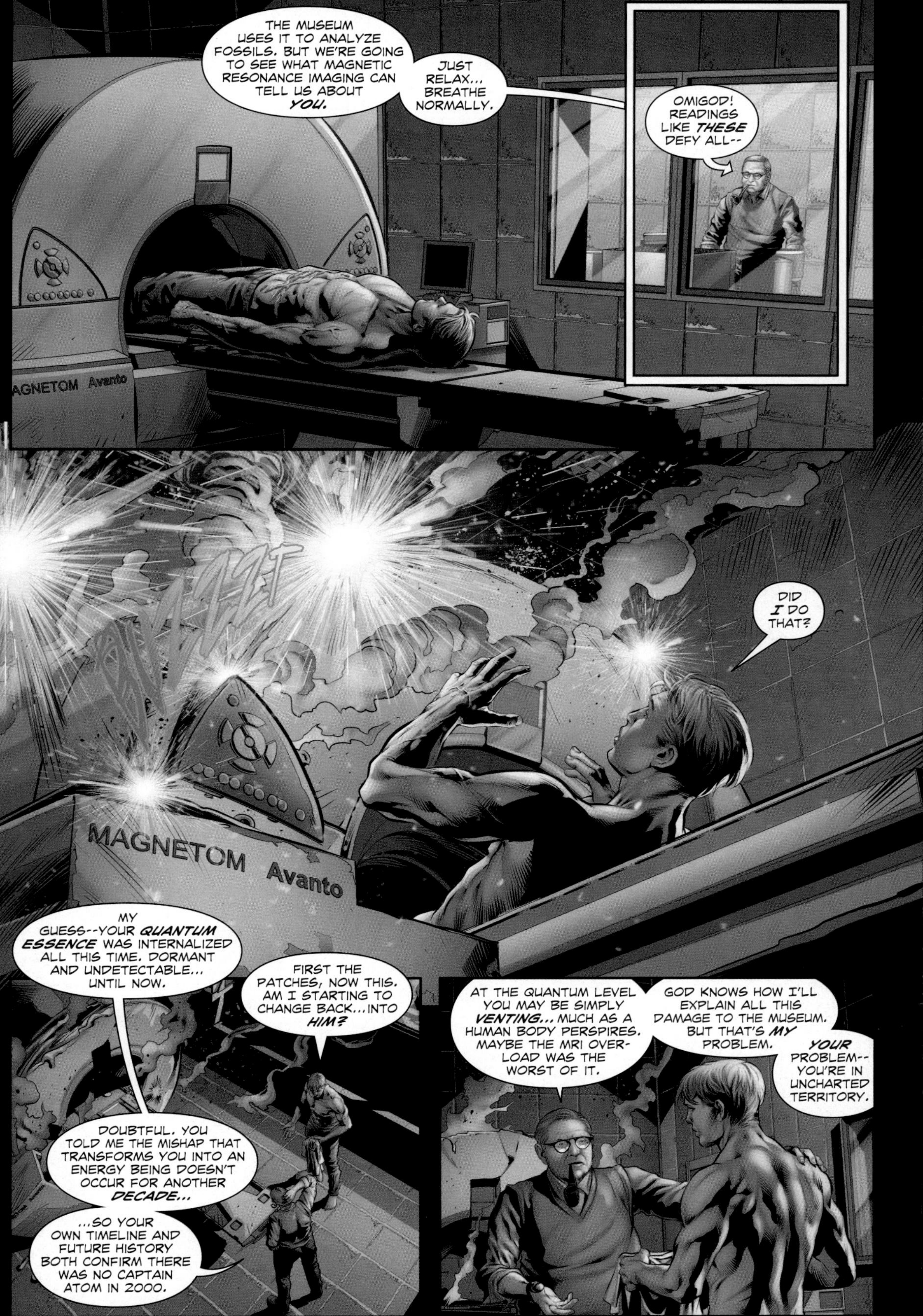
THE MUSEUM USES IT TO ANALYZE FOSSILS. BUT WE'RE GOING TO SEE WHAT MAGNETIC RESONANCE IMAGING CAN TELL US ABOUT *YOU.*
JUST RELAX... BREATHE NORMALLY.
MAGNETOM Avanto
OMIGOD! READINGS LIKE *THESE* DEFY ALL--
DID *I* DO THAT?
MAGNETOM Avanto
MY GUESS--YOUR *QUANTUM ESSENCE* WAS INTERNALIZED ALL THIS TIME. DORMANT AND UNDETECTABLE... UNTIL NOW.
FIRST THE PATCHES, NOW THIS. AM I STARTING TO CHANGE BACK... INTO *HIM?*
DOUBTFUL. YOU TOLD ME THE MISHAP THAT TRANSFORMS YOU INTO AN ENERGY BEING DOESN'T OCCUR FOR ANOTHER *DECADE...*
...SO YOUR OWN TIMELINE AND FUTURE HISTORY BOTH CONFIRM THERE WAS NO CAPTAIN ATOM IN 2000.
AT THE QUANTUM LEVEL YOU MAY BE SIMPLY *VENTING...* MUCH AS A HUMAN BODY PERSPIRES. MAYBE THE MRI OVER-LOAD WAS THE WORST OF IT.
GOD KNOWS HOW I'LL EXPLAIN ALL THIS DAMAGE TO THE MUSEUM. BUT THAT'S *MY* PROBLEM.
YOUR PROBLEM-- YOU'RE IN UNCHARTED TERRITORY.

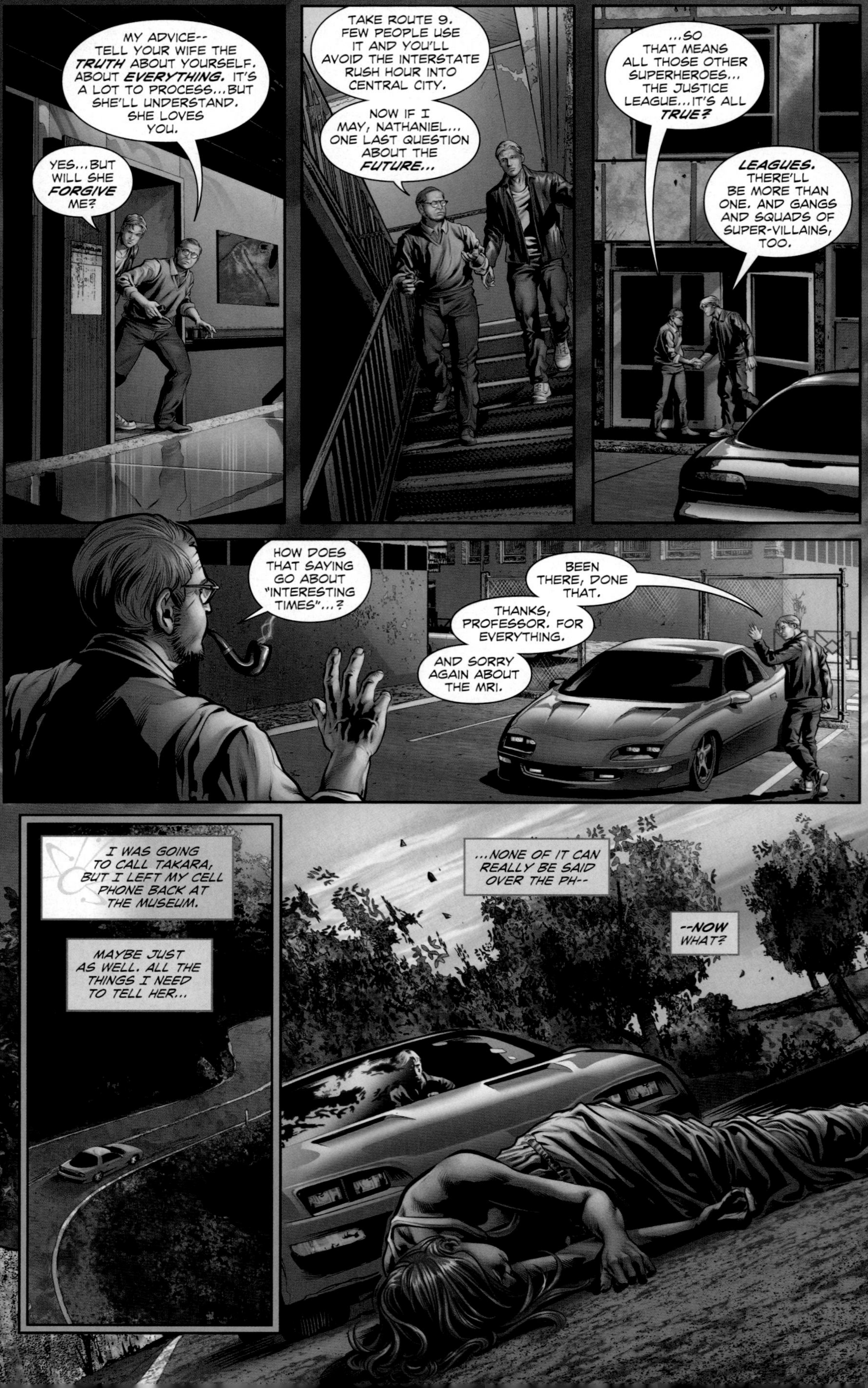
MY ADVICE-- TELL YOUR WIFE THE TRUTH ABOUT YOURSELF. ABOUT EVERYTHING. IT'S A LOT TO PROCESS...BUT SHE'LL UNDERSTAND. SHE LOVES YOU.
YES...BUT WILL SHE FORGIVE ME?
TAKE ROUTE 9. FEW PEOPLE USE IT AND YOU'LL AVOID THE INTERSTATE RUSH HOUR INTO CENTRAL CITY.
NOW IF I MAY, NATHANIEL... ONE LAST QUESTION ABOUT THE FUTURE...
...SO THAT MEANS ALL THOSE OTHER SUPERHEROES... THE JUSTICE LEAGUE...IT'S ALL TRUE?
LEAGUES. THERE'LL BE MORE THAN ONE. AND GANGS AND SQUADS OF SUPER-VILLAINS, TOO.
HOW DOES THAT SAYING GO ABOUT "INTERESTING TIMES"...?
BEEN THERE, DONE THAT.
THANKS, PROFESSOR. FOR EVERYTHING.
AND SORRY AGAIN ABOUT THE MRI.
I WAS GOING TO CALL TAKARA, BUT I LEFT MY CELL PHONE BACK AT THE MUSEUM.
MAYBE JUST AS WELL. ALL THE THINGS I NEED TO TELL HER...
...NONE OF IT CAN REALLY BE SAID OVER THE PH--
--NOW WHAT?

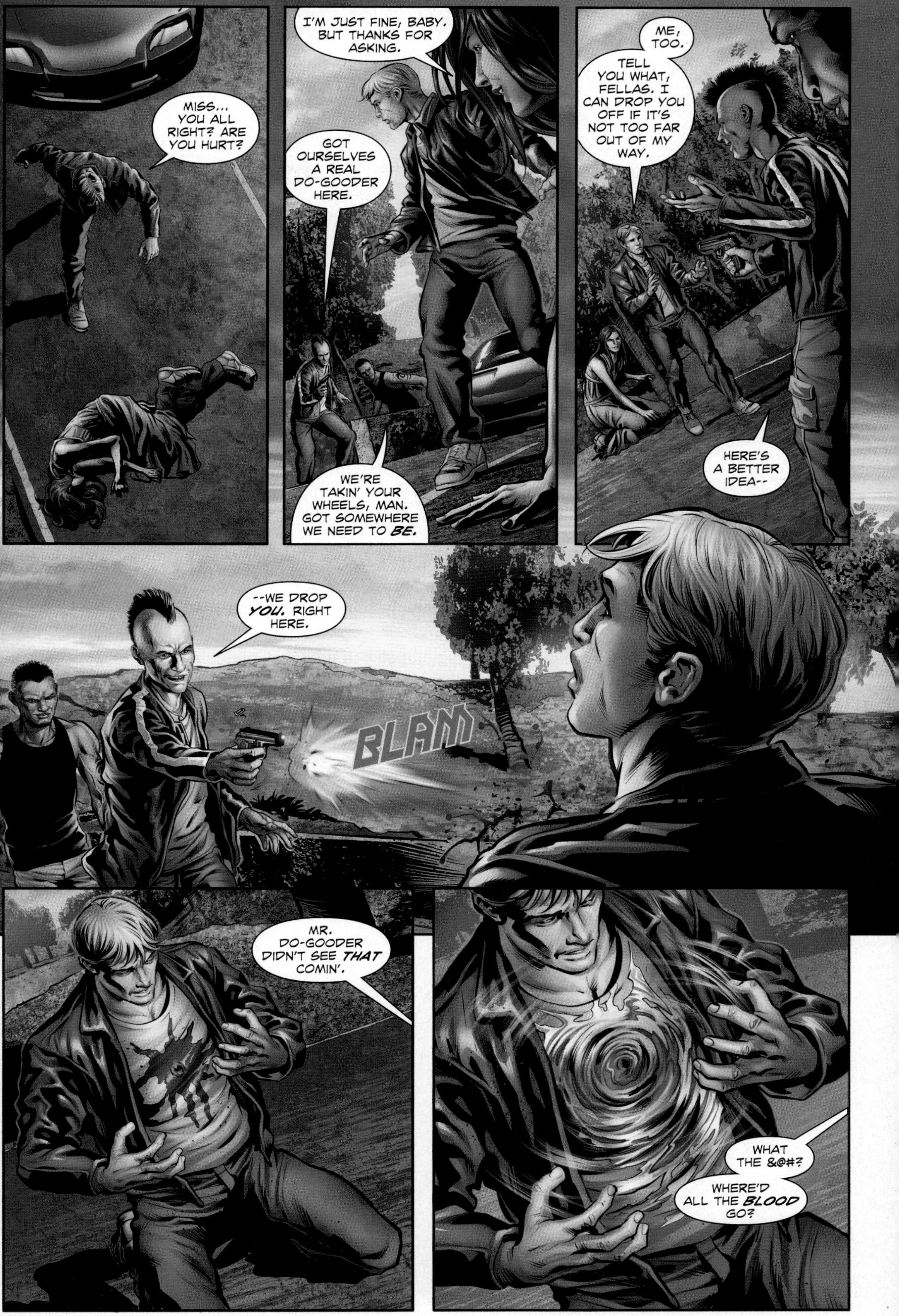
MISS... YOU ALL RIGHT? ARE YOU HURT?
I'M JUST FINE, BABY. BUT THANKS FOR ASKING.
GOT OURSELVES A REAL DO-GOODER HERE.
WE'RE TAKIN' YOUR WHEELS, MAN. GOT SOMEWHERE WE NEED TO BE.
ME, TOO.
TELL YOU WHAT, FELLAS. I CAN DROP YOU OFF IF IT'S NOT TOO FAR OUT OF MY WAY.
HERE'S A BETTER IDEA--
--WE DROP YOU. RIGHT HERE.
BLAM
MR. DO-GOODER DIDN'T SEE THAT COMIN'.
WHAT THE &@#?
WHERE'D ALL THE BLOOD GO?

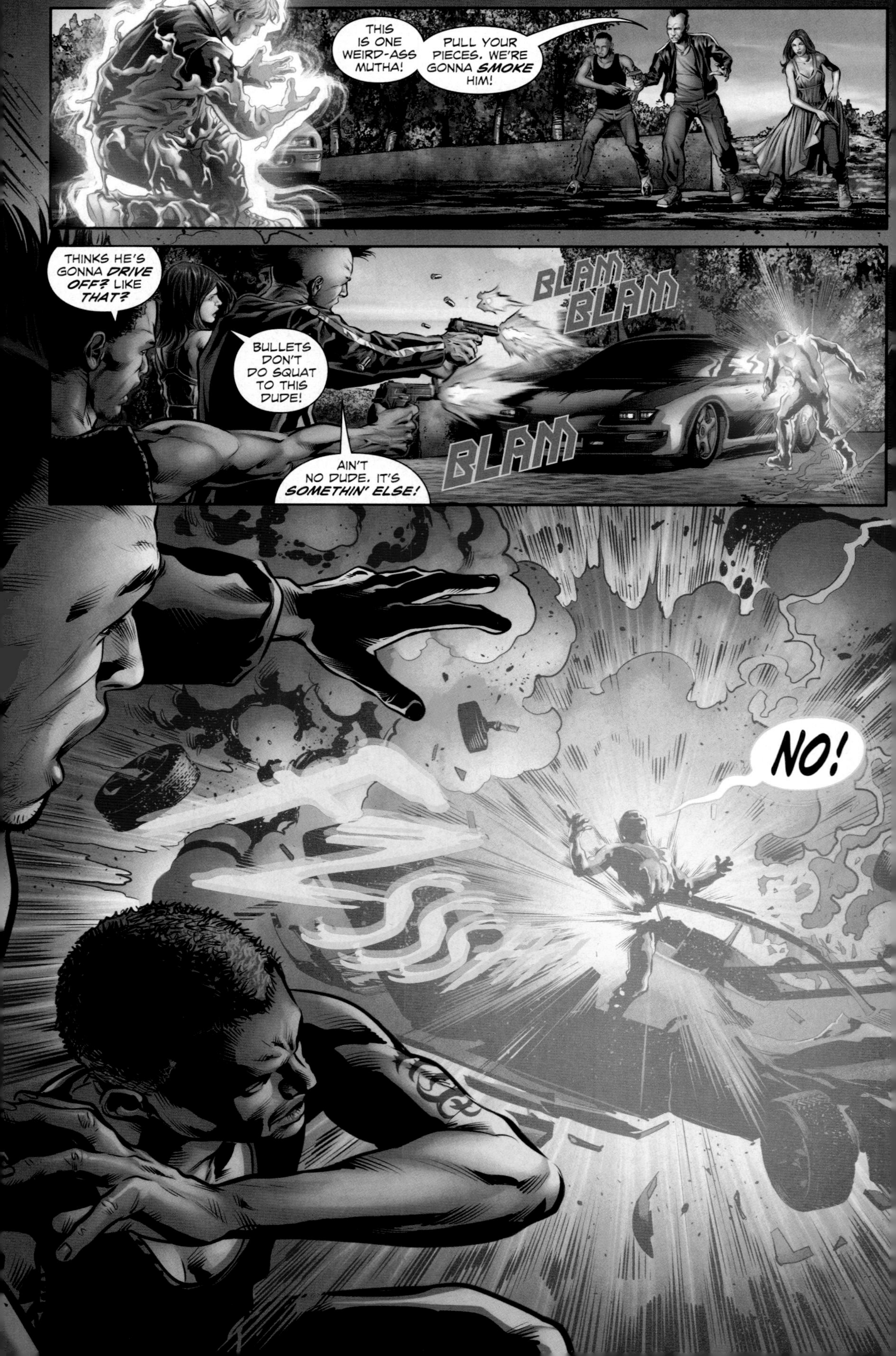
THIS IS ONE WEIRD-ASS MUTHA!
PULL YOUR PIECES. WE'RE GONNA SMOKE HIM!
THINKS HE'S GONNA DRIVE OFF? LIKE THAT?
BLAM BLAM
BULLETS DON'T DO SQUAT TO THIS DUDE!
BLAM
AIN'T NO DUDE. IT'S SOMETHIN' ELSE!
NO!

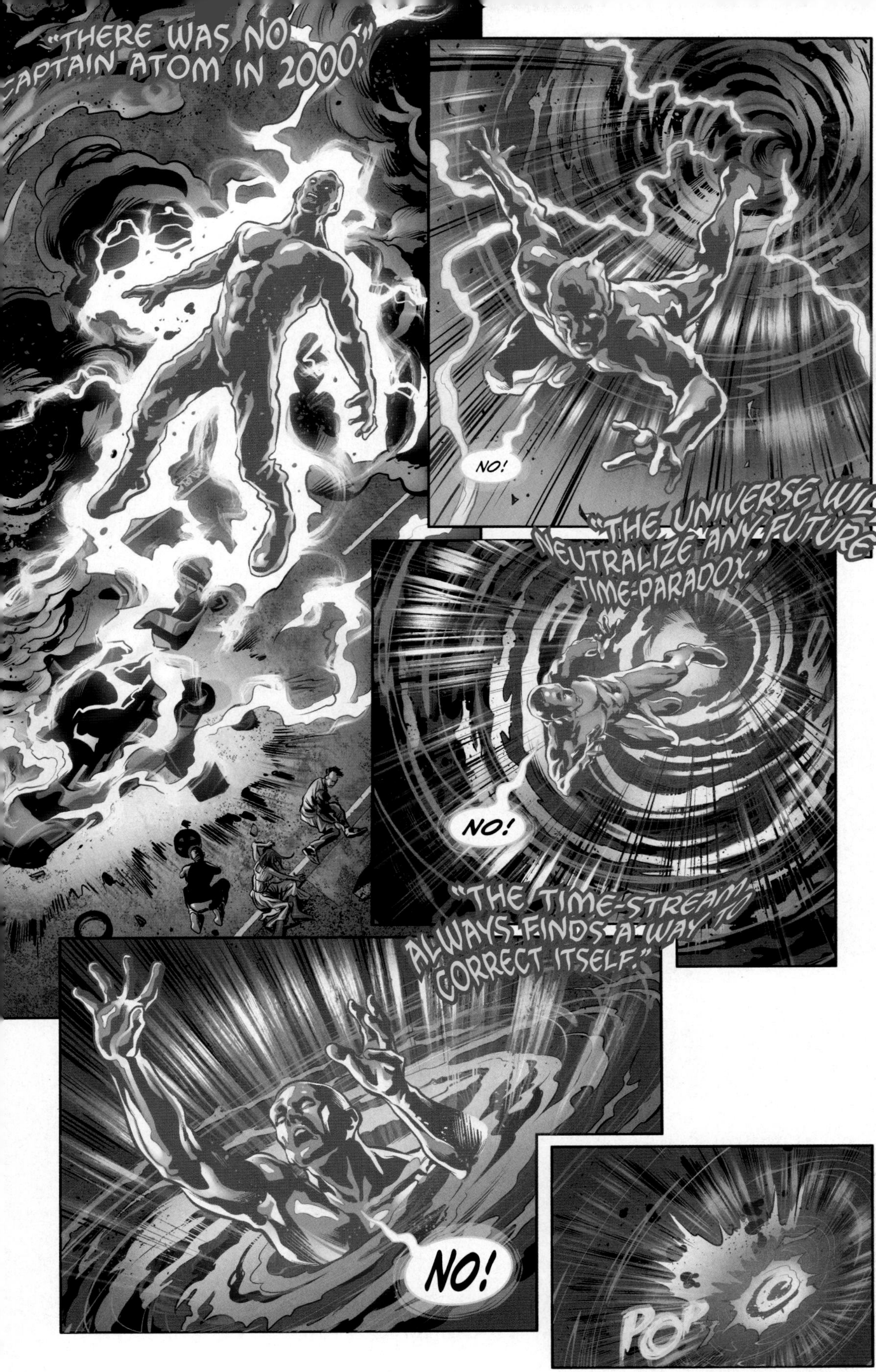
"THERE WAS NO CAPTAIN ATOM IN 2000."
NO!
"THE UNIVERSE WILL NEUTRALIZE ANY FUTURE TIME-PARADOX."
NO!
"THE TIME-STREAM ALWAYS FINDS A WAY TO CORRECT ITSELF."
NO!
POP

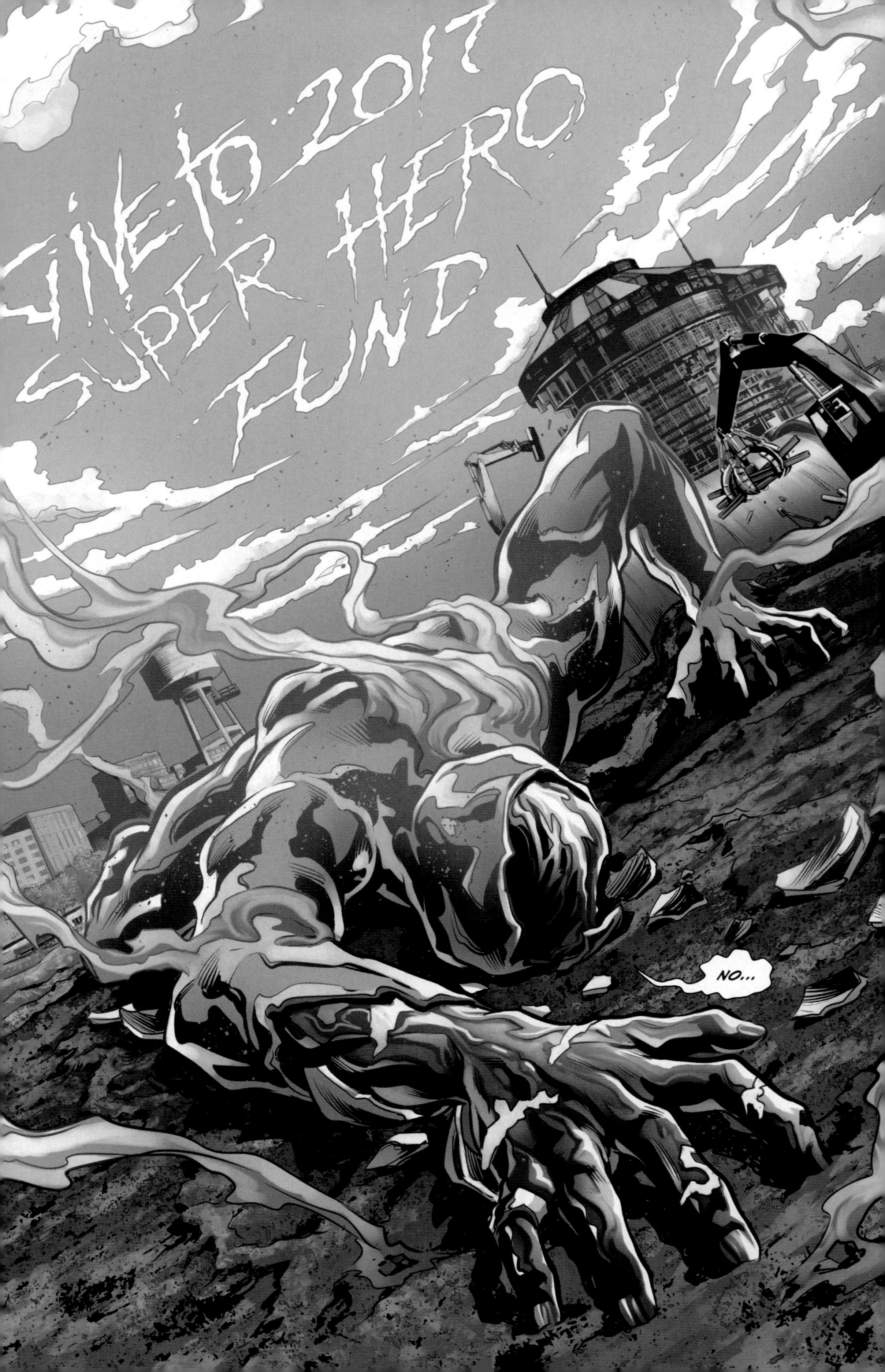
GIVE TO 2017 SUPER HERO FUND
NO...

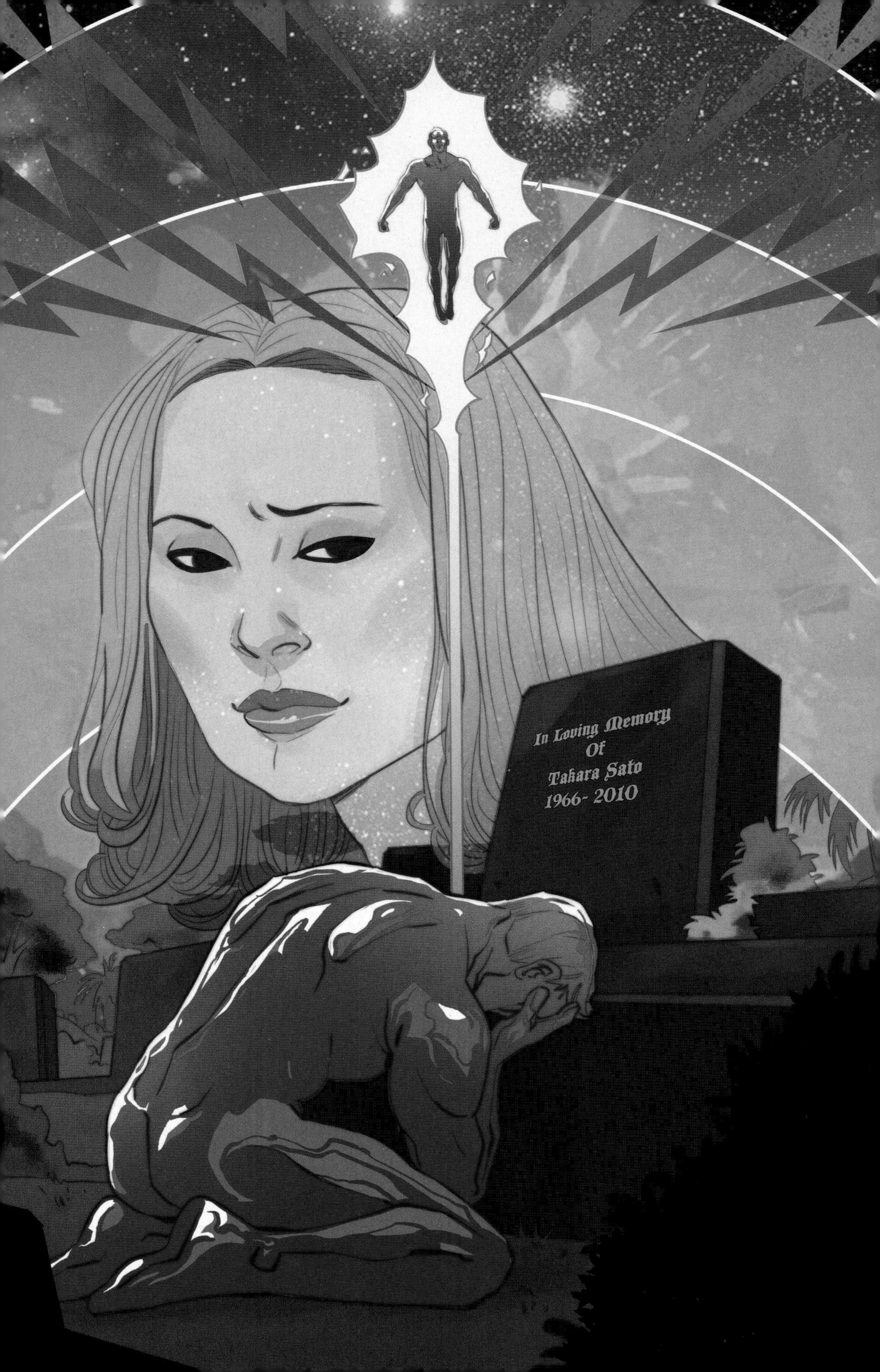
In Loving Memory
Of
Takara Sato
1966- 2010

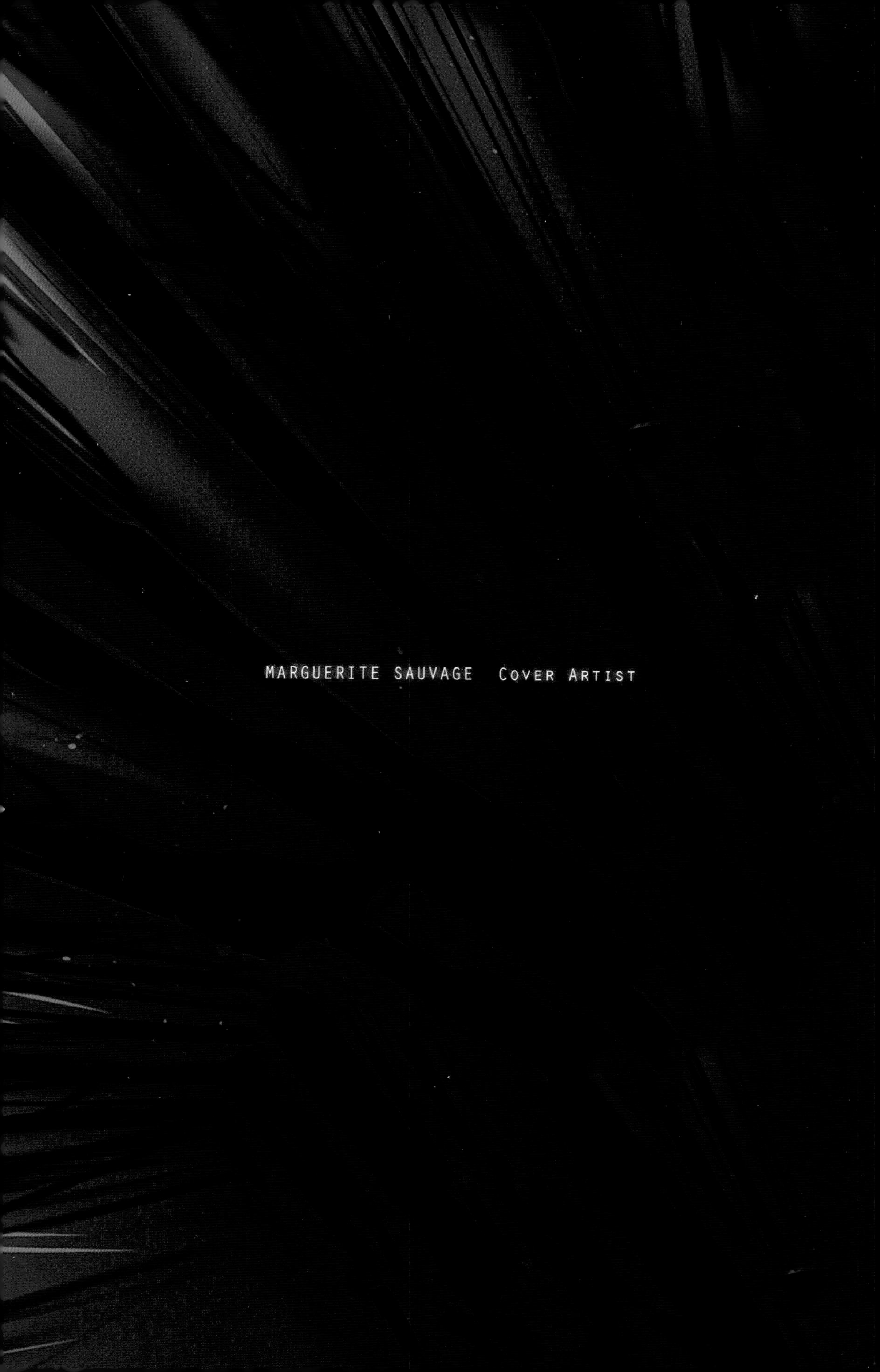
MARGUERITE SAUVAGE Cover Artist

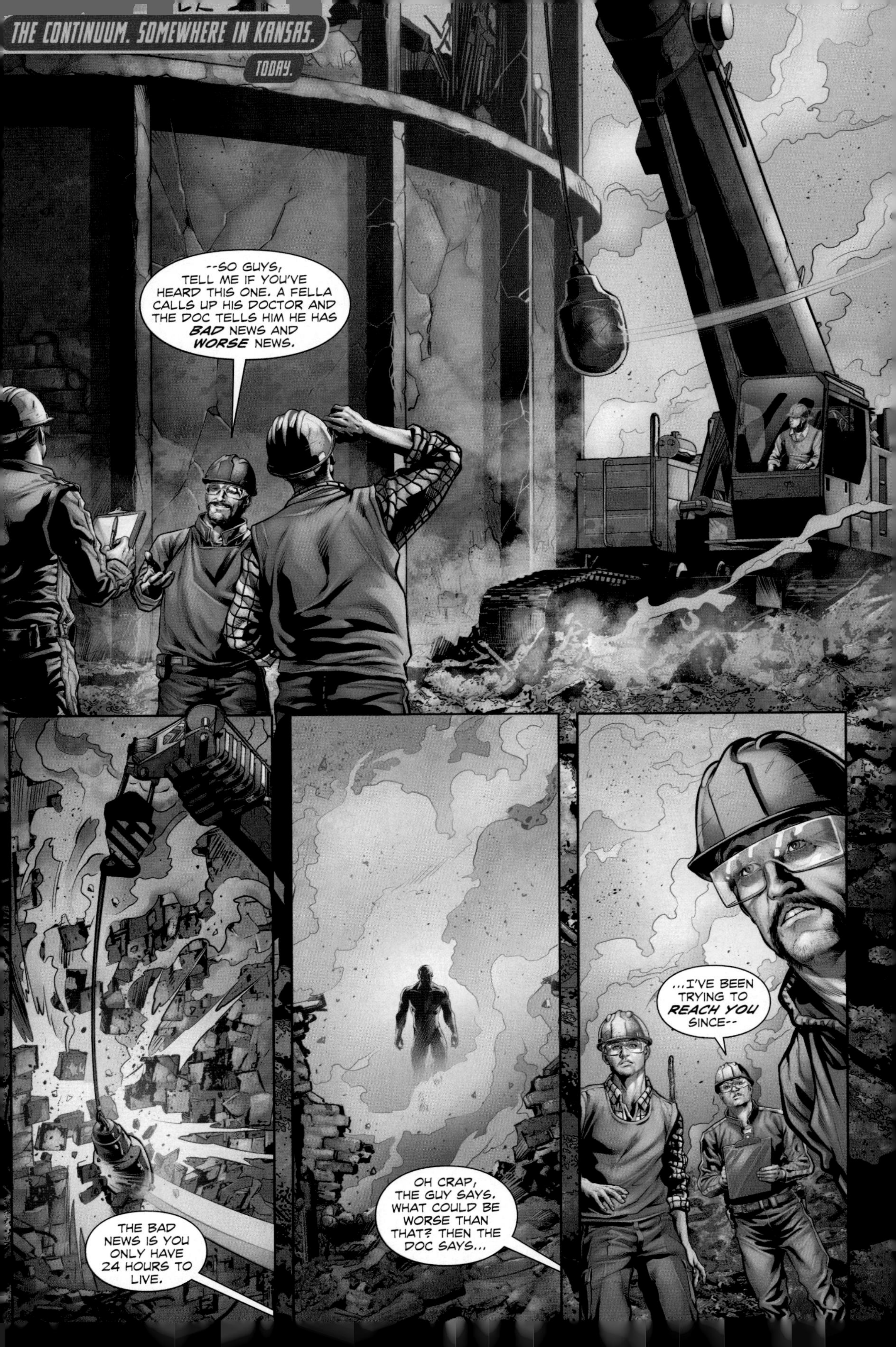
THE CONTINUUM. SOMEWHERE IN KANSAS.
TODAY.
--SO GUYS, TELL ME IF YOU'VE HEARD THIS ONE. A FELLA CALLS UP HIS DOCTOR AND THE DOC TELLS HIM HE HAS BAD NEWS AND WORSE NEWS.
THE BAD NEWS IS YOU ONLY HAVE 24 HOURS TO LIVE.
OH CRAP, THE GUY SAYS. WHAT COULD BE WORSE THAN THAT? THEN THE DOC SAYS...
...I'VE BEEN TRYING TO REACH YOU SINCE--

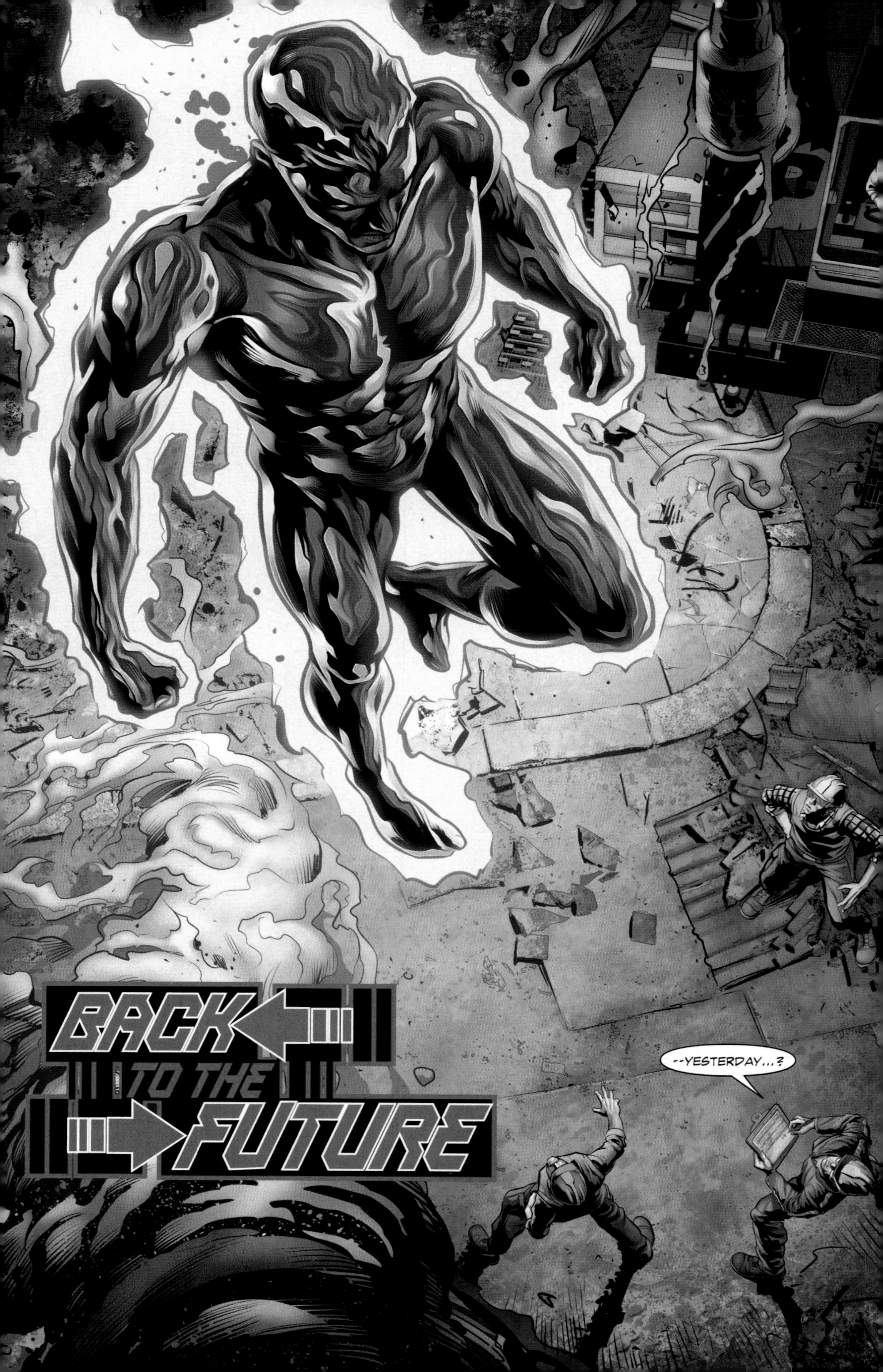
BACK TO THE FUTURE
--YESTERDAY...?

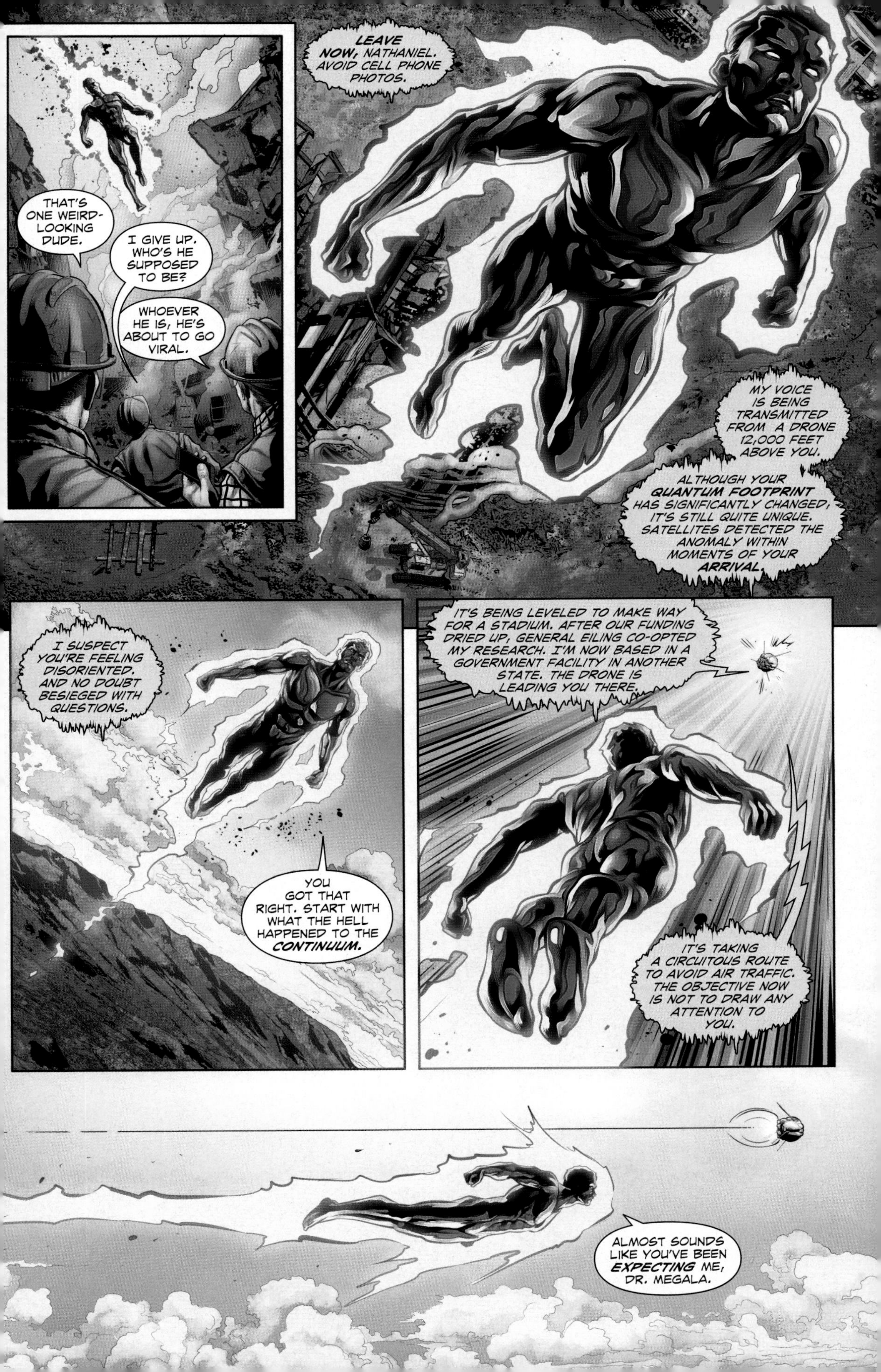
LEAVE NOW, NATHANIEL. AVOID CELL PHONE PHOTOS.
THAT'S ONE WEIRD-LOOKING DUDE.
I GIVE UP. WHO'S HE SUPPOSED TO BE?
WHOEVER HE IS, HE'S ABOUT TO GO VIRAL.
MY VOICE IS BEING TRANSMITTED FROM A DRONE 12,000 FEET ABOVE YOU.
ALTHOUGH YOUR QUANTUM FOOTPRINT HAS SIGNIFICANTLY CHANGED, IT'S STILL QUITE UNIQUE. SATELLITES DETECTED THE ANOMALY WITHIN MOMENTS OF YOUR ARRIVAL.
I SUSPECT YOU'RE FEELING DISORIENTED. AND NO DOUBT BESIEGED WITH QUESTIONS.
YOU GOT THAT RIGHT. START WITH WHAT THE HELL HAPPENED TO THE CONTINUUM.
IT'S BEING LEVELED TO MAKE WAY FOR A STADIUM. AFTER OUR FUNDING DRIED UP, GENERAL EILING CO-OPTED MY RESEARCH. I'M NOW BASED IN A GOVERNMENT FACILITY IN ANOTHER STATE. THE DRONE IS LEADING YOU THERE.
IT'S TAKING A CIRCUITOUS ROUTE TO AVOID AIR TRAFFIC. THE OBJECTIVE NOW IS NOT TO DRAW ANY ATTENTION TO YOU.
ALMOST SOUNDS LIKE YOU'VE BEEN EXPECTING ME, DR. MEGALA.

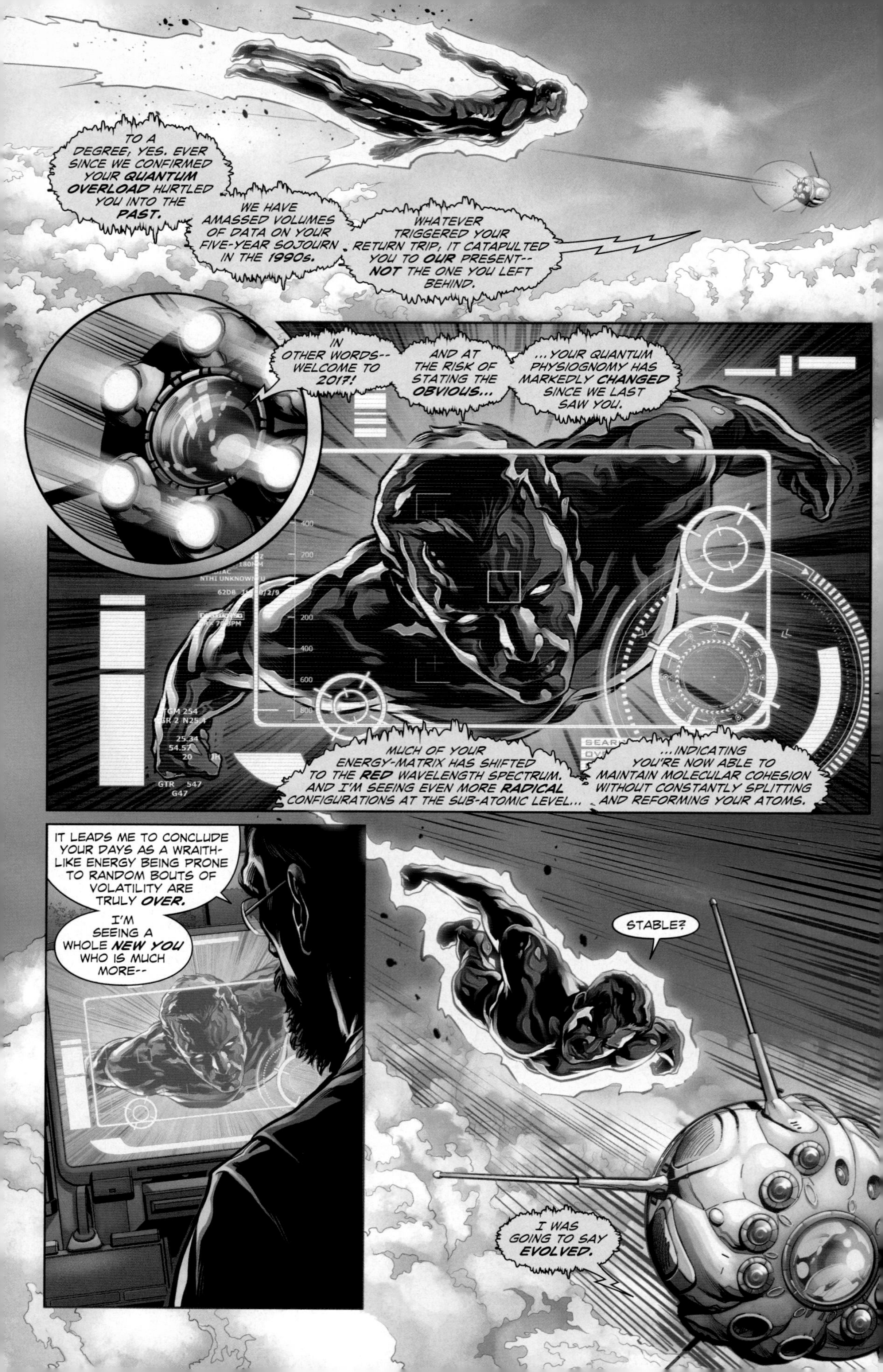
TO A DEGREE, YES. EVER SINCE WE CONFIRMED YOUR QUANTUM OVERLOAD HURTLED YOU INTO THE PAST.
WE HAVE AMASSED VOLUMES OF DATA ON YOUR FIVE-YEAR SOJOURN IN THE 1990s.
WHATEVER TRIGGERED YOUR RETURN TRIP, IT CATAPULTED YOU TO OUR PRESENT--NOT THE ONE YOU LEFT BEHIND.
IN OTHER WORDS--WELCOME TO 2017!
AND AT THE RISK OF STATING THE OBVIOUS...
...YOUR QUANTUM PHYSIOGNOMY HAS MARKEDLY CHANGED SINCE WE LAST SAW YOU.
MUCH OF YOUR ENERGY-MATRIX HAS SHIFTED TO THE RED WAVELENGTH SPECTRUM. AND I'M SEEING EVEN MORE RADICAL CONFIGURATIONS AT THE SUB-ATOMIC LEVEL...
...INDICATING YOU'RE NOW ABLE TO MAINTAIN MOLECULAR COHESION WITHOUT CONSTANTLY SPLITTING AND REFORMING YOUR ATOMS.
IT LEADS ME TO CONCLUDE YOUR DAYS AS A WRAITH-LIKE ENERGY BEING PRONE TO RANDOM BOUTS OF VOLATILITY ARE TRULY OVER.
I'M SEEING A WHOLE NEW YOU WHO IS MUCH MORE--
STABLE?
I WAS GOING TO SAY EVOLVED.

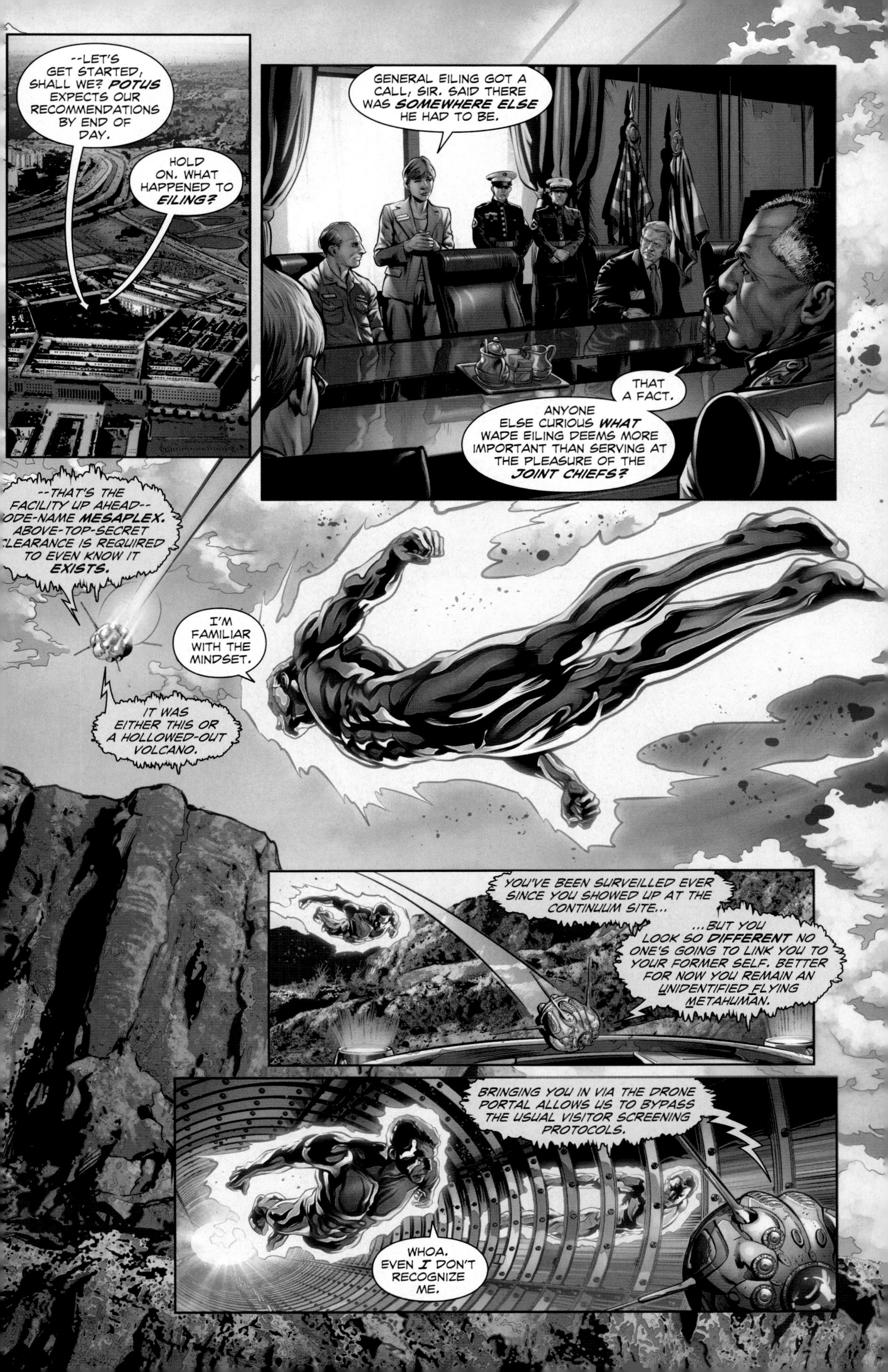
--LET'S GET STARTED, SHALL WE? POTUS EXPECTS OUR RECOMMENDATIONS BY END OF DAY.
HOLD ON. WHAT HAPPENED TO EILING?
GENERAL EILING GOT A CALL, SIR. SAID THERE WAS SOMEWHERE ELSE HE HAD TO BE.
THAT A FACT.
ANYONE ELSE CURIOUS WHAT WADE EILING DEEMS MORE IMPORTANT THAN SERVING AT THE PLEASURE OF THE JOINT CHIEFS?
--THAT'S THE FACILITY UP AHEAD-- CODE-NAME MESAPLEX. ABOVE-TOP-SECRET CLEARANCE IS REQUIRED TO EVEN KNOW IT EXISTS.
I'M FAMILIAR WITH THE MINDSET.
IT WAS EITHER THIS OR A HOLLOWED-OUT VOLCANO.
YOU'VE BEEN SURVEILLED EVER SINCE YOU SHOWED UP AT THE CONTINUUM SITE...
...BUT YOU LOOK SO DIFFERENT NO ONE'S GOING TO LINK YOU TO YOUR FORMER SELF. BETTER FOR NOW YOU REMAIN AN UNIDENTIFIED FLYING METAHUMAN.
BRINGING YOU IN VIA THE DRONE PORTAL ALLOWS US TO BYPASS THE USUAL VISITOR SCREENING PROTOCOLS.
WHOA. EVEN I DON'T RECOGNIZE ME.

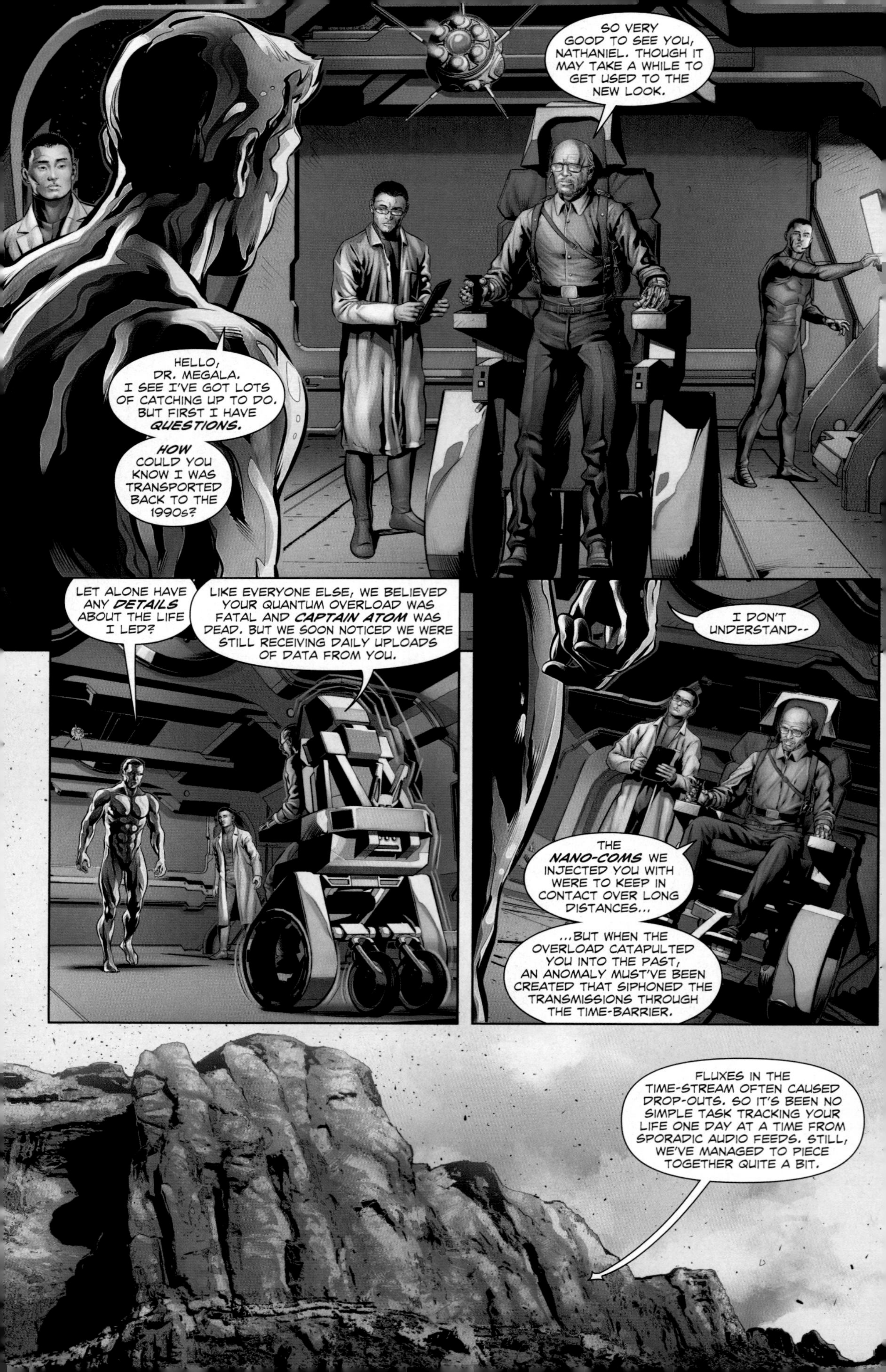

SO VERY GOOD TO SEE YOU, NATHANIEL. THOUGH IT MAY TAKE A WHILE TO GET USED TO THE NEW LOOK.
HELLO, DR. MEGALA. I SEE I'VE GOT LOTS OF CATCHING UP TO DO. BUT FIRST I HAVE *QUESTIONS.*
HOW COULD YOU KNOW I WAS TRANSPORTED BACK TO THE 1990s?
LET ALONE HAVE ANY *DETAILS* ABOUT THE LIFE I LED?
LIKE EVERYONE ELSE, WE BELIEVED YOUR QUANTUM OVERLOAD WAS FATAL AND *CAPTAIN ATOM* WAS DEAD. BUT WE SOON NOTICED WE WERE STILL RECEIVING DAILY UPLOADS OF DATA FROM YOU.
I DON'T UNDERSTAND--
THE *NANO-COMS* WE INJECTED YOU WITH WERE TO KEEP IN CONTACT OVER LONG DISTANCES...
...BUT WHEN THE OVERLOAD CATAPULTED YOU INTO THE PAST, AN ANOMALY MUST'VE BEEN CREATED THAT SIPHONED THE TRANSMISSIONS THROUGH THE TIME-BARRIER.
FLUXES IN THE TIME-STREAM OFTEN CAUSED DROP-OUTS. SO IT'S BEEN NO SIMPLE TASK TRACKING YOUR LIFE ONE DAY AT A TIME FROM SPORADIC AUDIO FEEDS. STILL, WE'VE MANAGED TO PIECE TOGETHER QUITE A BIT.

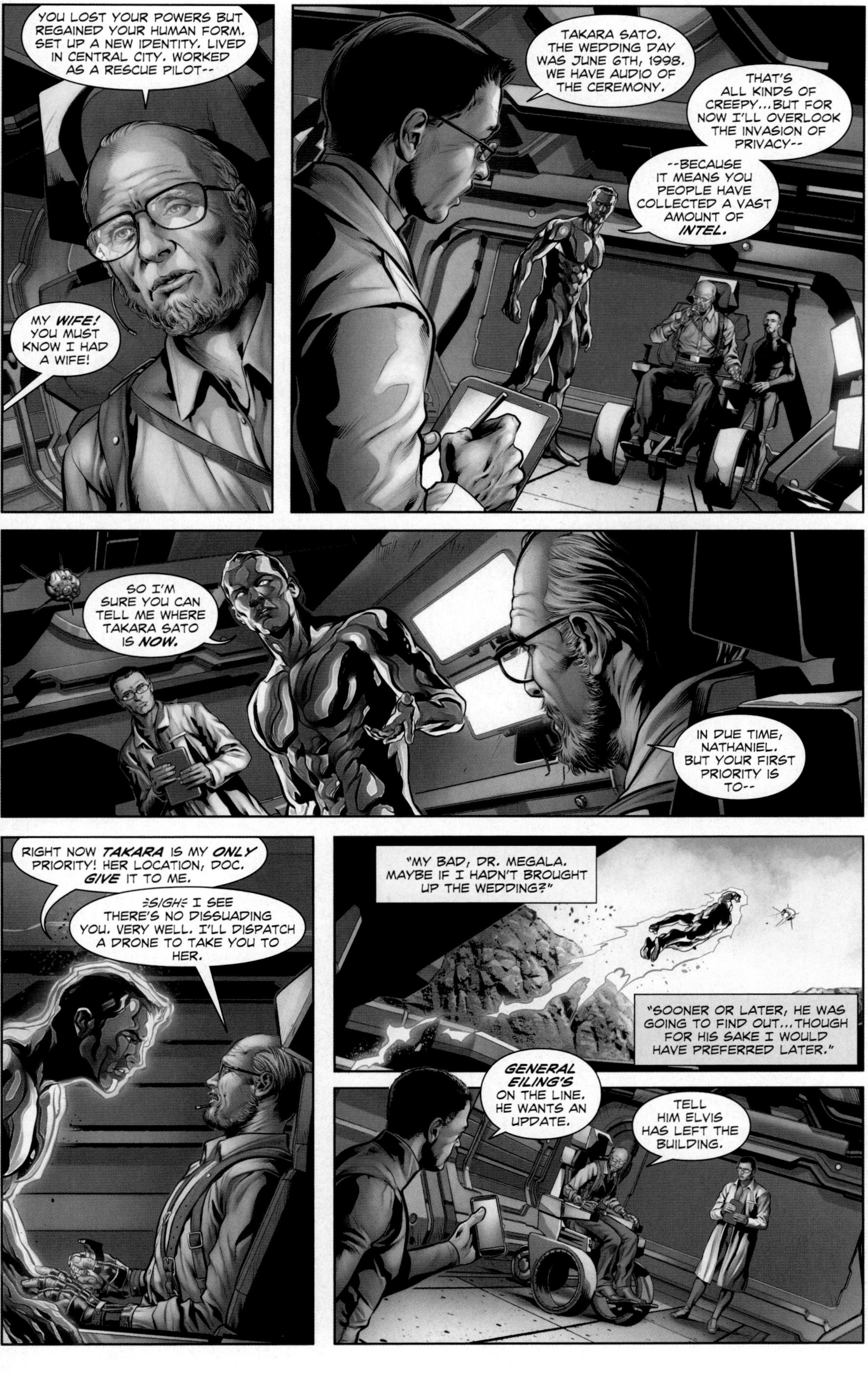
YOU LOST YOUR POWERS BUT REGAINED YOUR HUMAN FORM. SET UP A NEW IDENTITY. LIVED IN CENTRAL CITY. WORKED AS A RESCUE PILOT--
MY WIFE! YOU MUST KNOW I HAD A WIFE!
TAKARA SATO. THE WEDDING DAY WAS JUNE 6TH, 1998. WE HAVE AUDIO OF THE CEREMONY.
THAT'S ALL KINDS OF CREEPY...BUT FOR NOW I'LL OVERLOOK THE INVASION OF PRIVACY--
--BECAUSE IT MEANS YOU PEOPLE HAVE COLLECTED A VAST AMOUNT OF INTEL.
SO I'M SURE YOU CAN TELL ME WHERE TAKARA SATO IS NOW.
IN DUE TIME, NATHANIEL. BUT YOUR FIRST PRIORITY IS TO--
RIGHT NOW TAKARA IS MY ONLY PRIORITY! HER LOCATION, DOC. GIVE IT TO ME.
SIGH I SEE THERE'S NO DISSUADING YOU. VERY WELL. I'LL DISPATCH A DRONE TO TAKE YOU TO HER.
"MY BAD, DR. MEGALA. MAYBE IF I HADN'T BROUGHT UP THE WEDDING?"
"SOONER OR LATER, HE WAS GOING TO FIND OUT...THOUGH FOR HIS SAKE I WOULD HAVE PREFERRED LATER."
GENERAL EILING'S ON THE LINE. HE WANTS AN UPDATE.
TELL HIM ELVIS HAS LEFT THE BUILDING.

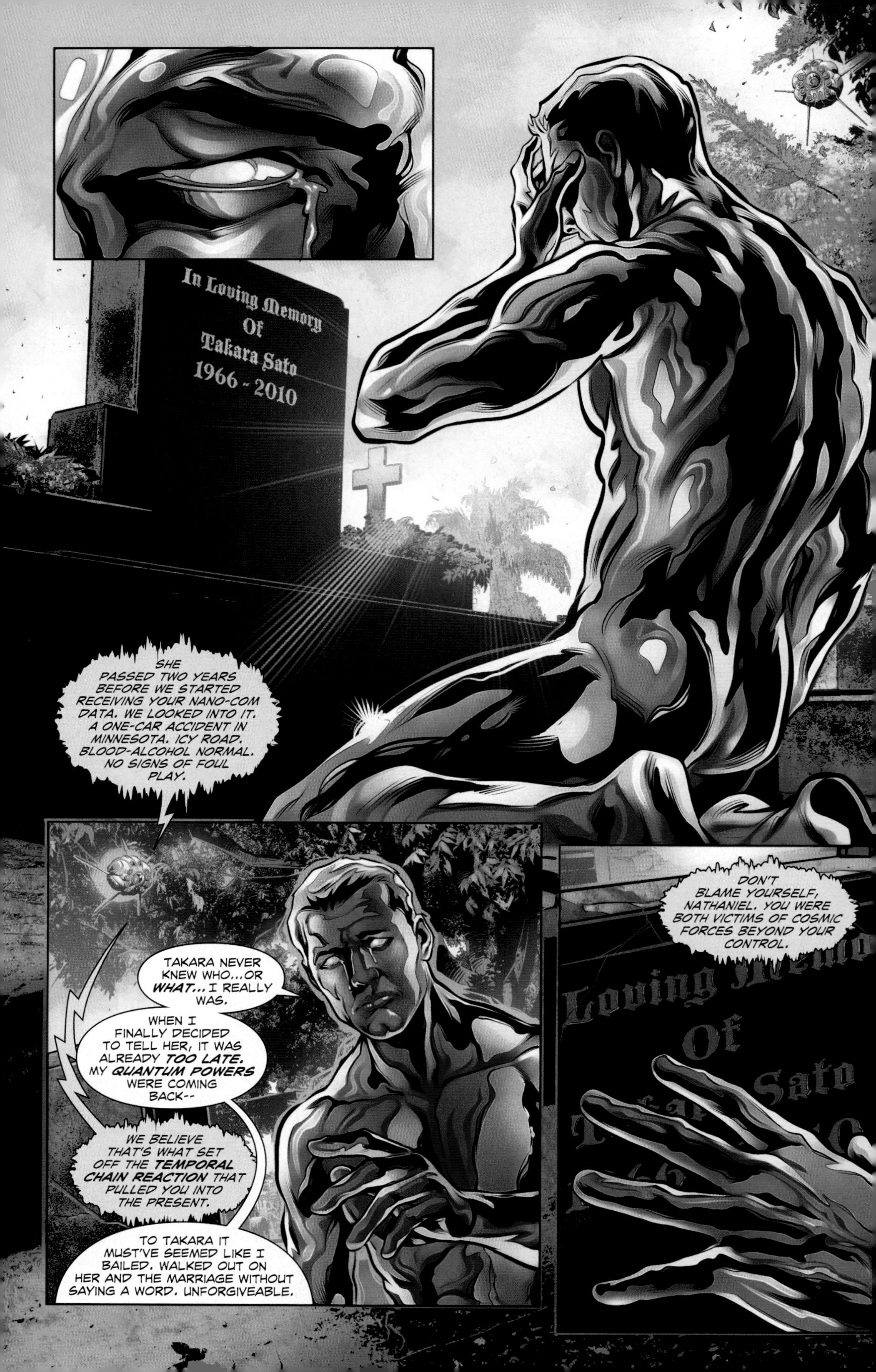

In Loving Memory Of Takara Sato 1966 - 2010
SHE PASSED TWO YEARS BEFORE WE STARTED RECEIVING YOUR NANO-COM DATA. WE LOOKED INTO IT. A ONE-CAR ACCIDENT IN MINNESOTA. ICY ROAD. BLOOD-ALCOHOL NORMAL. NO SIGNS OF FOUL PLAY.
TAKARA NEVER KNEW WHO...OR WHAT... I REALLY WAS.
WHEN I FINALLY DECIDED TO TELL HER, IT WAS ALREADY TOO LATE. MY QUANTUM POWERS WERE COMING BACK--
WE BELIEVE THAT'S WHAT SET OFF THE TEMPORAL CHAIN REACTION THAT PULLED YOU INTO THE PRESENT.
TO TAKARA IT MUST'VE SEEMED LIKE I BAILED. WALKED OUT ON HER AND THE MARRIAGE WITHOUT SAYING A WORD. UNFORGIVEABLE.
DON'T BLAME YOURSELF, NATHANIEL. YOU WERE BOTH VICTIMS OF COSMIC FORCES BEYOND YOUR CONTROL.

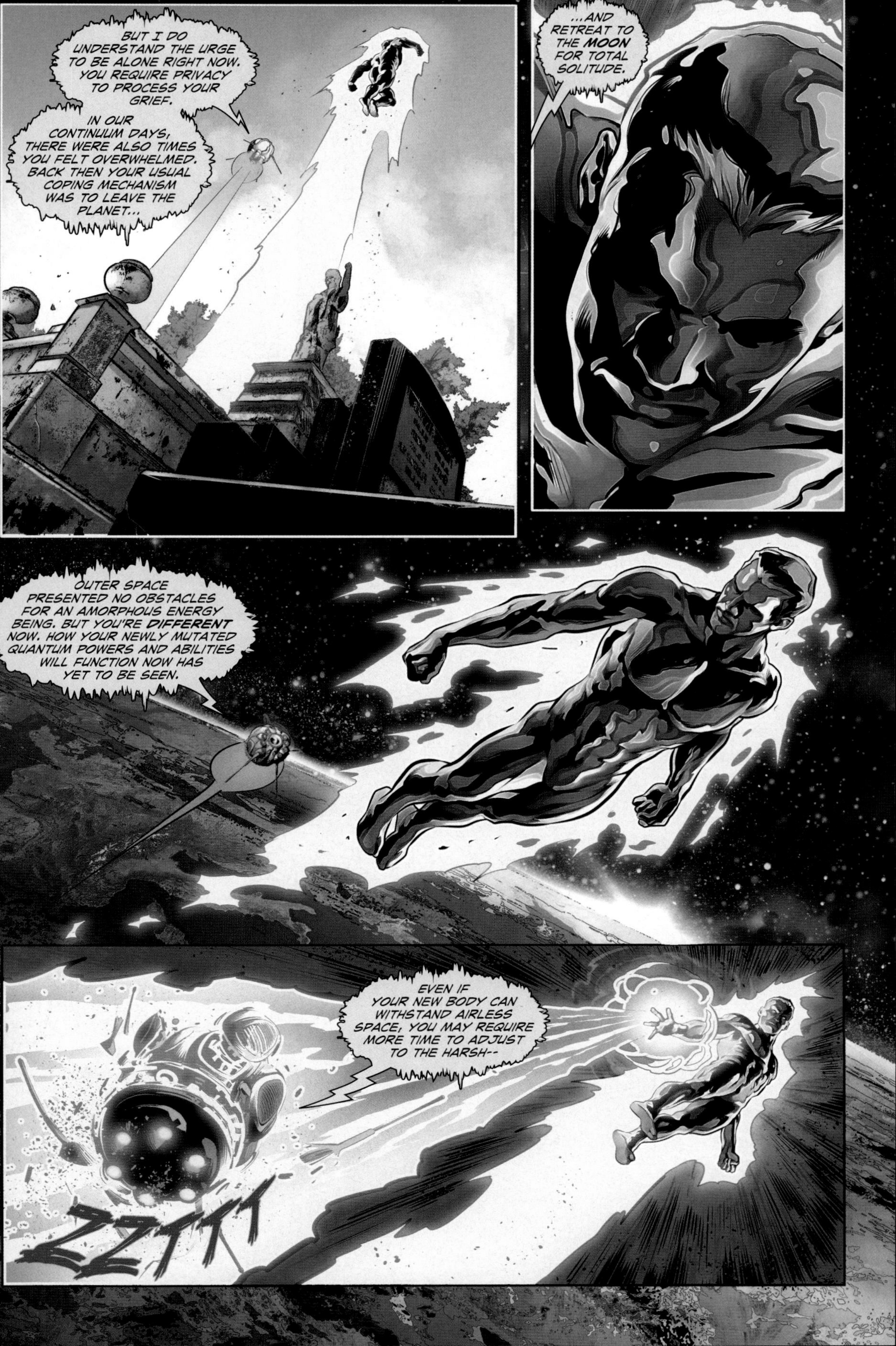
BUT I DO UNDERSTAND THE URGE TO BE ALONE RIGHT NOW. YOU REQUIRE PRIVACY TO PROCESS YOUR GRIEF.
IN OUR CONTINUUM DAYS, THERE WERE ALSO TIMES YOU FELT OVERWHELMED. BACK THEN YOUR USUAL COPING MECHANISM WAS TO LEAVE THE PLANET...
...AND RETREAT TO THE MOON FOR TOTAL SOLITUDE.
OUTER SPACE PRESENTED NO OBSTACLES FOR AN AMORPHOUS ENERGY BEING. BUT YOU'RE DIFFERENT NOW. HOW YOUR NEWLY MUTATED QUANTUM POWERS AND ABILITIES WILL FUNCTION NOW HAS YET TO BE SEEN.
EVEN IF YOUR NEW BODY CAN WITHSTAND AIRLESS SPACE, YOU MAY REQUIRE MORE TIME TO ADJUST TO THE HARSH--
ZZTTT

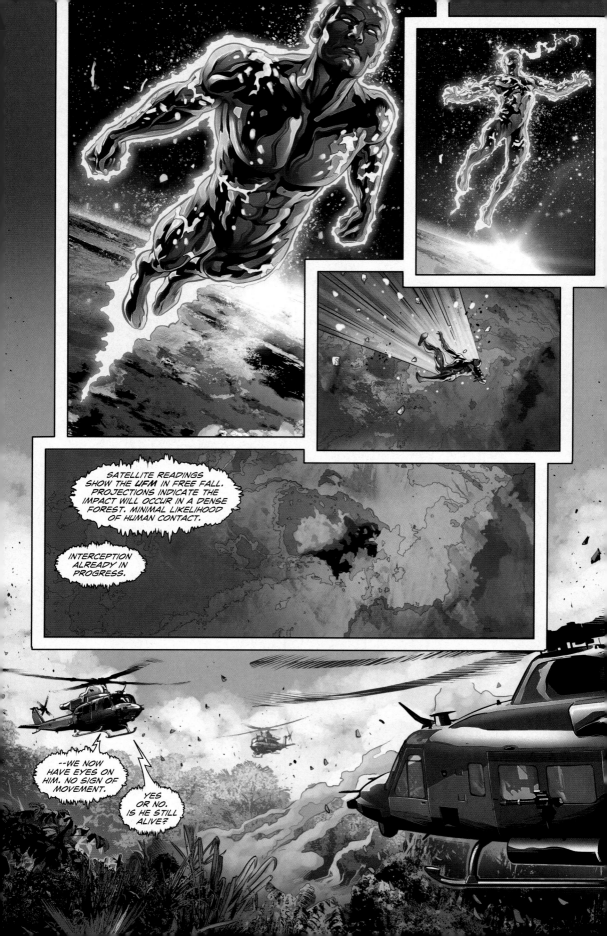

SATELLITE READINGS SHOW THE **UFM** IN FREE FALL. PROJECTIONS INDICATE THE IMPACT WILL OCCUR IN A DENSE FOREST. MINIMAL LIKELIHOOD OF HUMAN CONTACT.

INTERCEPTION ALREADY IN PROGRESS.

--WE NOW HAVE EYES ON HIM. NO SIGN OF MOVEMENT.

YES OR NO. IS HE STILL ALIVE?

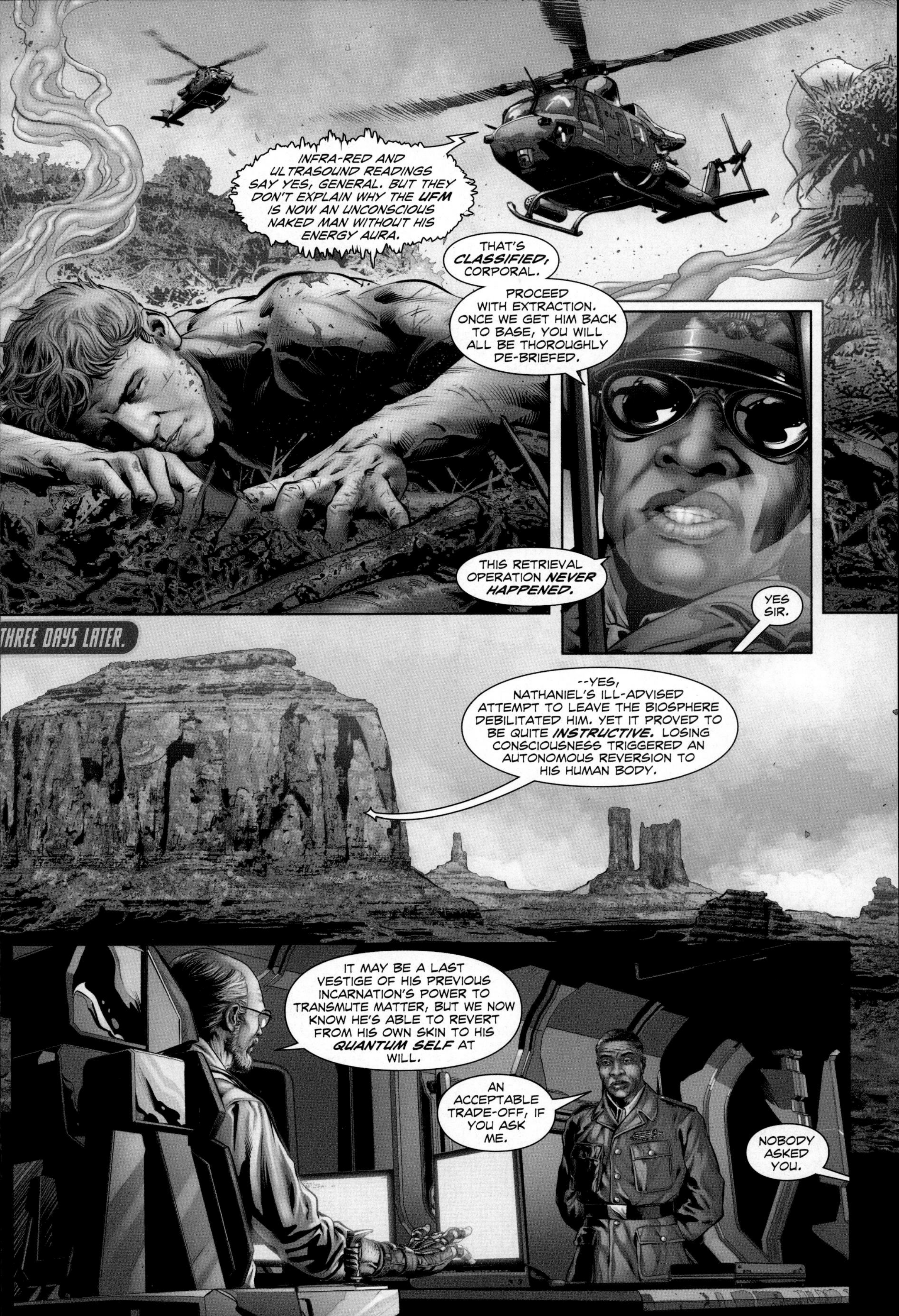
INFRA-RED AND ULTRASOUND READINGS SAY YES, GENERAL. BUT THEY DON'T EXPLAIN WHY THE UFM IS NOW AN UNCONSCIOUS NAKED MAN WITHOUT HIS ENERGY AURA.
THAT'S CLASSIFIED, CORPORAL.
PROCEED WITH EXTRACTION. ONCE WE GET HIM BACK TO BASE, YOU WILL ALL BE THOROUGHLY DE-BRIEFED.
THIS RETRIEVAL OPERATION NEVER HAPPENED.
YES SIR.
THREE DAYS LATER.
--YES, NATHANIEL'S ILL-ADVISED ATTEMPT TO LEAVE THE BIOSPHERE DEBILITATED HIM. YET IT PROVED TO BE QUITE INSTRUCTIVE. LOSING CONSCIOUSNESS TRIGGERED AN AUTONOMOUS REVERSION TO HIS HUMAN BODY.
IT MAY BE A LAST VESTIGE OF HIS PREVIOUS INCARNATION'S POWER TO TRANSMUTE MATTER, BUT WE NOW KNOW HE'S ABLE TO REVERT FROM HIS OWN SKIN TO HIS QUANTUM SELF AT WILL.
AN ACCEPTABLE TRADE-OFF, IF YOU ASK ME.
NOBODY ASKED YOU.

WE GET IT, SOLDIER. NOTHING MATTERS RIGHT NOW. YOU'RE STILL IN MOURNING OVER YOUR LATE WIFE.

KNOW THAT DR. MEGALA AND I ARE SORRY FOR YOUR LOSS. WE FEEL YOUR PAIN.

AND LOOKING AHEAD, WE BOTH WANT YOU TO BE ALL YOU CAN *BE.* BUT WE CAN'T REALLY TALK ABOUT WHAT THE FUTURE MAY HOLD--NOT WITHOUT FIRST ADDRESSING THE PAST.

YOUR PAST.

--WE NOW HAVE CONFIRMATION *CAPTAIN ATOM* IS DEAD, A VICTIM OF HIS OWN UNSTABLE POWERS.

AS DAMAGE REPORTS MOUNT, IT'S CLEAR THE *DEVASTATION* HE UNLEASHED TODAY WILL FOREVER BE HIS TRAGIC LEGACY.

IF NOT FOR *SUPERMAN, GREEN LANTERN* AND *CYBORG* THE WAKE OF DESTRUCTION WOULD HAVE BEEN EVEN *WORSE*--

DECEMBER

...ORTS STILL COMING, THE DEVASTA...

THE NEWSCASTS WERE UNRELENTING. YOUR CATASTROPHIC OVERLOAD ATTRACTED WORLD-WIDE MEDIA COVERAGE. NOW YOU SEE WHY WE'VE KEPT YOUR RETURN A SECRET.

THAT CAPTAIN ATOM WAS A PUBLIC MENACE AND RADIOACTIVE BOOGEYMAN. NO ONE WANTS TO SEE *HIM* COME BACK.

BUT THERE IS A SECOND OPTION.

WHILE YOU WERE CONVALESCING FROM YOUR HIGH-ALTITUDE FALL, MY INTERNAL PSYOPS TEAM WAS WORKING OVERTIME. WE CALL THIS *PROJECT RESURGENCE.*

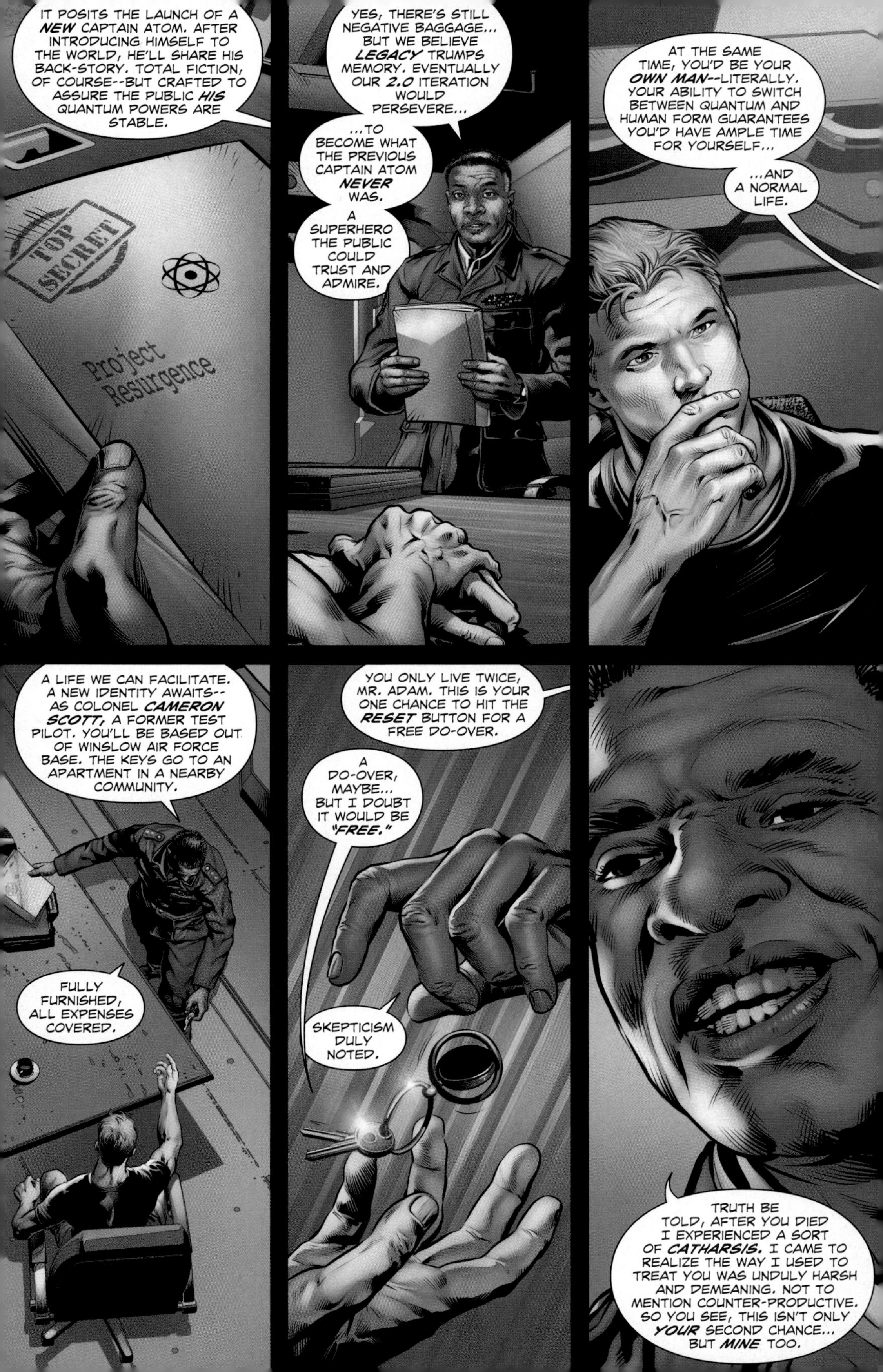

IT POSITS THE LAUNCH OF A NEW CAPTAIN ATOM. AFTER INTRODUCING HIMSELF TO THE WORLD, HE'LL SHARE HIS BACK-STORY. TOTAL FICTION, OF COURSE--BUT CRAFTED TO ASSURE THE PUBLIC HIS QUANTUM POWERS ARE STABLE.
TOP SECRET
Project Resurgence
YES, THERE'S STILL NEGATIVE BAGGAGE... BUT WE BELIEVE LEGACY TRUMPS MEMORY. EVENTUALLY OUR 2.0 ITERATION WOULD PERSEVERE...
...TO BECOME WHAT THE PREVIOUS CAPTAIN ATOM NEVER WAS.
A SUPERHERO THE PUBLIC COULD TRUST AND ADMIRE.
AT THE SAME TIME, YOU'D BE YOUR OWN MAN--LITERALLY. YOUR ABILITY TO SWITCH BETWEEN QUANTUM AND HUMAN FORM GUARANTEES YOU'D HAVE AMPLE TIME FOR YOURSELF...
...AND A NORMAL LIFE.
A LIFE WE CAN FACILITATE. A NEW IDENTITY AWAITS--AS COLONEL CAMERON SCOTT, A FORMER TEST PILOT. YOU'LL BE BASED OUT OF WINSLOW AIR FORCE BASE. THE KEYS GO TO AN APARTMENT IN A NEARBY COMMUNITY.
FULLY FURNISHED, ALL EXPENSES COVERED.
YOU ONLY LIVE TWICE, MR. ADAM. THIS IS YOUR ONE CHANCE TO HIT THE RESET BUTTON FOR A FREE DO-OVER.
A DO-OVER, MAYBE... BUT I DOUBT IT WOULD BE "FREE."
SKEPTICISM DULY NOTED.
TRUTH BE TOLD, AFTER YOU DIED I EXPERIENCED A SORT OF CATHARSIS. I CAME TO REALIZE THE WAY I USED TO TREAT YOU WAS UNDULY HARSH AND DEMEANING. NOT TO MENTION COUNTER-PRODUCTIVE. SO YOU SEE, THIS ISN'T ONLY YOUR SECOND CHANCE... BUT MINE TOO.

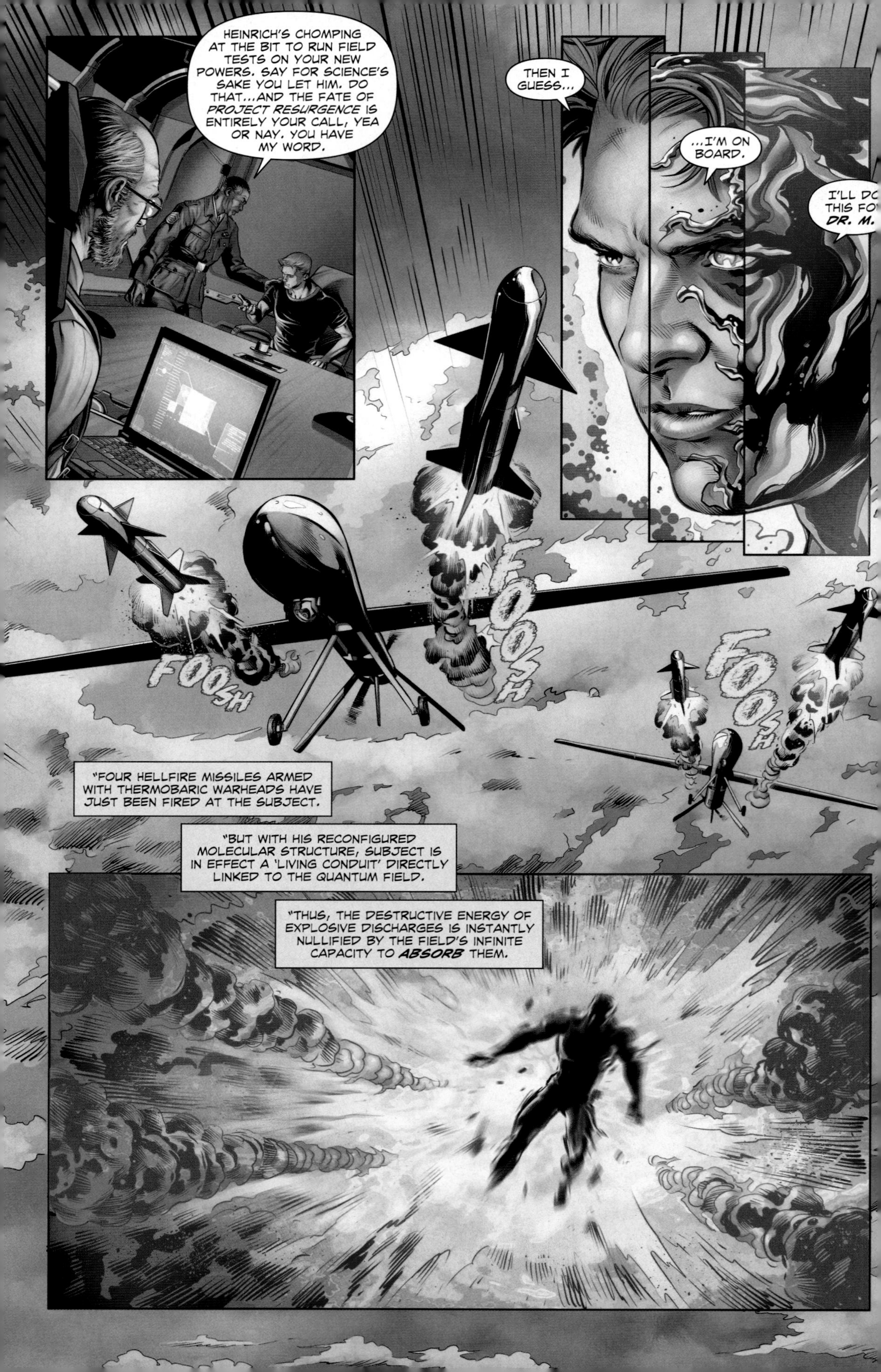
HEINRICH'S CHOMPING AT THE BIT TO RUN FIELD TESTS ON YOUR NEW POWERS. SAY FOR SCIENCE'S SAKE YOU LET HIM. DO THAT...AND THE FATE OF *PROJECT RESURGENCE* IS ENTIRELY YOUR CALL, YEA OR NAY. YOU HAVE MY WORD.
THEN I GUESS...
...I'M ON BOARD.
FOOSH
FOOSH
FOOSH
"FOUR HELLFIRE MISSILES ARMED WITH THERMOBARIC WARHEADS HAVE JUST BEEN FIRED AT THE SUBJECT.
"BUT WITH HIS RECONFIGURED MOLECULAR STRUCTURE, SUBJECT IS IN EFFECT A 'LIVING CONDUIT' DIRECTLY LINKED TO THE QUANTUM FIELD.
"THUS, THE DESTRUCTIVE ENERGY OF EXPLOSIVE DISCHARGES IS INSTANTLY NULLIFIED BY THE FIELD'S INFINITE CAPACITY TO ***ABSORB*** THEM.

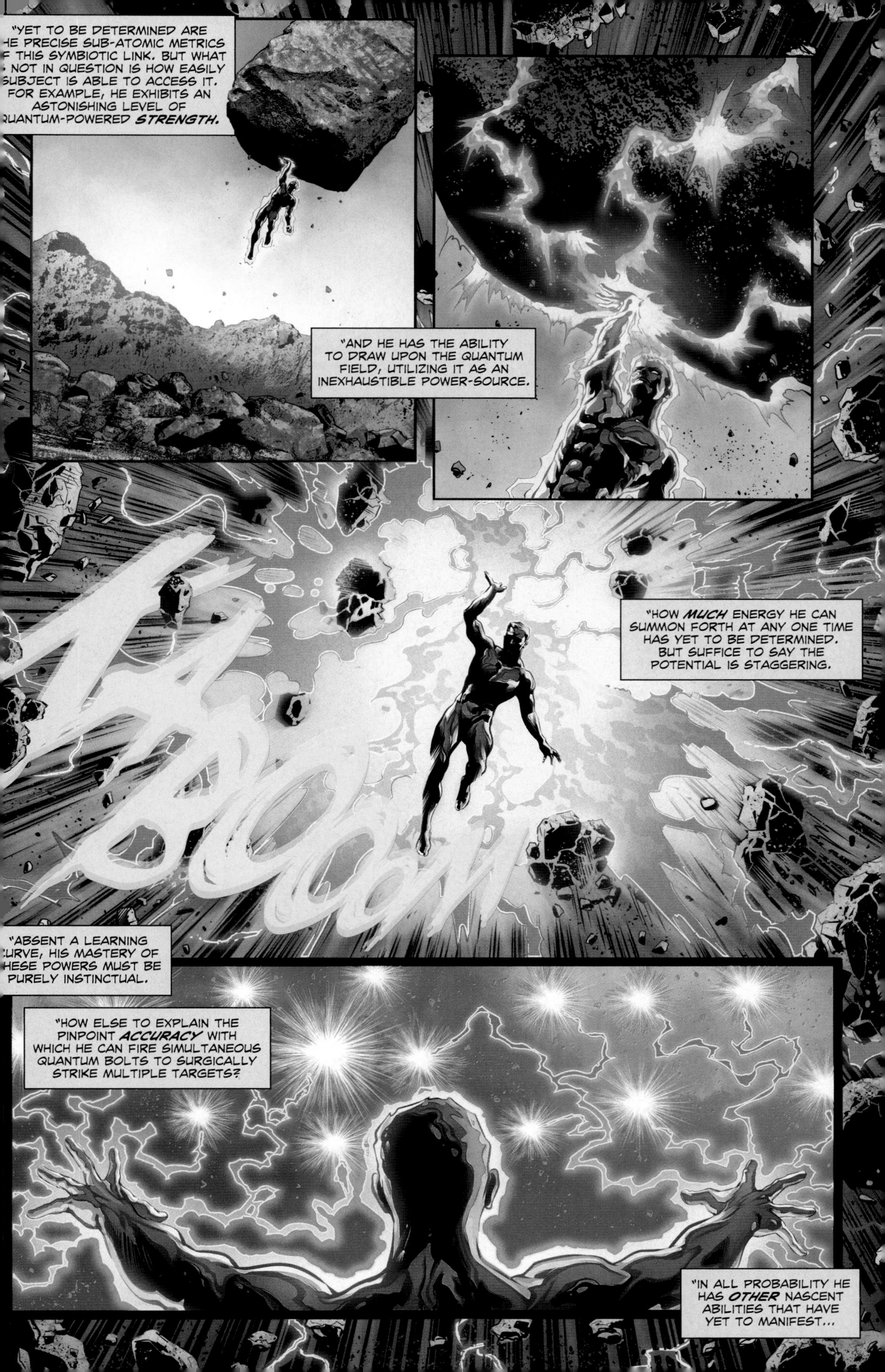
"YET TO BE DETERMINED ARE
HE PRECISE SUB-ATOMIC METRICS
F THIS SYMBIOTIC LINK. BUT WHAT
NOT IN QUESTION IS HOW EASILY
SUBJECT IS ABLE TO ACCESS IT.
FOR EXAMPLE, HE EXHIBITS AN
ASTONISHING LEVEL OF
QUANTUM-POWERED STRENGTH.
"AND HE HAS THE ABILITY TO DRAW UPON THE QUANTUM FIELD, UTILIZING IT AS AN INEXHAUSTIBLE POWER-SOURCE.
"HOW MUCH ENERGY HE CAN SUMMON FORTH AT ANY ONE TIME HAS YET TO BE DETERMINED. BUT SUFFICE TO SAY THE POTENTIAL IS STAGGERING.
KA-BOOOOM
"ABSENT A LEARNING
CURVE, HIS MASTERY OF
HESE POWERS MUST BE
PURELY INSTINCTUAL.
"HOW ELSE TO EXPLAIN THE PINPOINT ACCURACY WITH WHICH HE CAN FIRE SIMULTANEOUS QUANTUM BOLTS TO SURGICALLY STRIKE MULTIPLE TARGETS?
"IN ALL PROBABILITY HE HAS OTHER NASCENT ABILITIES THAT HAVE YET TO MANIFEST...

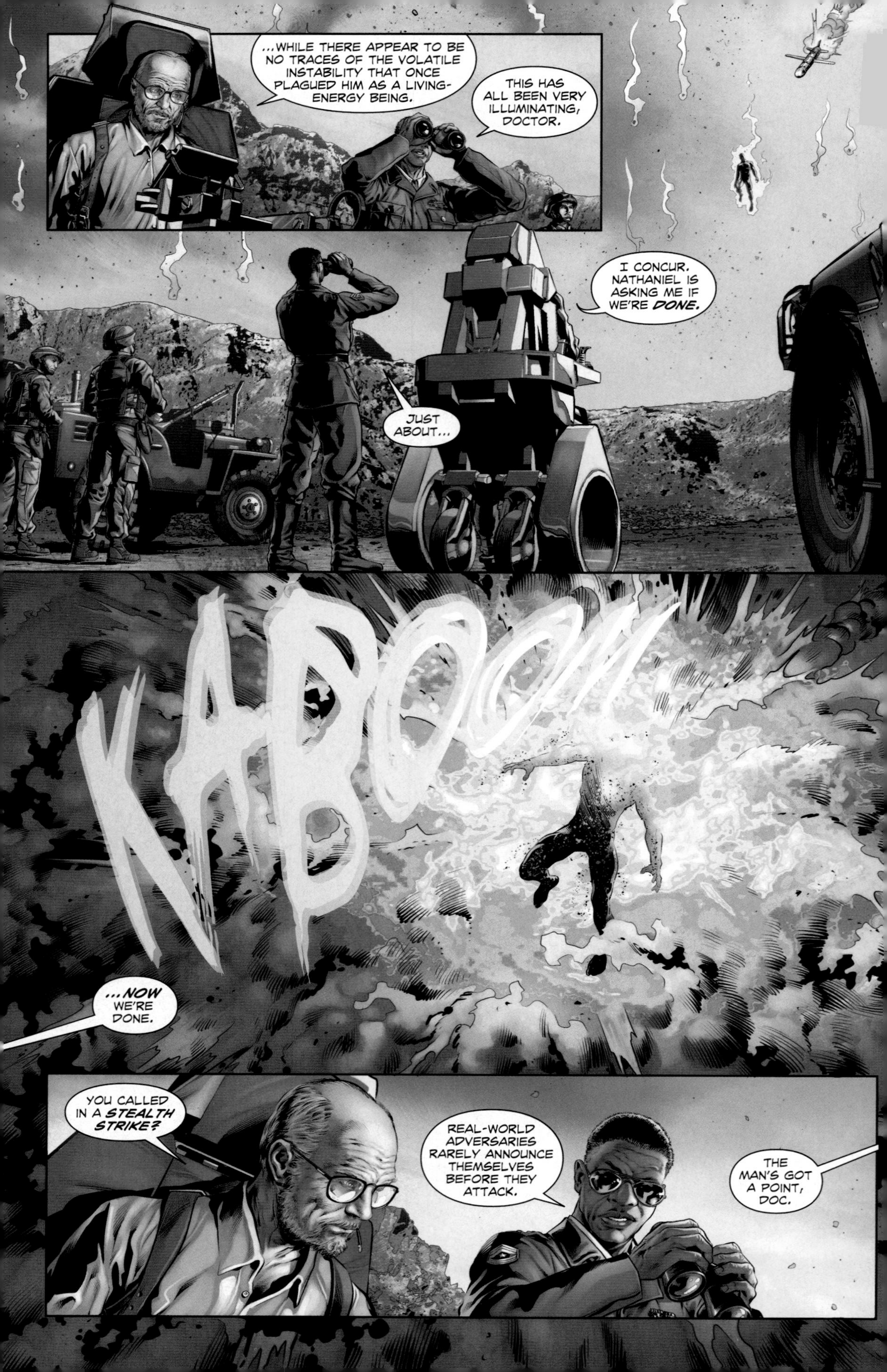
...WHILE THERE APPEAR TO BE NO TRACES OF THE VOLATILE INSTABILITY THAT ONCE PLAGUED HIM AS A LIVING-ENERGY BEING.
THIS HAS ALL BEEN VERY ILLUMINATING, DOCTOR.
I CONCUR. NATHANIEL IS ASKING ME IF WE'RE *DONE.*
JUST ABOUT...
KABOOM
...*NOW* WE'RE DONE.
YOU CALLED IN A *STEALTH STRIKE?*
REAL-WORLD ADVERSARIES RARELY ANNOUNCE THEMSELVES BEFORE THEY ATTACK.
THE MAN'S GOT A POINT, DOC.

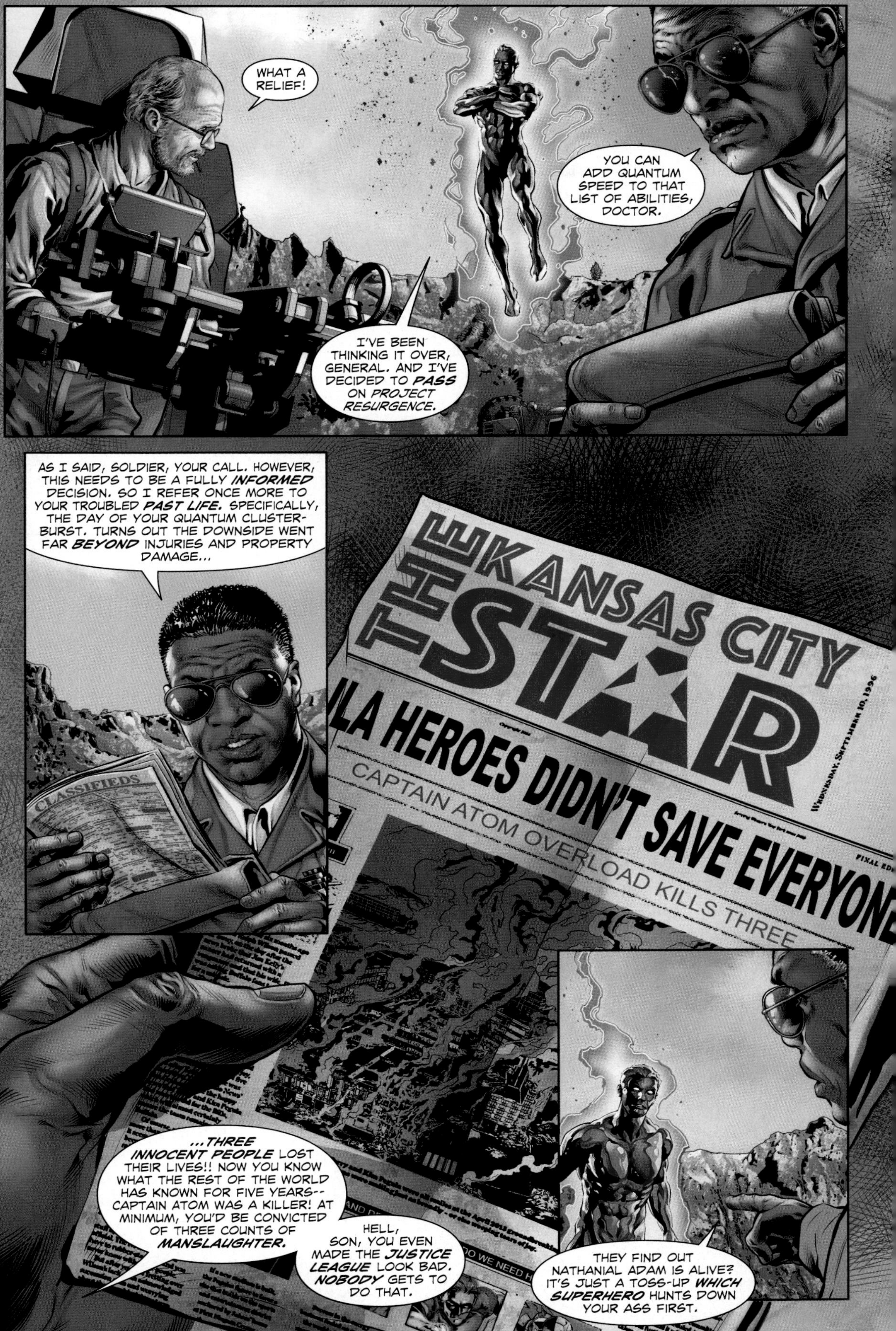
WHAT A RELIEF!
YOU CAN ADD QUANTUM SPEED TO THAT LIST OF ABILITIES, DOCTOR.
I'VE BEEN THINKING IT OVER, GENERAL. AND I'VE DECIDED TO PASS ON PROJECT RESURGENCE.
AS I SAID, SOLDIER, YOUR CALL. HOWEVER, THIS NEEDS TO BE A FULLY INFORMED DECISION. SO I REFER ONCE MORE TO YOUR TROUBLED PAST LIFE. SPECIFICALLY, THE DAY OF YOUR QUANTUM CLUSTER-BURST. TURNS OUT THE DOWNSIDE WENT FAR BEYOND INJURIES AND PROPERTY DAMAGE...
CLASSIFIEDS
THE KANSAS CITY STAR
WEDNESDAY, SEPTEMBER 10, 1996
JLA HEROES DIDN'T SAVE EVERYONE
CAPTAIN ATOM OVERLOAD KILLS THREE
...THREE INNOCENT PEOPLE LOST THEIR LIVES!! NOW YOU KNOW WHAT THE REST OF THE WORLD HAS KNOWN FOR FIVE YEARS-- CAPTAIN ATOM WAS A KILLER! AT MINIMUM, YOU'D BE CONVICTED OF THREE COUNTS OF MANSLAUGHTER.
HELL, SON, YOU EVEN MADE THE JUSTICE LEAGUE LOOK BAD. NOBODY GETS TO DO THAT.
THEY FIND OUT NATHANIAL ADAM IS ALIVE? IT'S JUST A TOSS-UP WHICH SUPERHERO HUNTS DOWN YOUR ASS FIRST.

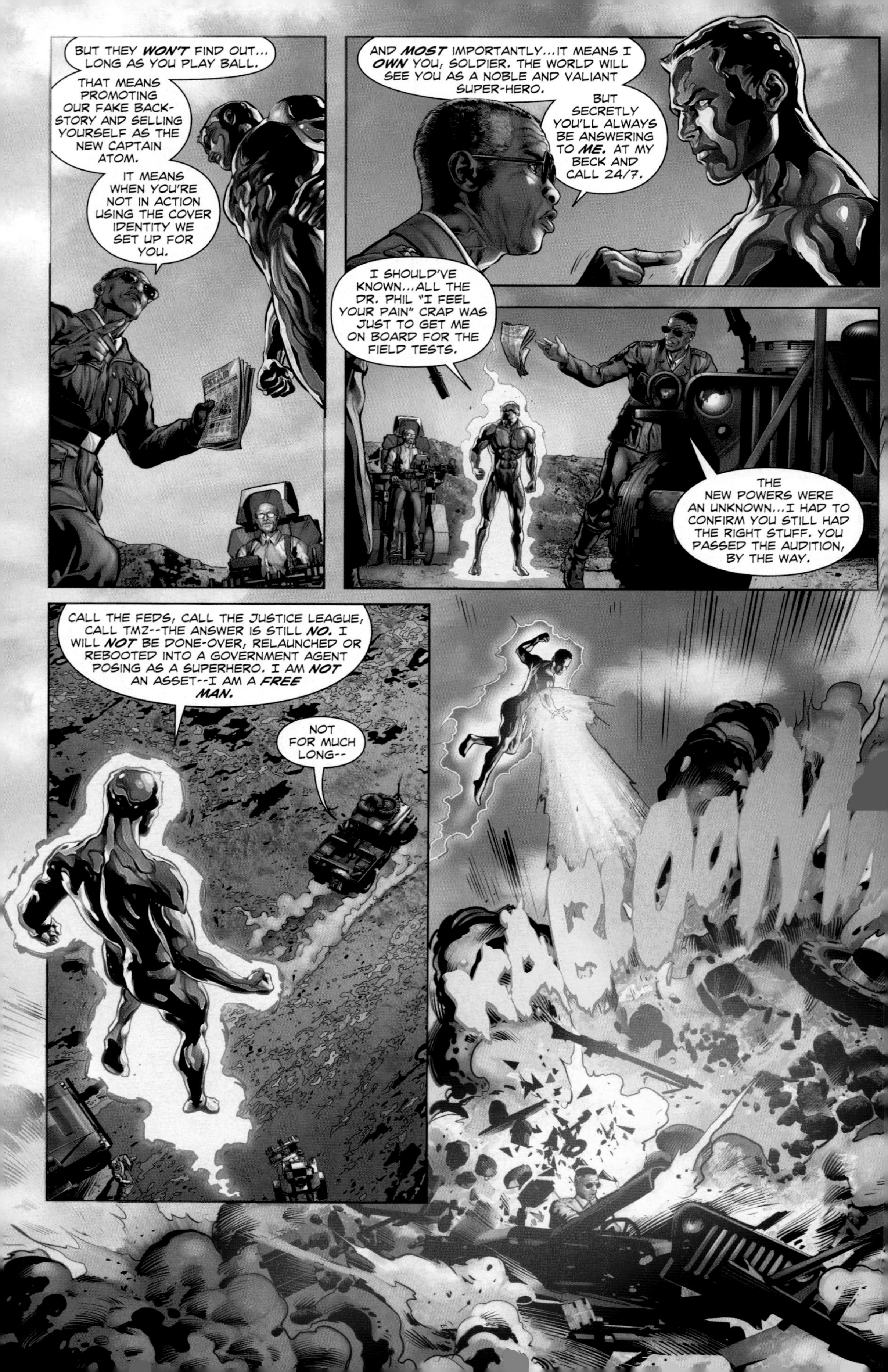
BUT THEY WON'T FIND OUT... LONG AS YOU PLAY BALL.
THAT MEANS PROMOTING OUR FAKE BACK-STORY AND SELLING YOURSELF AS THE NEW CAPTAIN ATOM.
IT MEANS WHEN YOU'RE NOT IN ACTION USING THE COVER IDENTITY WE SET UP FOR YOU.
AND MOST IMPORTANTLY...IT MEANS I OWN YOU, SOLDIER. THE WORLD WILL SEE YOU AS A NOBLE AND VALIANT SUPER-HERO.
BUT SECRETLY YOU'LL ALWAYS BE ANSWERING TO ME. AT MY BECK AND CALL 24/7.
I SHOULD'VE KNOWN...ALL THE DR. PHIL "I FEEL YOUR PAIN" CRAP WAS JUST TO GET ME ON BOARD FOR THE FIELD TESTS.
THE NEW POWERS WERE AN UNKNOWN...I HAD TO CONFIRM YOU STILL HAD THE RIGHT STUFF. YOU PASSED THE AUDITION, BY THE WAY.
CALL THE FEDS, CALL THE JUSTICE LEAGUE, CALL TMZ--THE ANSWER IS STILL NO. I WILL NOT BE DONE-OVER, RELAUNCHED OR REBOOTED INTO A GOVERNMENT AGENT POSING AS A SUPERHERO. I AM NOT AN ASSET--I AM A FREE MAN.
NOT FOR MUCH LONG--

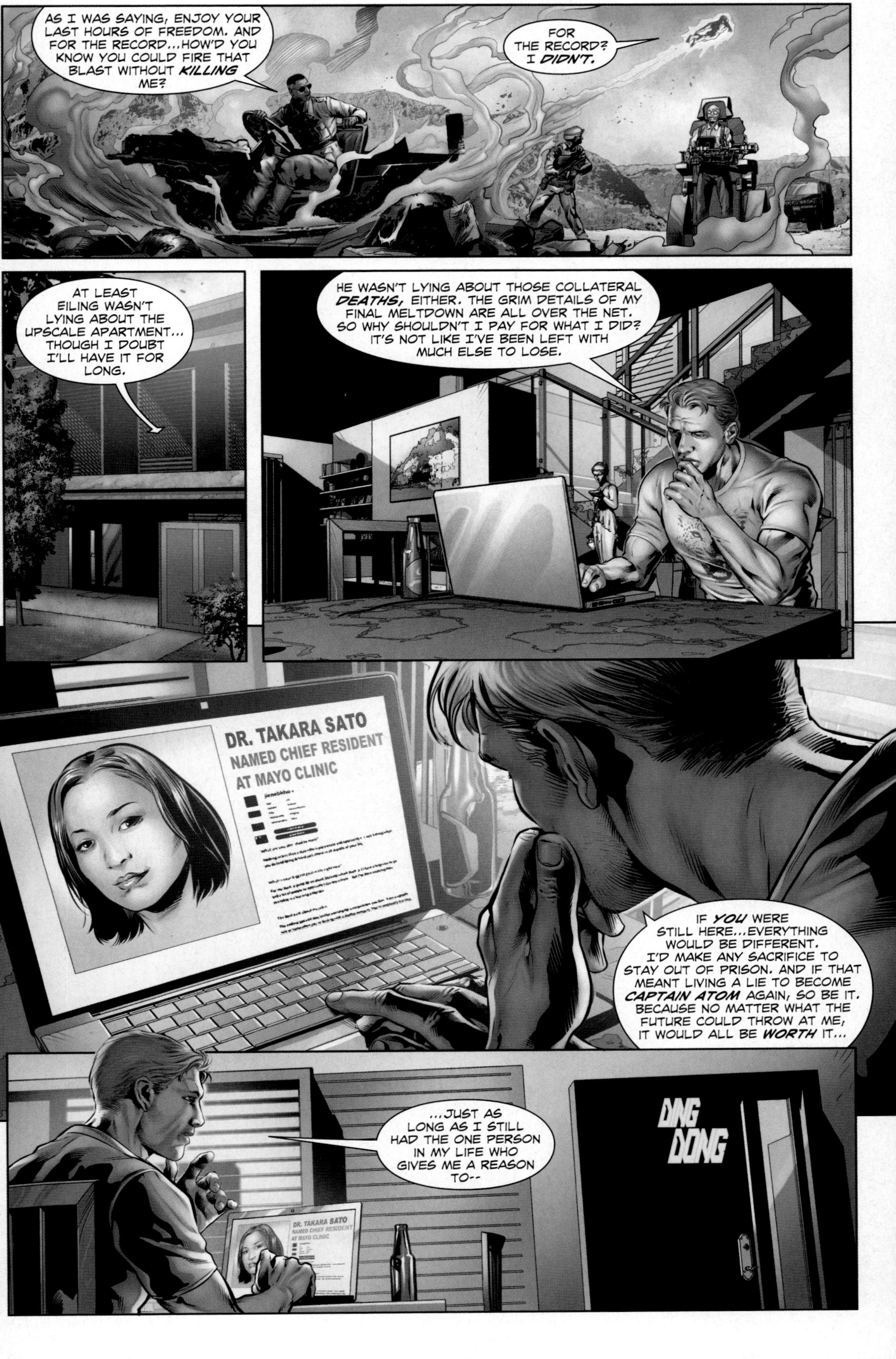

AS I WAS SAYING, ENJOY YOUR LAST HOURS OF FREEDOM. AND FOR THE RECORD...HOW'D YOU KNOW YOU COULD FIRE THAT BLAST WITHOUT KILLING ME?
FOR THE RECORD? I DIDN'T.
AT LEAST EILING WASN'T LYING ABOUT THE UPSCALE APARTMENT... THOUGH I DOUBT I'LL HAVE IT FOR LONG.
HE WASN'T LYING ABOUT THOSE COLLATERAL DEATHS, EITHER. THE GRIM DETAILS OF MY FINAL MELTDOWN ARE ALL OVER THE NET. SO WHY SHOULDN'T I PAY FOR WHAT I DID? IT'S NOT LIKE I'VE BEEN LEFT WITH MUCH ELSE TO LOSE.
DR. TAKARA SATO
NAMED CHIEF RESIDENT AT MAYO CLINIC
IF YOU WERE STILL HERE...EVERYTHING WOULD BE DIFFERENT. I'D MAKE ANY SACRIFICE TO STAY OUT OF PRISON. AND IF THAT MEANT LIVING A LIE TO BECOME CAPTAIN ATOM AGAIN, SO BE IT. BECAUSE NO MATTER WHAT THE FUTURE COULD THROW AT ME, IT WOULD ALL BE WORTH IT...
...JUST AS LONG AS I STILL HAD THE ONE PERSON IN MY LIFE WHO GIVES ME A REASON TO--
DING DONG
DR. TAKARA SATO
NAMED CHIEF RESIDENT AT MAYO CLINIC

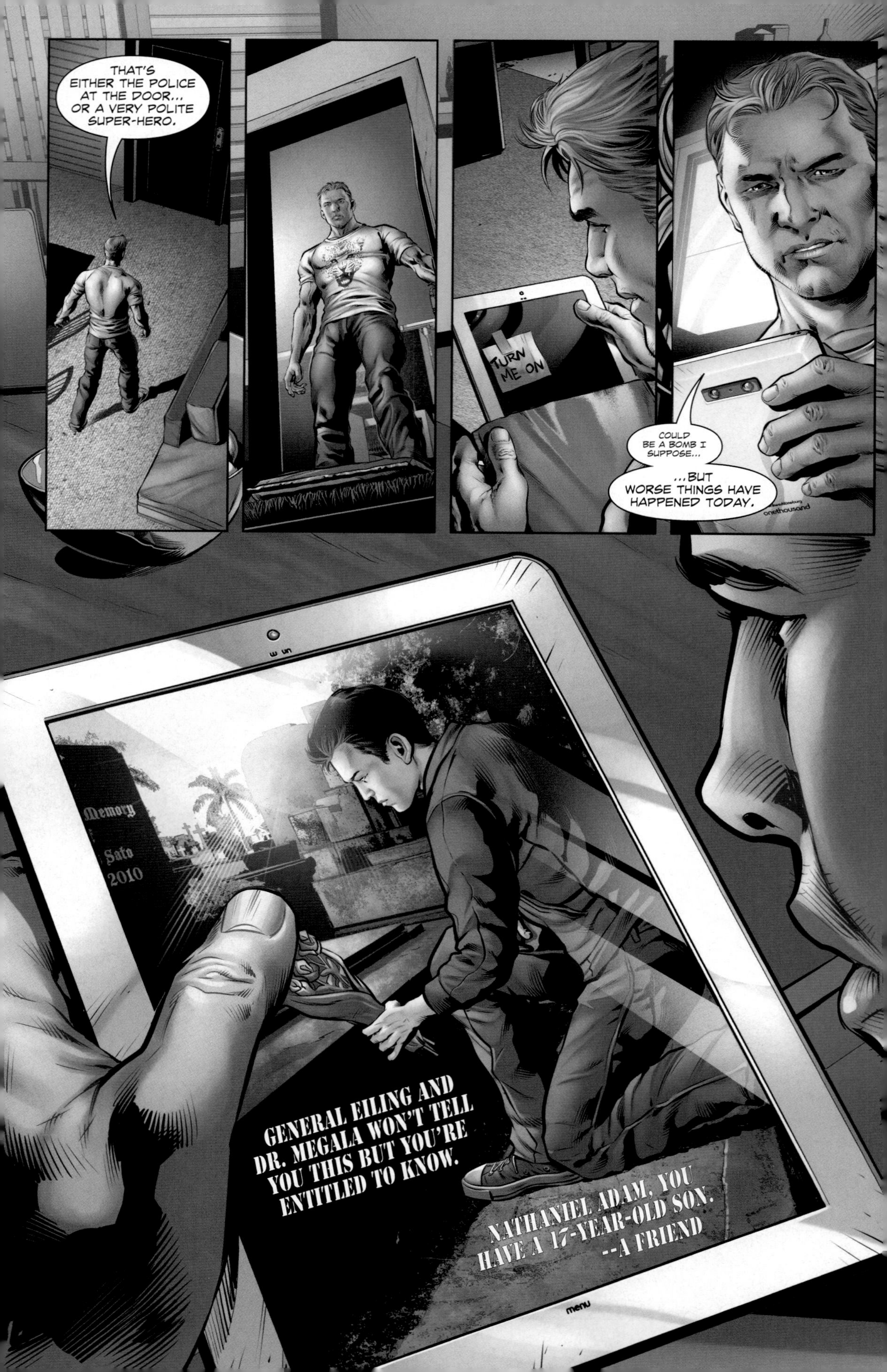
THAT'S EITHER THE POLICE AT THE DOOR... OR A VERY POLITE SUPER-HERO.
TURN ME ON
COULD BE A BOMB I SUPPOSE...
...BUT WORSE THINGS HAVE HAPPENED TODAY.
Memory
Sato
2010
GENERAL EILING AND DR. MEGALA WON'T TELL YOU THIS BUT YOU'RE ENTITLED TO KNOW.
NATHANIEL ADAM, YOU HAVE A 17-YEAR-OLD SON.
--A FRIEND
menu

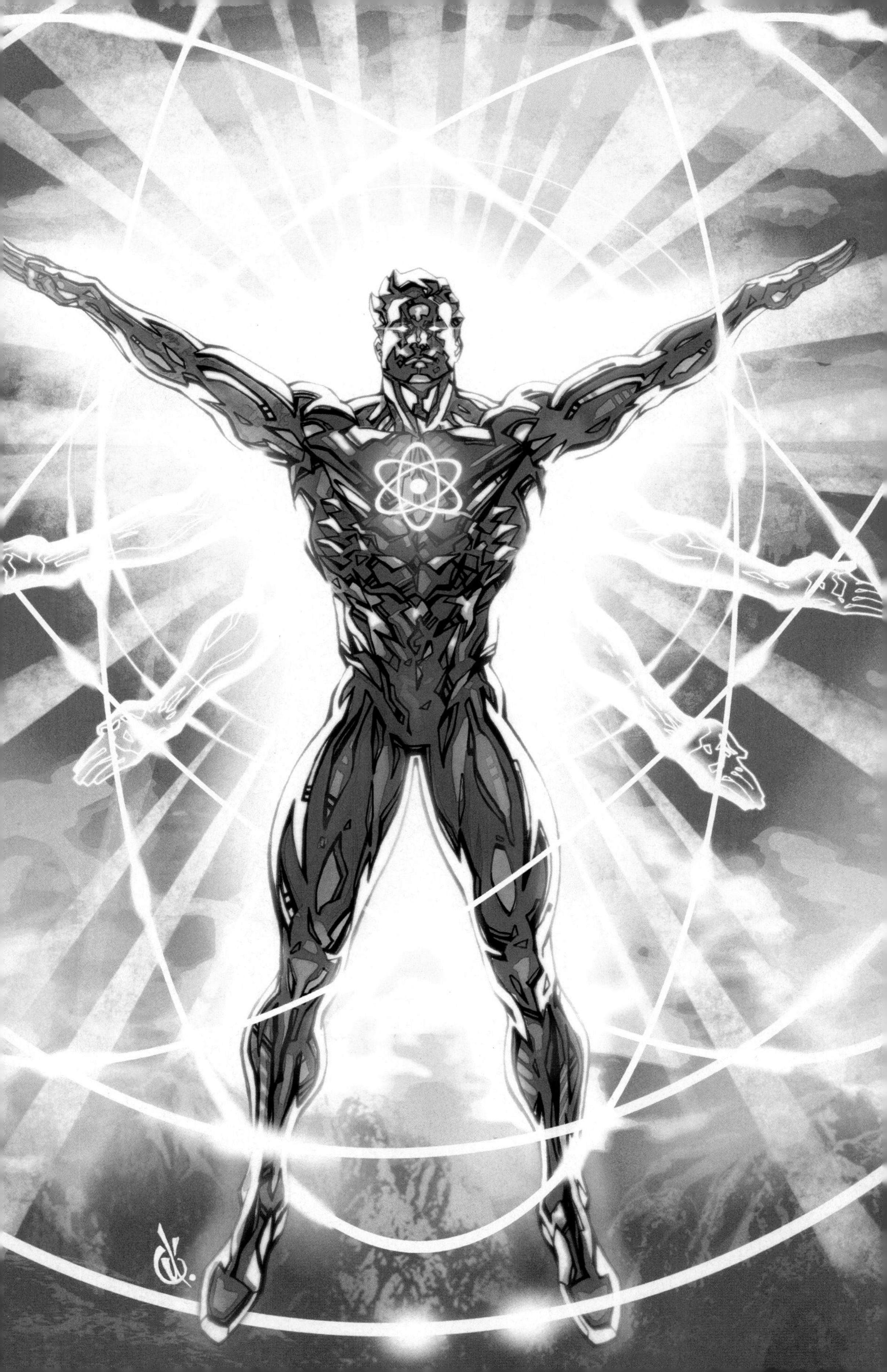

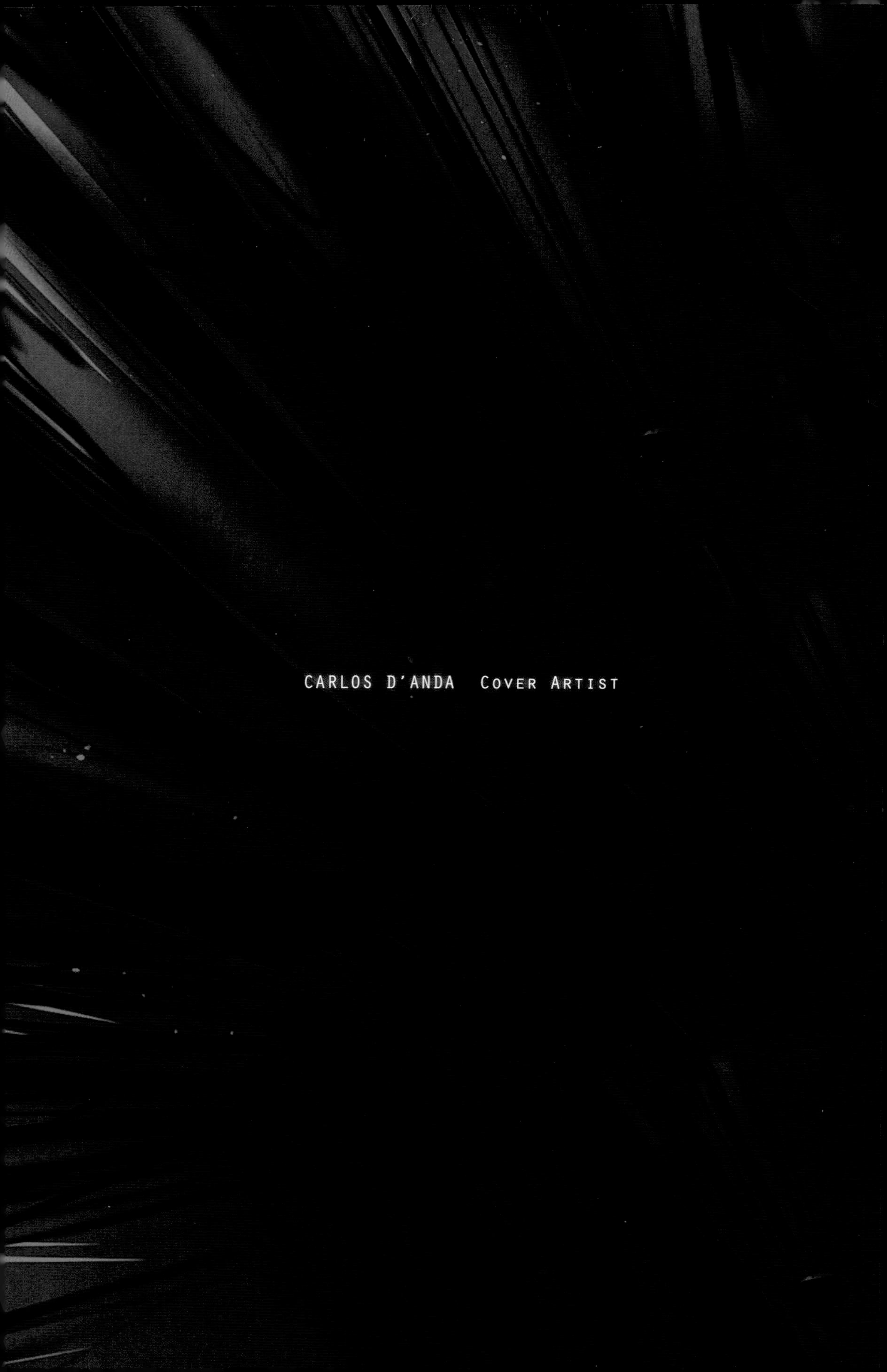
CARLOS D'ANDA Cover Artist

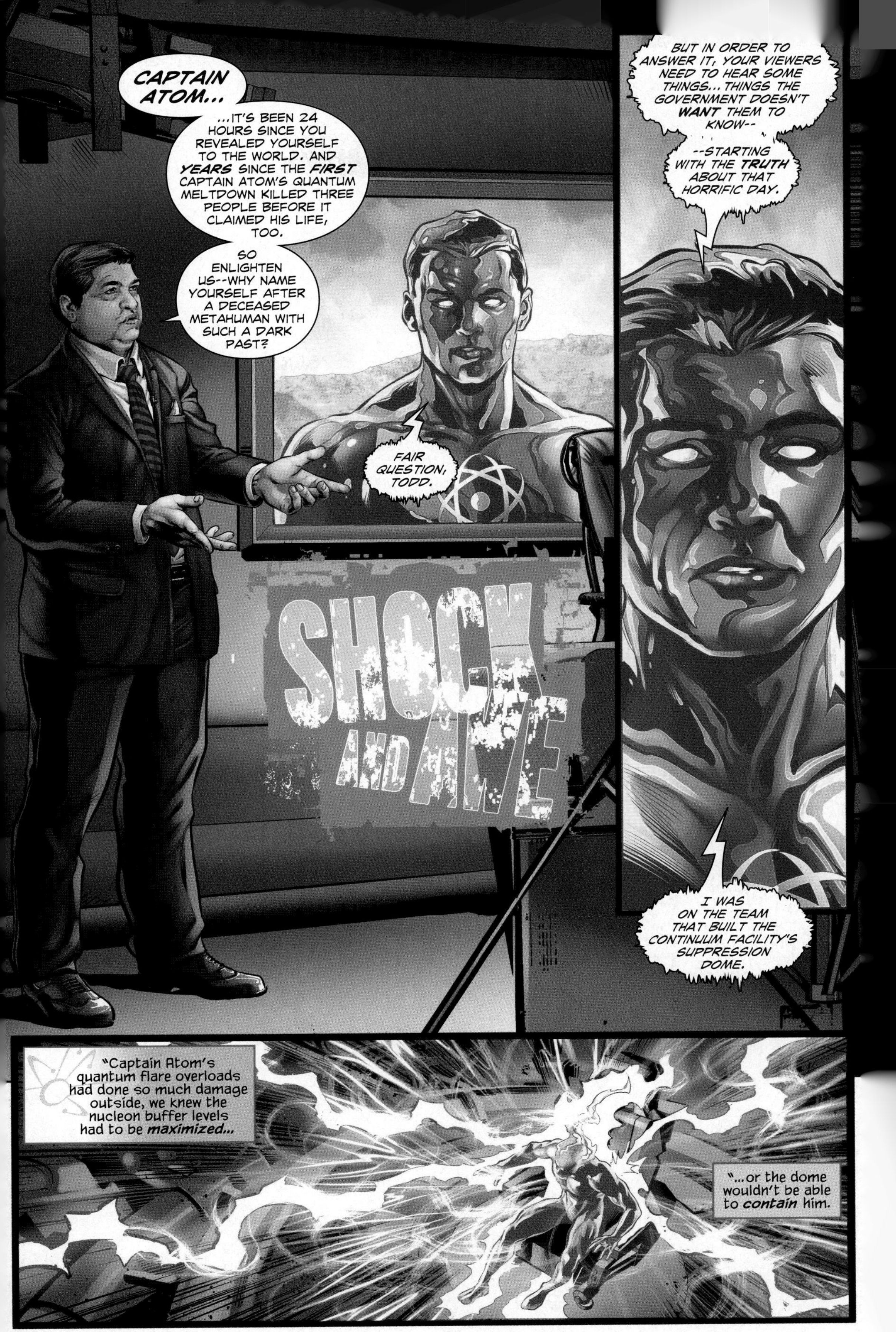
CAPTAIN ATOM...
...IT'S BEEN 24 HOURS SINCE YOU REVEALED YOURSELF TO THE WORLD. AND YEARS SINCE THE FIRST CAPTAIN ATOM'S QUANTUM MELTDOWN KILLED THREE PEOPLE BEFORE IT CLAIMED HIS LIFE, TOO.
SO ENLIGHTEN US--WHY NAME YOURSELF AFTER A DECEASED METAHUMAN WITH SUCH A DARK PAST?
FAIR QUESTION, TODD.
SHOCK AND AWE
BUT IN ORDER TO ANSWER IT, YOUR VIEWERS NEED TO HEAR SOME THINGS... THINGS THE GOVERNMENT DOESN'T WANT THEM TO KNOW--
--STARTING WITH THE TRUTH ABOUT THAT HORRIFIC DAY.
I WAS ON THE TEAM THAT BUILT THE CONTINUUM FACILITY'S SUPPRESSION DOME.
"Captain Atom's quantum flare overloads had done so much damage outside, we knew the nucleon buffer levels had to be maximized...
"...or the dome wouldn't be able to contain him.

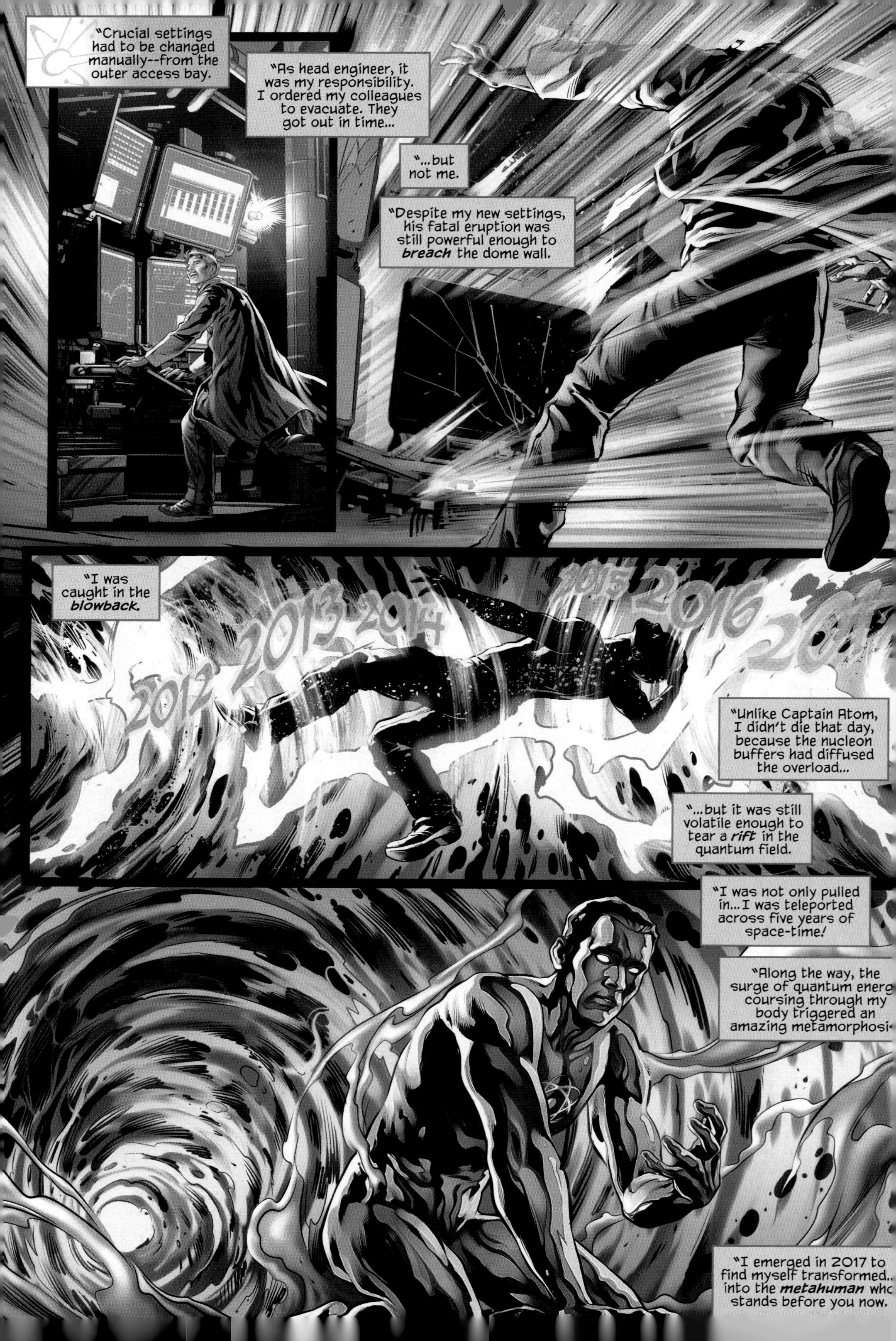
"Crucial settings had to be changed manually--from the outer access bay.
"As head engineer, it was my responsibility. I ordered my colleagues to evacuate. They got out in time...
"...but not me.
"Despite my new settings, his fatal eruption was still powerful enough to *breach* the dome wall.
"I was caught in the *blowback.*
2012 2013 2014 2015 2016
"Unlike Captain Atom, I didn't die that day, because the nucleon buffers had diffused the overload...
"...but it was still volatile enough to tear a *rift* in the quantum field.
"I was not only pulled in...I was teleported across five years of space-time!
"Along the way, the surge of quantum energ coursing through my body triggered an amazing metamorphosi
"I emerged in 2017 to find myself transformed.. into the *metahuman* whc stands before you now.

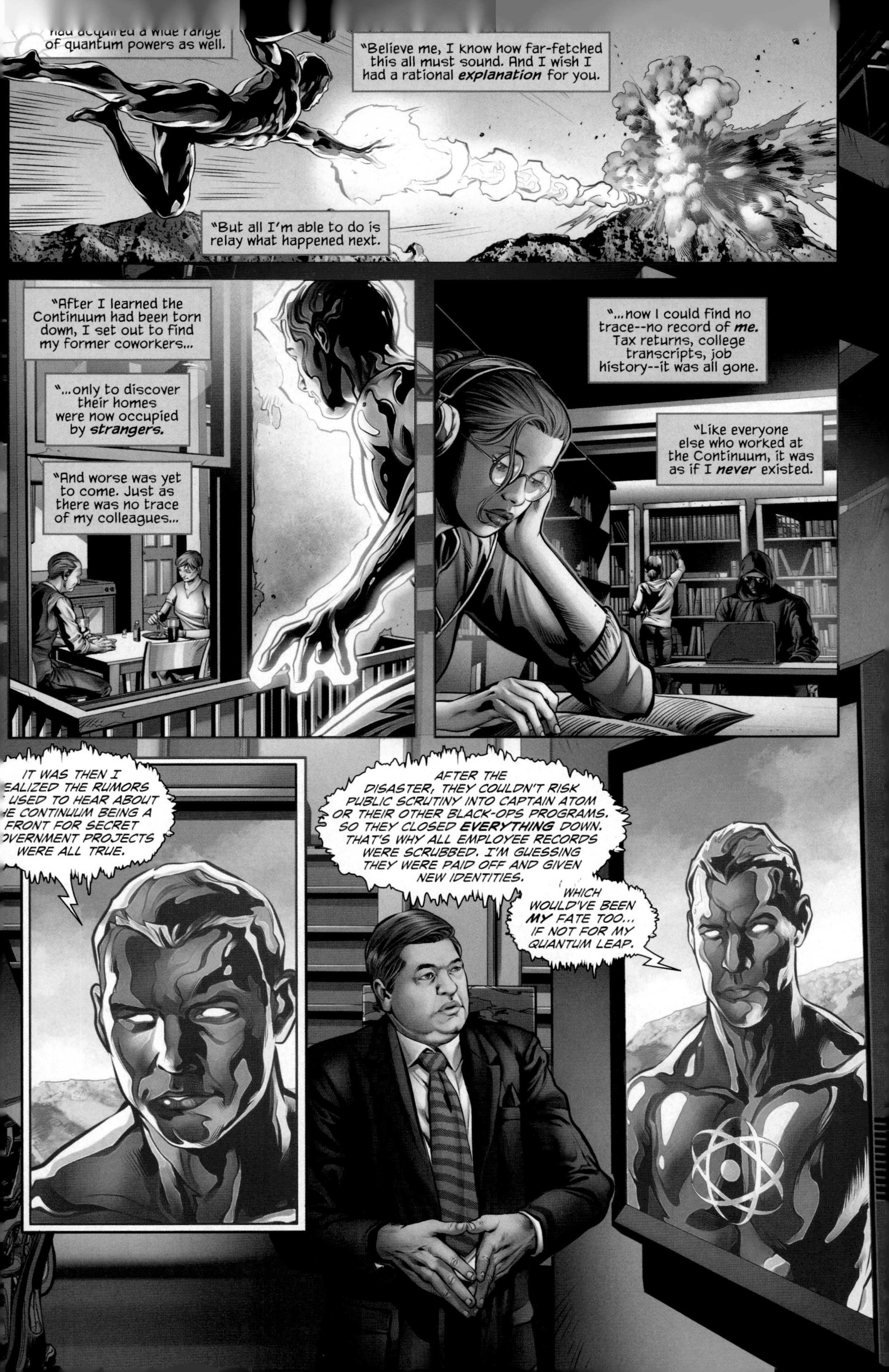
had acquired a wide range of quantum powers as well.
"Believe me, I know how far-fetched this all must sound. And I wish I had a rational *explanation* for you.
"But all I'm able to do is relay what happened next.
"After I learned the Continuum had been torn down, I set out to find my former coworkers...
"...only to discover their homes were now occupied by *strangers.*
"And worse was yet to come. Just as there was no trace of my colleagues...
"...now I could find no trace--no record of *me.* Tax returns, college transcripts, job history--it was all gone.
"Like everyone else who worked at the Continuum, it was as if I *never* existed.
IT WAS THEN I EALIZED THE RUMORS USED TO HEAR ABOUT HE CONTINUUM BEING A FRONT FOR SECRET OVERNMENT PROJECTS WERE ALL TRUE.
AFTER THE DISASTER, THEY COULDN'T RISK PUBLIC SCRUTINY INTO CAPTAIN ATOM OR THEIR OTHER BLACK-OPS PROGRAMS. SO THEY CLOSED **EVERYTHING** DOWN. THAT'S WHY ALL EMPLOYEE RECORDS WERE SCRUBBED. I'M GUESSING THEY WERE PAID OFF AND GIVEN NEW IDENTITIES.
WHICH WOULD'VE BEEN **MY** FATE TOO... IF NOT FOR MY QUANTUM LEAP.

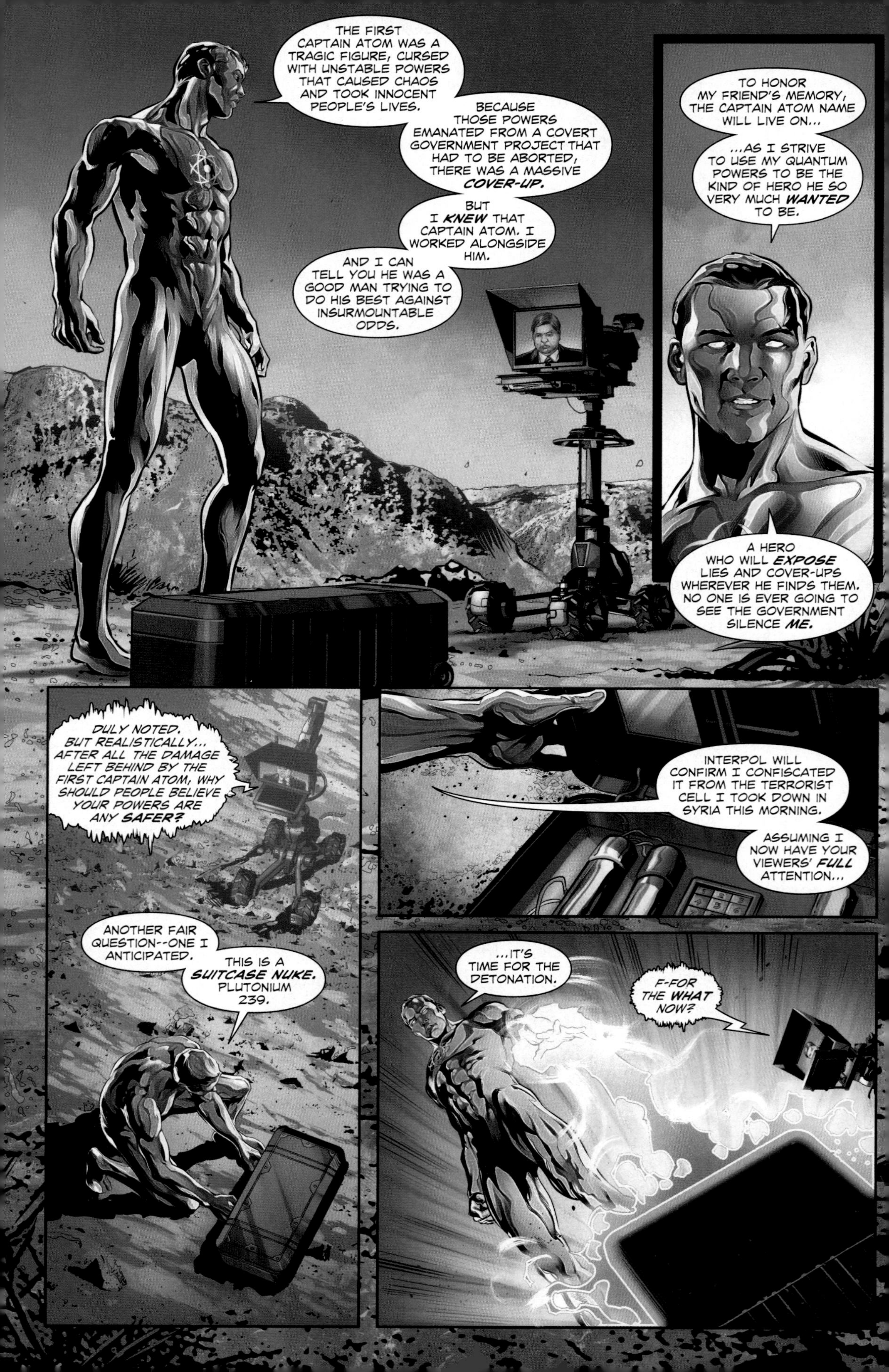
THE FIRST CAPTAIN ATOM WAS A TRAGIC FIGURE, CURSED WITH UNSTABLE POWERS THAT CAUSED CHAOS AND TOOK INNOCENT PEOPLE'S LIVES.
BECAUSE THOSE POWERS EMANATED FROM A COVERT GOVERNMENT PROJECT THAT HAD TO BE ABORTED, THERE WAS A MASSIVE **COVER-UP.**
BUT I **KNEW** THAT CAPTAIN ATOM. I WORKED ALONGSIDE HIM.
AND I CAN TELL YOU HE WAS A GOOD MAN TRYING TO DO HIS BEST AGAINST INSURMOUNTABLE ODDS.
TO HONOR MY FRIEND'S MEMORY, THE CAPTAIN ATOM NAME WILL LIVE ON...
...AS I STRIVE TO USE MY QUANTUM POWERS TO BE THE KIND OF HERO HE SO VERY MUCH **WANTED** TO BE.
A HERO WHO WILL **EXPOSE** LIES AND COVER-UPS WHEREVER HE FINDS THEM. NO ONE IS EVER GOING TO SEE THE GOVERNMENT SILENCE **ME.**
DULY NOTED. BUT REALISTICALLY... AFTER ALL THE DAMAGE LEFT BEHIND BY THE FIRST CAPTAIN ATOM, WHY SHOULD PEOPLE BELIEVE YOUR POWERS ARE ANY ***SAFER?***
ANOTHER FAIR QUESTION--ONE I ANTICIPATED.
THIS IS A **SUITCASE NUKE.** PLUTONIUM 239.
INTERPOL WILL CONFIRM I CONFISCATED IT FROM THE TERRORIST CELL I TOOK DOWN IN SYRIA THIS MORNING.
ASSUMING I NOW HAVE YOUR VIEWERS' **FULL** ATTENTION...
...IT'S TIME FOR THE DETONATION.
F-FOR THE ***WHAT*** *NOW?*

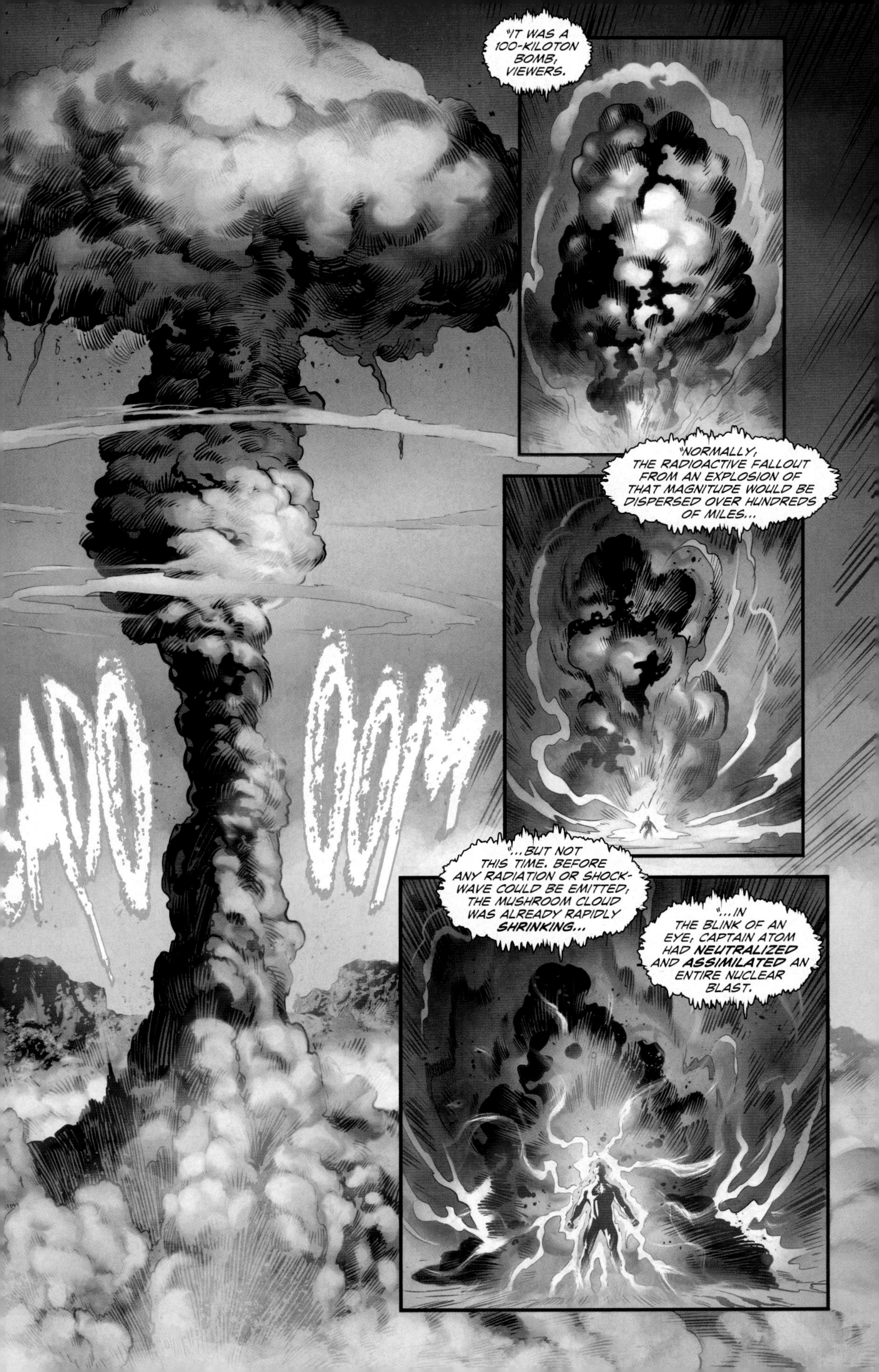
"IT WAS A 100-KILOTON BOMB, VIEWERS.
"NORMALLY, THE RADIOACTIVE FALLOUT FROM AN EXPLOSION OF THAT MAGNITUDE WOULD BE DISPERSED OVER HUNDREDS OF MILES...
...BUT NOT THIS TIME. BEFORE ANY RADIATION OR SHOCK-WAVE COULD BE EMITTED, THE MUSHROOM CLOUD WAS ALREADY RAPIDLY **SHRINKING...**
"...IN THE BLINK OF AN EYE, CAPTAIN ATOM HAD **NEUTRALIZED** AND **ASSIMILATED** AN ENTIRE NUCLEAR BLAST.

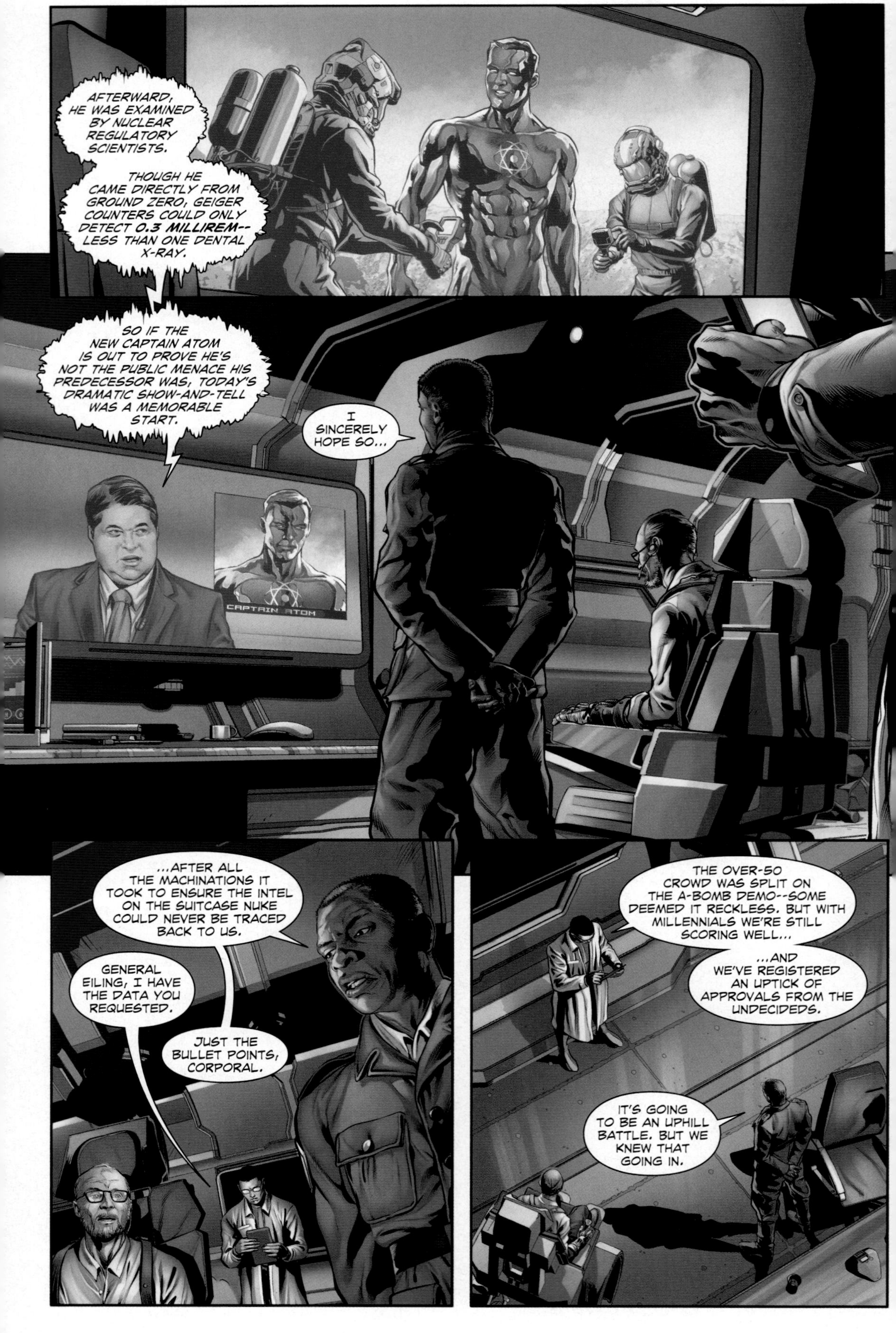
AFTERWARD, HE WAS EXAMINED BY NUCLEAR REGULATORY SCIENTISTS.
THOUGH HE CAME DIRECTLY FROM GROUND ZERO, GEIGER COUNTERS COULD ONLY DETECT 0.3 MILLIREM-- LESS THAN ONE DENTAL X-RAY.
SO IF THE NEW CAPTAIN ATOM IS OUT TO PROVE HE'S NOT THE PUBLIC MENACE HIS PREDECESSOR WAS, TODAY'S DRAMATIC SHOW-AND-TELL WAS A MEMORABLE START.
I SINCERELY HOPE SO...
CAPTAIN ATOM
...AFTER ALL THE MACHINATIONS IT TOOK TO ENSURE THE INTEL ON THE SUITCASE NUKE COULD NEVER BE TRACED BACK TO US.
GENERAL EILING, I HAVE THE DATA YOU REQUESTED.
JUST THE BULLET POINTS, CORPORAL.
THE OVER-50 CROWD WAS SPLIT ON THE A-BOMB DEMO--SOME DEEMED IT RECKLESS. BUT WITH MILLENNIALS WE'RE STILL SCORING WELL...
...AND WE'VE REGISTERED AN UPTICK OF APPROVALS FROM THE UNDECIDEDS.
IT'S GOING TO BE AN UPHILL BATTLE. BUT WE KNEW THAT GOING IN.

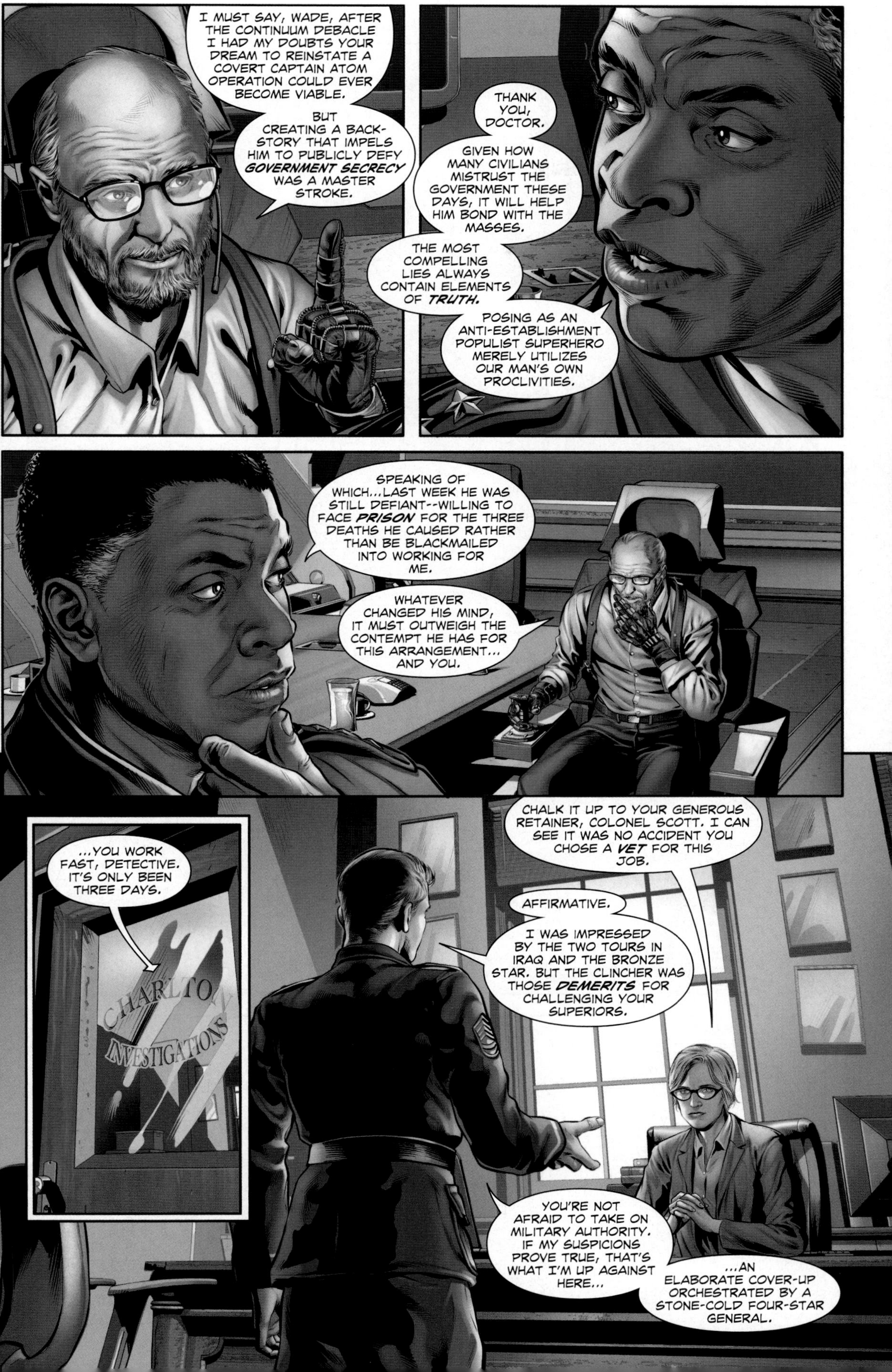
I MUST SAY, WADE, AFTER THE CONTINUUM DEBACLE I HAD MY DOUBTS YOUR DREAM TO REINSTATE A COVERT CAPTAIN ATOM OPERATION COULD EVER BECOME VIABLE.
BUT CREATING A BACK-STORY THAT IMPELS HIM TO PUBLICLY DEFY GOVERNMENT SECRECY WAS A MASTER STROKE.
THANK YOU, DOCTOR.
GIVEN HOW MANY CIVILIANS MISTRUST THE GOVERNMENT THESE DAYS, IT WILL HELP HIM BOND WITH THE MASSES.
THE MOST COMPELLING LIES ALWAYS CONTAIN ELEMENTS OF TRUTH.
POSING AS AN ANTI-ESTABLISHMENT POPULIST SUPERHERO MERELY UTILIZES OUR MAN'S OWN PROCLIVITIES.
SPEAKING OF WHICH...LAST WEEK HE WAS STILL DEFIANT--WILLING TO FACE PRISON FOR THE THREE DEATHS HE CAUSED RATHER THAN BE BLACKMAILED INTO WORKING FOR ME.
WHATEVER CHANGED HIS MIND, IT MUST OUTWEIGH THE CONTEMPT HE HAS FOR THIS ARRANGEMENT... AND YOU.
...YOU WORK FAST, DETECTIVE. IT'S ONLY BEEN THREE DAYS.
CHARLTON INVESTIGATIONS
CHALK IT UP TO YOUR GENEROUS RETAINER, COLONEL SCOTT. I CAN SEE IT WAS NO ACCIDENT YOU CHOSE A VET FOR THIS JOB.
AFFIRMATIVE.
I WAS IMPRESSED BY THE TWO TOURS IN IRAQ AND THE BRONZE STAR. BUT THE CLINCHER WAS THOSE DEMERITS FOR CHALLENGING YOUR SUPERIORS.
YOU'RE NOT AFRAID TO TAKE ON MILITARY AUTHORITY. IF MY SUSPICIONS PROVE TRUE, THAT'S WHAT I'M UP AGAINST HERE...
...AN ELABORATE COVER-UP ORCHESTRATED BY A STONE-COLD FOUR-STAR GENERAL.

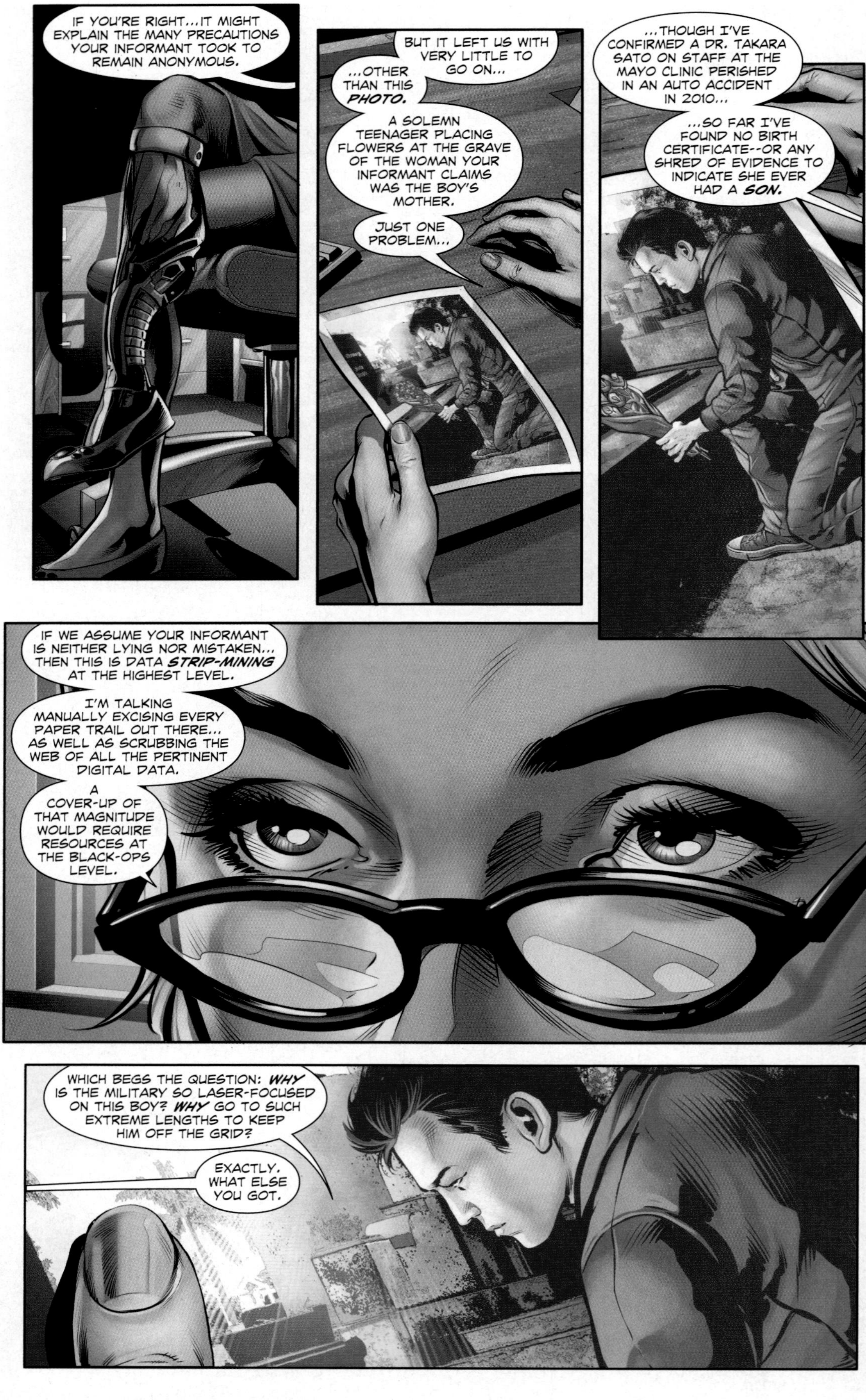
IF YOU'RE RIGHT...IT MIGHT EXPLAIN THE MANY PRECAUTIONS YOUR INFORMANT TOOK TO REMAIN ANONYMOUS.
BUT IT LEFT US WITH VERY LITTLE TO GO ON...
...OTHER THAN THIS PHOTO.
A SOLEMN TEENAGER PLACING FLOWERS AT THE GRAVE OF THE WOMAN YOUR INFORMANT CLAIMS WAS THE BOY'S MOTHER.
JUST ONE PROBLEM...
...THOUGH I'VE CONFIRMED A DR. TAKARA SATO ON STAFF AT THE MAYO CLINIC PERISHED IN AN AUTO ACCIDENT IN 2010...
...SO FAR I'VE FOUND NO BIRTH CERTIFICATE--OR ANY SHRED OF EVIDENCE TO INDICATE SHE EVER HAD A SON.
IF WE ASSUME YOUR INFORMANT IS NEITHER LYING NOR MISTAKEN... THEN THIS IS DATA STRIP-MINING AT THE HIGHEST LEVEL.
I'M TALKING MANUALLY EXCISING EVERY PAPER TRAIL OUT THERE... AS WELL AS SCRUBBING THE WEB OF ALL THE PERTINENT DIGITAL DATA.
A COVER-UP OF THAT MAGNITUDE WOULD REQUIRE RESOURCES AT THE BLACK-OPS LEVEL.
WHICH BEGS THE QUESTION: WHY IS THE MILITARY SO LASER-FOCUSED ON THIS BOY? WHY GO TO SUCH EXTREME LENGTHS TO KEEP HIM OFF THE GRID?
EXACTLY. WHAT ELSE YOU GOT.

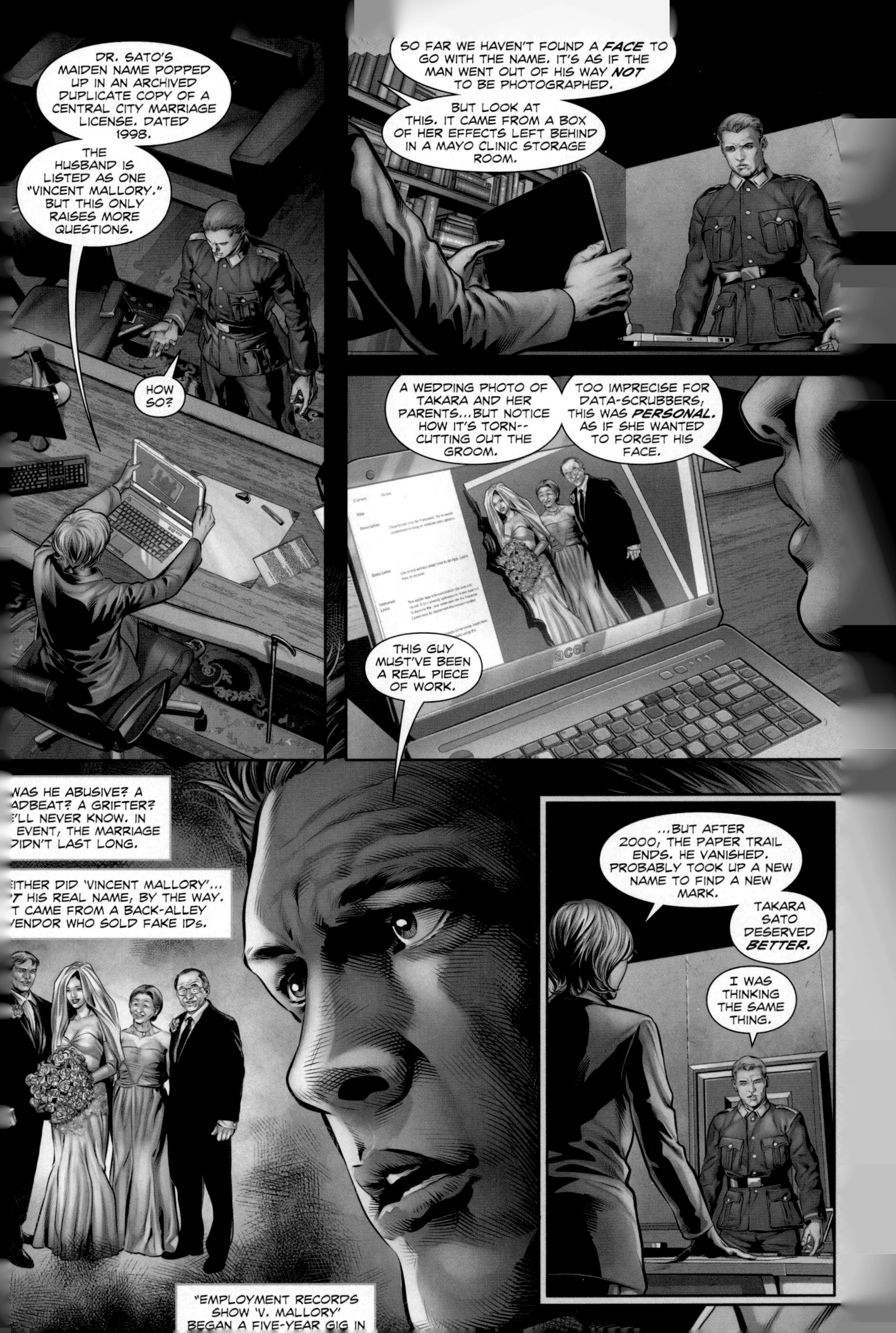

DR. SATO'S MAIDEN NAME POPPED UP IN AN ARCHIVED DUPLICATE COPY OF A CENTRAL CITY MARRIAGE LICENSE. DATED 1998.
THE HUSBAND IS LISTED AS ONE "VINCENT MALLORY." BUT THIS ONLY RAISES MORE QUESTIONS.
HOW SO?
SO FAR WE HAVEN'T FOUND A *FACE* TO GO WITH THE NAME. IT'S AS IF THE MAN WENT OUT OF HIS WAY *NOT* TO BE PHOTOGRAPHED.
BUT LOOK AT THIS. IT CAME FROM A BOX OF HER EFFECTS LEFT BEHIND IN A MAYO CLINIC STORAGE ROOM.
A WEDDING PHOTO OF TAKARA AND HER PARENTS...BUT NOTICE HOW IT'S TORN--CUTTING OUT THE GROOM.
TOO IMPRECISE FOR DATA-SCRUBBERS, THIS WAS *PERSONAL.* AS IF SHE WANTED TO FORGET HIS FACE.
acer
THIS GUY MUST'VE BEEN A REAL PIECE OF WORK.
WAS HE ABUSIVE? A
ADBEAT? A GRIFTER?
'LL NEVER KNOW. IN
EVENT, THE MARRIAGE
DIDN'T LAST LONG.
EITHER DID 'VINCENT MALLORY'...
T HIS REAL NAME, BY THE WAY.
T CAME FROM A BACK-ALLEY
VENDOR WHO SOLD FAKE IDs.
"EMPLOYMENT RECORDS SHOW 'V. MALLORY' BEGAN A FIVE-YEAR GIG IN
...BUT AFTER 2000, THE PAPER TRAIL ENDS. HE VANISHED. PROBABLY TOOK UP A NEW NAME TO FIND A NEW MARK.
TAKARA SATO DESERVED *BETTER.*
I WAS THINKING THE SAME THING.

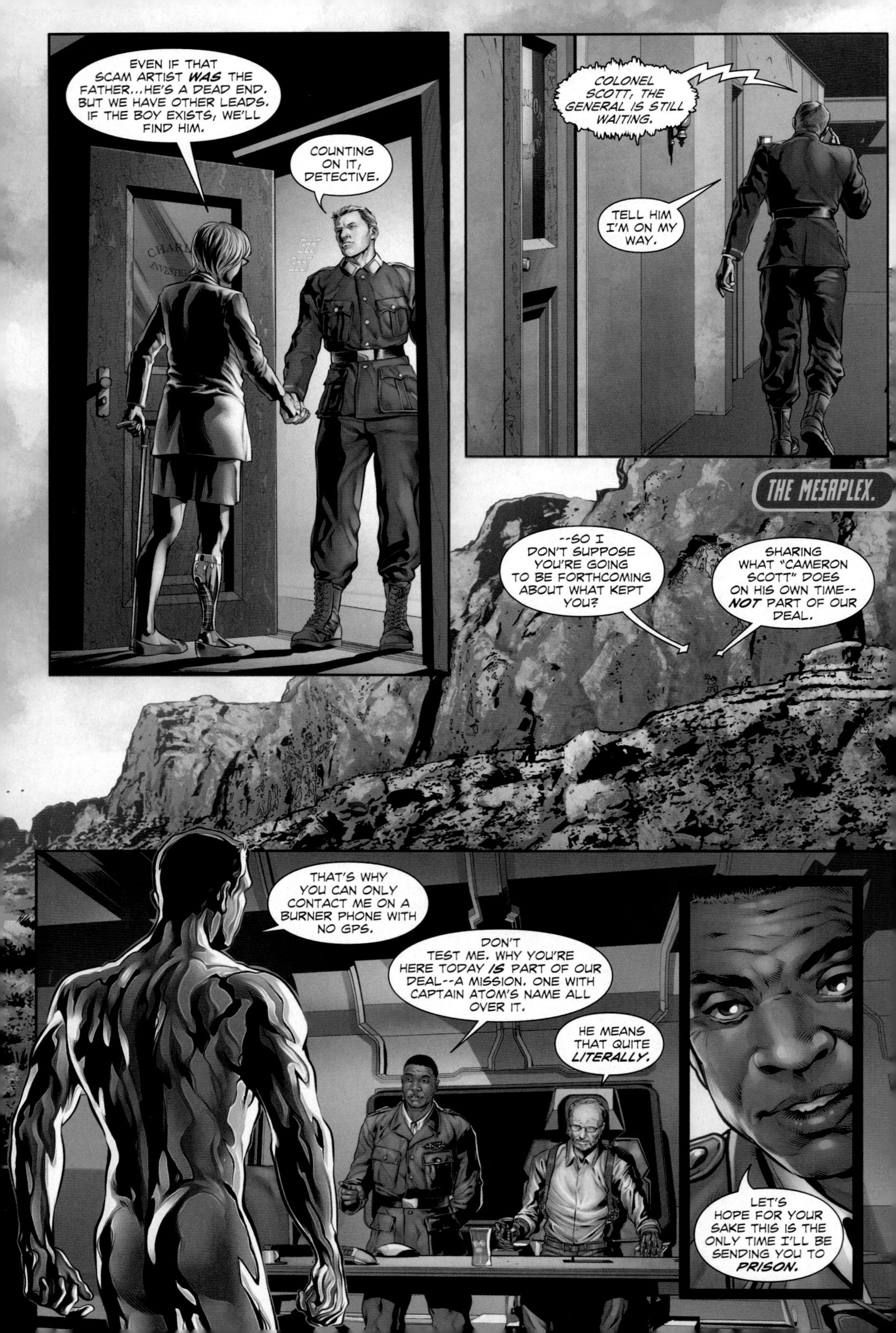
EVEN IF THAT SCAM ARTIST WAS THE FATHER...HE'S A DEAD END. BUT WE HAVE OTHER LEADS. IF THE BOY EXISTS, WE'LL FIND HIM.
COUNTING ON IT, DETECTIVE.
BZZT BZZT
COLONEL SCOTT, THE GENERAL IS STILL WAITING.
TELL HIM I'M ON MY WAY.
THE MESAPLEX.
--SO I DON'T SUPPOSE YOU'RE GOING TO BE FORTHCOMING ABOUT WHAT KEPT YOU?
SHARING WHAT "CAMERON SCOTT" DOES ON HIS OWN TIME--NOT PART OF OUR DEAL.
THAT'S WHY YOU CAN ONLY CONTACT ME ON A BURNER PHONE WITH NO GPS.
DON'T TEST ME. WHY YOU'RE HERE TODAY IS PART OF OUR DEAL--A MISSION. ONE WITH CAPTAIN ATOM'S NAME ALL OVER IT.
HE MEANS THAT QUITE LITERALLY.
LET'S HOPE FOR YOUR SAKE THIS IS THE ONLY TIME I'LL BE SENDING YOU TO PRISON.

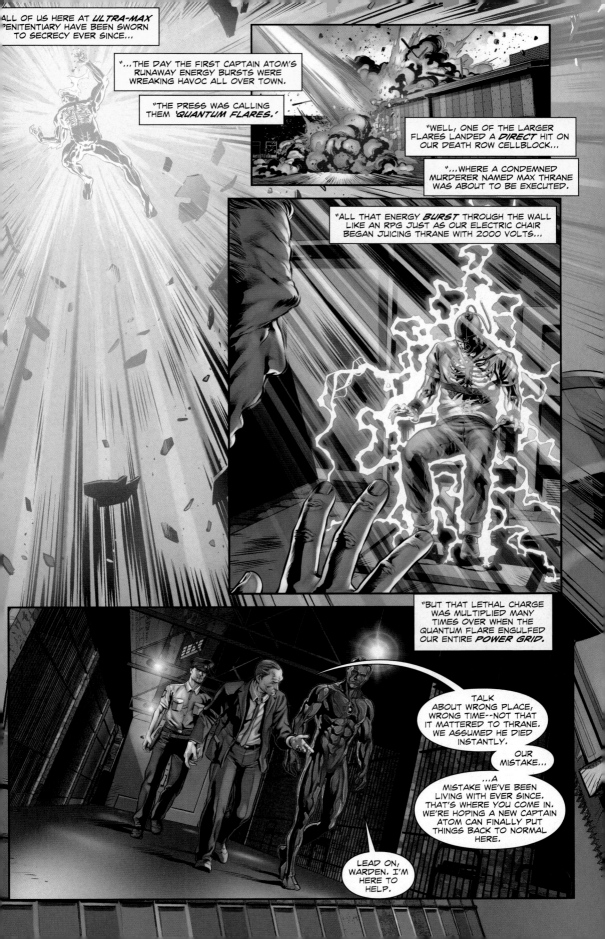

ALL OF US HERE AT *ULTRA-MAX* PENITENTIARY HAVE BEEN SWORN TO SECRECY EVER SINCE...

"...THE DAY THE FIRST CAPTAIN ATOM'S RUNAWAY ENERGY BURSTS WERE WREAKING HAVOC ALL OVER TOWN.

"THE PRESS WAS CALLING THEM *'QUANTUM FLARES.'*

"WELL, ONE OF THE LARGER FLARES LANDED A *DIRECT* HIT ON OUR DEATH ROW CELLBLOCK...

"...WHERE A CONDEMNED MURDERER NAMED MAX THRANE WAS ABOUT TO BE EXECUTED.

"ALL THAT ENERGY *BURST* THROUGH THE WALL LIKE AN RPG JUST AS OUR ELECTRIC CHAIR BEGAN JUICING THRANE WITH 2000 VOLTS...

"BUT THAT LETHAL CHARGE WAS MULTIPLIED MANY TIMES OVER WHEN THE QUANTUM FLARE ENGULFED OUR ENTIRE *POWER GRID.*

TALK ABOUT WRONG PLACE, WRONG TIME--NOT THAT IT MATTERED TO THRANE. WE ASSUMED HE DIED INSTANTLY.

OUR MISTAKE...

...A MISTAKE WE'VE BEEN LIVING WITH EVER SINCE. THAT'S WHERE YOU COME IN. WE'RE HOPING A NEW CAPTAIN ATOM CAN FINALLY PUT THINGS BACK TO NORMAL HERE.

LEAD ON, WARDEN. I'M HERE TO HELP.

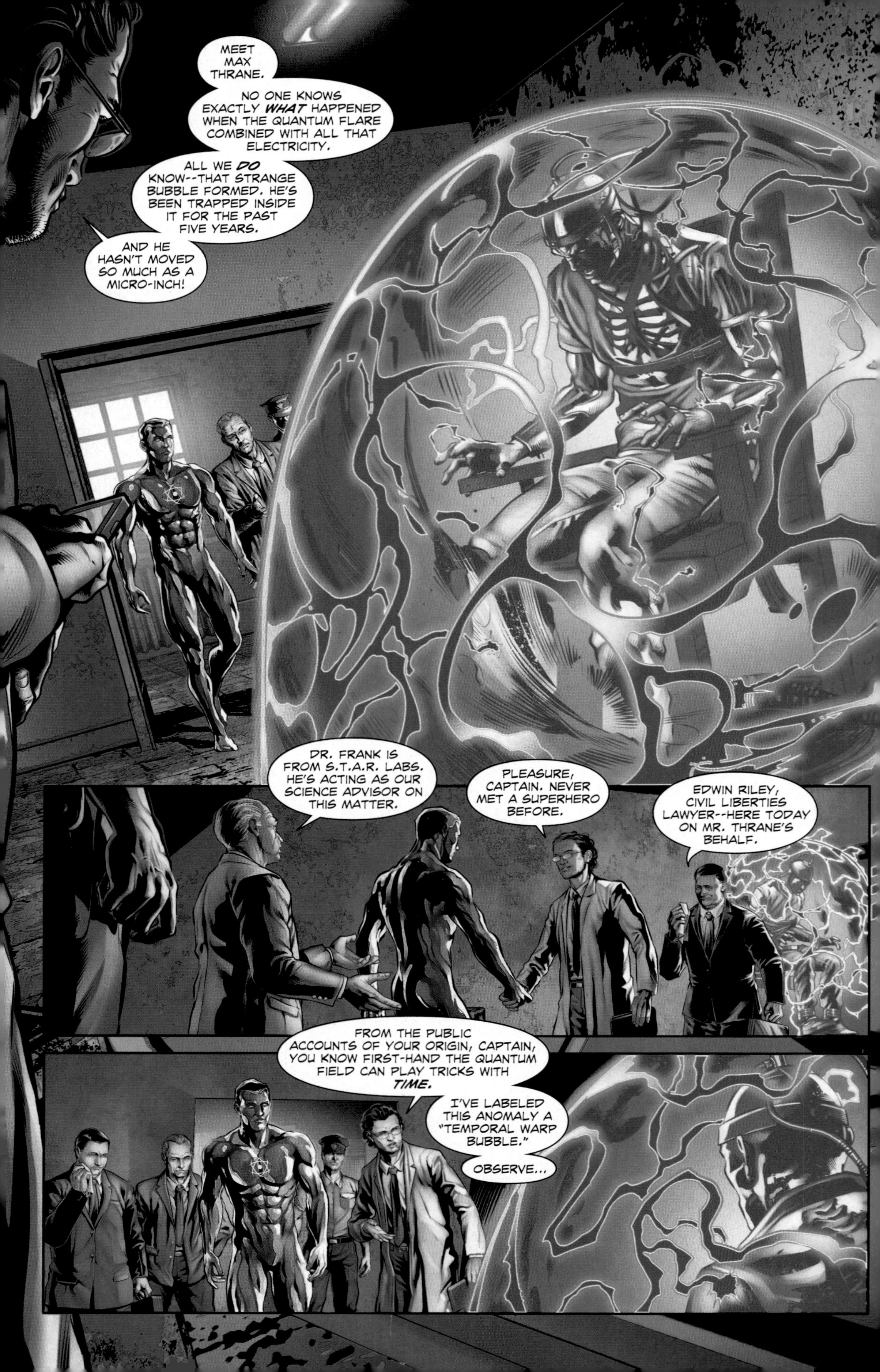
MEET MAX THRANE.
NO ONE KNOWS EXACTLY WHAT HAPPENED WHEN THE QUANTUM FLARE COMBINED WITH ALL THAT ELECTRICITY.
ALL WE DO KNOW--THAT STRANGE BUBBLE FORMED. HE'S BEEN TRAPPED INSIDE IT FOR THE PAST FIVE YEARS.
AND HE HASN'T MOVED SO MUCH AS A MICRO-INCH!
DR. FRANK IS FROM S.T.A.R. LABS. HE'S ACTING AS OUR SCIENCE ADVISOR ON THIS MATTER.
PLEASURE, CAPTAIN. NEVER MET A SUPERHERO BEFORE.
EDWIN RILEY, CIVIL LIBERTIES LAWYER--HERE TODAY ON MR. THRANE'S BEHALF.
FROM THE PUBLIC ACCOUNTS OF YOUR ORIGIN, CAPTAIN, YOU KNOW FIRST-HAND THE QUANTUM FIELD CAN PLAY TRICKS WITH TIME.
I'VE LABELED THIS ANOMALY A "TEMPORAL WARP BUBBLE."
OBSERVE...

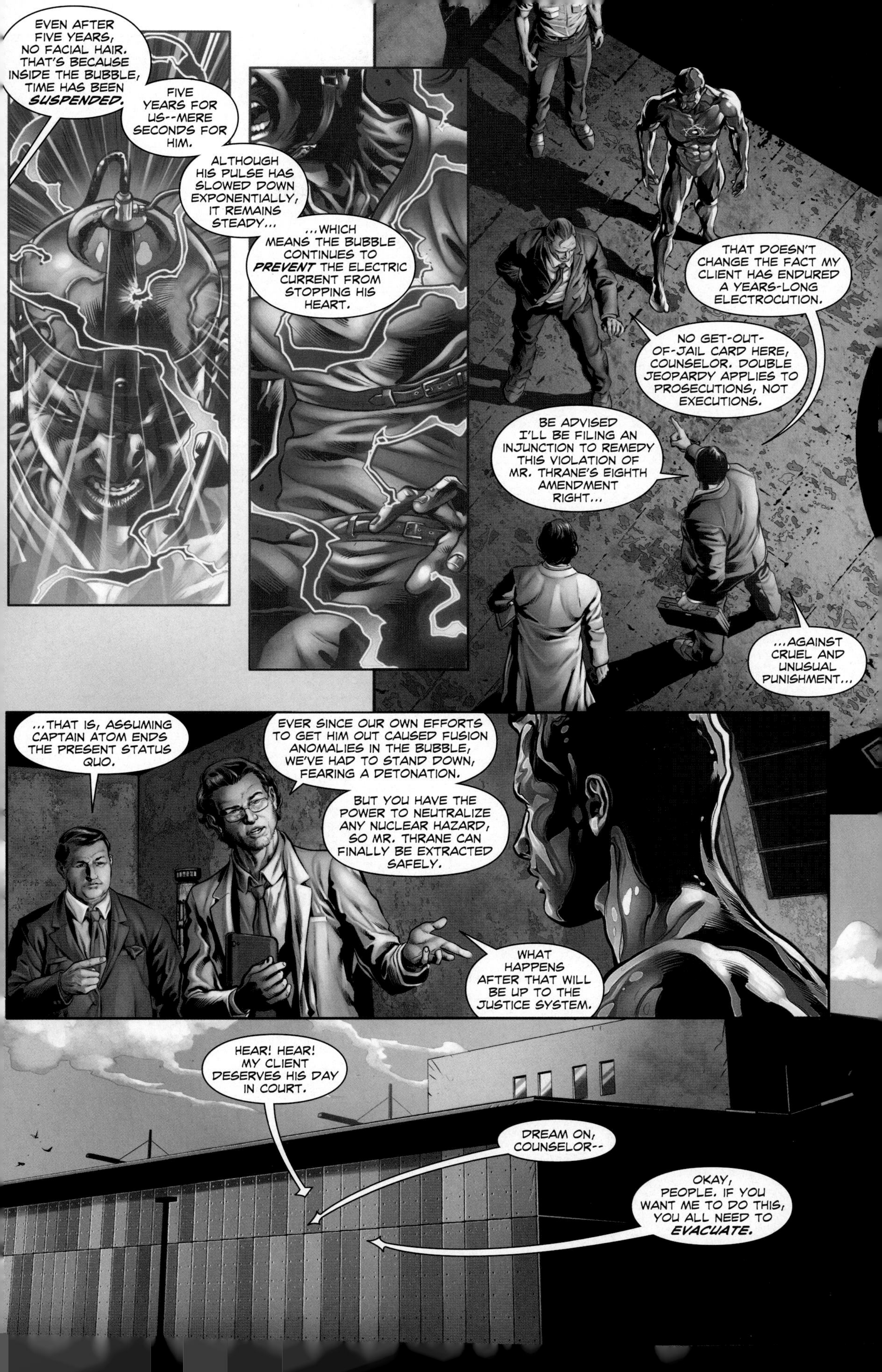

EVEN AFTER FIVE YEARS, NO FACIAL HAIR. THAT'S BECAUSE INSIDE THE BUBBLE, TIME HAS BEEN SUSPENDED.
FIVE YEARS FOR US--MERE SECONDS FOR HIM.
ALTHOUGH HIS PULSE HAS SLOWED DOWN EXPONENTIALLY, IT REMAINS STEADY...
...WHICH MEANS THE BUBBLE CONTINUES TO PREVENT THE ELECTRIC CURRENT FROM STOPPING HIS HEART.
THAT DOESN'T CHANGE THE FACT MY CLIENT HAS ENDURED A YEARS-LONG ELECTROCUTION.
NO GET-OUT-OF-JAIL CARD HERE, COUNSELOR. DOUBLE JEOPARDY APPLIES TO PROSECUTIONS, NOT EXECUTIONS.
BE ADVISED I'LL BE FILING AN INJUNCTION TO REMEDY THIS VIOLATION OF MR. THRANE'S EIGHTH AMENDMENT RIGHT...
...AGAINST CRUEL AND UNUSUAL PUNISHMENT...
...THAT IS, ASSUMING CAPTAIN ATOM ENDS THE PRESENT STATUS QUO.
EVER SINCE OUR OWN EFFORTS TO GET HIM OUT CAUSED FUSION ANOMALIES IN THE BUBBLE, WE'VE HAD TO STAND DOWN, FEARING A DETONATION.
BUT YOU HAVE THE POWER TO NEUTRALIZE ANY NUCLEAR HAZARD, SO MR. THRANE CAN FINALLY BE EXTRACTED SAFELY.
WHAT HAPPENS AFTER THAT WILL BE UP TO THE JUSTICE SYSTEM.
HEAR! HEAR! MY CLIENT DESERVES HIS DAY IN COURT.
DREAM ON, COUNSELOR--
OKAY, PEOPLE. IF YOU WANT ME TO DO THIS, YOU ALL NEED TO EVACUATE.

HERE WE GO. I'LL START SLOW, DISPENSING MY BEAMS GRADUALLY AT FIRST...

...UNTIL I SEE HOW MUCH ENERGY IS NEEDED FOR THE BUBBLE TO IMPLODE SO IT CAN BE REASSIMILATED INTO THE QUANTUM FIELD.

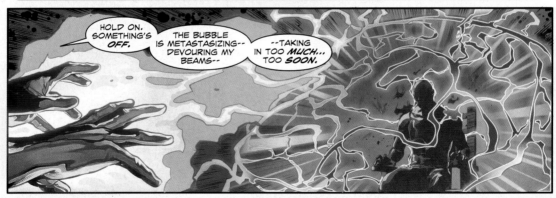

HOLD ON. SOMETHING'S *OFF*.

THE BUBBLE IS METASTASIZING-- DEVOURING MY BEAMS--

--TAKING IN TOO *MUCH*... TOO *SOON*.

WAY TOO SOON!

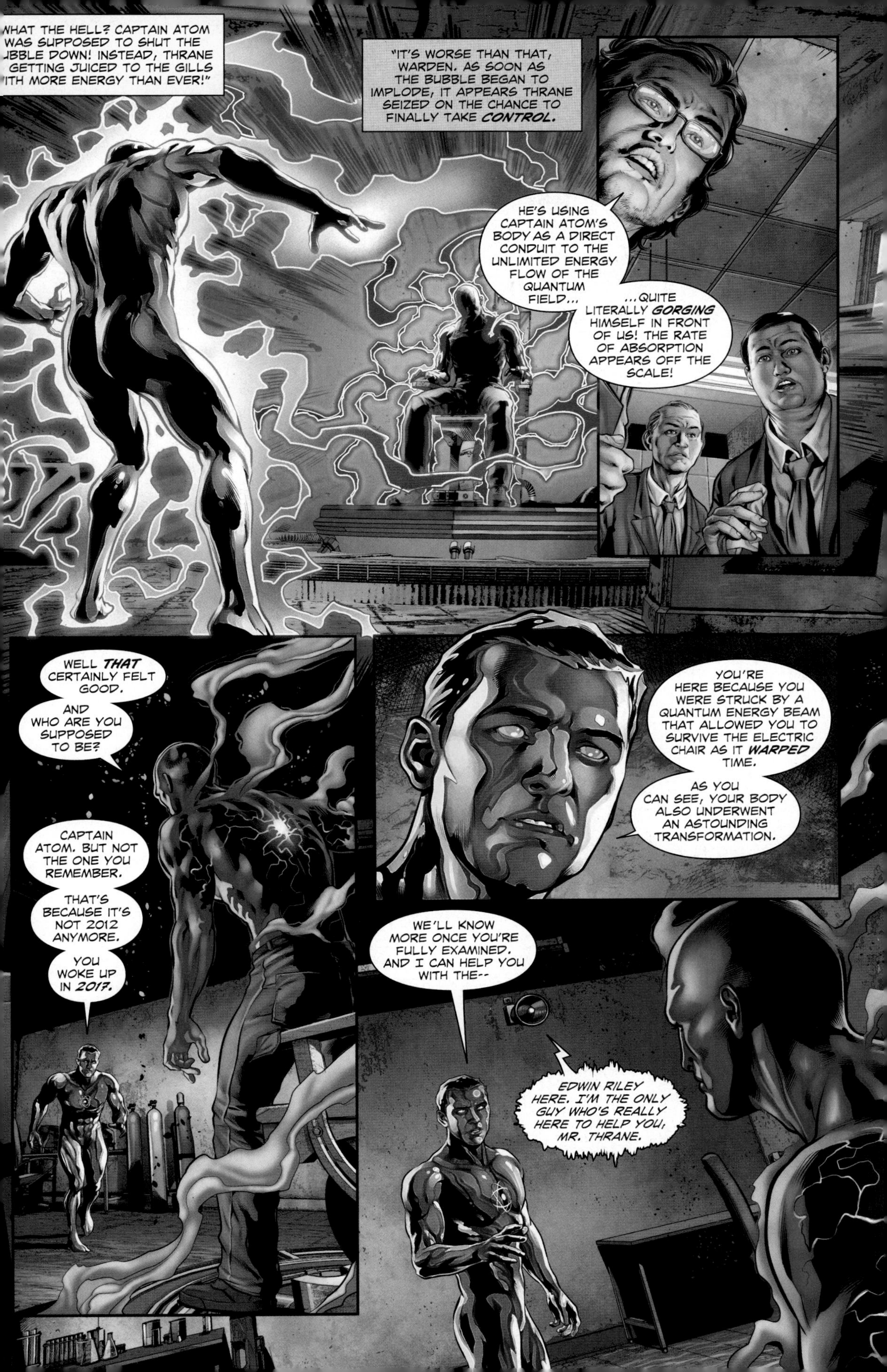
WHAT THE HELL? CAPTAIN ATOM WAS SUPPOSED TO SHUT THE BUBBLE DOWN! INSTEAD, THRANE IS GETTING JUICED TO THE GILLS WITH MORE ENERGY THAN EVER!"
"IT'S WORSE THAN THAT, WARDEN. AS SOON AS THE BUBBLE BEGAN TO IMPLODE, IT APPEARS THRANE SEIZED ON THE CHANCE TO FINALLY TAKE CONTROL.
HE'S USING CAPTAIN ATOM'S BODY AS A DIRECT CONDUIT TO THE UNLIMITED ENERGY FLOW OF THE QUANTUM FIELD...
...QUITE LITERALLY GORGING HIMSELF IN FRONT OF US! THE RATE OF ABSORPTION APPEARS OFF THE SCALE!
WELL THAT CERTAINLY FELT GOOD.
AND WHO ARE YOU SUPPOSED TO BE?
CAPTAIN ATOM. BUT NOT THE ONE YOU REMEMBER.
THAT'S BECAUSE IT'S NOT 2012 ANYMORE.
YOU WOKE UP IN 2017.
YOU'RE HERE BECAUSE YOU WERE STRUCK BY A QUANTUM ENERGY BEAM THAT ALLOWED YOU TO SURVIVE THE ELECTRIC CHAIR AS IT WARPED TIME.
AS YOU CAN SEE, YOUR BODY ALSO UNDERWENT AN ASTOUNDING TRANSFORMATION.
WE'LL KNOW MORE ONCE YOU'RE FULLY EXAMINED. AND I CAN HELP YOU WITH THE--
EDWIN RILEY HERE. I'M THE ONLY GUY WHO'S REALLY HERE TO HELP YOU, MR. THRANE.

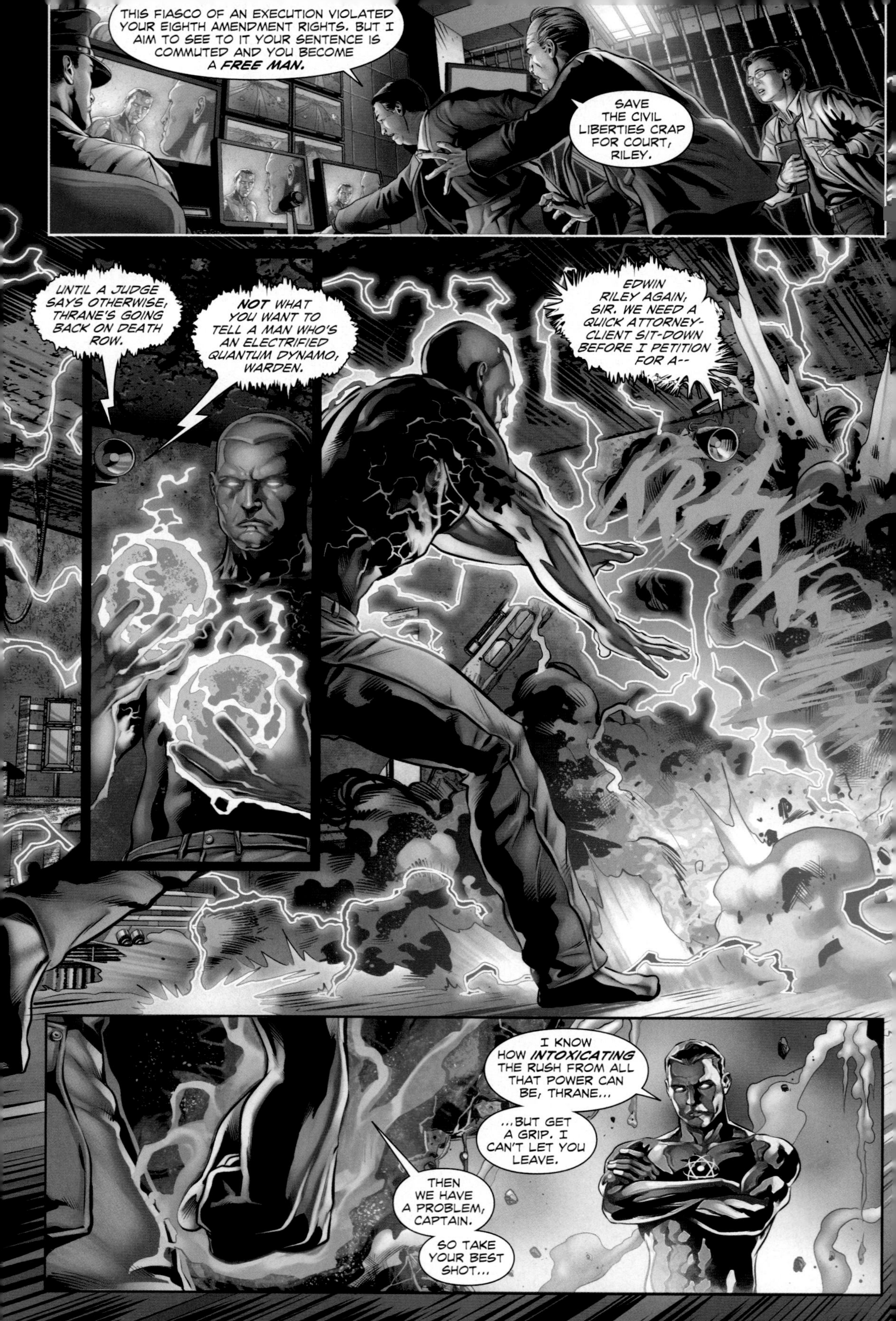
THIS FIASCO OF AN EXECUTION VIOLATED YOUR EIGHTH AMENDMENT RIGHTS. BUT I AIM TO SEE TO IT YOUR SENTENCE IS COMMUTED AND YOU BECOME A FREE MAN.
SAVE THE CIVIL LIBERTIES CRAP FOR COURT, RILEY.
UNTIL A JUDGE SAYS OTHERWISE, THRANE'S GOING BACK ON DEATH ROW.
NOT WHAT YOU WANT TO TELL A MAN WHO'S AN ELECTRIFIED QUANTUM DYNAMO, WARDEN.
EDWIN RILEY AGAIN, SIR. WE NEED A QUICK ATTORNEY-CLIENT SIT-DOWN BEFORE I PETITION FOR A--
KRAK
I KNOW HOW INTOXICATING THE RUSH FROM ALL THAT POWER CAN BE, THRANE...
...BUT GET A GRIP. I CAN'T LET YOU LEAVE.
THEN WE HAVE A PROBLEM, CAPTAIN.
SO TAKE YOUR BEST SHOT...

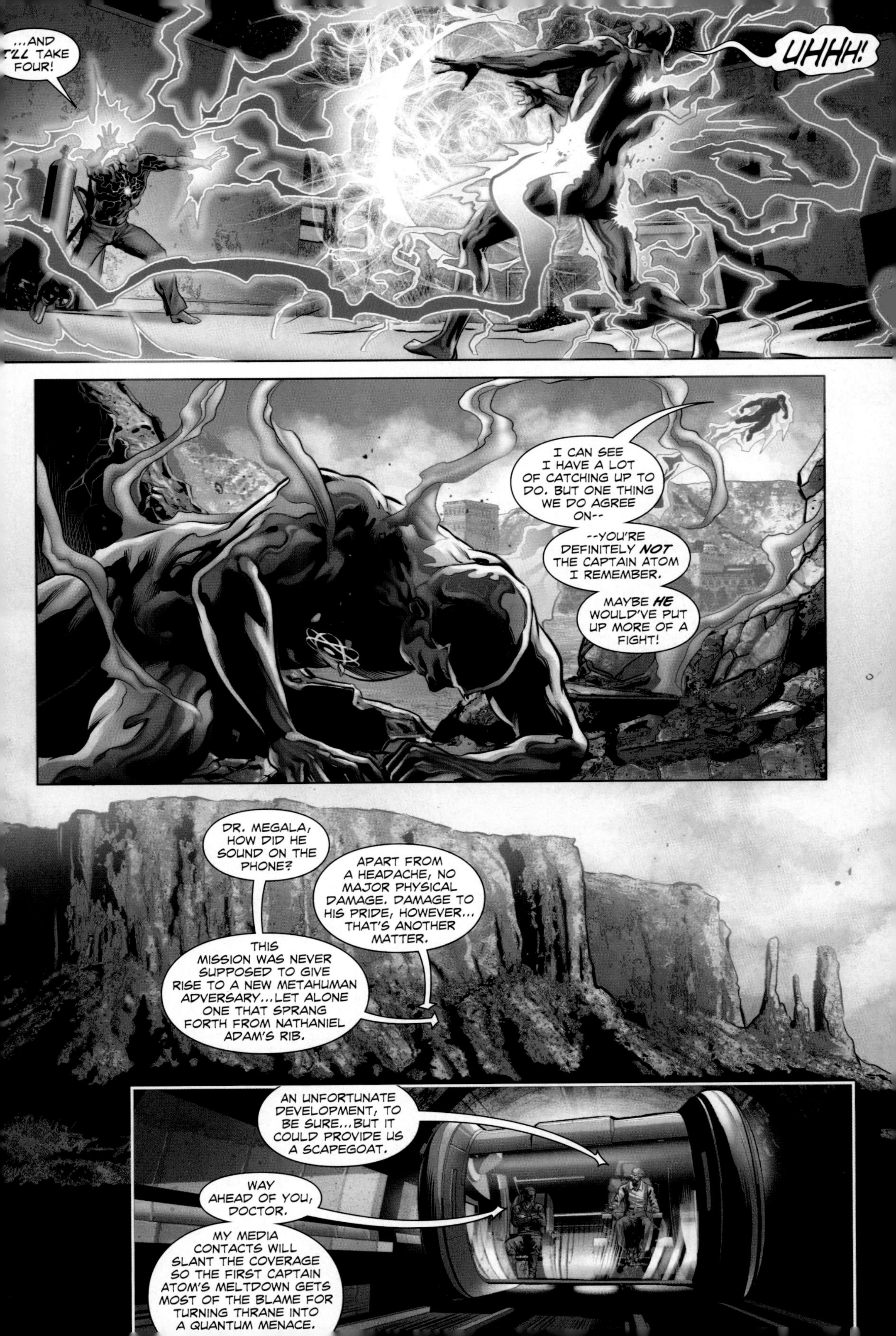
...AND I'LL TAKE FOUR!
UHHH!
I CAN SEE I HAVE A LOT OF CATCHING UP TO DO. BUT ONE THING WE DO AGREE ON--
--YOU'RE DEFINITELY NOT THE CAPTAIN ATOM I REMEMBER.
MAYBE HE WOULD'VE PUT UP MORE OF A FIGHT!
DR. MEGALA, HOW DID HE SOUND ON THE PHONE?
APART FROM A HEADACHE, NO MAJOR PHYSICAL DAMAGE. DAMAGE TO HIS PRIDE, HOWEVER... THAT'S ANOTHER MATTER.
THIS MISSION WAS NEVER SUPPOSED TO GIVE RISE TO A NEW METAHUMAN ADVERSARY...LET ALONE ONE THAT SPRANG FORTH FROM NATHANIEL ADAM'S RIB.
AN UNFORTUNATE DEVELOPMENT, TO BE SURE...BUT IT COULD PROVIDE US A SCAPEGOAT.
WAY AHEAD OF YOU, DOCTOR.
MY MEDIA CONTACTS WILL SLANT THE COVERAGE SO THE FIRST CAPTAIN ATOM'S MELTDOWN GETS MOST OF THE BLAME FOR TURNING THRANE INTO A QUANTUM MENACE.

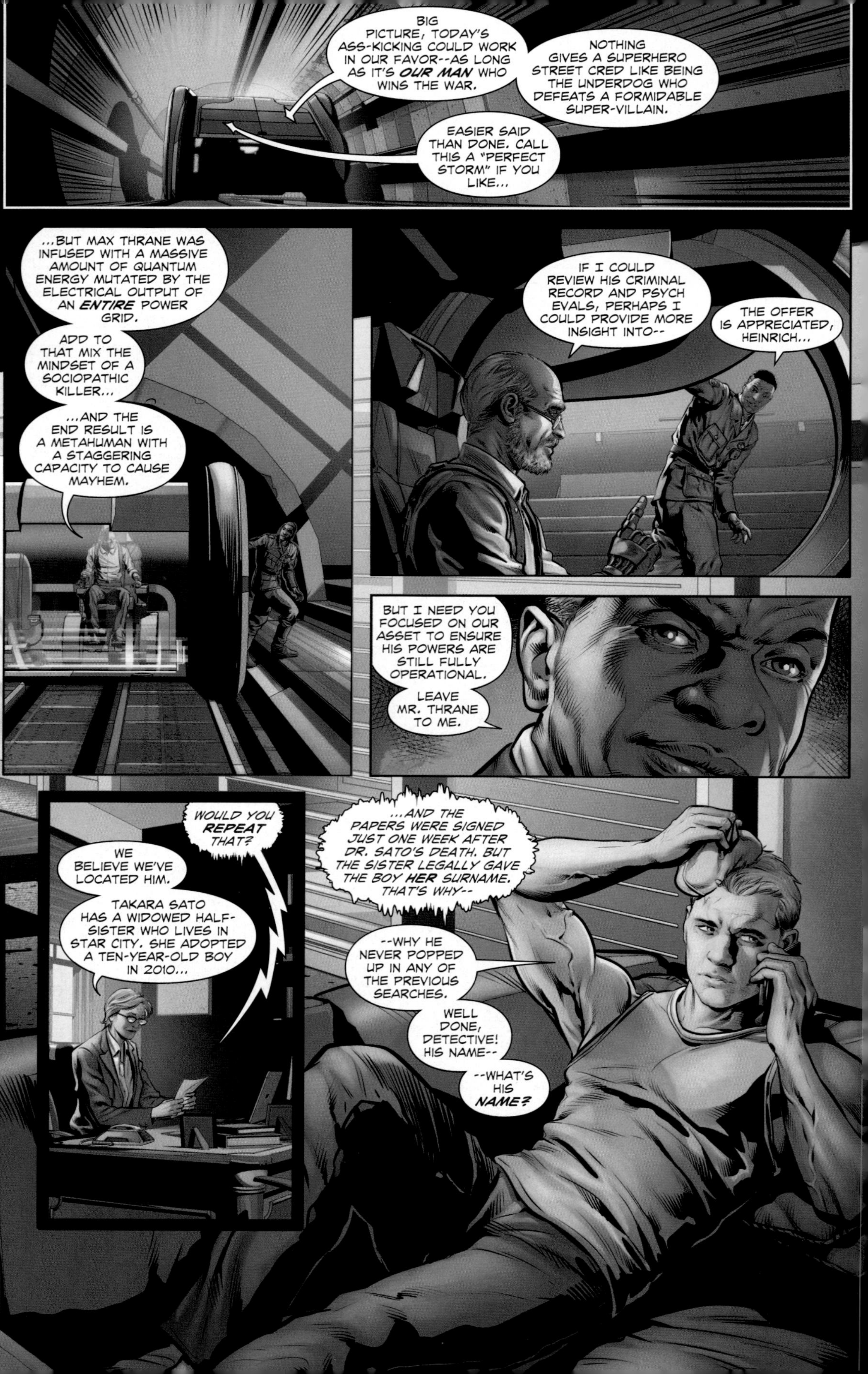
BIG PICTURE, TODAY'S ASS-KICKING COULD WORK IN OUR FAVOR--AS LONG AS IT'S **OUR MAN** WHO WINS THE WAR.
NOTHING GIVES A SUPERHERO STREET CRED LIKE BEING THE UNDERDOG WHO DEFEATS A FORMIDABLE SUPER-VILLAIN.
EASIER SAID THAN DONE. CALL THIS A "PERFECT STORM" IF YOU LIKE...
...BUT MAX THRANE WAS INFUSED WITH A MASSIVE AMOUNT OF QUANTUM ENERGY MUTATED BY THE ELECTRICAL OUTPUT OF AN **ENTIRE** POWER GRID.
ADD TO THAT MIX THE MINDSET OF A SOCIOPATHIC KILLER...
...AND THE END RESULT IS A METAHUMAN WITH A STAGGERING CAPACITY TO CAUSE MAYHEM.
IF I COULD REVIEW HIS CRIMINAL RECORD AND PSYCH EVALS, PERHAPS I COULD PROVIDE MORE INSIGHT INTO--
THE OFFER IS APPRECIATED, HEINRICH...
BUT I NEED YOU FOCUSED ON OUR ASSET TO ENSURE HIS POWERS ARE STILL FULLY OPERATIONAL.
LEAVE MR. THRANE TO ME.
WE BELIEVE WE'VE LOCATED HIM.
*WOULD YOU **REPEAT** THAT?*
TAKARA SATO HAS A WIDOWED HALF-SISTER WHO LIVES IN STAR CITY. SHE ADOPTED A TEN-YEAR-OLD BOY IN 2010...
*...AND THE PAPERS WERE SIGNED JUST ONE WEEK AFTER DR. SATO'S DEATH. BUT THE SISTER LEGALLY GAVE THE BOY **HER** SURNAME. THAT'S WHY--*
--WHY HE NEVER POPPED UP IN ANY OF THE PREVIOUS SEARCHES.
WELL DONE, DETECTIVE! HIS NAME--
--WHAT'S HIS **NAME?**

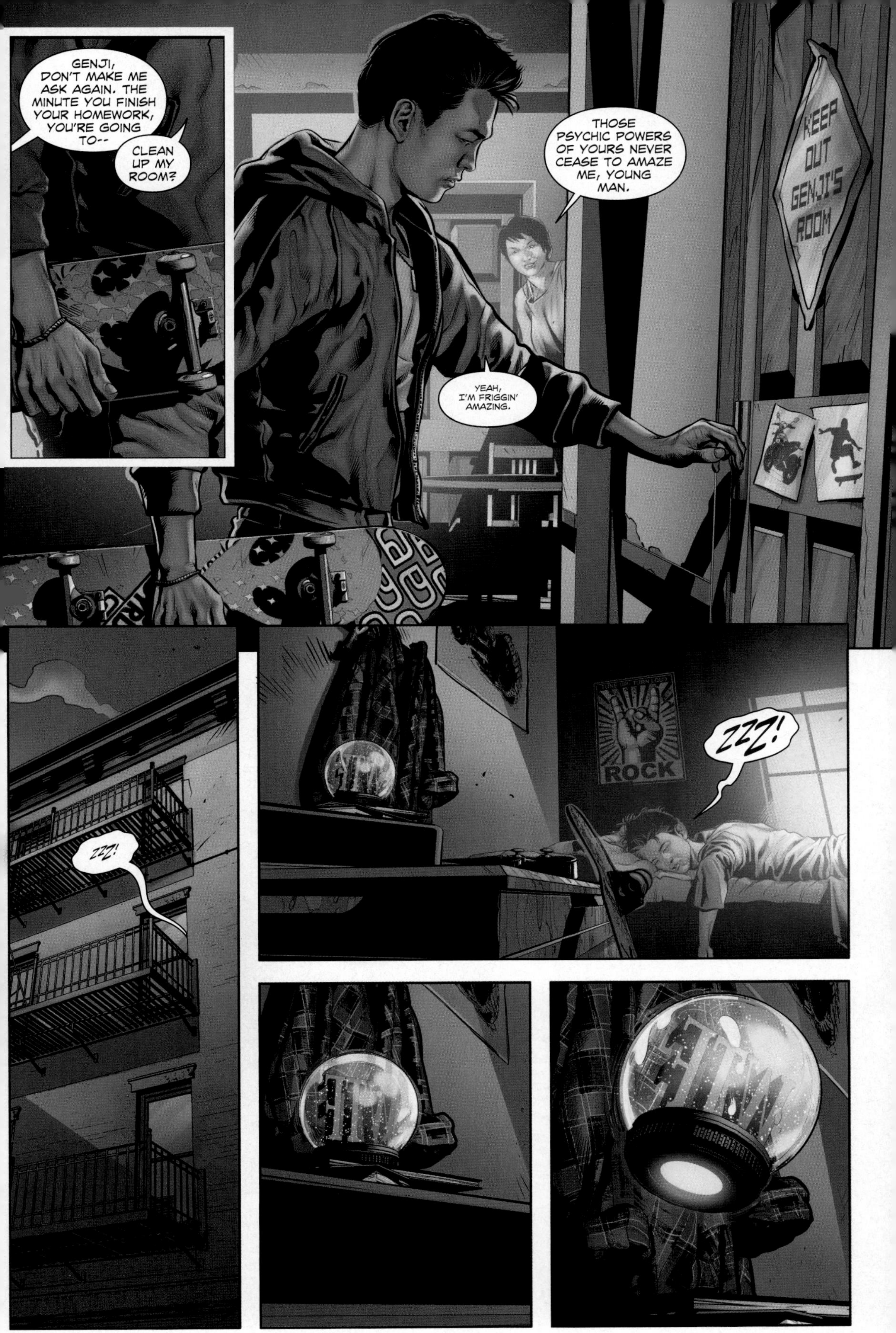
GENJI, DON'T MAKE ME ASK AGAIN. THE MINUTE YOU FINISH YOUR HOMEWORK, YOU'RE GOING TO--
CLEAN UP MY ROOM?
THOSE PSYCHIC POWERS OF YOURS NEVER CEASE TO AMAZE ME, YOUNG MAN.
YEAH, I'M FRIGGIN' AMAZING.
KEEP OUT GENJI'S ROOM
ZZZ!
ROCK
ZZZ!

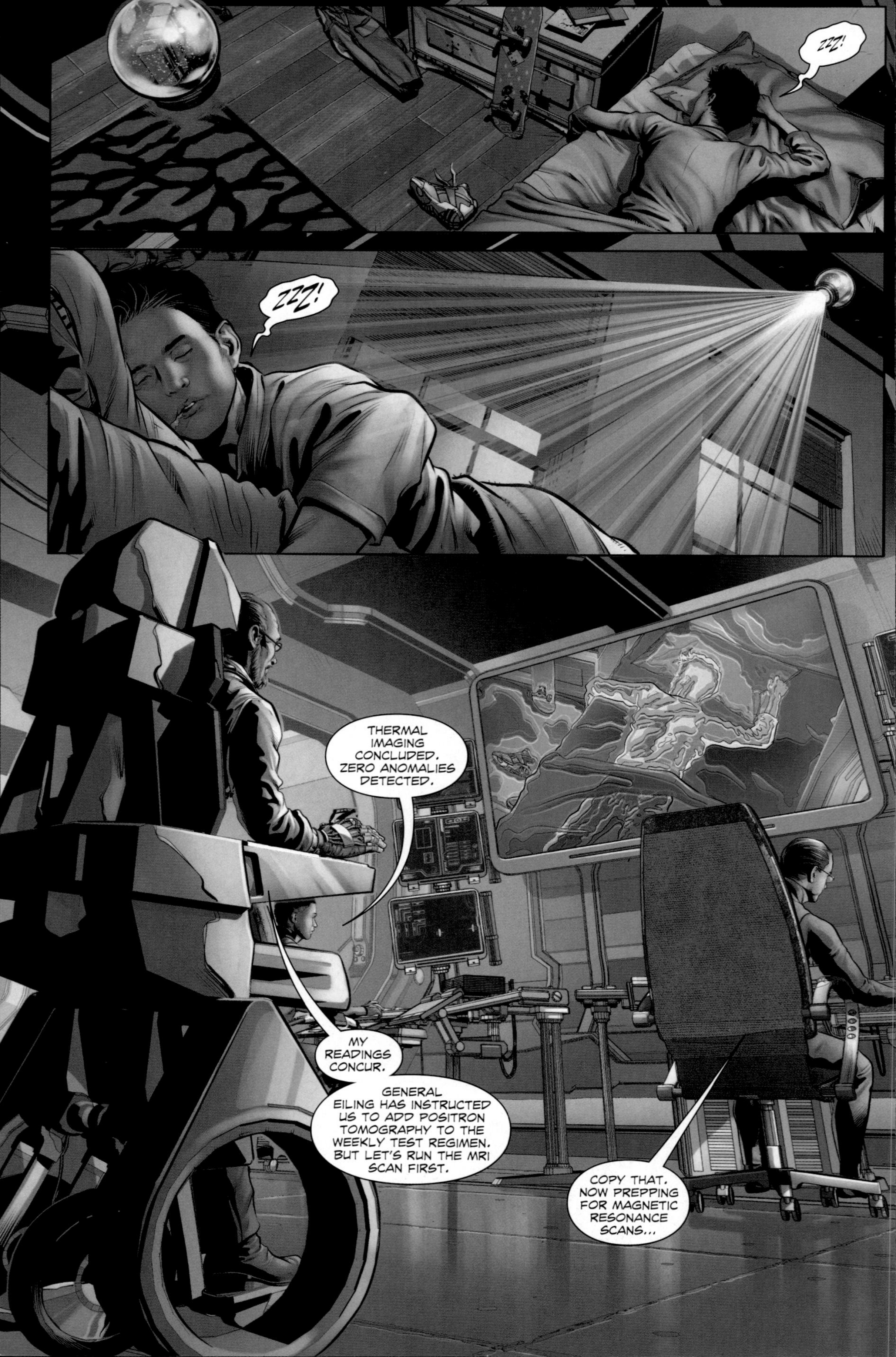
ZZZ!
ZZZ!
THERMAL IMAGING CONCLUDED. ZERO ANOMALIES DETECTED.
MY READINGS CONCUR.
GENERAL EILING HAS INSTRUCTED US TO ADD POSITRON TOMOGRAPHY TO THE WEEKLY TEST REGIMEN. BUT LET'S RUN THE MRI SCAN FIRST.
COPY THAT. NOW PREPPING FOR MAGNETIC RESONANCE SCANS...

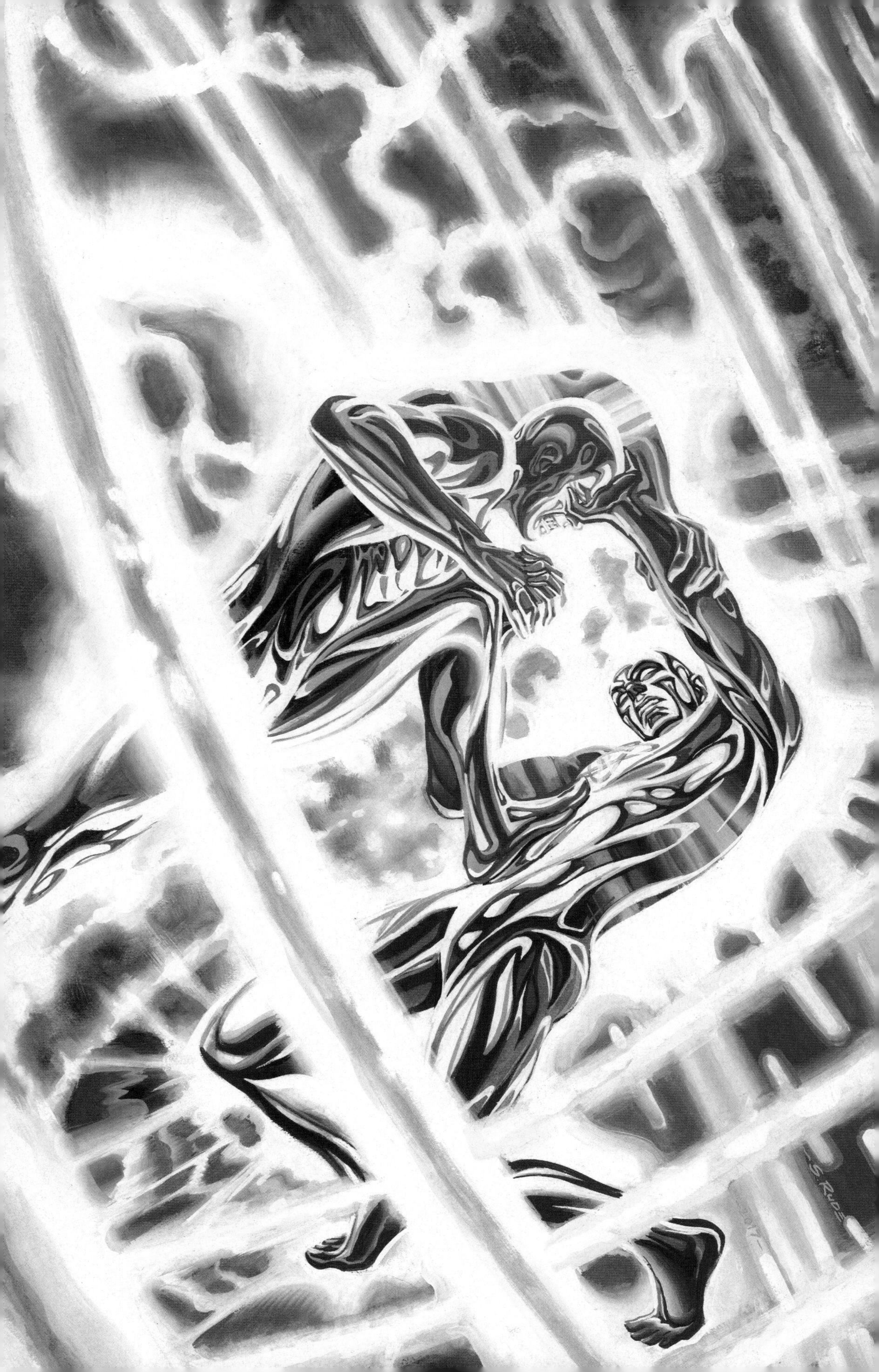

STEVE RUDE Cover Artist

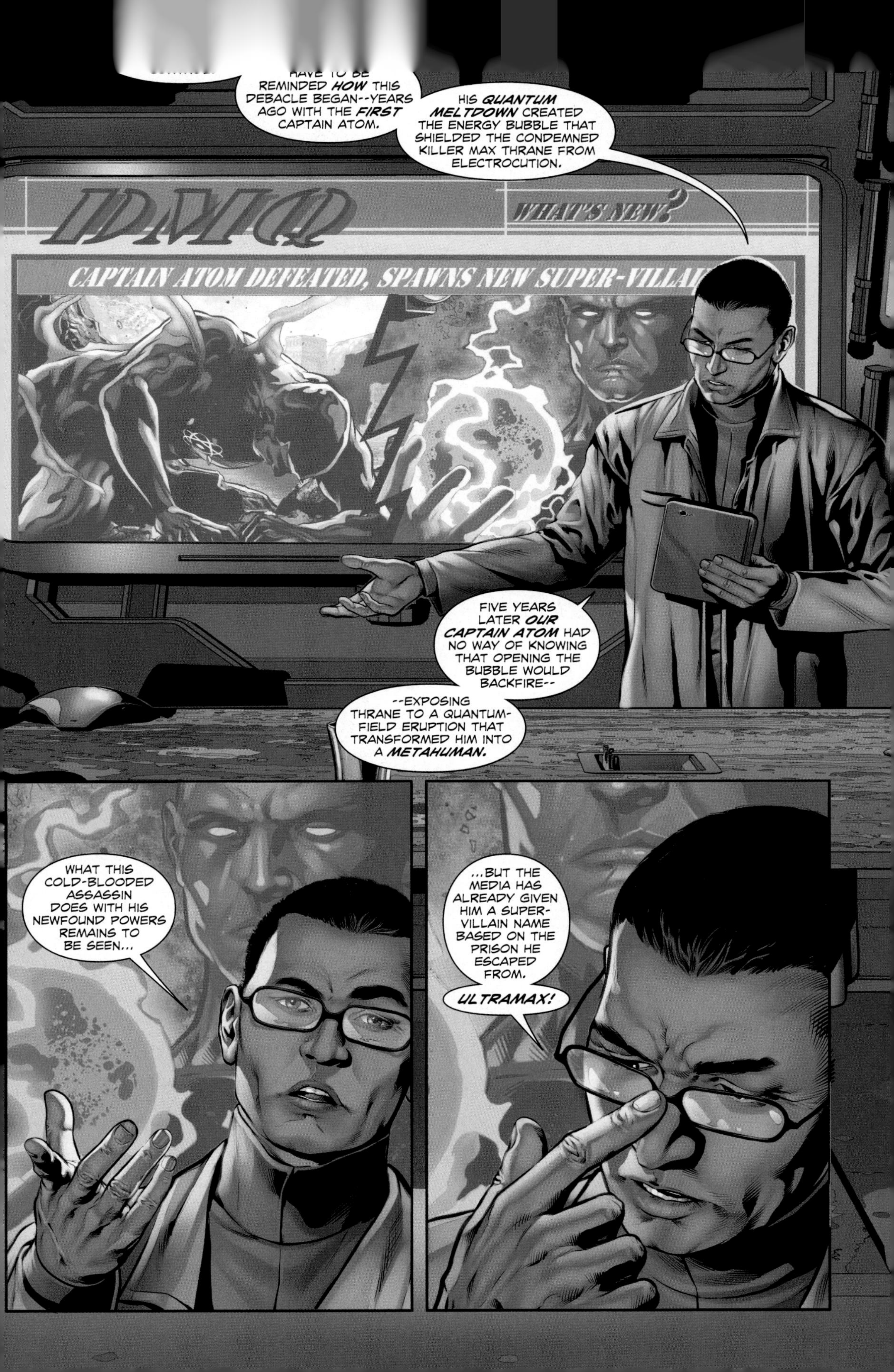
HAVE TO BE REMINDED HOW THIS DEBACLE BEGAN--YEARS AGO WITH THE FIRST CAPTAIN ATOM.
HIS QUANTUM MELTDOWN CREATED THE ENERGY BUBBLE THAT SHIELDED THE CONDEMNED KILLER MAX THRANE FROM ELECTROCUTION.
DMQ
WHAT'S NEW?
CAPTAIN ATOM DEFEATED, SPAWNS NEW SUPER-VILLAI
FIVE YEARS LATER OUR CAPTAIN ATOM HAD NO WAY OF KNOWING THAT OPENING THE BUBBLE WOULD BACKFIRE--
--EXPOSING THRANE TO A QUANTUM-FIELD ERUPTION THAT TRANSFORMED HIM INTO A METAHUMAN.
WHAT THIS COLD-BLOODED ASSASSIN DOES WITH HIS NEWFOUND POWERS REMAINS TO BE SEEN...
...BUT THE MEDIA HAS ALREADY GIVEN HIM A SUPER-VILLAIN NAME BASED ON THE PRISON HE ESCAPED FROM.
ULTRAMAX!

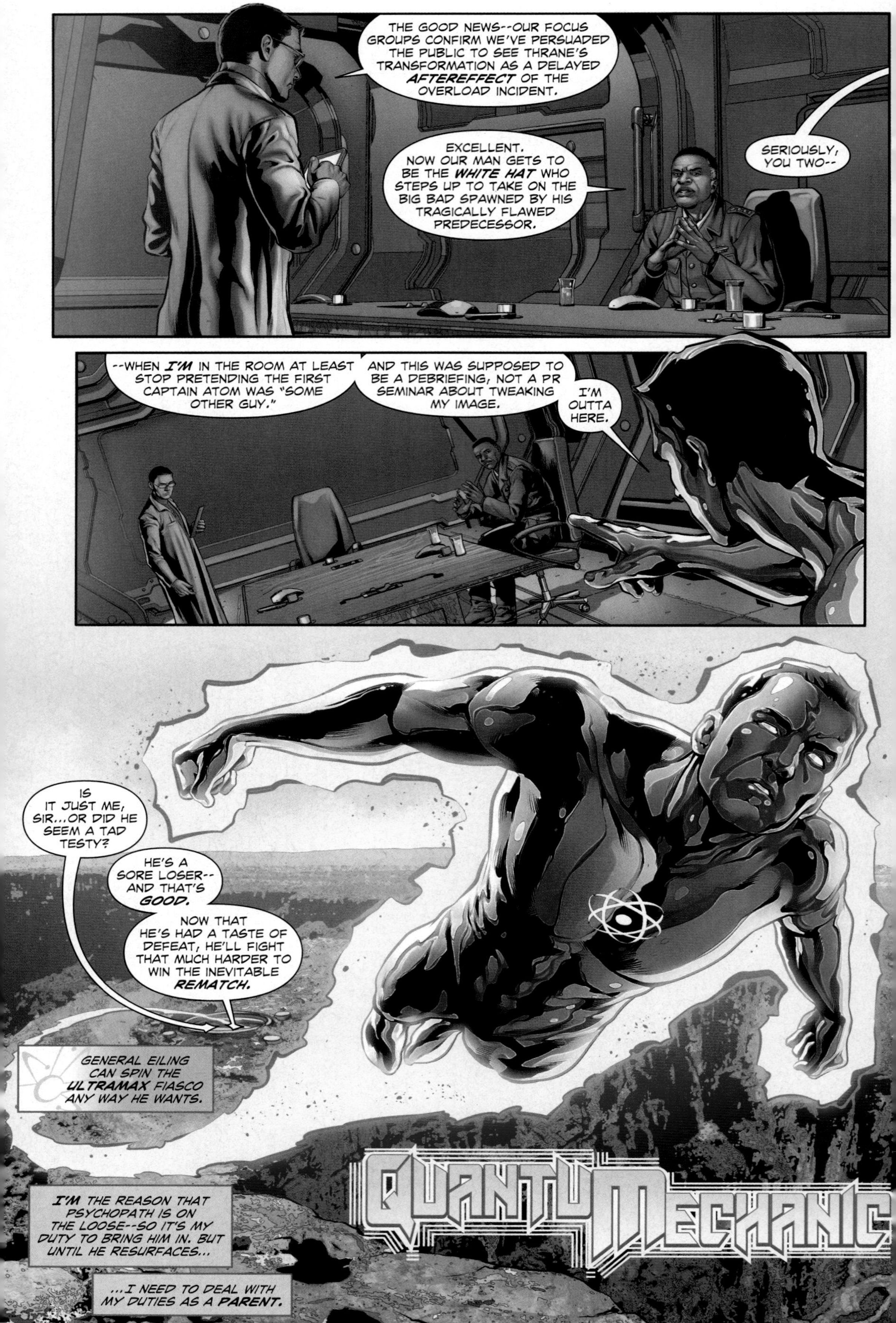

THE GOOD NEWS--OUR FOCUS GROUPS CONFIRM WE'VE PERSUADED THE PUBLIC TO SEE THRANE'S TRANSFORMATION AS A DELAYED AFTEREFFECT OF THE OVERLOAD INCIDENT.
EXCELLENT. NOW OUR MAN GETS TO BE THE WHITE HAT WHO STEPS UP TO TAKE ON THE BIG BAD SPAWNED BY HIS TRAGICALLY FLAWED PREDECESSOR.
SERIOUSLY, YOU TWO--
--WHEN I'M IN THE ROOM AT LEAST STOP PRETENDING THE FIRST CAPTAIN ATOM WAS "SOME OTHER GUY."
AND THIS WAS SUPPOSED TO BE A DEBRIEFING, NOT A PR SEMINAR ABOUT TWEAKING MY IMAGE.
I'M OUTTA HERE.
IS IT JUST ME, SIR...OR DID HE SEEM A TAD TESTY?
HE'S A SORE LOSER-- AND THAT'S GOOD.
NOW THAT HE'S HAD A TASTE OF DEFEAT, HE'LL FIGHT THAT MUCH HARDER TO WIN THE INEVITABLE REMATCH.
GENERAL EILING CAN SPIN THE ULTRAMAX FIASCO ANY WAY HE WANTS.
QUANTUM MECHANIC
I'M THE REASON THAT PSYCHOPATH IS ON THE LOOSE--SO IT'S MY DUTY TO BRING HIM IN. BUT UNTIL HE RESURFACES...
...I NEED TO DEAL WITH MY DUTIES AS A PARENT.

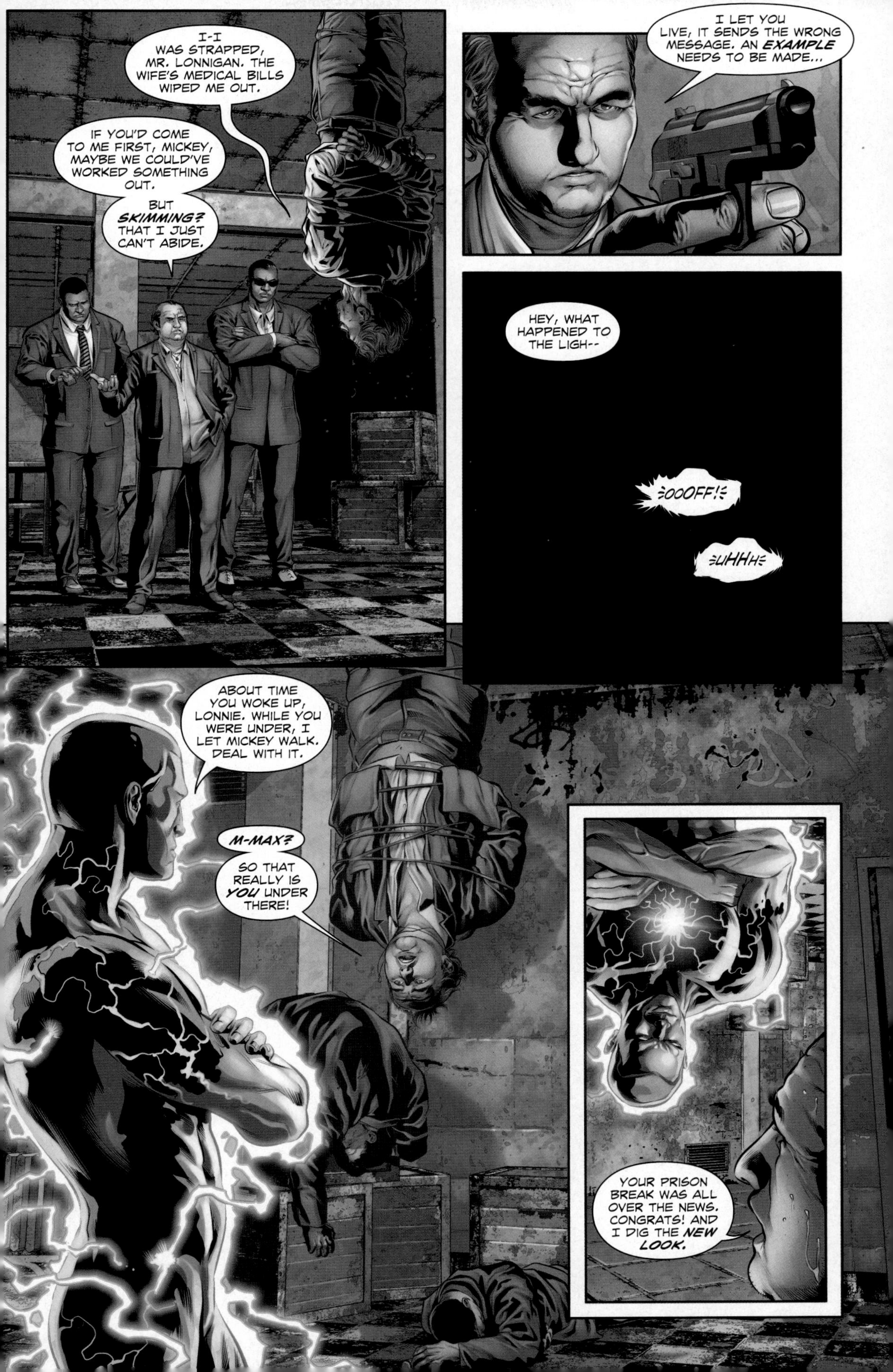
I-I WAS STRAPPED, MR. LONNIGAN. THE WIFE'S MEDICAL BILLS WIPED ME OUT.
IF YOU'D COME TO ME FIRST, MICKEY, MAYBE WE COULD'VE WORKED SOMETHING OUT.
BUT SKIMMING? THAT I JUST CAN'T ABIDE.
I LET YOU LIVE, IT SENDS THE WRONG MESSAGE. AN EXAMPLE NEEDS TO BE MADE...
HEY, WHAT HAPPENED TO THE LIGH--
OOOFF!
UHHH
ABOUT TIME YOU WOKE UP, LONNIE. WHILE YOU WERE UNDER, I LET MICKEY WALK. DEAL WITH IT.
M-MAX?
SO THAT REALLY IS YOU UNDER THERE!
YOUR PRISON BREAK WAS ALL OVER THE NEWS. CONGRATS! AND I DIG THE NEW LOOK.

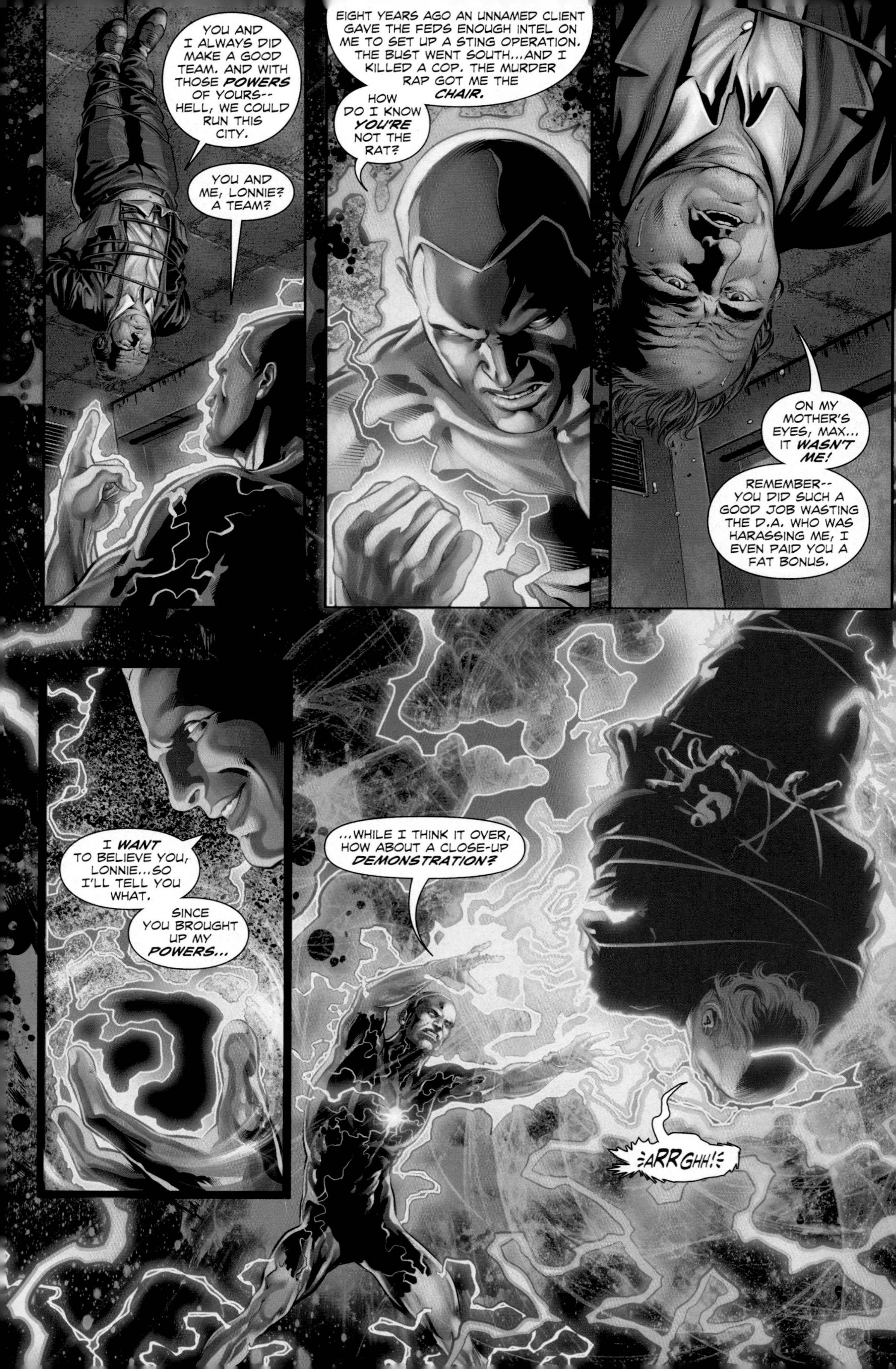
YOU AND I ALWAYS DID MAKE A GOOD TEAM. AND WITH THOSE POWERS OF YOURS-- HELL, WE COULD RUN THIS CITY.
YOU AND ME, LONNIE? A TEAM?
EIGHT YEARS AGO AN UNNAMED CLIENT GAVE THE FEDS ENOUGH INTEL ON ME TO SET UP A STING OPERATION. THE BUST WENT SOUTH...AND I KILLED A COP. THE MURDER RAP GOT ME THE CHAIR.
HOW DO I KNOW YOU'RE NOT THE RAT?
ON MY MOTHER'S EYES, MAX... IT WASN'T ME!
REMEMBER-- YOU DID SUCH A GOOD JOB WASTING THE D.A. WHO WAS HARASSING ME, I EVEN PAID YOU A FAT BONUS.
I WANT TO BELIEVE YOU, LONNIE...SO I'LL TELL YOU WHAT.
SINCE YOU BROUGHT UP MY POWERS...
...WHILE I THINK IT OVER, HOW ABOUT A CLOSE-UP DEMONSTRATION?
AARRGHH!

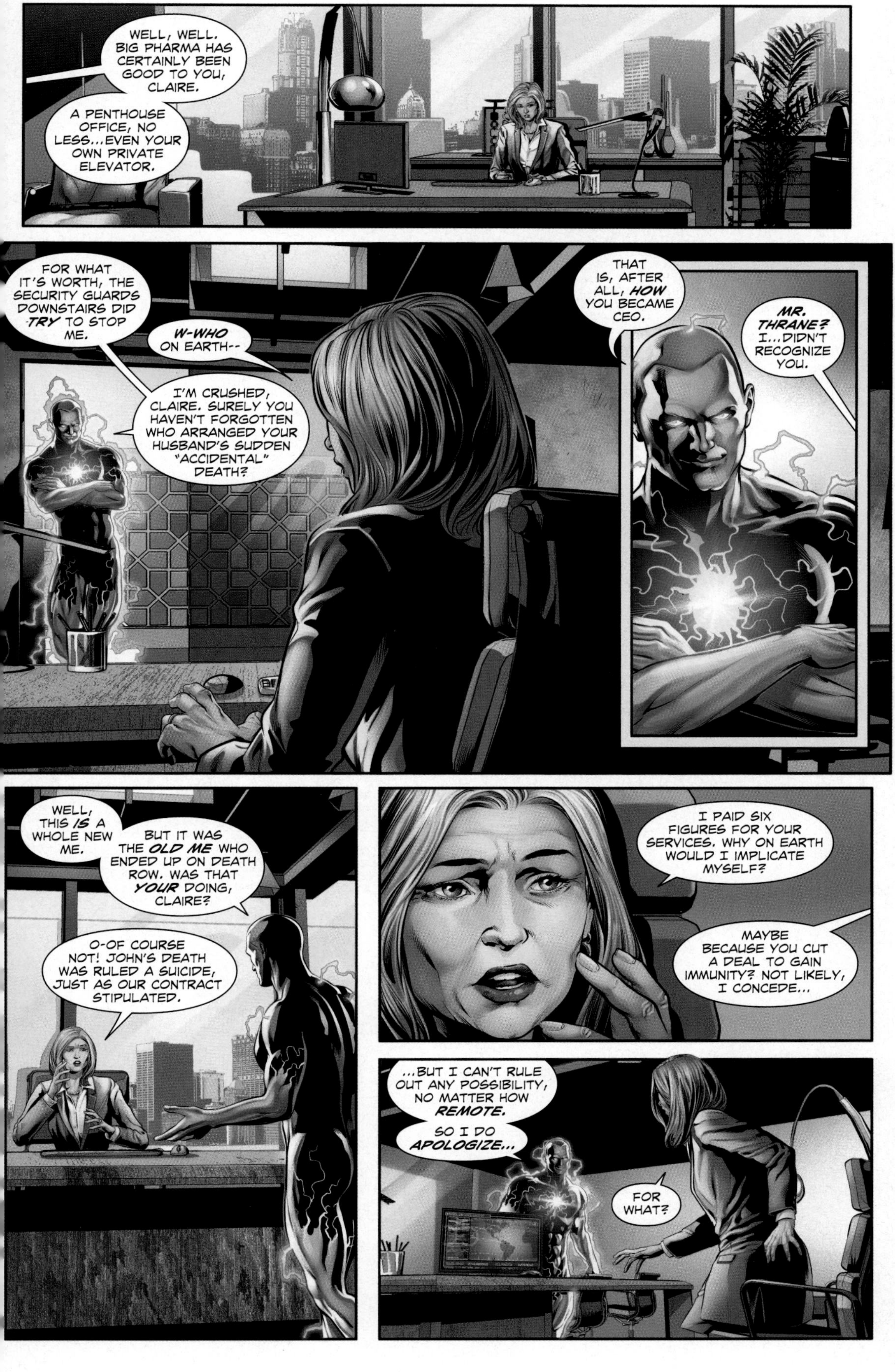
WELL, WELL. BIG PHARMA HAS CERTAINLY BEEN GOOD TO YOU, CLAIRE.
A PENTHOUSE OFFICE, NO LESS...EVEN YOUR OWN PRIVATE ELEVATOR.
FOR WHAT IT'S WORTH, THE SECURITY GUARDS DOWNSTAIRS DID TRY TO STOP ME.
W-WHO ON EARTH--
I'M CRUSHED, CLAIRE. SURELY YOU HAVEN'T FORGOTTEN WHO ARRANGED YOUR HUSBAND'S SUDDEN "ACCIDENTAL" DEATH?
THAT IS, AFTER ALL, HOW YOU BECAME CEO.
MR. THRANE? I...DIDN'T RECOGNIZE YOU.
WELL, THIS IS A WHOLE NEW ME.
BUT IT WAS THE OLD ME WHO ENDED UP ON DEATH ROW. WAS THAT YOUR DOING, CLAIRE?
O-OF COURSE NOT! JOHN'S DEATH WAS RULED A SUICIDE, JUST AS OUR CONTRACT STIPULATED.
I PAID SIX FIGURES FOR YOUR SERVICES. WHY ON EARTH WOULD I IMPLICATE MYSELF?
MAYBE BECAUSE YOU CUT A DEAL TO GAIN IMMUNITY? NOT LIKELY, I CONCEDE...
...BUT I CAN'T RULE OUT ANY POSSIBILITY, NO MATTER HOW REMOTE.
SO I DO APOLOGIZE...
FOR WHAT?

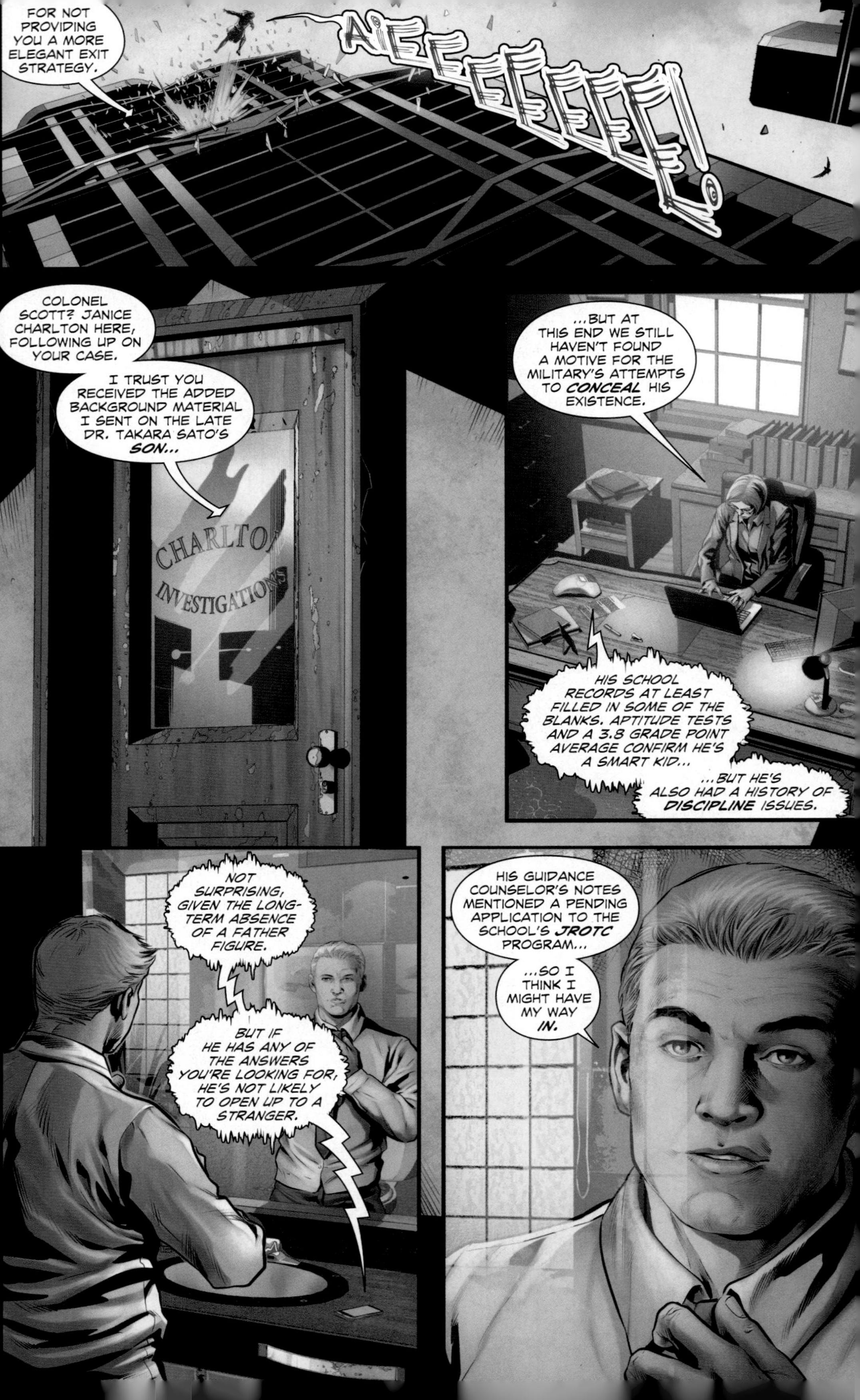
FOR NOT PROVIDING YOU A MORE ELEGANT EXIT STRATEGY.
AIEEEEEEEE!
COLONEL SCOTT? JANICE CHARLTON HERE, FOLLOWING UP ON YOUR CASE.
I TRUST YOU RECEIVED THE ADDED BACKGROUND MATERIAL I SENT ON THE LATE DR. TAKARA SATO'S SON...
CHARLTON INVESTIGATIONS
...BUT AT THIS END WE STILL HAVEN'T FOUND A MOTIVE FOR THE MILITARY'S ATTEMPTS TO CONCEAL HIS EXISTENCE.
HIS SCHOOL RECORDS AT LEAST FILLED IN SOME OF THE BLANKS. APTITUDE TESTS AND A 3.8 GRADE POINT AVERAGE CONFIRM HE'S A SMART KID...
...BUT HE'S ALSO HAD A HISTORY OF DISCIPLINE ISSUES.
NOT SURPRISING, GIVEN THE LONG-TERM ABSENCE OF A FATHER FIGURE.
BUT IF HE HAS ANY OF THE ANSWERS YOU'RE LOOKING FOR, HE'S NOT LIKELY TO OPEN UP TO A STRANGER.
HIS GUIDANCE COUNSELOR'S NOTES MENTIONED A PENDING APPLICATION TO THE SCHOOL'S JROTC PROGRAM...
...SO I THINK I MIGHT HAVE MY WAY IN.

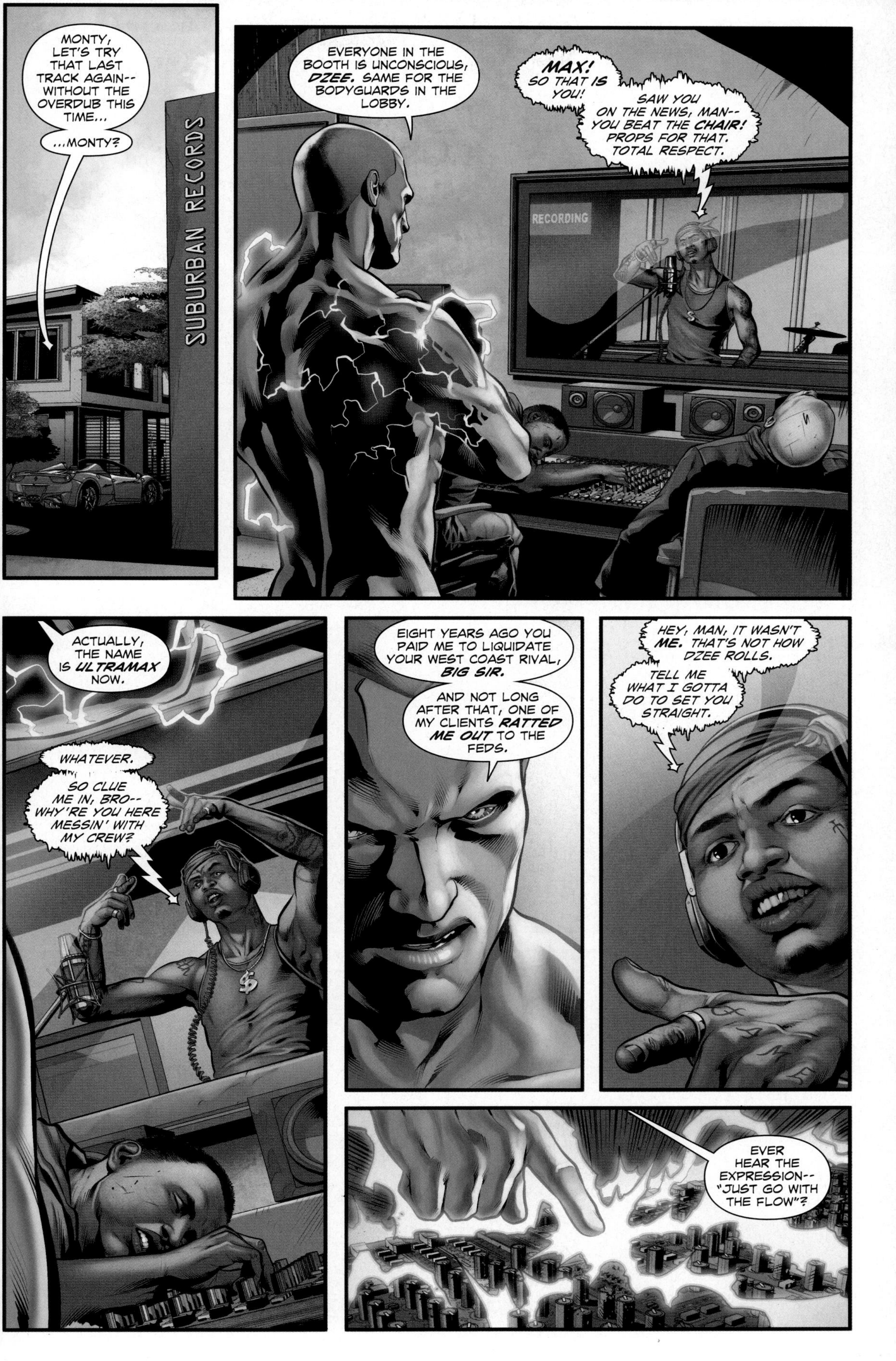
MONTY, LET'S TRY THAT LAST TRACK AGAIN-- WITHOUT THE OVERDUB THIS TIME...
...MONTY?
SUBURBAN RECORDS
EVERYONE IN THE BOOTH IS UNCONSCIOUS, DZEE. SAME FOR THE BODYGUARDS IN THE LOBBY.
MAX! SO THAT IS YOU!
SAW YOU ON THE NEWS, MAN-- YOU BEAT THE CHAIR! PROPS FOR THAT. TOTAL RESPECT.
RECORDING
ACTUALLY, THE NAME IS ULTRAMAX NOW.
WHATEVER.
SO CLUE ME IN, BRO-- WHY'RE YOU HERE MESSIN' WITH MY CREW?
EIGHT YEARS AGO YOU PAID ME TO LIQUIDATE YOUR WEST COAST RIVAL, BIG SIR.
AND NOT LONG AFTER THAT, ONE OF MY CLIENTS RATTED ME OUT TO THE FEDS.
HEY, MAN, IT WASN'T ME. THAT'S NOT HOW DZEE ROLLS.
TELL ME WHAT I GOTTA DO TO SET YOU STRAIGHT.
EVER HEAR THE EXPRESSION-- "JUST GO WITH THE FLOW"?

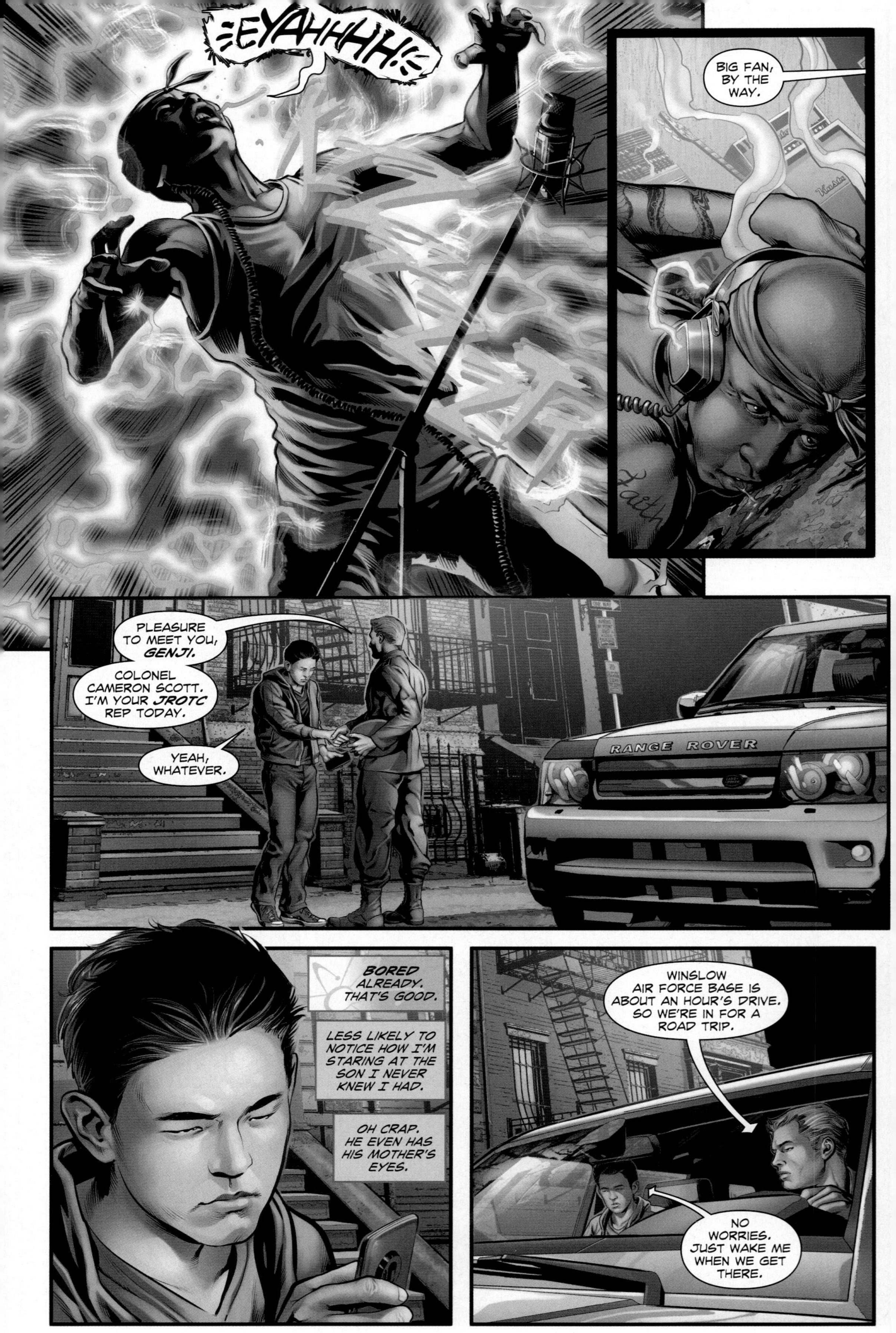
EYAHHHH!
BIG FAN, BY THE WAY.
PLEASURE TO MEET YOU, GENJI.
COLONEL CAMERON SCOTT. I'M YOUR JROTC REP TODAY.
YEAH, WHATEVER.
RANGE ROVER
BORED ALREADY. THAT'S GOOD.
LESS LIKELY TO NOTICE HOW I'M STARING AT THE SON I NEVER KNEW I HAD.
OH CRAP. HE EVEN HAS HIS MOTHER'S EYES.
WINSLOW AIR FORCE BASE IS ABOUT AN HOUR'S DRIVE. SO WE'RE IN FOR A ROAD TRIP.
NO WORRIES. JUST WAKE ME WHEN WE GET THERE.

--MOB BOSS **LONNIE LONNIGAN**, BIG PHARMA CZAR **CLAIRE VAN NESS** AND THE RAP ARTIST **DZEE**.

THREE MURDERS WITHIN EIGHT HOURS--WITH TWO OTHERS YET TO BE CONFIRMED. BEYOND THE VICTIMS' HIGH PROFILES, POLICE HAVE FOUND NO COMMON LINK.

"BOSS" LONNIGAN

CLAIRE VAN NESS

RAPPER DZEE

NO LINK-- BUT A SINGULAR **PERSON OF INTEREST**.

REPORTS ARE COMING IN THAT THE FUGITIVE MAX THRANE--ALSO KNOWN NOW AS **ULTRAMAX**-- WAS SIGHTED NEAR **ALL** THE CRIME SCENE VICINITIES.

BEFORE ENDING UP ON DEATH ROW, THRANE WAS A HIGH-PAID *"MECHANIC"*-- A PROFESSIONAL HIT MAN.

POLICE SPECULATE HE MAY BE SELLING HIS SERVICES AGAIN--ONLY NOW USING **METAHUMAN POWERS** TO KILL.

CLAIRE VAN NESS

WRONG.

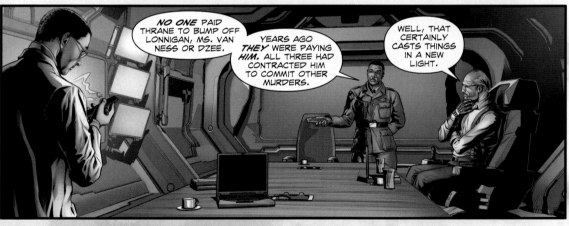

NO ONE PAID THRANE TO BUMP OFF LONNIGAN, MS. VAN NESS OR DZEE.

YEARS AGO **THEY** WERE PAYING **HIM.** ALL THREE HAD CONTRACTED HIM TO COMMIT OTHER MURDERS.

WELL, THAT CERTAINLY CASTS THINGS IN A NEW LIGHT.

THRANE COULD ONLY BE HIRED BY REFERRAL.

BACK IN 2008, IN EXCHANGE FOR ANONYMITY, A FORMER CLIENT GAVE THE POLICE ENOUGH INSIDE INTEL TO SET UP A **STING** OPERATION...

...WHICH LED TO HIS EVENTUAL CONVICTION AND DEATH SENTENCE.

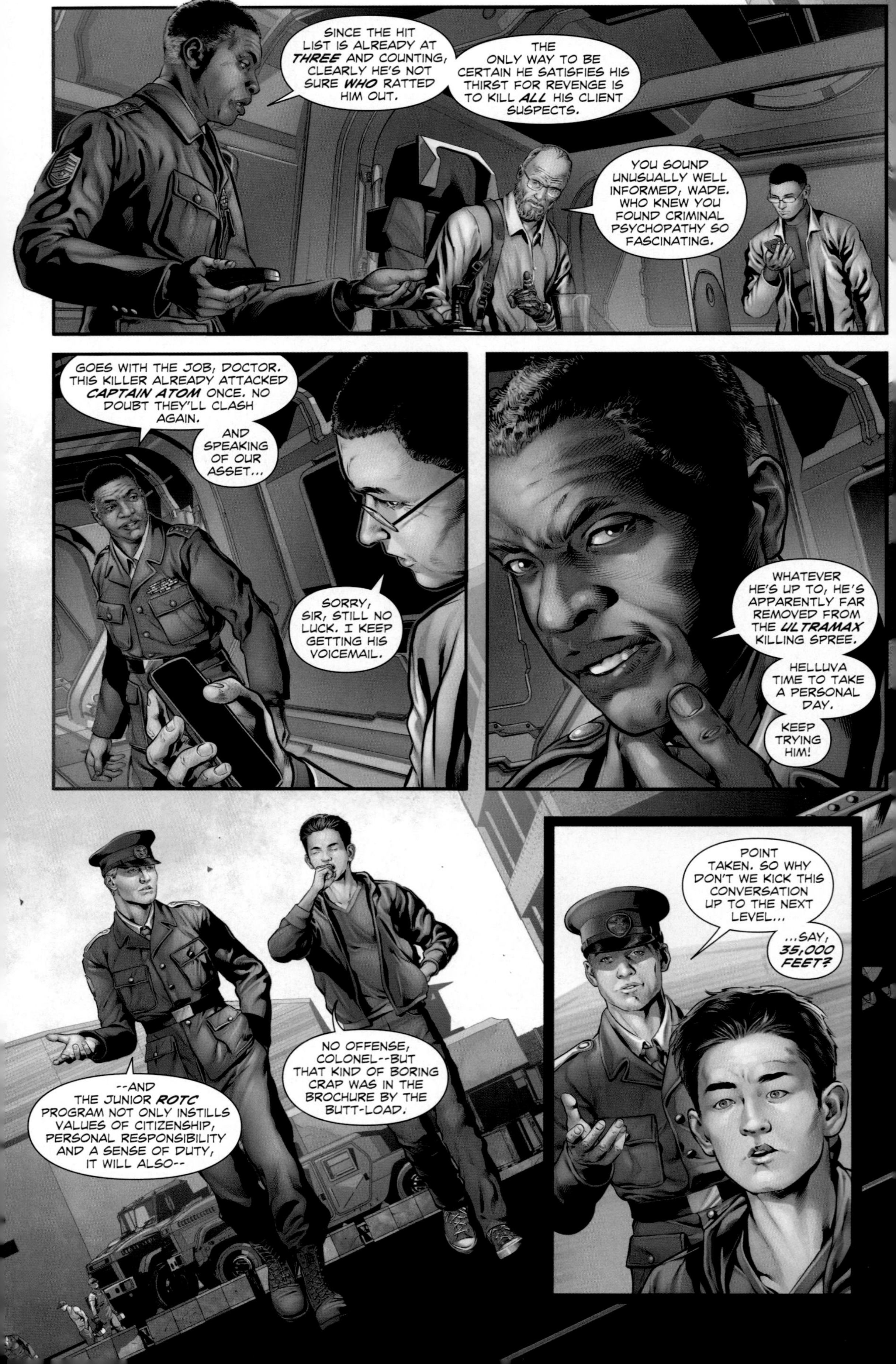
SINCE THE HIT LIST IS ALREADY AT THREE AND COUNTING, CLEARLY HE'S NOT SURE WHO RATTED HIM OUT.
THE ONLY WAY TO BE CERTAIN HE SATISFIES HIS THIRST FOR REVENGE IS TO KILL ALL HIS CLIENT SUSPECTS.
YOU SOUND UNUSUALLY WELL INFORMED, WADE. WHO KNEW YOU FOUND CRIMINAL PSYCHOPATHY SO FASCINATING.
GOES WITH THE JOB, DOCTOR. THIS KILLER ALREADY ATTACKED CAPTAIN ATOM ONCE. NO DOUBT THEY'LL CLASH AGAIN.
AND SPEAKING OF OUR ASSET...
SORRY, SIR, STILL NO LUCK. I KEEP GETTING HIS VOICEMAIL.
WHATEVER HE'S UP TO, HE'S APPARENTLY FAR REMOVED FROM THE ULTRAMAX KILLING SPREE.
HELLUVA TIME TO TAKE A PERSONAL DAY.
KEEP TRYING HIM!
--AND THE JUNIOR ROTC PROGRAM NOT ONLY INSTILLS VALUES OF CITIZENSHIP, PERSONAL RESPONSIBILITY AND A SENSE OF DUTY, IT WILL ALSO--
NO OFFENSE, COLONEL--BUT THAT KIND OF BORING CRAP WAS IN THE BROCHURE BY THE BUTT-LOAD.
POINT TAKEN. SO WHY DON'T WE KICK THIS CONVERSATION UP TO THE NEXT LEVEL...
...SAY, 35,000 FEET?

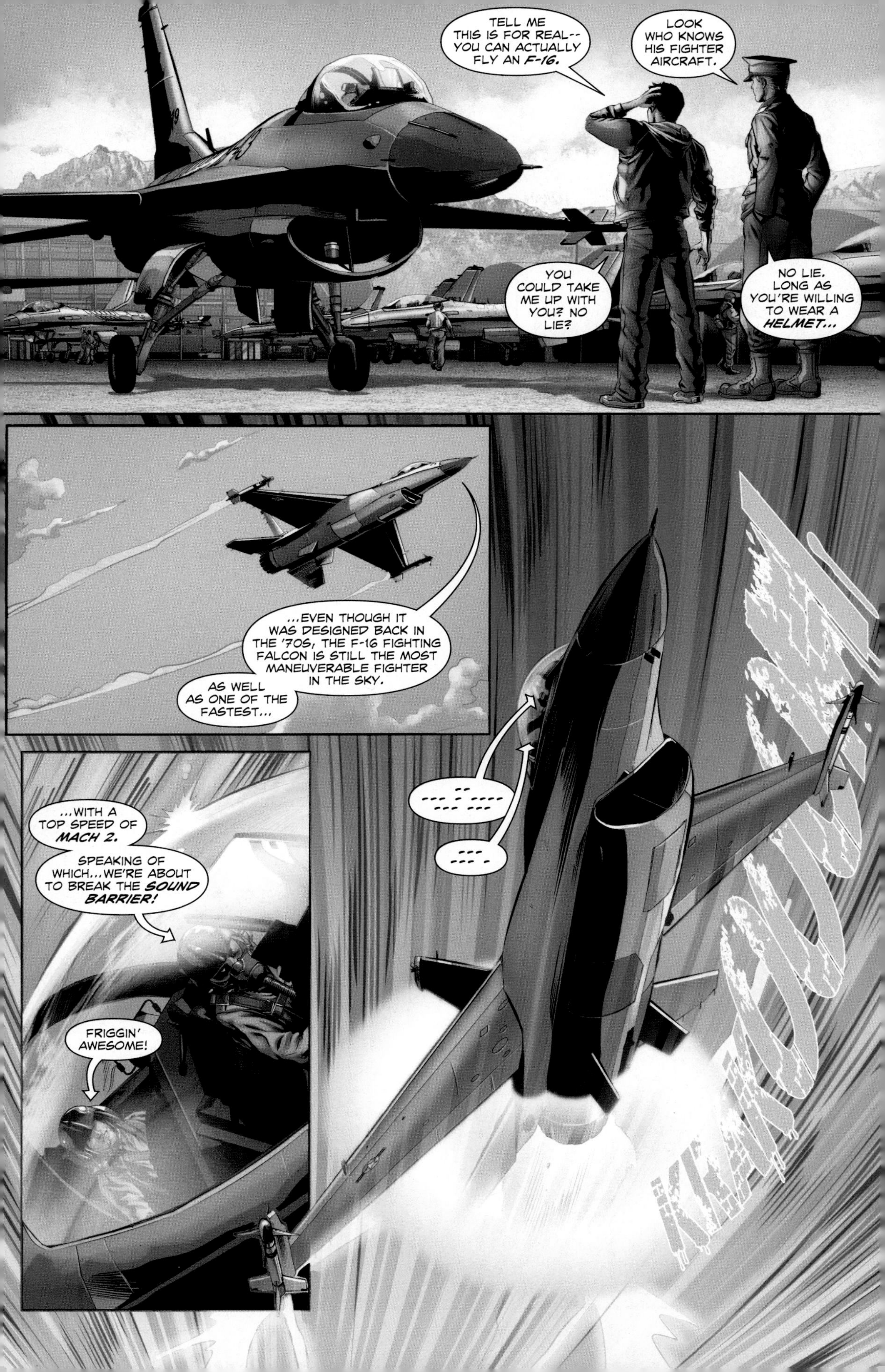
TELL ME THIS IS FOR REAL-- YOU CAN ACTUALLY FLY AN F-16.
LOOK WHO KNOWS HIS FIGHTER AIRCRAFT.
YOU COULD TAKE ME UP WITH YOU? NO LIE?
NO LIE. LONG AS YOU'RE WILLING TO WEAR A HELMET...
...EVEN THOUGH IT WAS DESIGNED BACK IN THE '70S, THE F-16 FIGHTING FALCON IS STILL THE MOST MANEUVERABLE FIGHTER IN THE SKY.
AS WELL AS ONE OF THE FASTEST...
...WITH A TOP SPEED OF MACH 2.
SPEAKING OF WHICH...WE'RE ABOUT TO BREAK THE SOUND BARRIER!
FRIGGIN' AWESOME!

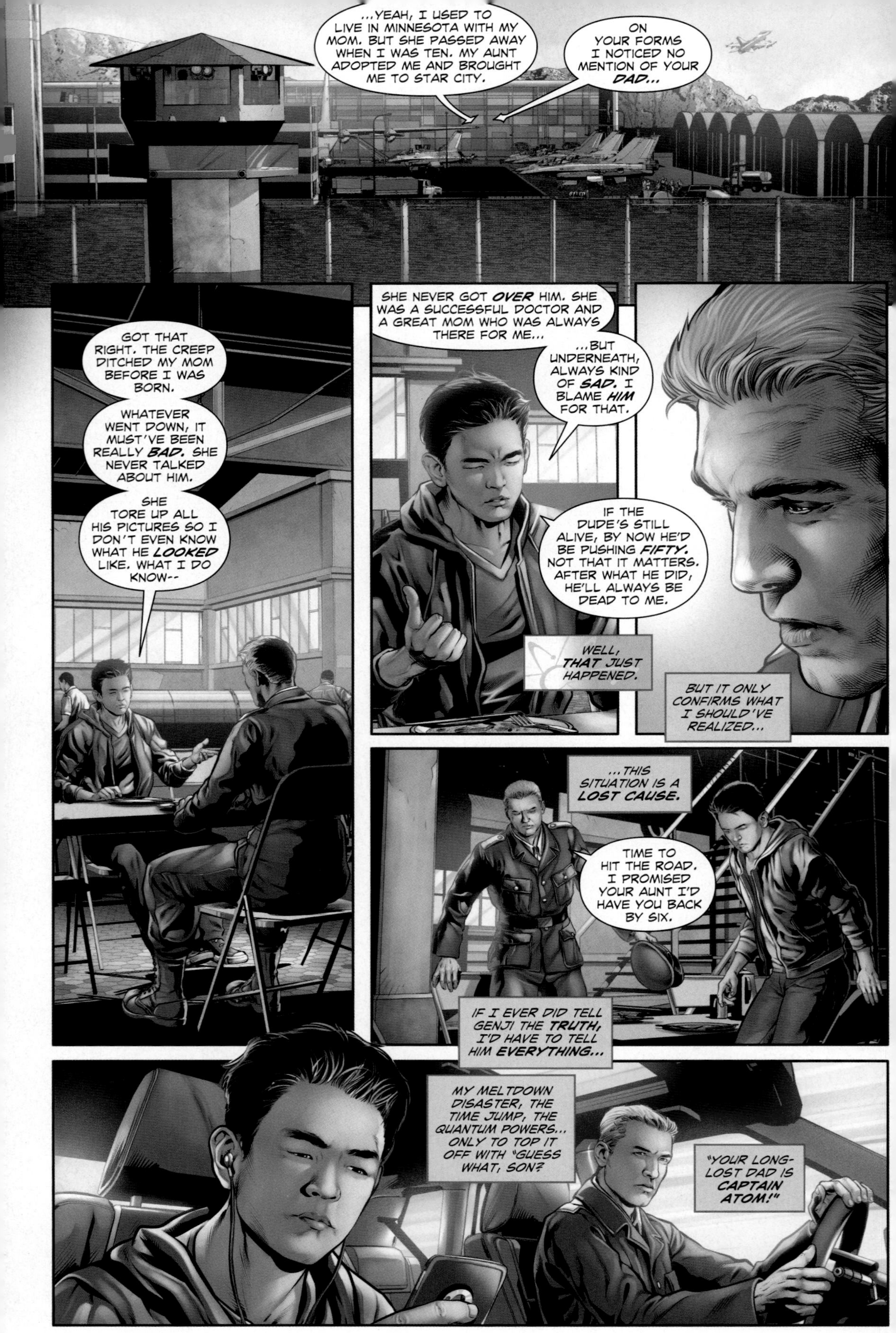
...YEAH, I USED TO LIVE IN MINNESOTA WITH MY MOM. BUT SHE PASSED AWAY WHEN I WAS TEN. MY AUNT ADOPTED ME AND BROUGHT ME TO STAR CITY.
ON YOUR FORMS I NOTICED NO MENTION OF YOUR DAD...
GOT THAT RIGHT. THE CREEP DITCHED MY MOM BEFORE I WAS BORN.
WHATEVER WENT DOWN, IT MUST'VE BEEN REALLY BAD. SHE NEVER TALKED ABOUT HIM.
SHE TORE UP ALL HIS PICTURES SO I DON'T EVEN KNOW WHAT HE LOOKED LIKE. WHAT I DO KNOW--
SHE NEVER GOT OVER HIM. SHE WAS A SUCCESSFUL DOCTOR AND A GREAT MOM WHO WAS ALWAYS THERE FOR ME...
...BUT UNDERNEATH, ALWAYS KIND OF SAD. I BLAME HIM FOR THAT.
IF THE DUDE'S STILL ALIVE, BY NOW HE'D BE PUSHING FIFTY. NOT THAT IT MATTERS. AFTER WHAT HE DID, HE'LL ALWAYS BE DEAD TO ME.
WELL, THAT JUST HAPPENED.
BUT IT ONLY CONFIRMS WHAT I SHOULD'VE REALIZED...
...THIS SITUATION IS A LOST CAUSE.
TIME TO HIT THE ROAD. I PROMISED YOUR AUNT I'D HAVE YOU BACK BY SIX.
IF I EVER DID TELL GENJI THE TRUTH, I'D HAVE TO TELL HIM EVERYTHING...
MY MELTDOWN DISASTER, THE TIME JUMP, THE QUANTUM POWERS... ONLY TO TOP IT OFF WITH "GUESS WHAT, SON?
"YOUR LONG-LOST DAD IS CAPTAIN ATOM!"

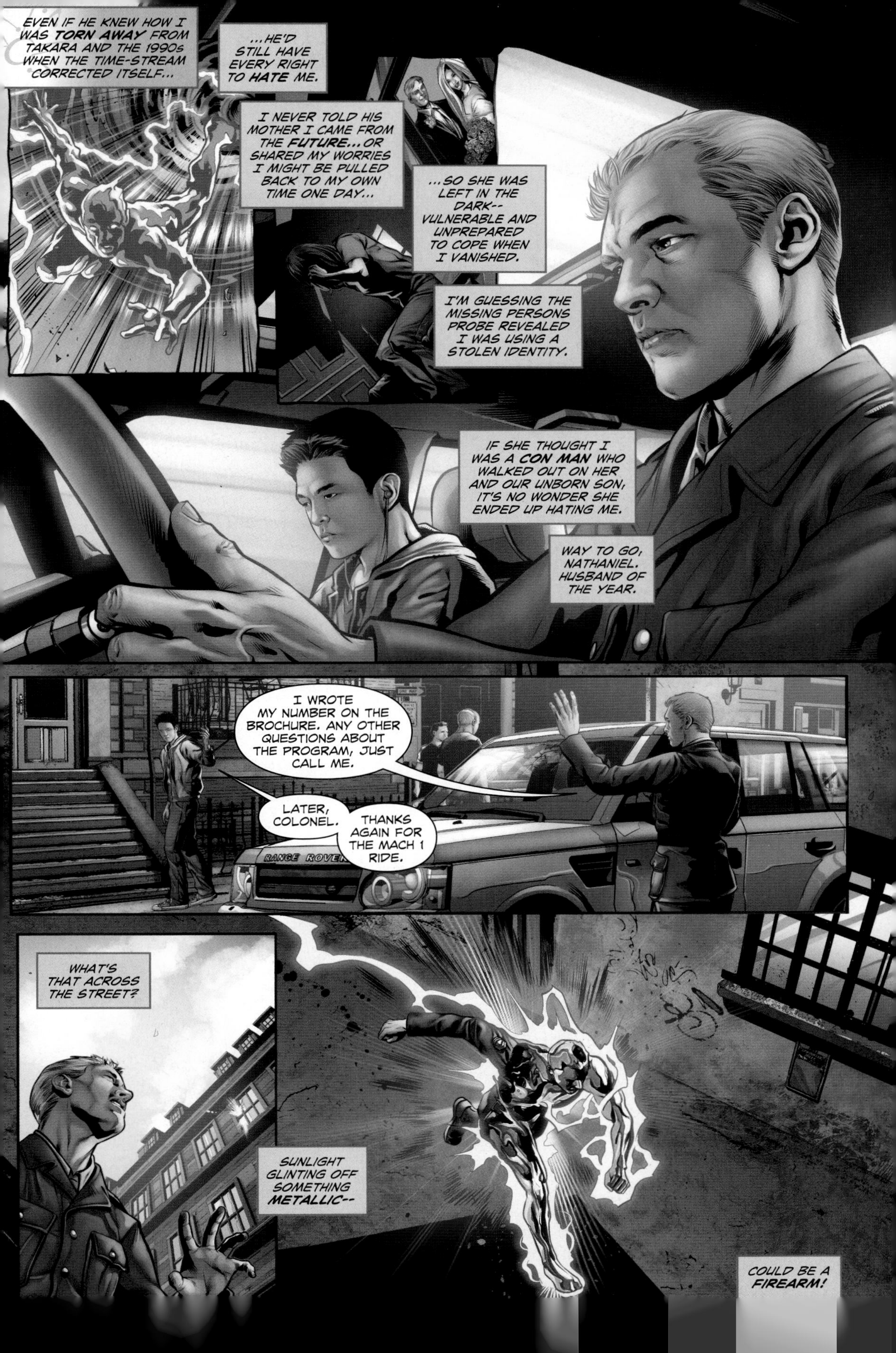
EVEN IF HE KNEW HOW I WAS TORN AWAY FROM TAKARA AND THE 1990s WHEN THE TIME-STREAM CORRECTED ITSELF...
...HE'D STILL HAVE EVERY RIGHT TO HATE ME.
I NEVER TOLD HIS MOTHER I CAME FROM THE FUTURE...OR SHARED MY WORRIES I MIGHT BE PULLED BACK TO MY OWN TIME ONE DAY...
...SO SHE WAS LEFT IN THE DARK-- VULNERABLE AND UNPREPARED TO COPE WHEN I VANISHED.
I'M GUESSING THE MISSING PERSONS PROBE REVEALED I WAS USING A STOLEN IDENTITY.
IF SHE THOUGHT I WAS A CON MAN WHO WALKED OUT ON HER AND OUR UNBORN SON, IT'S NO WONDER SHE ENDED UP HATING ME.
WAY TO GO, NATHANIEL. HUSBAND OF THE YEAR.
I WROTE MY NUMBER ON THE BROCHURE. ANY OTHER QUESTIONS ABOUT THE PROGRAM, JUST CALL ME.
LATER, COLONEL.
THANKS AGAIN FOR THE MACH 1 RIDE.
RANGE ROVER
WHAT'S THAT ACROSS THE STREET?
SUNLIGHT GLINTING OFF SOMETHING METALLIC--
COULD BE A FIREARM!

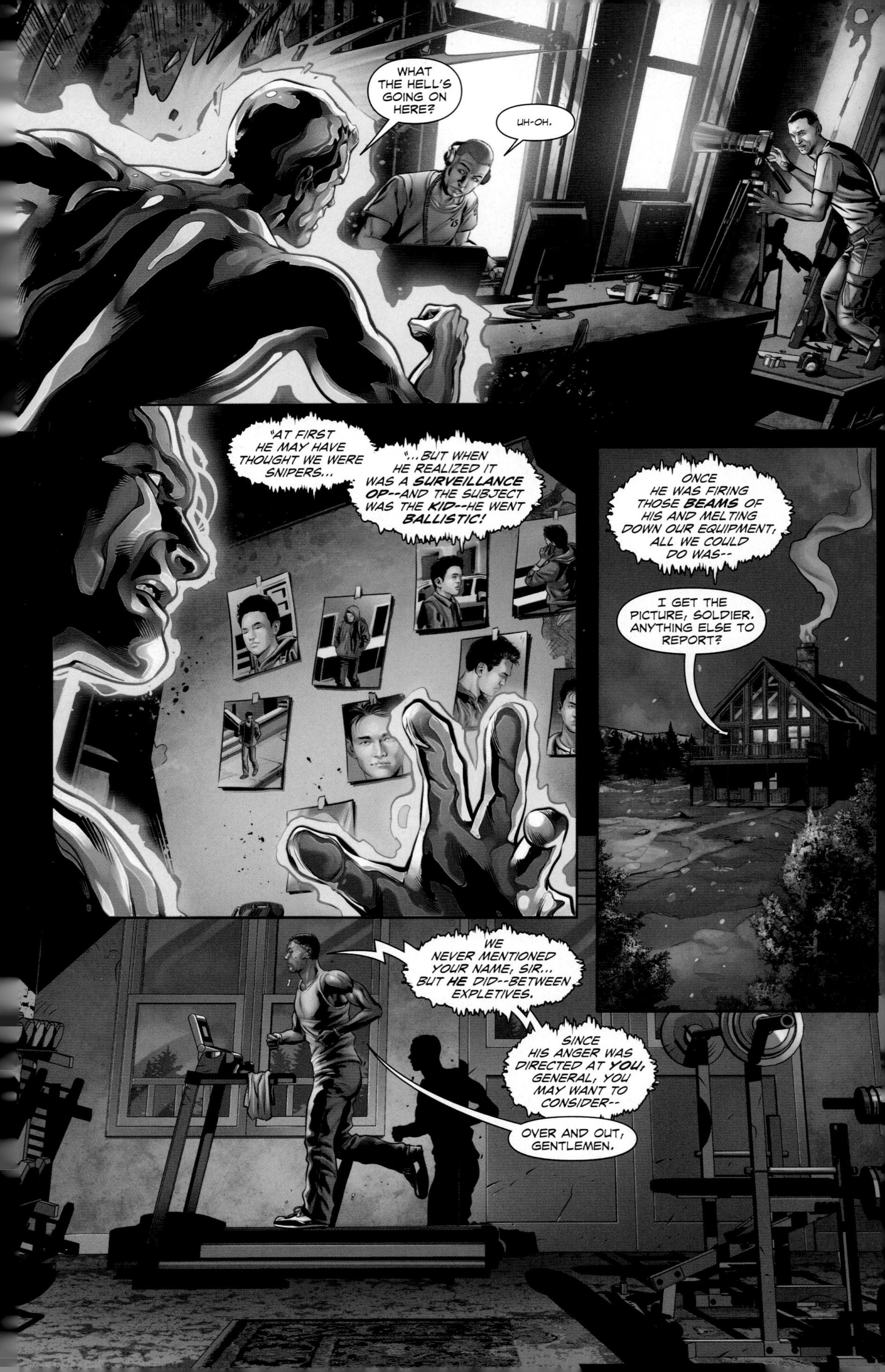
WHAT THE HELL'S GOING ON HERE?
UH-OH.
"AT FIRST HE MAY HAVE THOUGHT WE WERE SNIPERS...
"...BUT WHEN HE REALIZED IT WAS A SURVEILLANCE OP--AND THE SUBJECT WAS THE KID--HE WENT BALLISTIC!
ONCE HE WAS FIRING THOSE BEAMS OF HIS AND MELTING DOWN OUR EQUIPMENT, ALL WE COULD DO WAS--
I GET THE PICTURE, SOLDIER. ANYTHING ELSE TO REPORT?
WE NEVER MENTIONED YOUR NAME, SIR... BUT HE DID--BETWEEN EXPLETIVES.
SINCE HIS ANGER WAS DIRECTED AT YOU, GENERAL, YOU MAY WANT TO CONSIDER--
OVER AND OUT, GENTLEMEN.

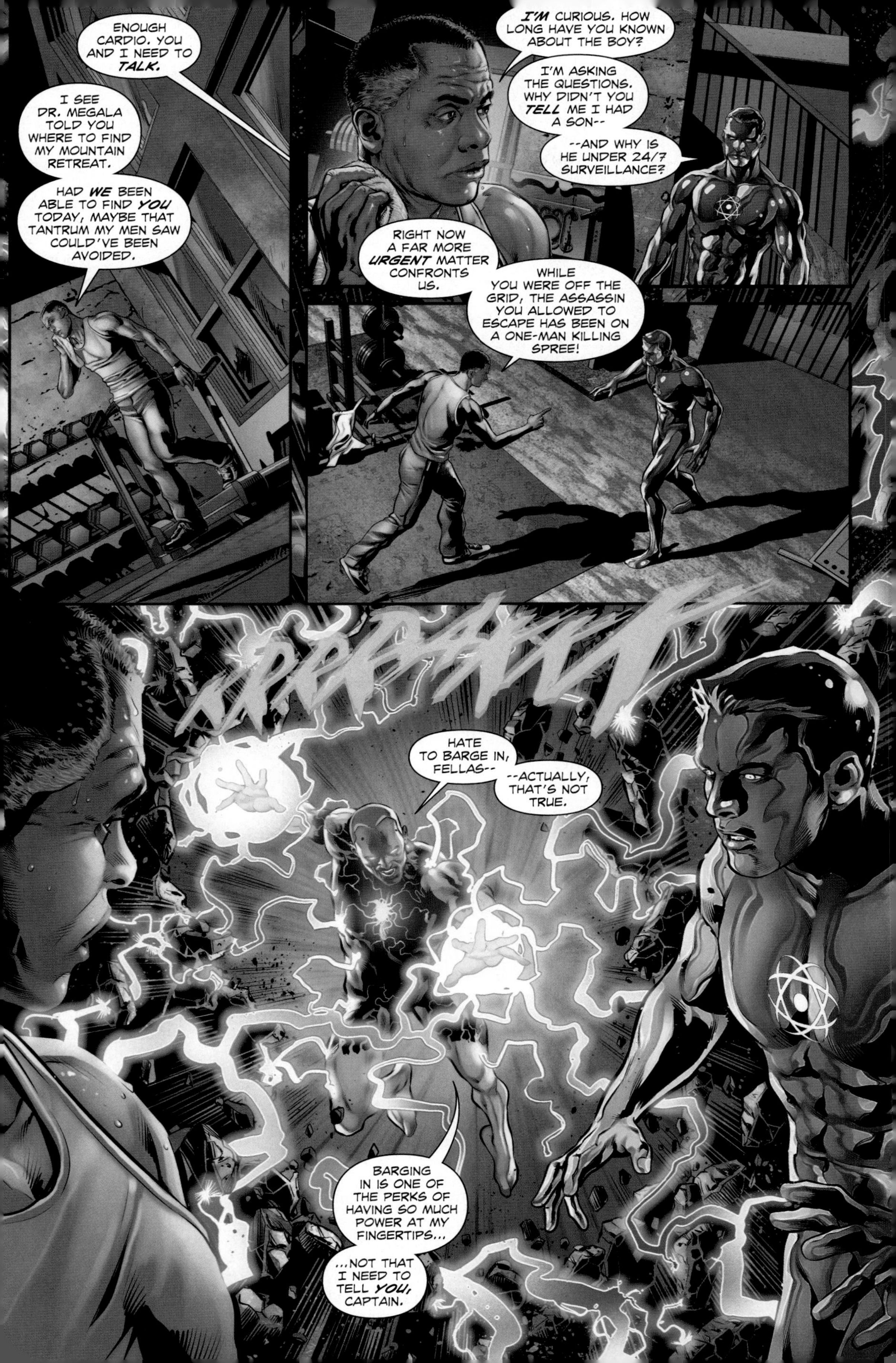
ENOUGH CARDIO. YOU AND I NEED TO **TALK.**
I SEE DR. MEGALA TOLD YOU WHERE TO FIND MY MOUNTAIN RETREAT.
HAD **WE** BEEN ABLE TO FIND **YOU** TODAY, MAYBE THAT TANTRUM MY MEN SAW COULD'VE BEEN AVOIDED.
I'M CURIOUS. HOW LONG HAVE YOU KNOWN ABOUT THE BOY?
I'M ASKING THE QUESTIONS. WHY DIDN'T YOU **TELL** ME I HAD A SON--
--AND WHY IS HE UNDER 24/7 SURVEILLANCE?
RIGHT NOW A FAR MORE **URGENT** MATTER CONFRONTS US.
WHILE YOU WERE OFF THE GRID, THE ASSASSIN YOU ALLOWED TO ESCAPE HAS BEEN ON A ONE-MAN KILLING SPREE!
HATE TO BARGE IN, FELLAS--
--ACTUALLY, THAT'S NOT TRUE.
BARGING IN IS ONE OF THE PERKS OF HAVING SO MUCH POWER AT MY FINGERTIPS...
...NOT THAT I NEED TO TELL **YOU**, CAPTAIN.

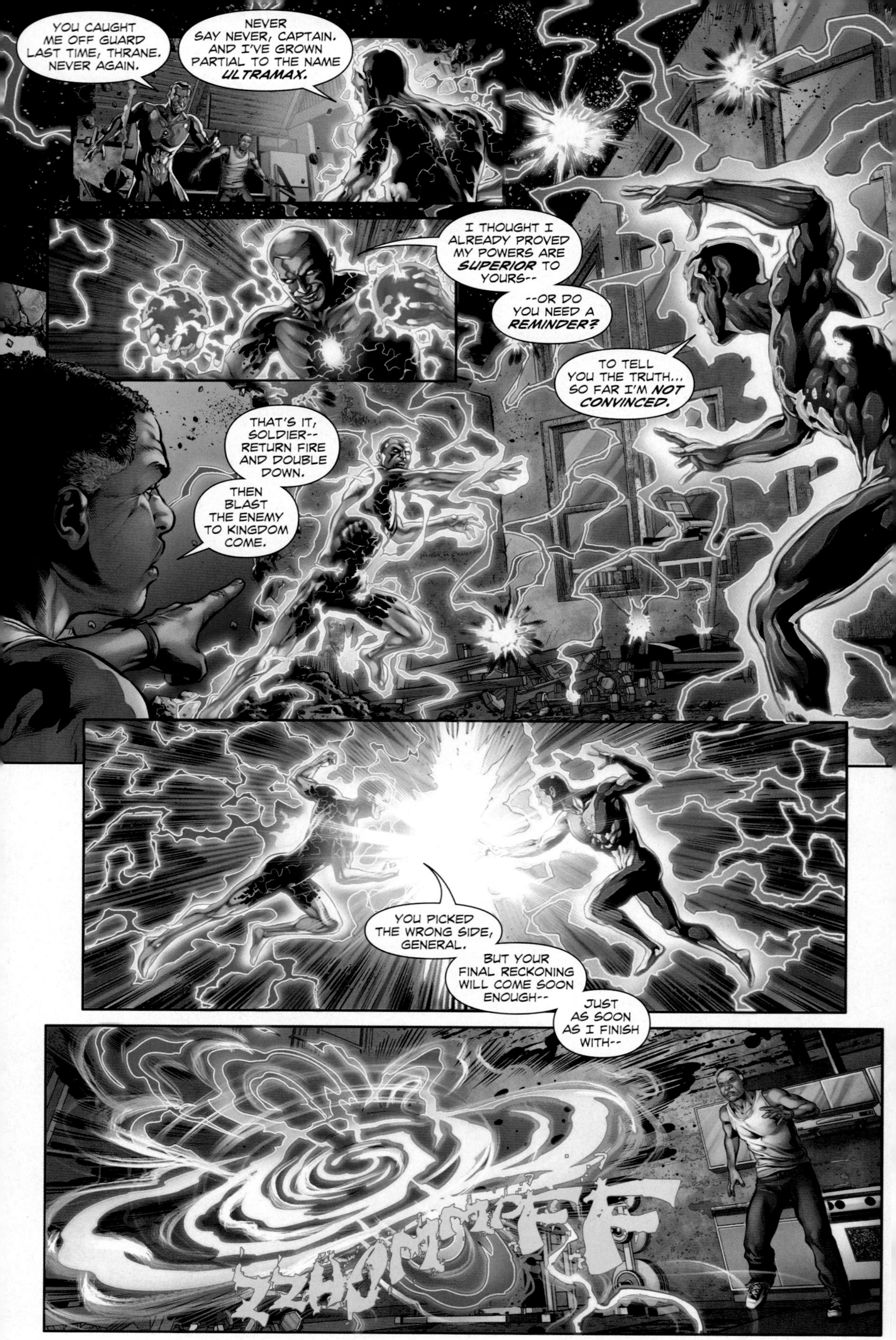
YOU CAUGHT ME OFF GUARD LAST TIME, THRANE. NEVER AGAIN.
NEVER SAY NEVER, CAPTAIN. AND I'VE GROWN PARTIAL TO THE NAME ULTRAMAX.
I THOUGHT I ALREADY PROVED MY POWERS ARE SUPERIOR TO YOURS--
--OR DO YOU NEED A REMINDER?
TO TELL YOU THE TRUTH... SO FAR I'M NOT CONVINCED.
THAT'S IT, SOLDIER-- RETURN FIRE AND DOUBLE DOWN.
THEN BLAST THE ENEMY TO KINGDOM COME.
YOU PICKED THE WRONG SIDE, GENERAL.
BUT YOUR FINAL RECKONING WILL COME SOON ENOUGH--
JUST AS SOON AS I FINISH WITH--
ZZHOOMMFFF

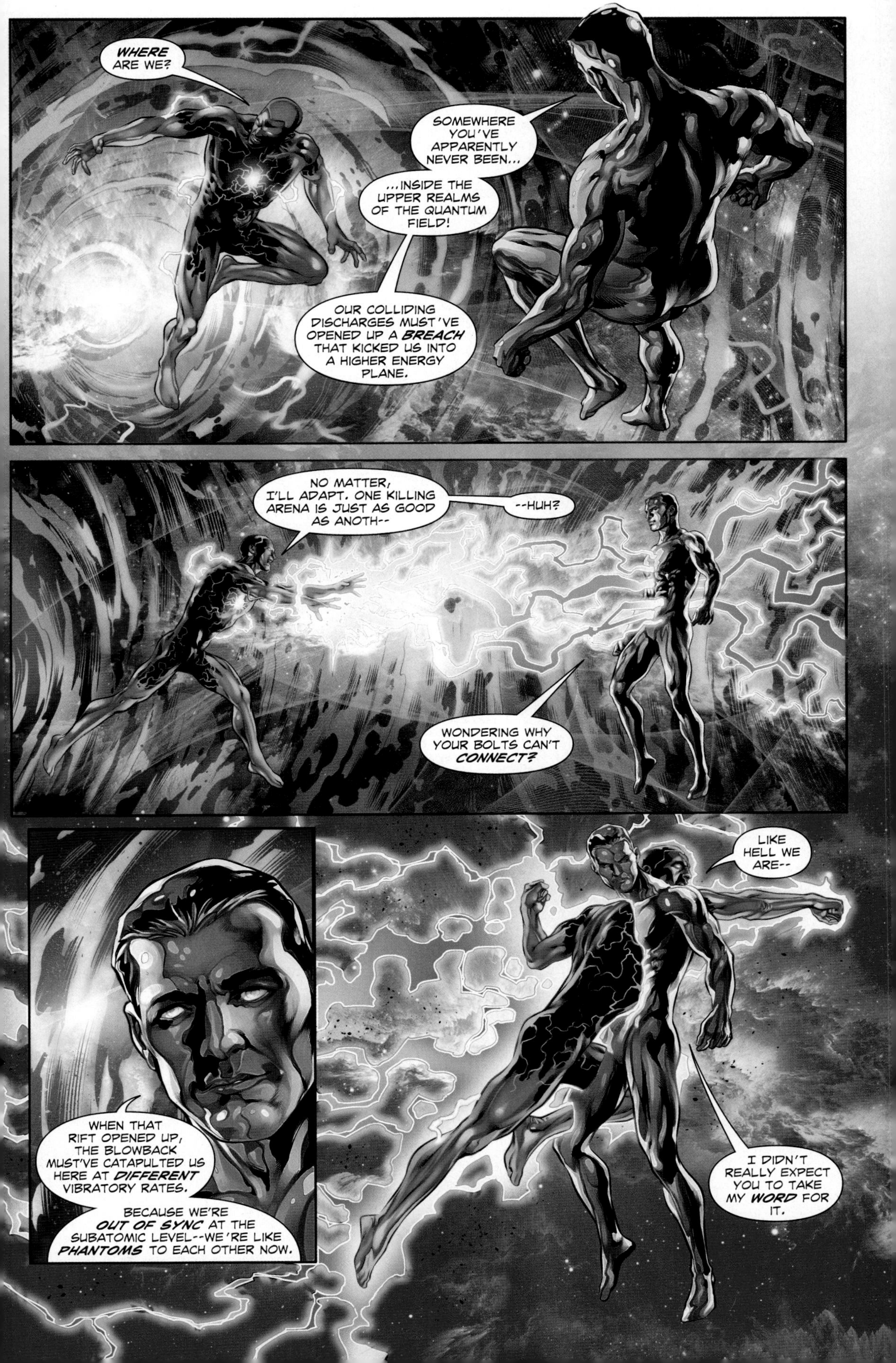
WHERE ARE WE?
SOMEWHERE YOU'VE APPARENTLY NEVER BEEN...
...INSIDE THE UPPER REALMS OF THE QUANTUM FIELD!
OUR COLLIDING DISCHARGES MUST'VE OPENED UP A BREACH THAT KICKED US INTO A HIGHER ENERGY PLANE.
NO MATTER, I'LL ADAPT. ONE KILLING ARENA IS JUST AS GOOD AS ANOTH--
--HUH?
WONDERING WHY YOUR BOLTS CAN'T CONNECT?
WHEN THAT RIFT OPENED UP, THE BLOWBACK MUST'VE CATAPULTED US HERE AT DIFFERENT VIBRATORY RATES.
BECAUSE WE'RE OUT OF SYNC AT THE SUBATOMIC LEVEL--WE'RE LIKE PHANTOMS TO EACH OTHER NOW.
LIKE HELL WE ARE--
I DIDN'T REALLY EXPECT YOU TO TAKE MY WORD FOR IT.

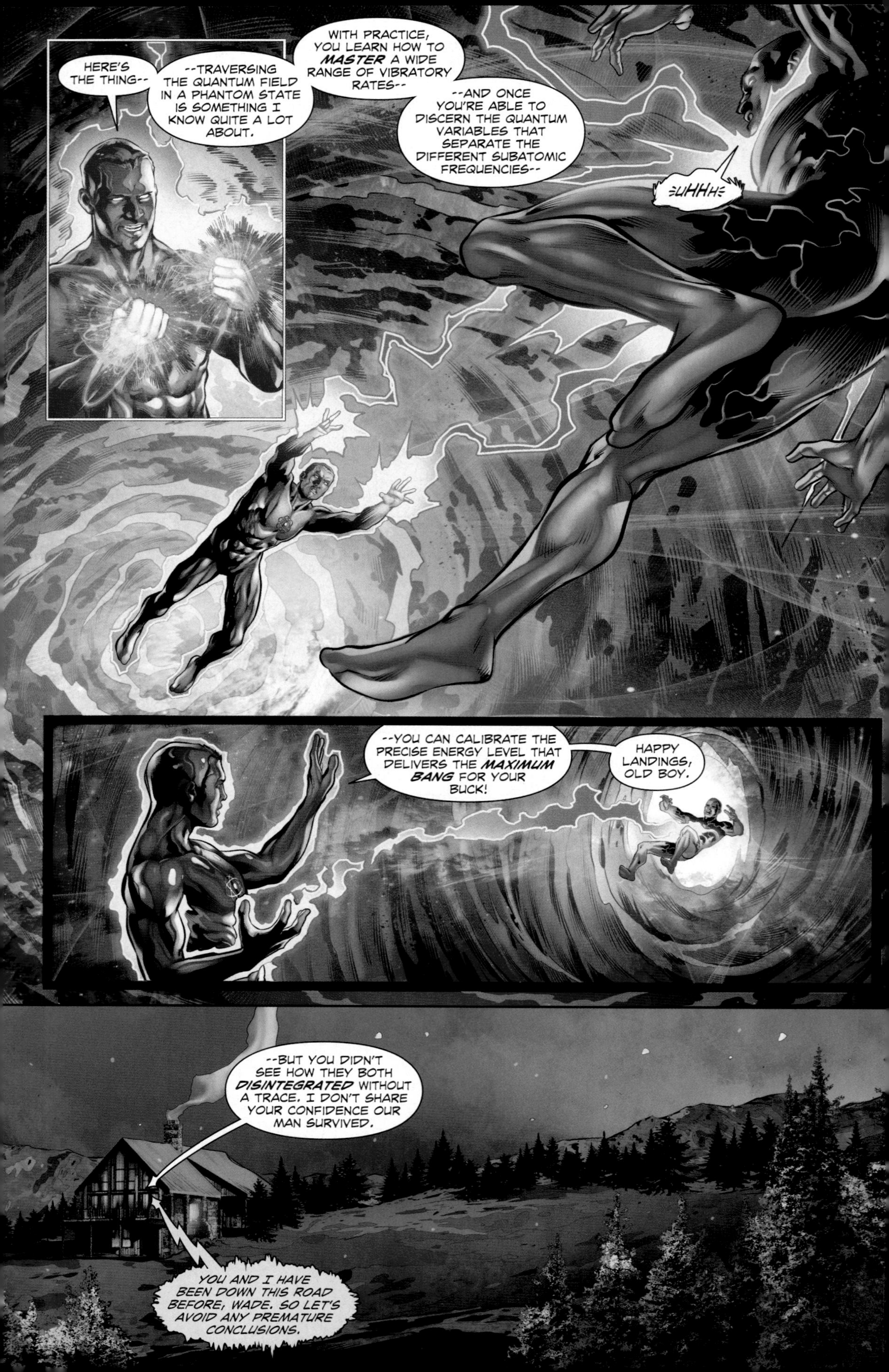
HERE'S THE THING--
--TRAVERSING THE QUANTUM FIELD IN A PHANTOM STATE IS SOMETHING I KNOW QUITE A LOT ABOUT.
WITH PRACTICE, YOU LEARN HOW TO MASTER A WIDE RANGE OF VIBRATORY RATES--
--AND ONCE YOU'RE ABLE TO DISCERN THE QUANTUM VARIABLES THAT SEPARATE THE DIFFERENT SUBATOMIC FREQUENCIES--
UHHH
--YOU CAN CALIBRATE THE PRECISE ENERGY LEVEL THAT DELIVERS THE MAXIMUM BANG FOR YOUR BUCK!
HAPPY LANDINGS, OLD BOY.
--BUT YOU DIDN'T SEE HOW THEY BOTH DISINTEGRATED WITHOUT A TRACE. I DON'T SHARE YOUR CONFIDENCE OUR MAN SURVIVED.
YOU AND I HAVE BEEN DOWN THIS ROAD BEFORE, WADE. SO LET'S AVOID ANY PREMATURE CONCLUSIONS.

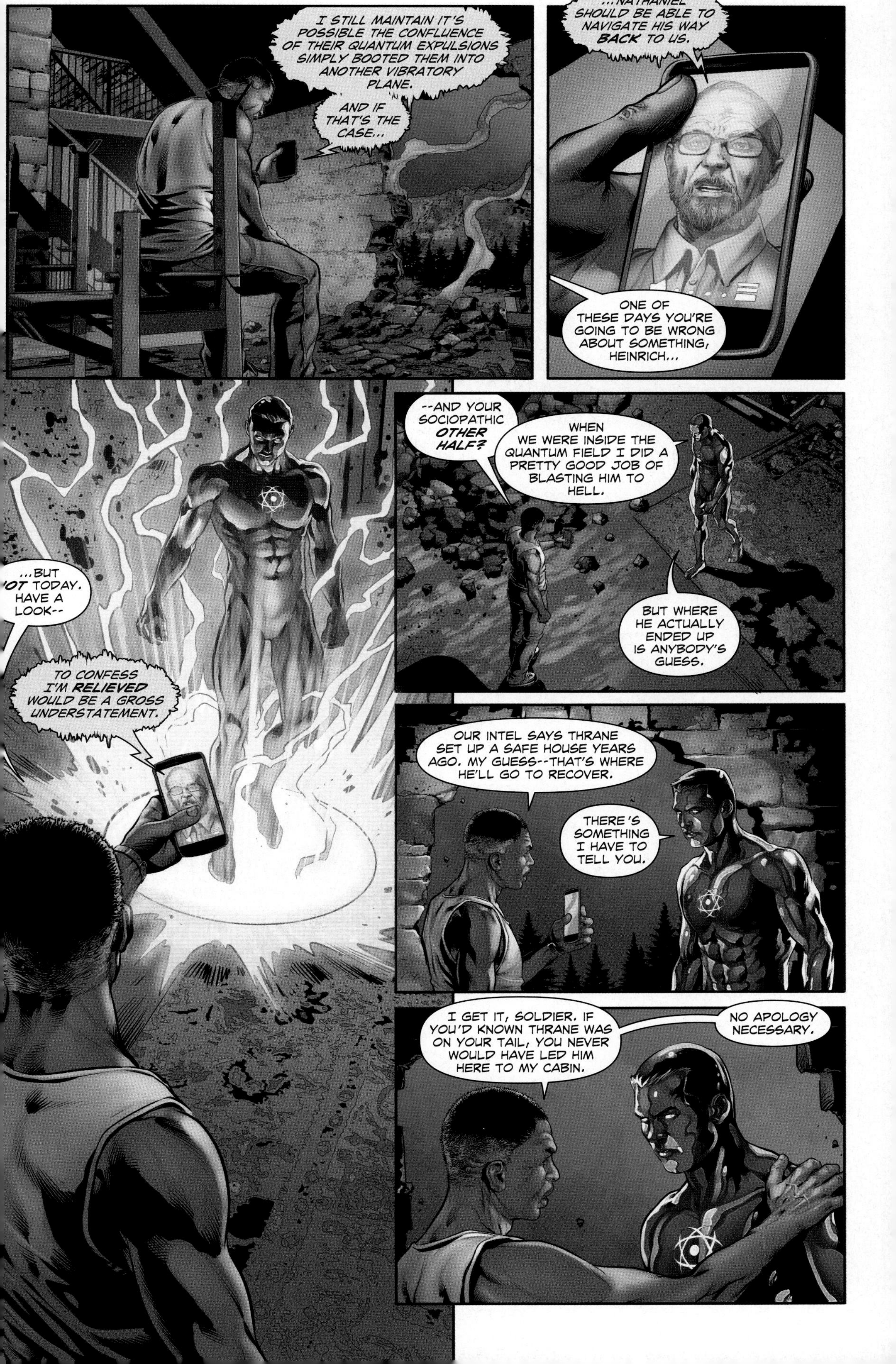
I STILL MAINTAIN IT'S POSSIBLE THE CONFLUENCE OF THEIR QUANTUM EXPULSIONS SIMPLY BOOTED THEM INTO ANOTHER VIBRATORY PLANE.
AND IF THAT'S THE CASE...
...NATHANIEL SHOULD BE ABLE TO NAVIGATE HIS WAY BACK TO US.
ONE OF THESE DAYS YOU'RE GOING TO BE WRONG ABOUT SOMETHING, HEINRICH...
...BUT NOT TODAY. HAVE A LOOK--
TO CONFESS I'M RELIEVED WOULD BE A GROSS UNDERSTATEMENT.
--AND YOUR SOCIOPATHIC OTHER HALF?
WHEN WE WERE INSIDE THE QUANTUM FIELD I DID A PRETTY GOOD JOB OF BLASTING HIM TO HELL.
BUT WHERE HE ACTUALLY ENDED UP IS ANYBODY'S GUESS.
OUR INTEL SAYS THRANE SET UP A SAFE HOUSE YEARS AGO. MY GUESS--THAT'S WHERE HE'LL GO TO RECOVER.
THERE'S SOMETHING I HAVE TO TELL YOU.
I GET IT, SOLDIER. IF YOU'D KNOWN THRANE WAS ON YOUR TAIL, YOU NEVER WOULD HAVE LED HIM HERE TO MY CABIN.
NO APOLOGY NECESSARY.

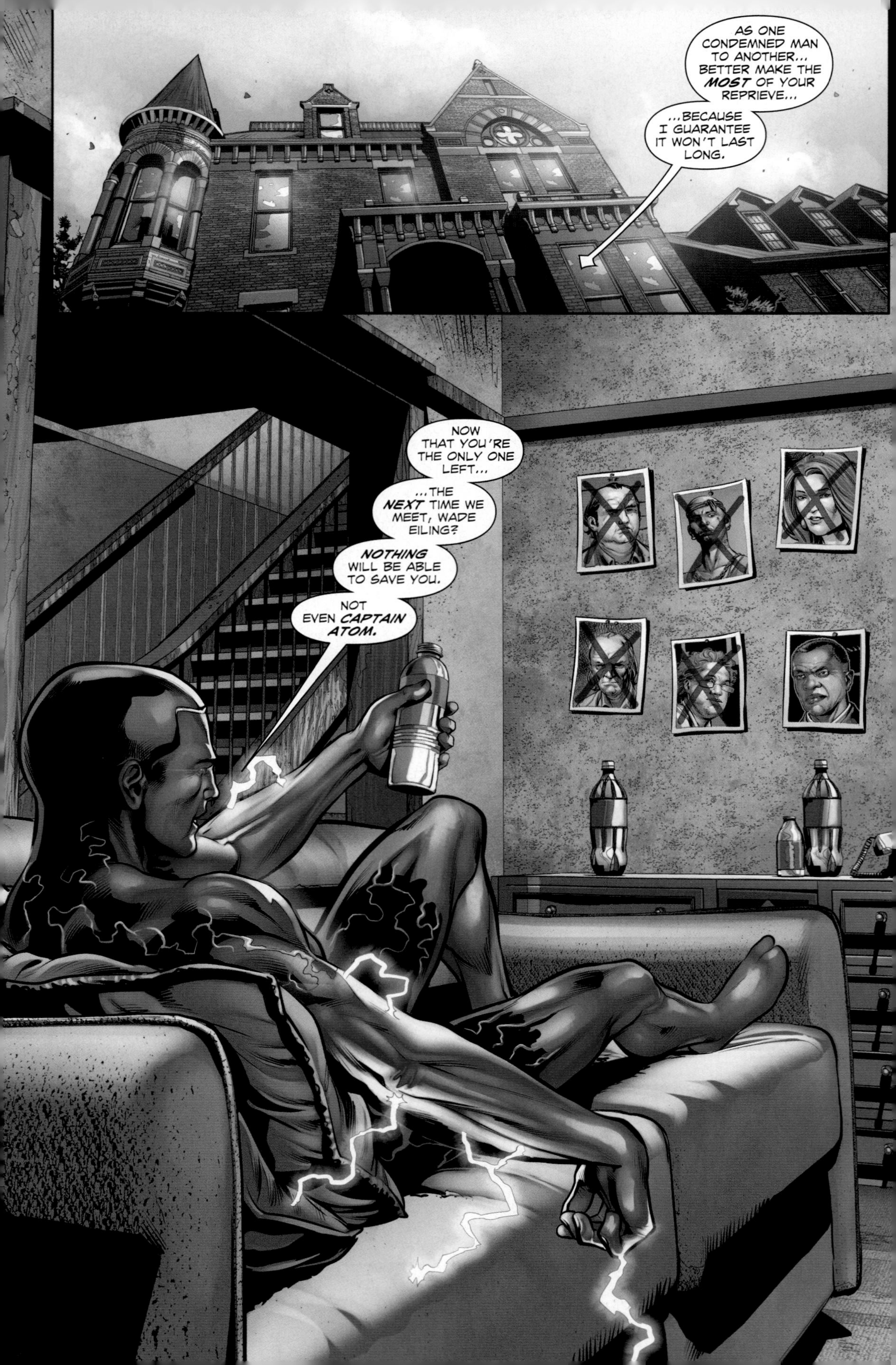

AS ONE CONDEMNED MAN TO ANOTHER... BETTER MAKE THE MOST OF YOUR REPRIEVE...
...BECAUSE I GUARANTEE IT WON'T LAST LONG.
NOW THAT YOU'RE THE ONLY ONE LEFT...
...THE NEXT TIME WE MEET, WADE EILING?
NOTHING WILL BE ABLE TO SAVE YOU.
NOT EVEN CAPTAIN ATOM.

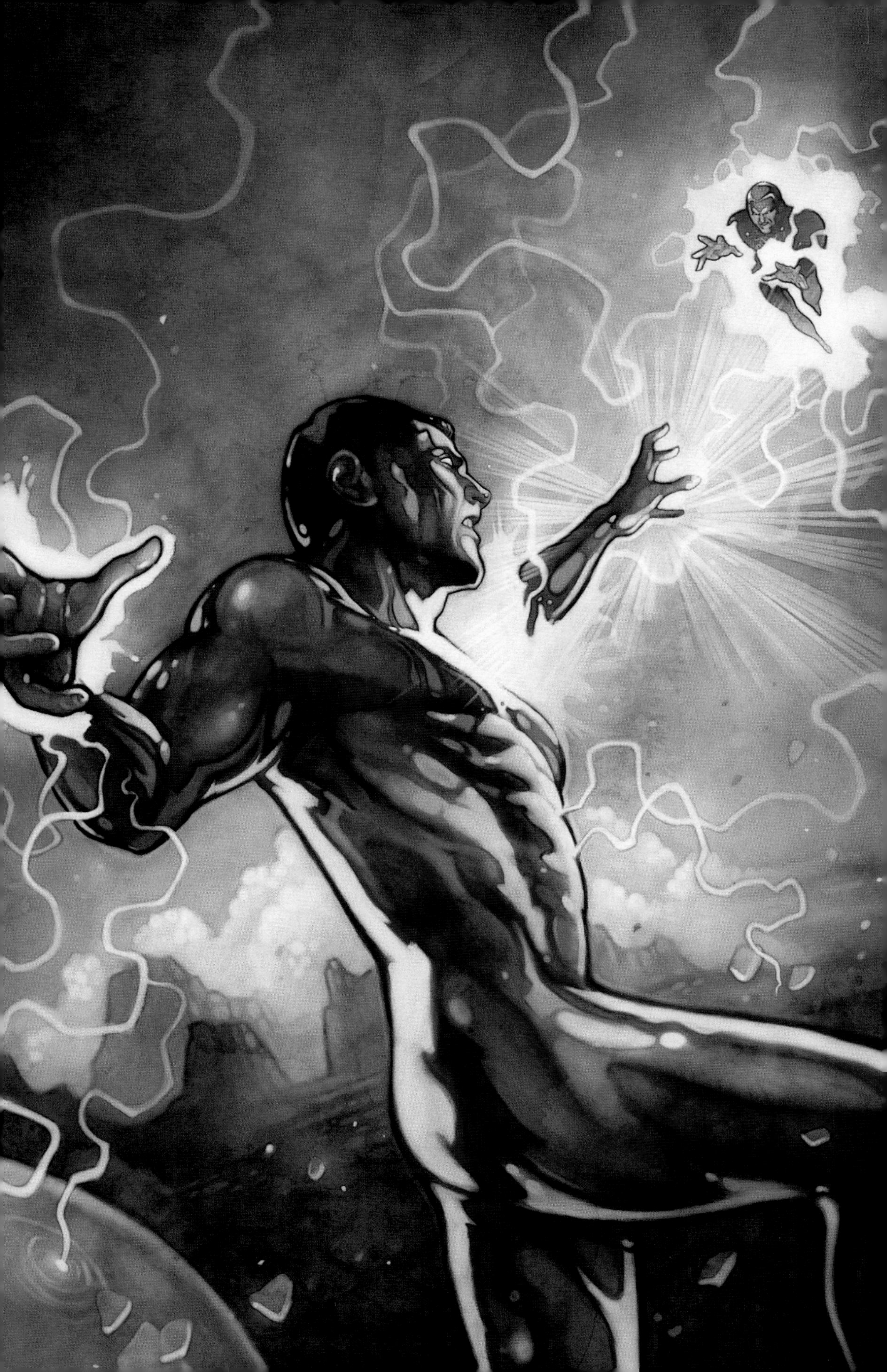

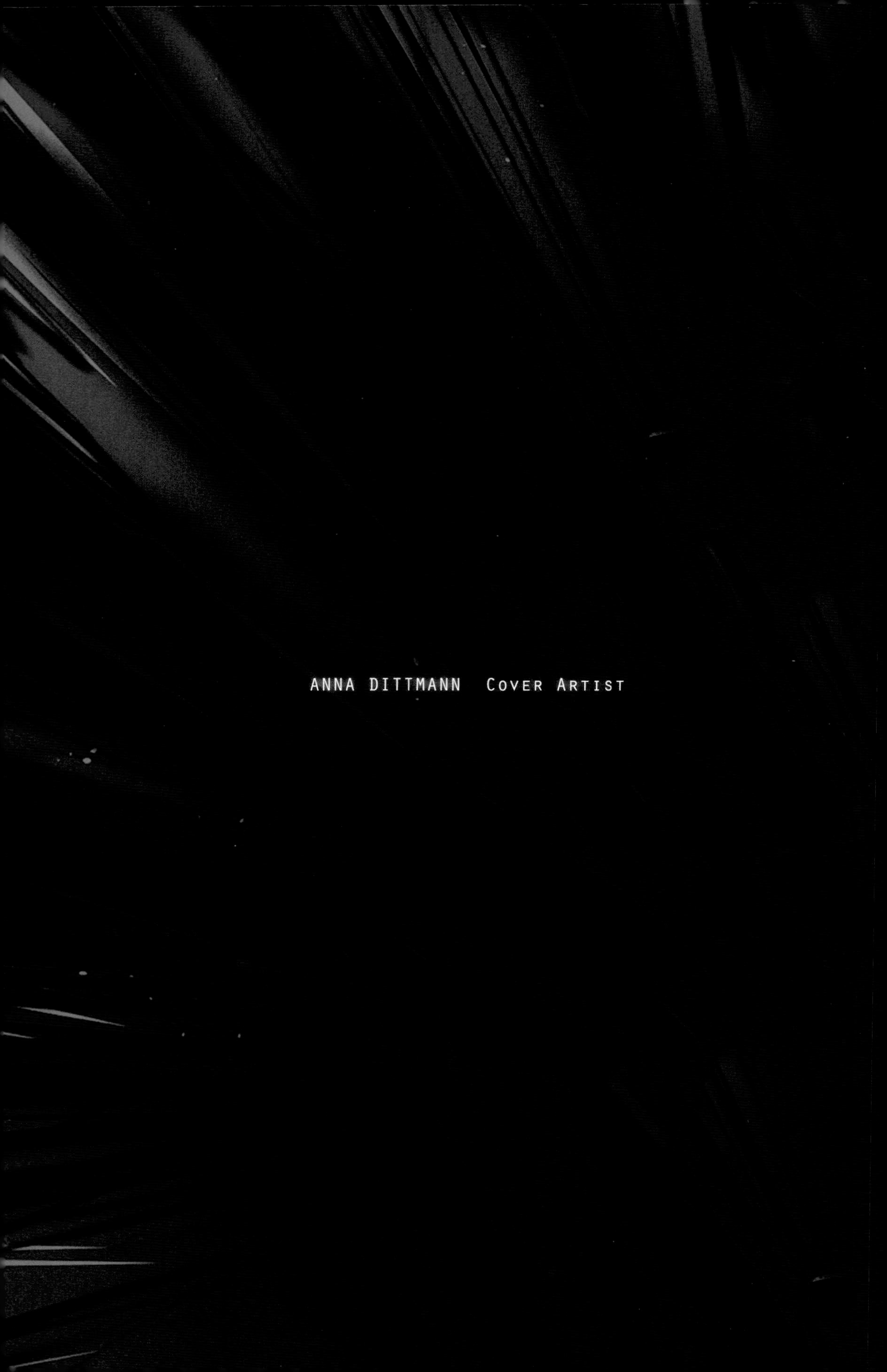

ANNA DITTMANN Cover Artist

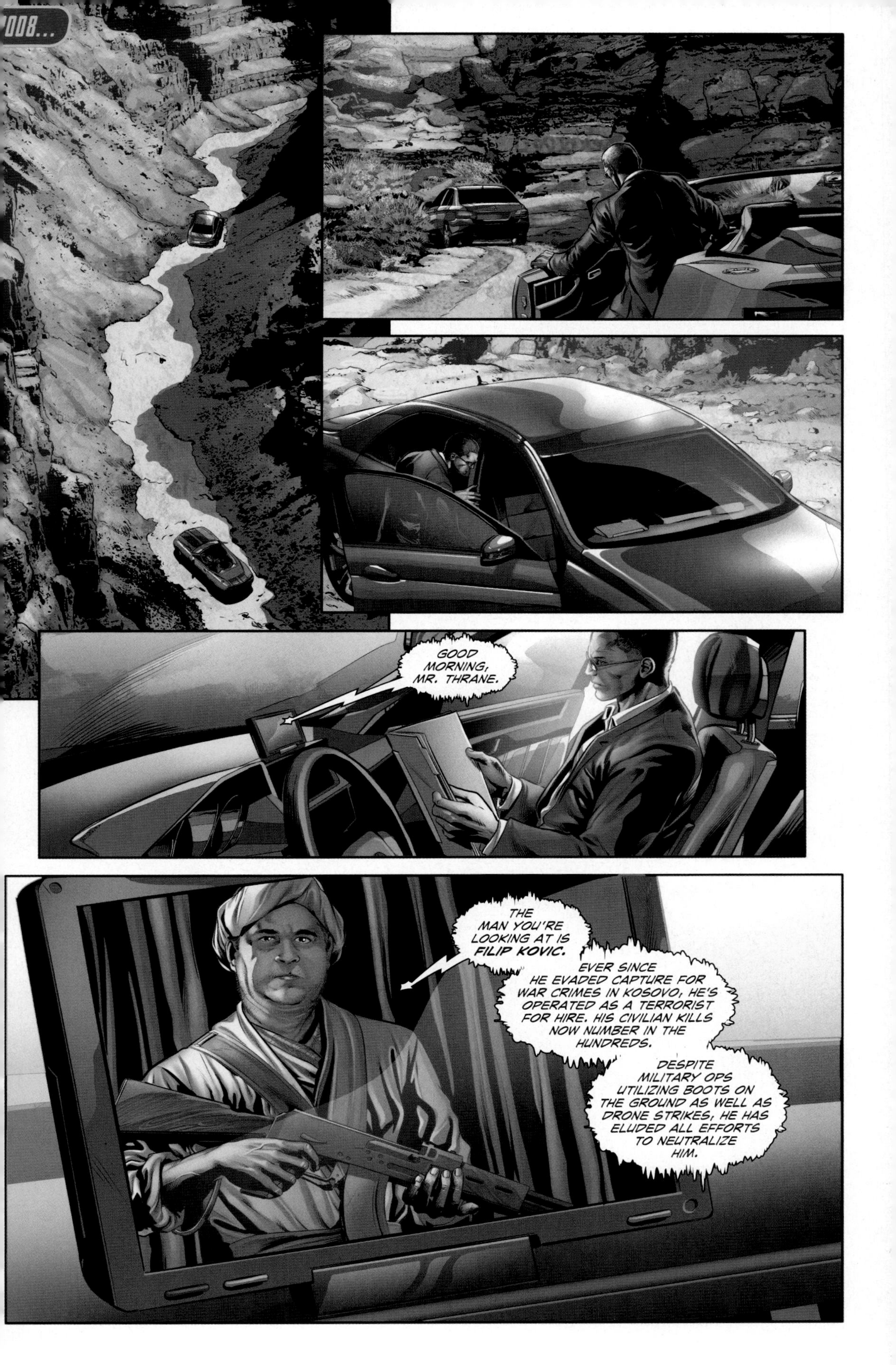
GOOD MORNING, MR. THRANE.
THE MAN YOU'RE LOOKING AT IS FILIP KOVIC.
EVER SINCE HE EVADED CAPTURE FOR WAR CRIMES IN KOSOVO, HE'S OPERATED AS A TERRORIST FOR HIRE. HIS CIVILIAN KILLS NOW NUMBER IN THE HUNDREDS.
DESPITE MILITARY OPS UTILIZING BOOTS ON THE GROUND AS WELL AS DRONE STRIKES, HE HAS ELUDED ALL EFFORTS TO NEUTRALIZE HIM.

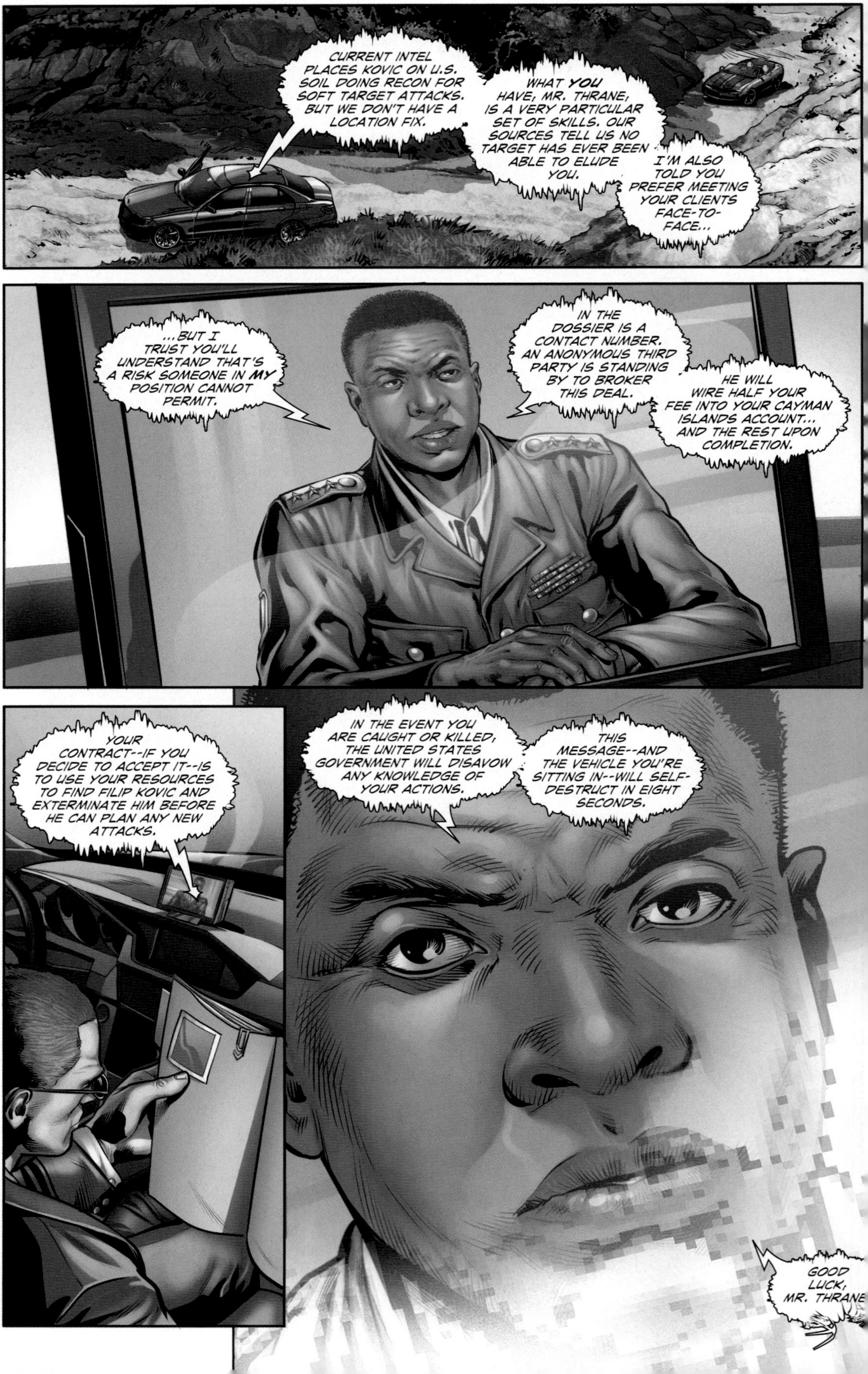
CURRENT INTEL PLACES KOVIC ON U.S. SOIL DOING RECON FOR SOFT TARGET ATTACKS. BUT WE DON'T HAVE A LOCATION FIX.
WHAT YOU HAVE, MR. THRANE, IS A VERY PARTICULAR SET OF SKILLS. OUR SOURCES TELL US NO TARGET HAS EVER BEEN ABLE TO ELUDE YOU.
I'M ALSO TOLD YOU PREFER MEETING YOUR CLIENTS FACE-TO-FACE...
...BUT I TRUST YOU'LL UNDERSTAND THAT'S A RISK SOMEONE IN MY POSITION CANNOT PERMIT.
IN THE DOSSIER IS A CONTACT NUMBER. AN ANONYMOUS THIRD PARTY IS STANDING BY TO BROKER THIS DEAL.
HE WILL WIRE HALF YOUR FEE INTO YOUR CAYMAN ISLANDS ACCOUNT... AND THE REST UPON COMPLETION.
YOUR CONTRACT--IF YOU DECIDE TO ACCEPT IT--IS TO USE YOUR RESOURCES TO FIND FILIP KOVIC AND EXTERMINATE HIM BEFORE HE CAN PLAN ANY NEW ATTACKS.
IN THE EVENT YOU ARE CAUGHT OR KILLED, THE UNITED STATES GOVERNMENT WILL DISAVOW ANY KNOWLEDGE OF YOUR ACTIONS.
THIS MESSAGE--AND THE VEHICLE YOU'RE SITTING IN--WILL SELF-DESTRUCT IN EIGHT SECONDS.
GOOD LUCK, MR. THRANE

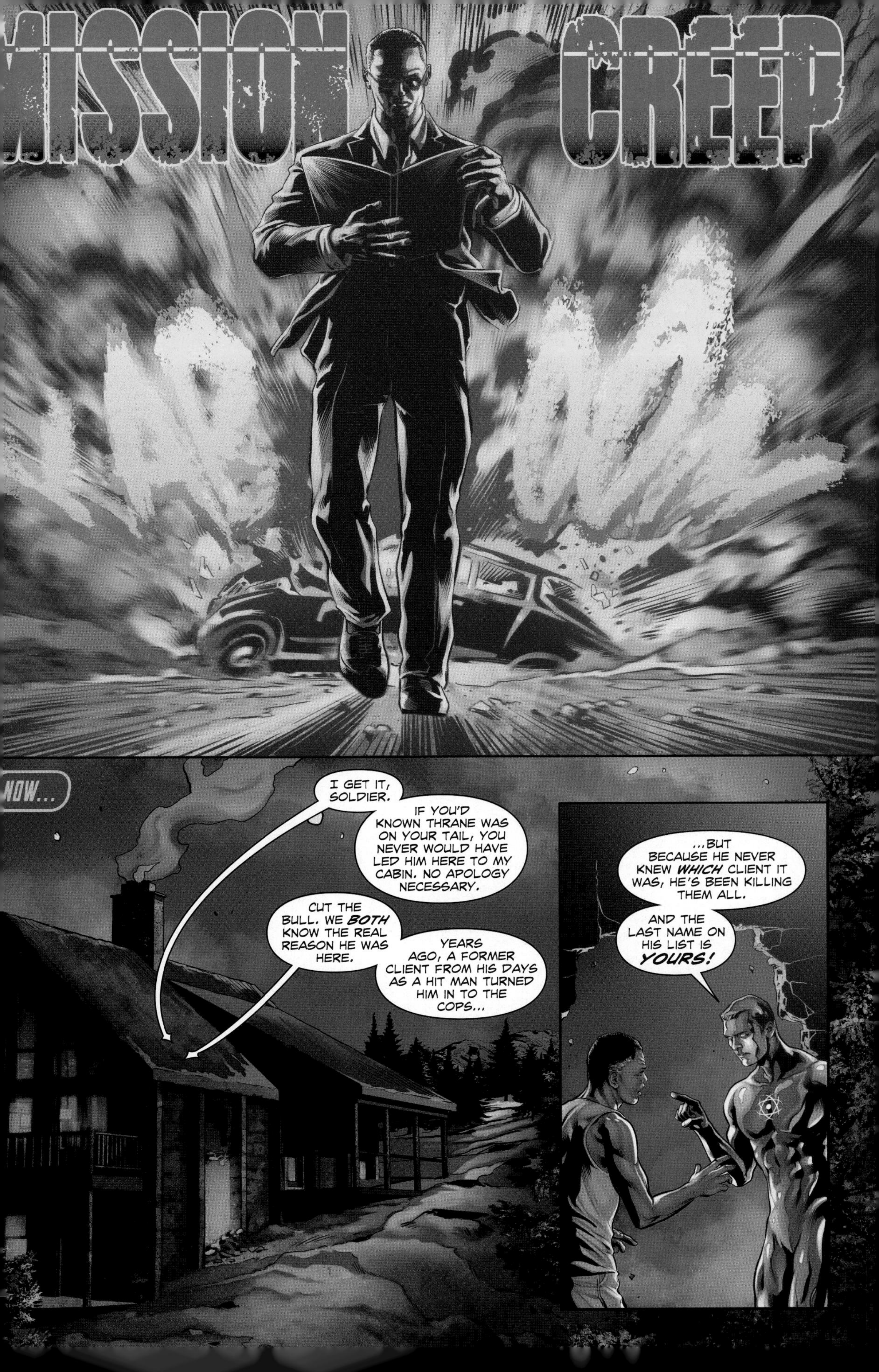
MISSION CREEP
NOW...
I GET IT, SOLDIER.
IF YOU'D KNOWN THRANE WAS ON YOUR TAIL, YOU NEVER WOULD HAVE LED HIM HERE TO MY CABIN. NO APOLOGY NECESSARY.
CUT THE BULL. WE *BOTH* KNOW THE REAL REASON HE WAS HERE.
YEARS AGO, A FORMER CLIENT FROM HIS DAYS AS A HIT MAN TURNED HIM IN TO THE COPS...
...BUT BECAUSE HE NEVER KNEW *WHICH* CLIENT IT WAS, HE'S BEEN KILLING THEM ALL.
AND THE LAST NAME ON HIS LIST IS ***YOURS!***

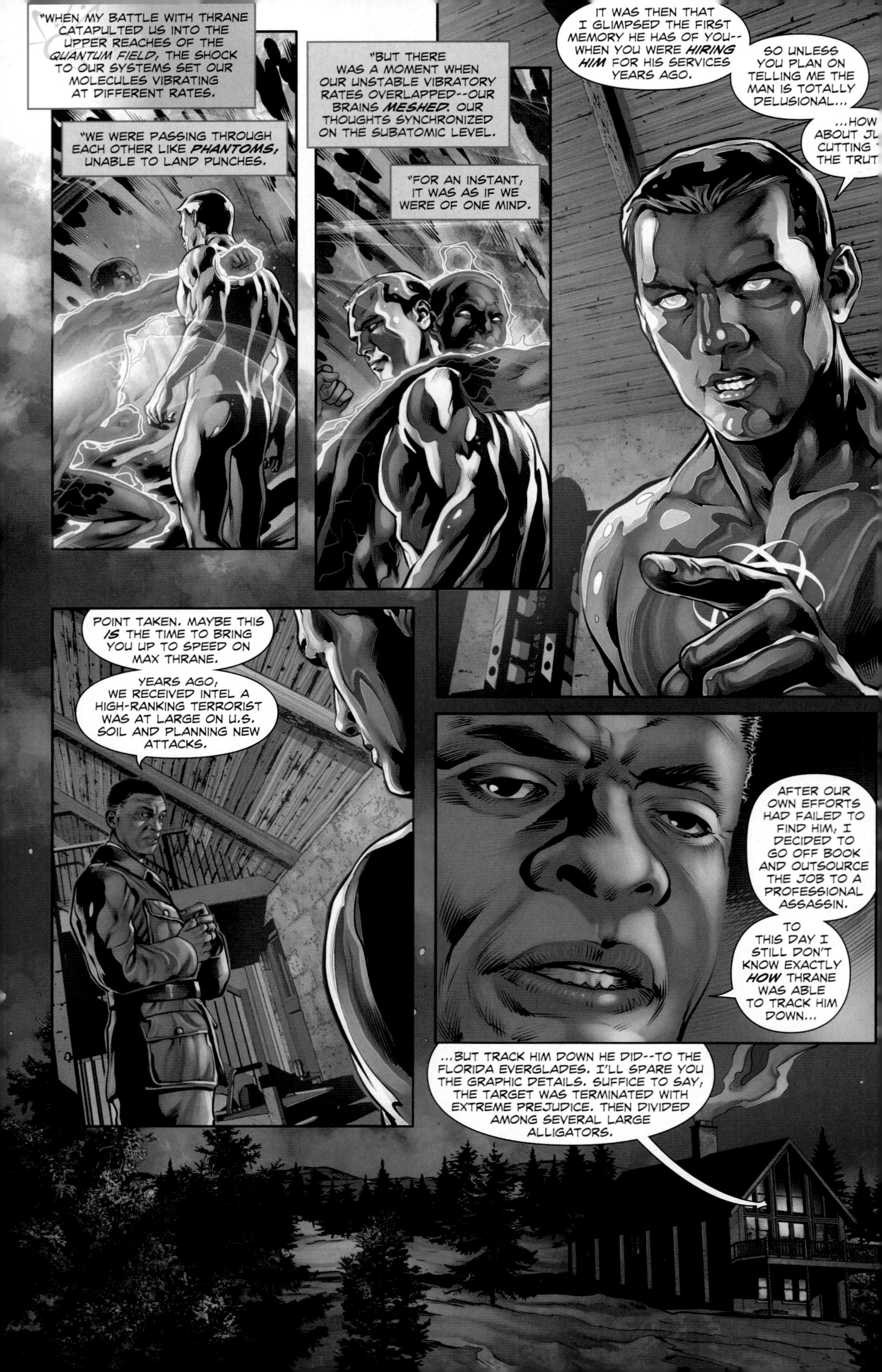
"WHEN MY BATTLE WITH THRANE CATAPULTED US INTO THE UPPER REACHES OF THE QUANTUM FIELD, THE SHOCK TO OUR SYSTEMS SET OUR MOLECULES VIBRATING AT DIFFERENT RATES.
"WE WERE PASSING THROUGH EACH OTHER LIKE PHANTOMS, UNABLE TO LAND PUNCHES.
"BUT THERE WAS A MOMENT WHEN OUR UNSTABLE VIBRATORY RATES OVERLAPPED--OUR BRAINS MESHED. OUR THOUGHTS SYNCHRONIZED ON THE SUBATOMIC LEVEL.
"FOR AN INSTANT, IT WAS AS IF WE WERE OF ONE MIND.
IT WAS THEN THAT I GLIMPSED THE FIRST MEMORY HE HAS OF YOU--WHEN YOU WERE HIRING HIM FOR HIS SERVICES YEARS AGO.
SO UNLESS YOU PLAN ON TELLING ME THE MAN IS TOTALLY DELUSIONAL...
...HOW ABOUT JU CUTTING THE TRUT
POINT TAKEN. MAYBE THIS IS THE TIME TO BRING YOU UP TO SPEED ON MAX THRANE.
YEARS AGO, WE RECEIVED INTEL A HIGH-RANKING TERRORIST WAS AT LARGE ON U.S. SOIL AND PLANNING NEW ATTACKS.
AFTER OUR OWN EFFORTS HAD FAILED TO FIND HIM, I DECIDED TO GO OFF BOOK AND OUTSOURCE THE JOB TO A PROFESSIONAL ASSASSIN.
TO THIS DAY I STILL DON'T KNOW EXACTLY HOW THRANE WAS ABLE TO TRACK HIM DOWN...
...BUT TRACK HIM DOWN HE DID--TO THE FLORIDA EVERGLADES. I'LL SPARE YOU THE GRAPHIC DETAILS. SUFFICE TO SAY, THE TARGET WAS TERMINATED WITH EXTREME PREJUDICE. THEN DIVIDED AMONG SEVERAL LARGE ALLIGATORS.

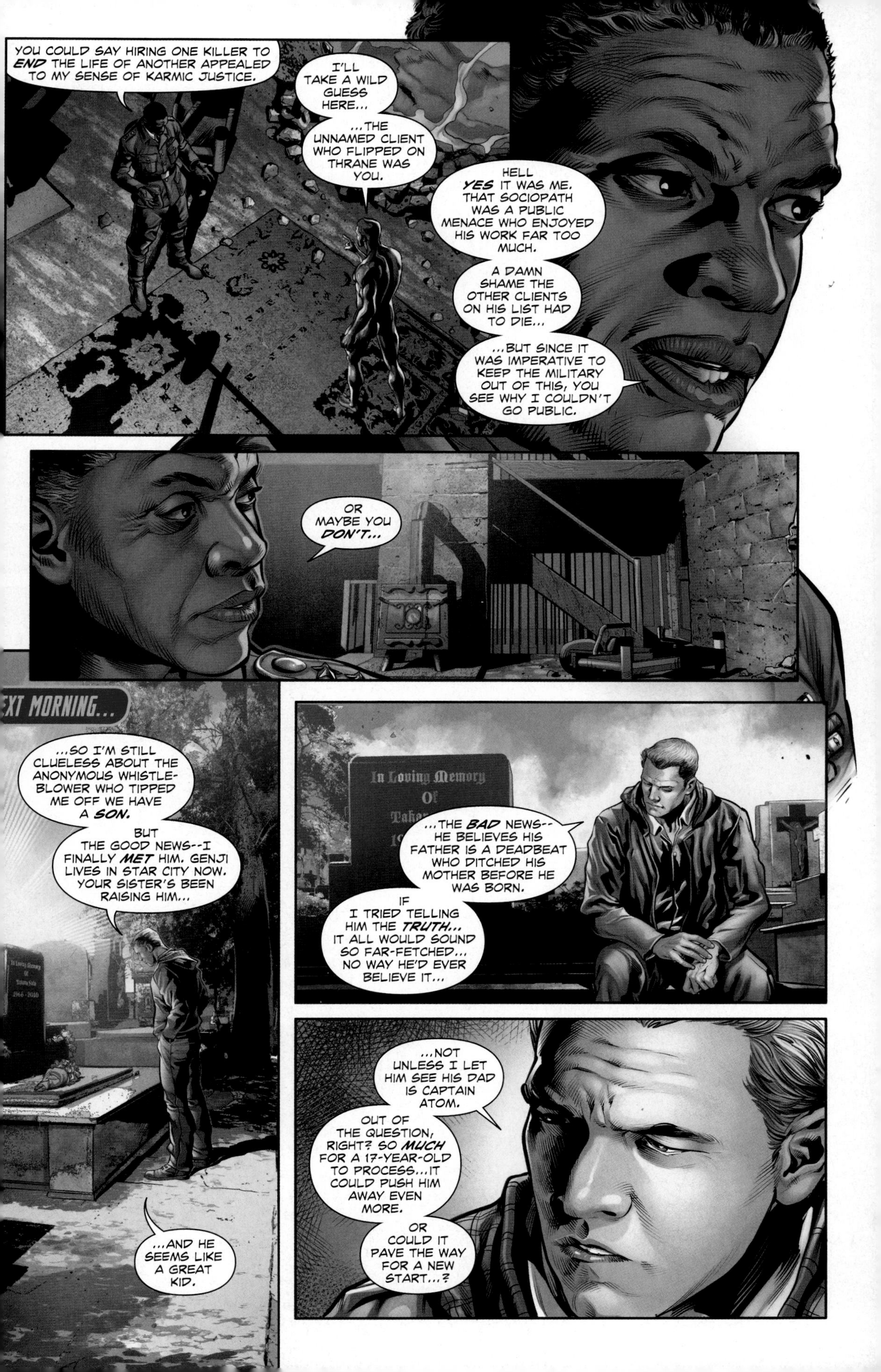

YOU COULD SAY HIRING ONE KILLER TO END THE LIFE OF ANOTHER APPEALED TO MY SENSE OF KARMIC JUSTICE.
I'LL TAKE A WILD GUESS HERE...
...THE UNNAMED CLIENT WHO FLIPPED ON THRANE WAS YOU.
HELL YES IT WAS ME. THAT SOCIOPATH WAS A PUBLIC MENACE WHO ENJOYED HIS WORK FAR TOO MUCH.
A DAMN SHAME THE OTHER CLIENTS ON HIS LIST HAD TO DIE...
...BUT SINCE IT WAS IMPERATIVE TO KEEP THE MILITARY OUT OF THIS, YOU SEE WHY I COULDN'T GO PUBLIC.
OR MAYBE YOU DON'T...
EXT MORNING...
...SO I'M STILL CLUELESS ABOUT THE ANONYMOUS WHISTLE-BLOWER WHO TIPPED ME OFF WE HAVE A SON.
BUT THE GOOD NEWS--I FINALLY MET HIM. GENJI LIVES IN STAR CITY NOW. YOUR SISTER'S BEEN RAISING HIM...
...AND HE SEEMS LIKE A GREAT KID.
In Loving Memory Of
...THE BAD NEWS--HE BELIEVES HIS FATHER IS A DEADBEAT WHO DITCHED HIS MOTHER BEFORE HE WAS BORN.
IF I TRIED TELLING HIM THE TRUTH... IT ALL WOULD SOUND SO FAR-FETCHED... NO WAY HE'D EVER BELIEVE IT...
...NOT UNLESS I LET HIM SEE HIS DAD IS CAPTAIN ATOM.
OUT OF THE QUESTION, RIGHT? SO MUCH FOR A 17-YEAR-OLD TO PROCESS...IT COULD PUSH HIM AWAY EVEN MORE.
OR COULD IT PAVE THE WAY FOR A NEW START...?

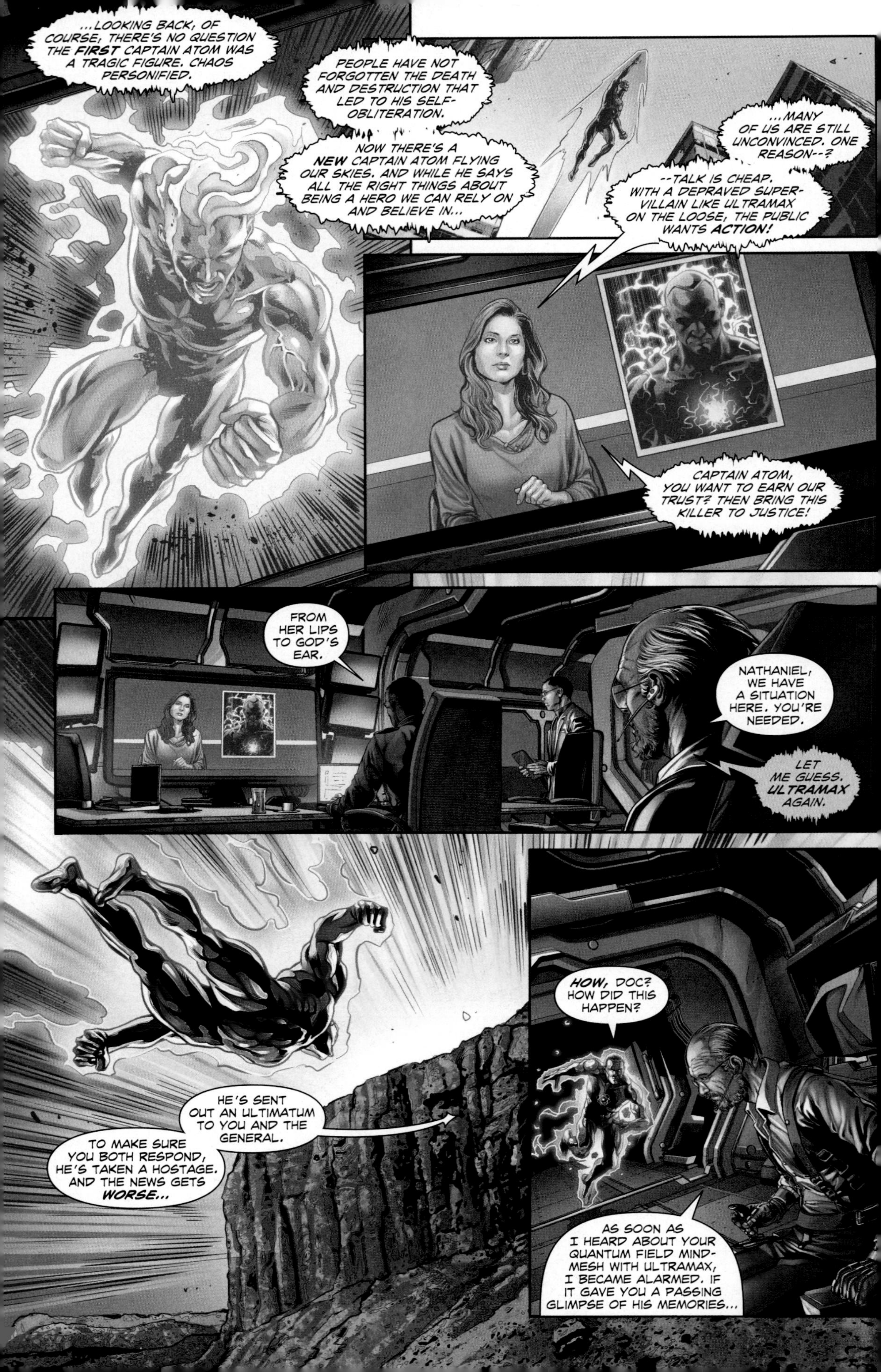
...LOOKING BACK, OF COURSE, THERE'S NO QUESTION THE FIRST CAPTAIN ATOM WAS A TRAGIC FIGURE. CHAOS PERSONIFIED.
PEOPLE HAVE NOT FORGOTTEN THE DEATH AND DESTRUCTION THAT LED TO HIS SELF-OBLITERATION.
NOW THERE'S A NEW CAPTAIN ATOM FLYING OUR SKIES. AND WHILE HE SAYS ALL THE RIGHT THINGS ABOUT BEING A HERO WE CAN RELY ON AND BELIEVE IN...
...MANY OF US ARE STILL UNCONVINCED. ONE REASON--?
--TALK IS CHEAP. WITH A DEPRAVED SUPER-VILLAIN LIKE ULTRAMAX ON THE LOOSE, THE PUBLIC WANTS ACTION!
CAPTAIN ATOM, YOU WANT TO EARN OUR TRUST? THEN BRING THIS KILLER TO JUSTICE!
FROM HER LIPS TO GOD'S EAR.
NATHANIEL, WE HAVE A SITUATION HERE. YOU'RE NEEDED.
LET ME GUESS. ULTRAMAX AGAIN.
HE'S SENT OUT AN ULTIMATUM TO YOU AND THE GENERAL.
TO MAKE SURE YOU BOTH RESPOND, HE'S TAKEN A HOSTAGE. AND THE NEWS GETS WORSE...
HOW, DOC? HOW DID THIS HAPPEN?
AS SOON AS I HEARD ABOUT YOUR QUANTUM FIELD MIND-MESH WITH ULTRAMAX, I BECAME ALARMED. IF IT GAVE YOU A PASSING GLIMPSE OF HIS MEMORIES...

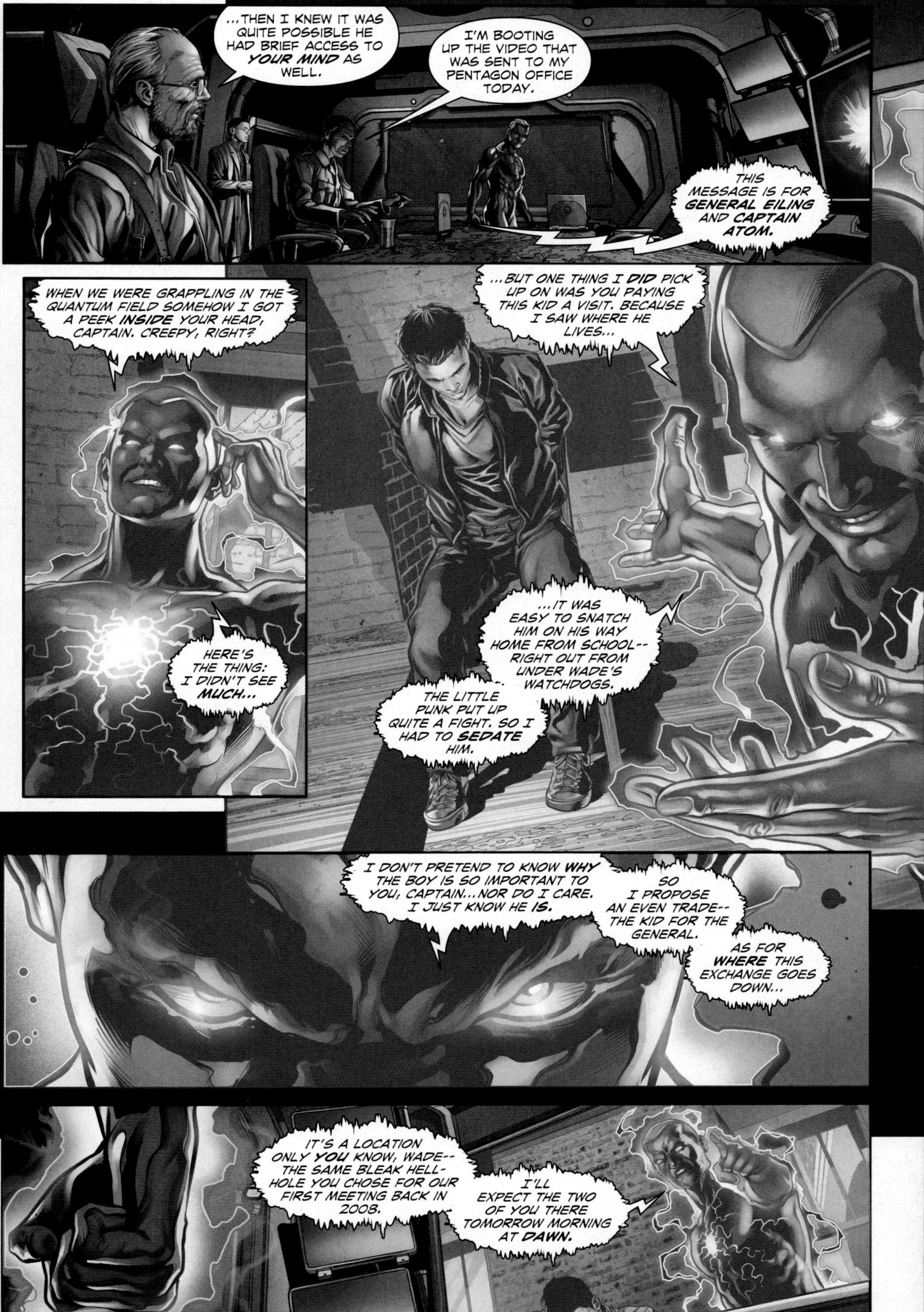
...THEN I KNEW IT WAS QUITE POSSIBLE HE HAD BRIEF ACCESS TO YOUR MIND AS WELL.
I'M BOOTING UP THE VIDEO THAT WAS SENT TO MY PENTAGON OFFICE TODAY.
THIS MESSAGE IS FOR GENERAL EILING AND CAPTAIN ATOM.
WHEN WE WERE GRAPPLING IN THE QUANTUM FIELD SOMEHOW I GOT A PEEK INSIDE YOUR HEAD, CAPTAIN. CREEPY, RIGHT?
HERE'S THE THING: I DIDN'T SEE MUCH...
...BUT ONE THING I DID PICK UP ON WAS YOU PAYING THIS KID A VISIT. BECAUSE I SAW WHERE HE LIVES...
...IT WAS EASY TO SNATCH HIM ON HIS WAY HOME FROM SCHOOL-- RIGHT OUT FROM UNDER WADE'S WATCHDOGS.
THE LITTLE PUNK PUT UP QUITE A FIGHT. SO I HAD TO SEDATE HIM.
I DON'T PRETEND TO KNOW WHY THE BOY IS SO IMPORTANT TO YOU, CAPTAIN...NOR DO I CARE. I JUST KNOW HE IS.
SO I PROPOSE AN EVEN TRADE-- THE KID FOR THE GENERAL.
AS FOR WHERE THIS EXCHANGE GOES DOWN...
IT'S A LOCATION ONLY YOU KNOW, WADE-- THE SAME BLEAK HELL-HOLE YOU CHOSE FOR OUR FIRST MEETING BACK IN 2008.
I'LL EXPECT THE TWO OF YOU THERE TOMORROW MORNING AT DAWN.

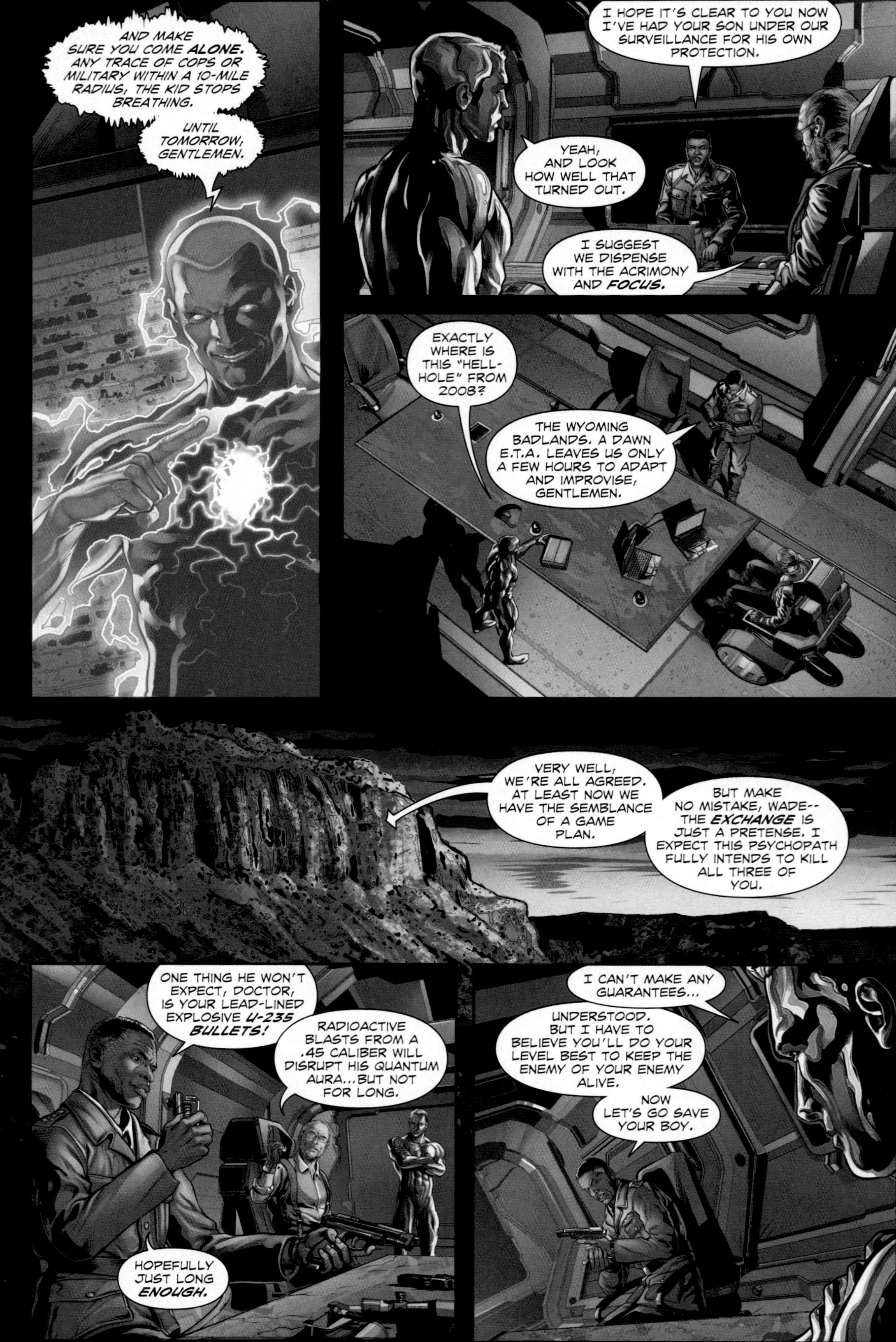
AND MAKE SURE YOU COME ALONE. ANY TRACE OF COPS OR MILITARY WITHIN A 10-MILE RADIUS, THE KID STOPS BREATHING.
UNTIL TOMORROW, GENTLEMEN.
I HOPE IT'S CLEAR TO YOU NOW I'VE HAD YOUR SON UNDER OUR SURVEILLANCE FOR HIS OWN PROTECTION.
YEAH, AND LOOK HOW WELL THAT TURNED OUT.
I SUGGEST WE DISPENSE WITH THE ACRIMONY AND FOCUS.
EXACTLY WHERE IS THIS "HELL-HOLE" FROM 2008?
THE WYOMING BADLANDS. A DAWN E.T.A. LEAVES US ONLY A FEW HOURS TO ADAPT AND IMPROVISE, GENTLEMEN.
VERY WELL, WE'RE ALL AGREED. AT LEAST NOW WE HAVE THE SEMBLANCE OF A GAME PLAN.
BUT MAKE NO MISTAKE, WADE-- THE EXCHANGE IS JUST A PRETENSE. I EXPECT THIS PSYCHOPATH FULLY INTENDS TO KILL ALL THREE OF YOU.
ONE THING HE WON'T EXPECT, DOCTOR, IS YOUR LEAD-LINED EXPLOSIVE U-235 BULLETS!
RADIOACTIVE BLASTS FROM A .45 CALIBER WILL DISRUPT HIS QUANTUM AURA...BUT NOT FOR LONG.
HOPEFULLY JUST LONG ENOUGH.
I CAN'T MAKE ANY GUARANTEES...
UNDERSTOOD. BUT I HAVE TO BELIEVE YOU'LL DO YOUR LEVEL BEST TO KEEP THE ENEMY OF YOUR ENEMY ALIVE.
NOW LET'S GO SAVE YOUR BOY.

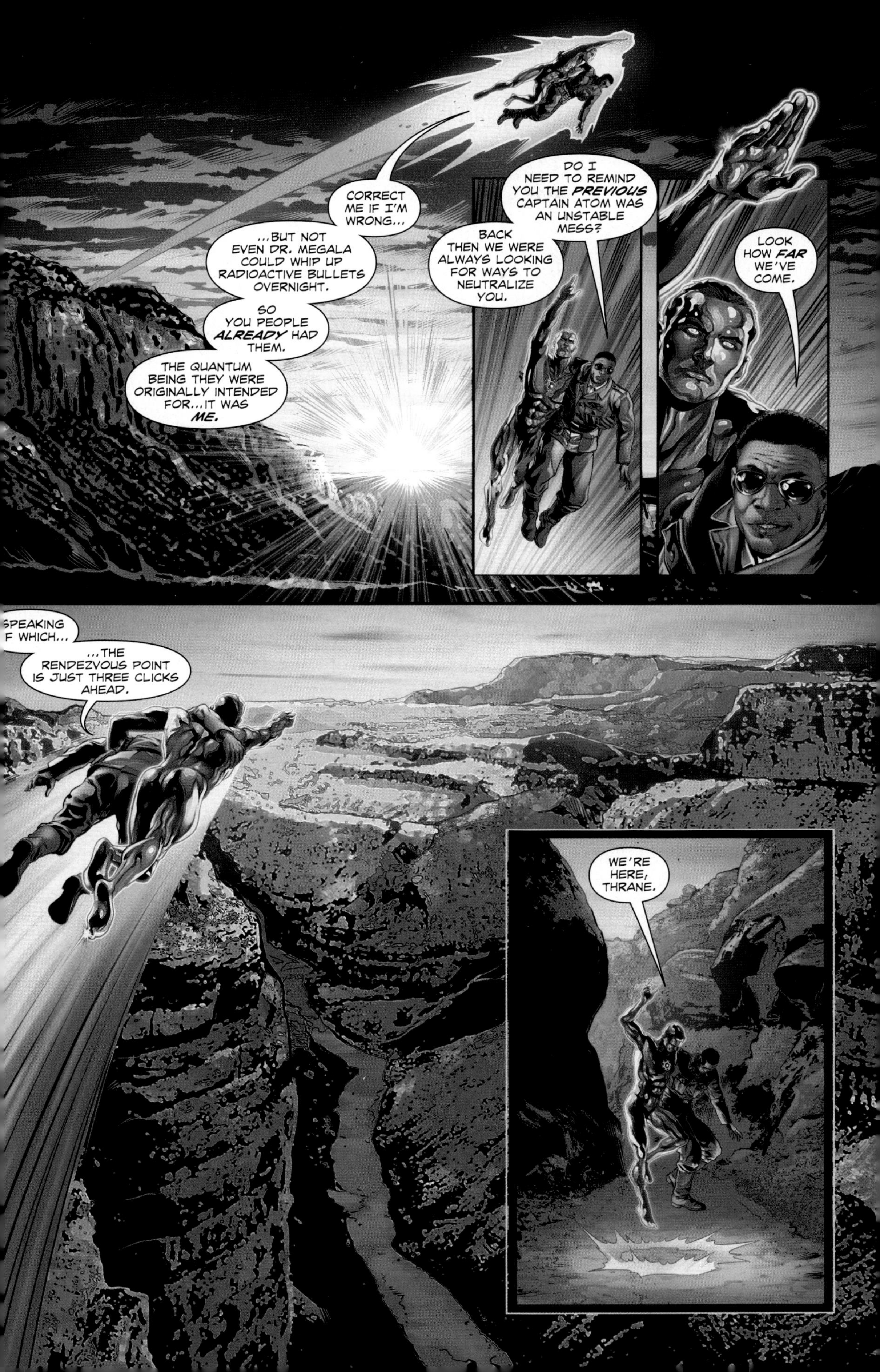
CORRECT ME IF I'M WRONG...
...BUT NOT EVEN DR. MEGALA COULD WHIP UP RADIOACTIVE BULLETS OVERNIGHT.
SO YOU PEOPLE ALREADY HAD THEM.
THE QUANTUM BEING THEY WERE ORIGINALLY INTENDED FOR...IT WAS ME.
DO I NEED TO REMIND YOU THE PREVIOUS CAPTAIN ATOM WAS AN UNSTABLE MESS?
BACK THEN WE WERE ALWAYS LOOKING FOR WAYS TO NEUTRALIZE YOU.
LOOK HOW FAR WE'VE COME.
SPEAKING F WHICH...
...THE RENDEZVOUS POINT IS JUST THREE CLICKS AHEAD.
WE'RE HERE, THRANE.

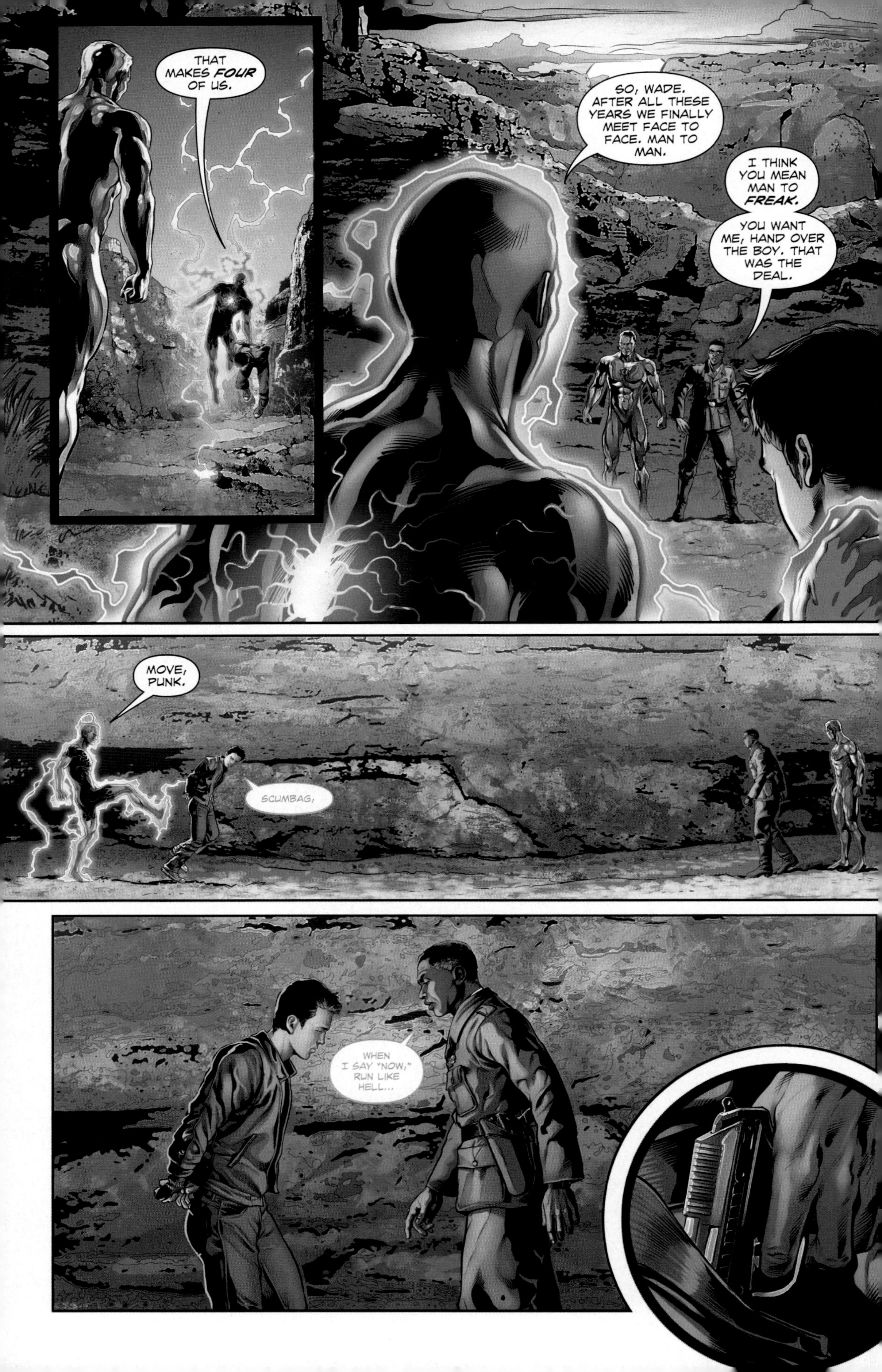
THAT MAKES FOUR OF US.
SO, WADE. AFTER ALL THESE YEARS WE FINALLY MEET FACE TO FACE. MAN TO MAN.
I THINK YOU MEAN MAN TO FREAK.
YOU WANT ME, HAND OVER THE BOY. THAT WAS THE DEAL.
MOVE, PUNK.
SCUMBAG,
WHEN I SAY "NOW," RUN LIKE HELL...

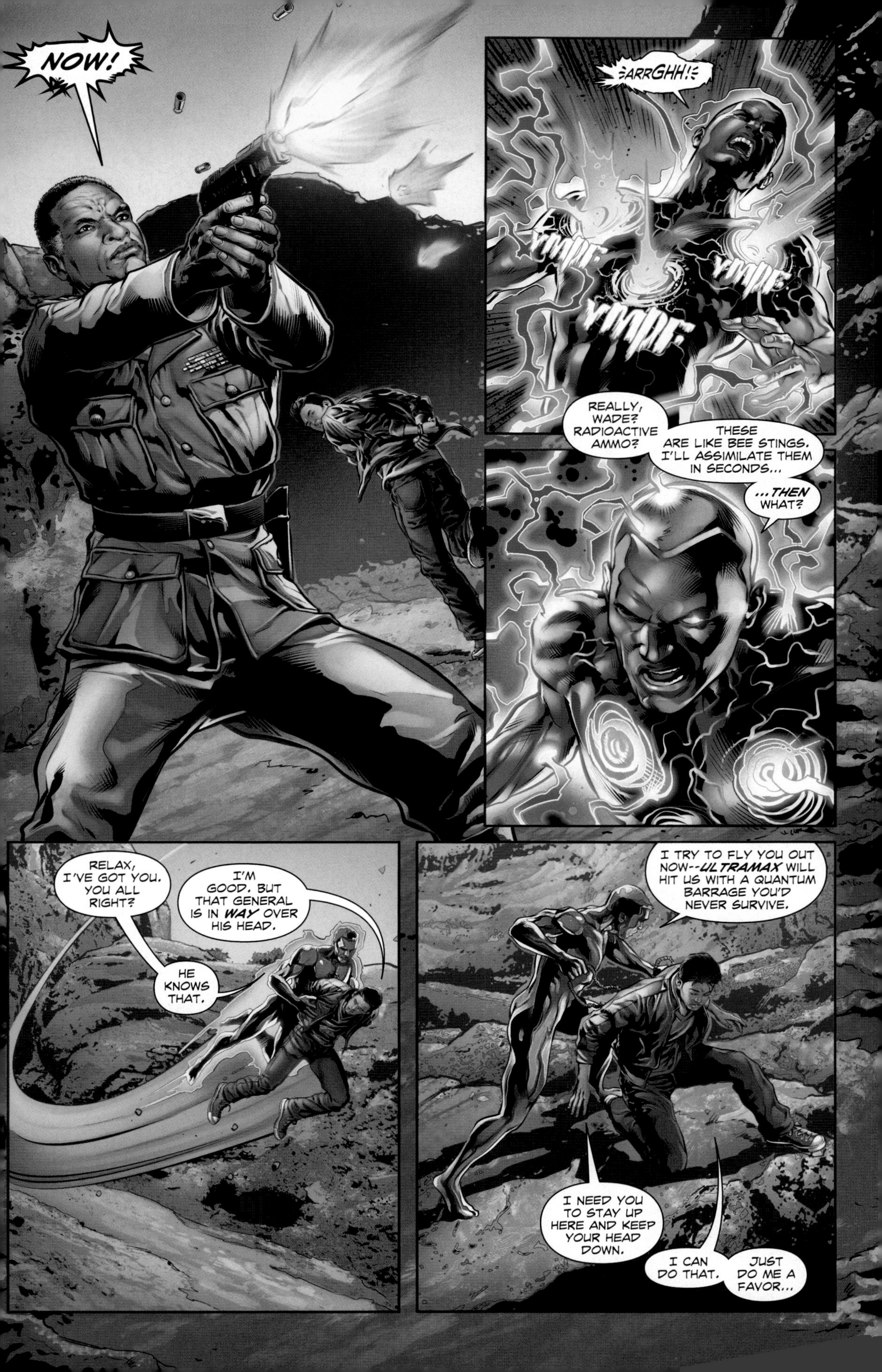
NOW!
ARRGHH!
YMPF
YMPF
YMPF
REALLY, WADE? RADIOACTIVE AMMO?
THESE ARE LIKE BEE STINGS. I'LL ASSIMILATE THEM IN SECONDS...
...THEN WHAT?
RELAX, I'VE GOT YOU. YOU ALL RIGHT?
I'M GOOD. BUT THAT GENERAL IS IN WAY OVER HIS HEAD.
HE KNOWS THAT.
I TRY TO FLY YOU OUT NOW--ULTRAMAX WILL HIT US WITH A QUANTUM BARRAGE YOU'D NEVER SURVIVE.
I NEED YOU TO STAY UP HERE AND KEEP YOUR HEAD DOWN.
I CAN DO THAT.
JUST DO ME A FAVOR...

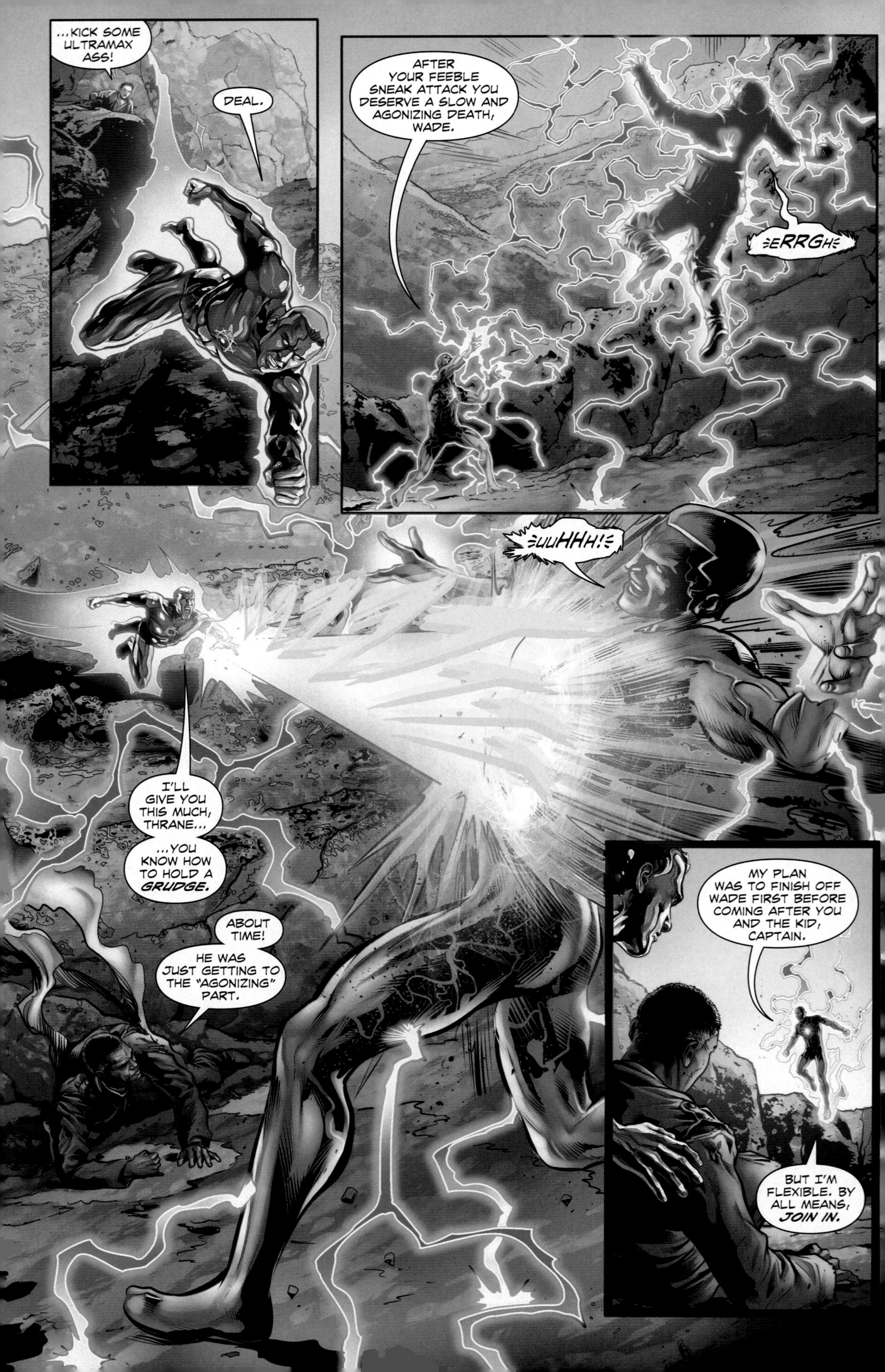
...KICK SOME ULTRAMAX ASS!
DEAL.
AFTER YOUR FEEBLE SNEAK ATTACK YOU DESERVE A SLOW AND AGONIZING DEATH, WADE.
eRRGh
uuHHH!
I'LL GIVE YOU THIS MUCH, THRANE...
...YOU KNOW HOW TO HOLD A GRUDGE.
ABOUT TIME!
HE WAS JUST GETTING TO THE "AGONIZING" PART.
MY PLAN WAS TO FINISH OFF WADE FIRST BEFORE COMING AFTER YOU AND THE KID, CAPTAIN.
BUT I'M FLEXIBLE. BY ALL MEANS, JOIN IN.

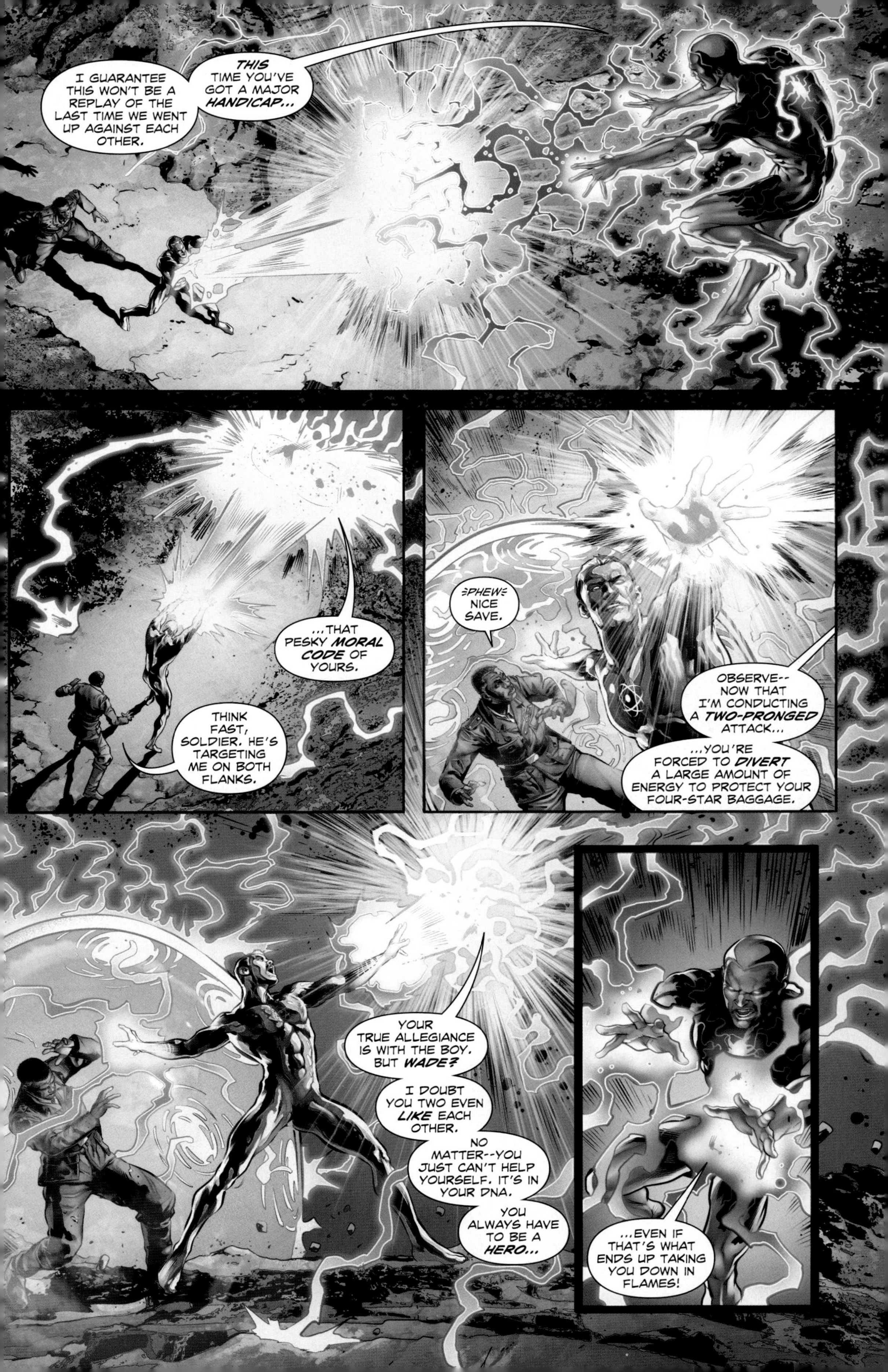
I GUARANTEE THIS WON'T BE A REPLAY OF THE LAST TIME WE WENT UP AGAINST EACH OTHER.
THIS TIME YOU'VE GOT A MAJOR HANDICAP...
...THAT PESKY MORAL CODE OF YOURS.
THINK FAST, SOLDIER. HE'S TARGETING ME ON BOTH FLANKS.
PHEW NICE SAVE.
OBSERVE-- NOW THAT I'M CONDUCTING A TWO-PRONGED ATTACK...
...YOU'RE FORCED TO DIVERT A LARGE AMOUNT OF ENERGY TO PROTECT YOUR FOUR-STAR BAGGAGE.
YOUR TRUE ALLEGIANCE IS WITH THE BOY. BUT WADE?
I DOUBT YOU TWO EVEN LIKE EACH OTHER.
NO MATTER--YOU JUST CAN'T HELP YOURSELF. IT'S IN YOUR DNA.
YOU ALWAYS HAVE TO BE A HERO...
...EVEN IF THAT'S WHAT ENDS UP TAKING YOU DOWN IN FLAMES!

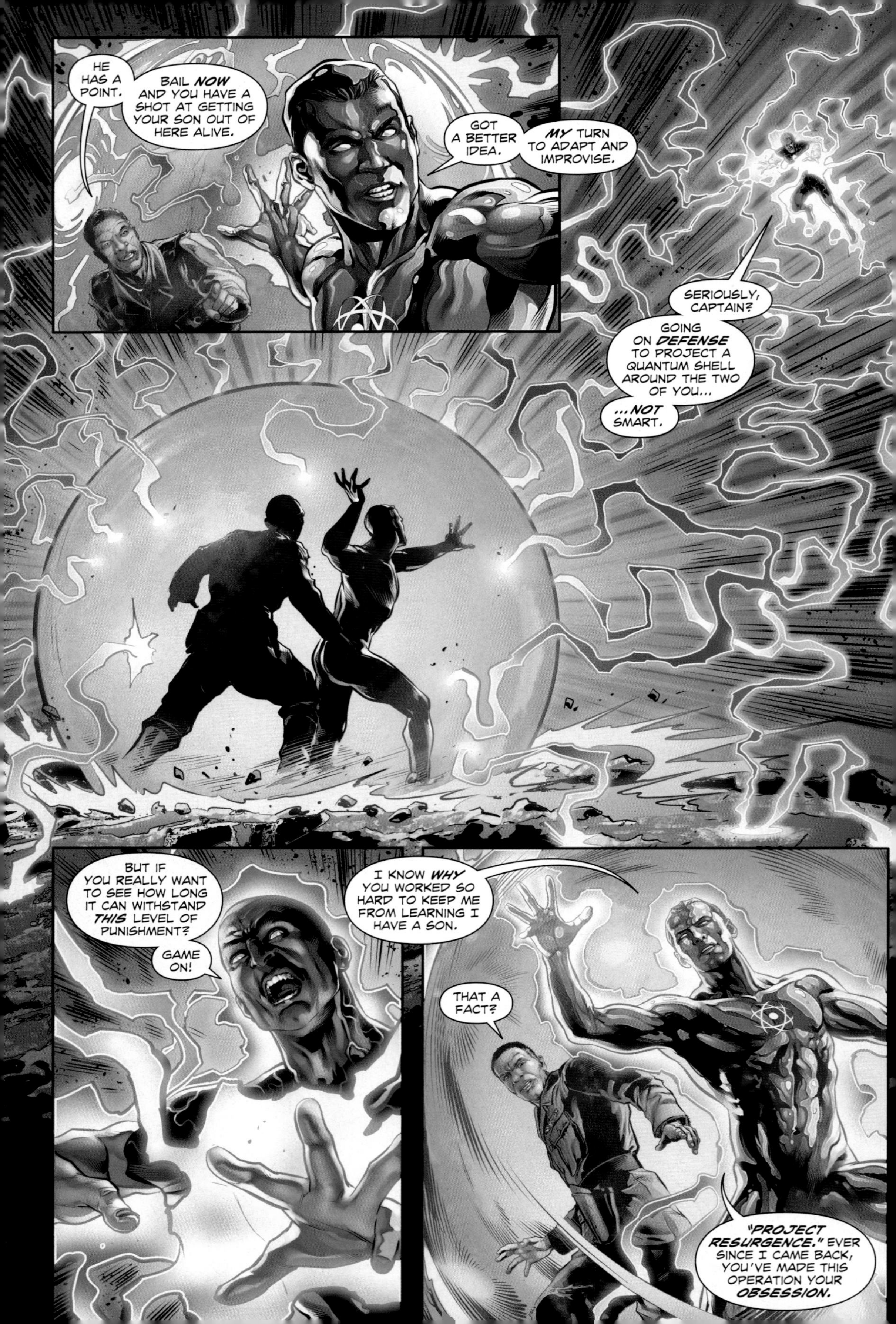
HE HAS A POINT.
BAIL NOW AND YOU HAVE A SHOT AT GETTING YOUR SON OUT OF HERE ALIVE.
GOT A BETTER IDEA.
MY TURN TO ADAPT AND IMPROVISE.
SERIOUSLY, CAPTAIN?
GOING ON DEFENSE TO PROJECT A QUANTUM SHELL AROUND THE TWO OF YOU...
...NOT SMART.
BUT IF YOU REALLY WANT TO SEE HOW LONG IT CAN WITHSTAND THIS LEVEL OF PUNISHMENT?
GAME ON!
I KNOW WHY YOU WORKED SO HARD TO KEEP ME FROM LEARNING I HAVE A SON.
THAT A FACT?
"PROJECT RESURGENCE." EVER SINCE I CAME BACK, YOU'VE MADE THIS OPERATION YOUR OBSESSION.

SINCE OUR LAST RUN-IN, I'VE LEARNED SOME NEW TRICKS--LIKE HOW TO SPEED-SIPHON ENERGY STREAMS FROM THE QUANTUM FIELD.

JUST A MATTER OF SECONDS NOW BEFORE THEY BURST YOUR *BUBBLE!*

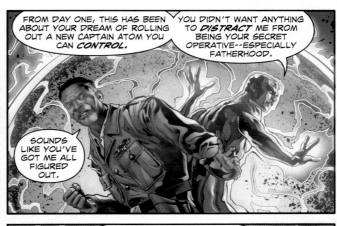

FROM DAY ONE, THIS HAS BEEN ABOUT YOUR DREAM OF ROLLING OUT A NEW CAPTAIN ATOM YOU CAN *CONTROL.*

YOU DIDN'T WANT ANYTHING TO *DISTRACT* ME FROM BEING YOUR SECRET OPERATIVE--ESPECIALLY FATHERHOOD.

SOUNDS LIKE YOU'VE GOT ME ALL FIGURED OUT.

NOW WHY DON'T YOU FIGURE A WAY *OUT* OF THIS MESS BEFORE IT'S TOO LATE FOR BOTH OF US?

ALREADY ON IT.

FOR THE PAST FEW MINUTES ULTRAMAX HAS BEEN STEADILY *AMPING UP* HIS QUANTUM ENERGY BOMBARDMENT...

...JUST WHAT I WAS *COUNTING* ON.

NOW BRACE YOURSELF FOR ONE LAST CHANGE-UP.

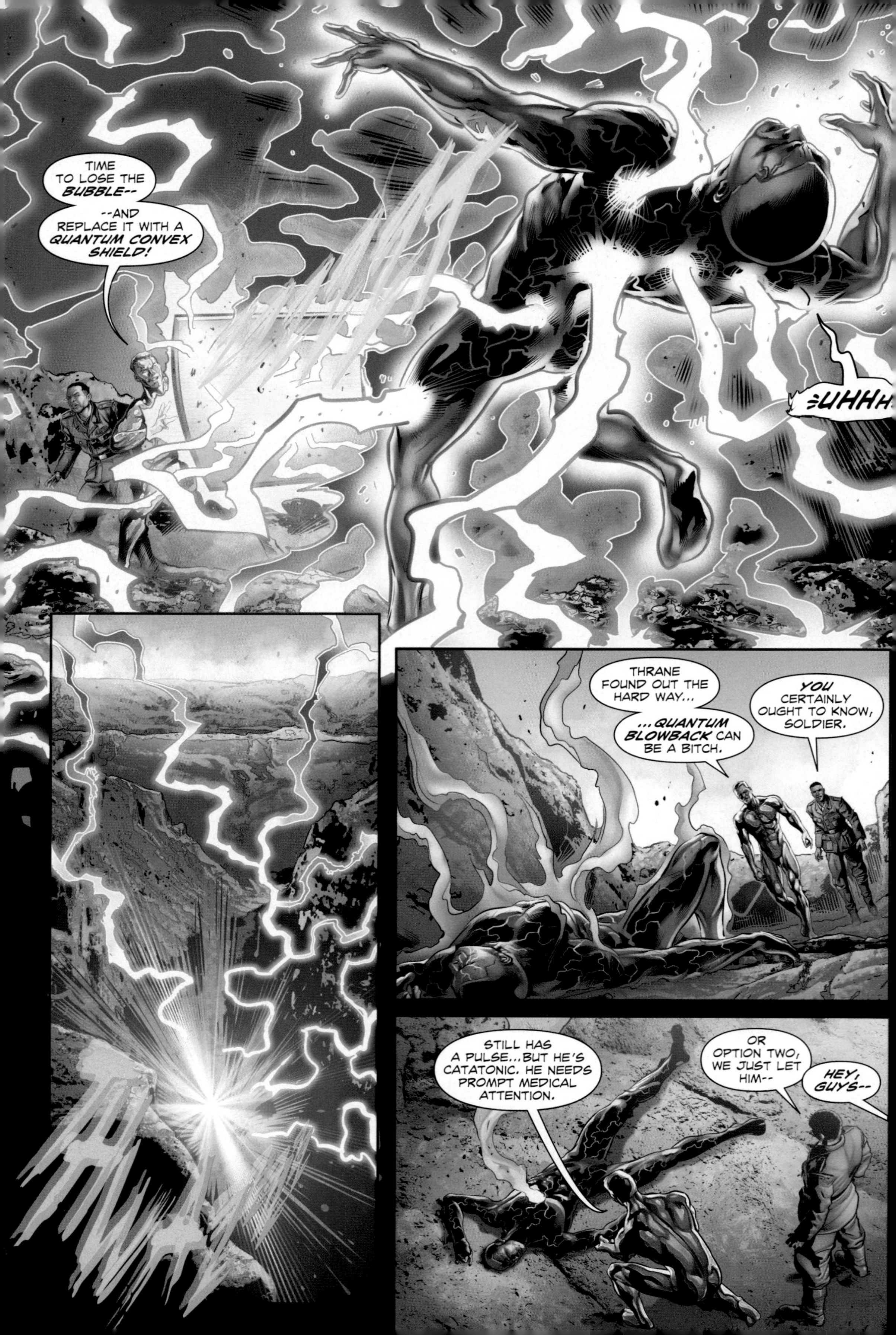
TIME TO LOSE THE BUBBLE--
--AND REPLACE IT WITH A QUANTUM CONVEX SHIELD!
UHHH
THRANE FOUND OUT THE HARD WAY...
...QUANTUM BLOWBACK CAN BE A BITCH.
YOU CERTAINLY OUGHT TO KNOW, SOLDIER.
STILL HAS A PULSE...BUT HE'S CATATONIC. HE NEEDS PROMPT MEDICAL ATTENTION.
OR OPTION TWO, WE JUST LET HIM--
HEY, GUYS--

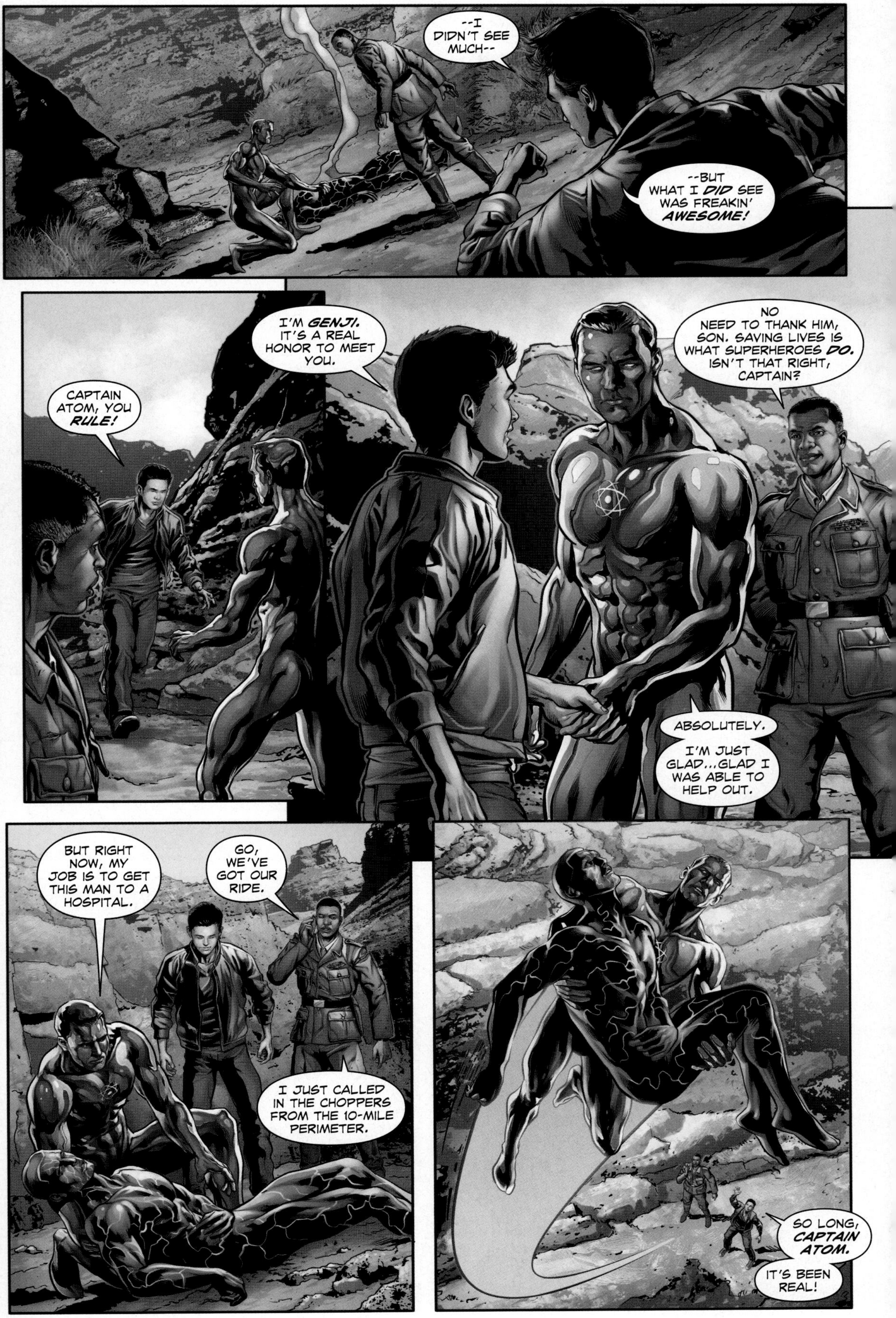
--I DIDN'T SEE MUCH--
--BUT WHAT I *DID* SEE WAS FREAKIN' ***AWESOME!***
CAPTAIN ATOM, YOU ***RULE!***
I'M ***GENJI.*** IT'S A REAL HONOR TO MEET YOU.
NO NEED TO THANK HIM, SON. SAVING LIVES IS WHAT SUPERHEROES ***DO.*** ISN'T THAT RIGHT, CAPTAIN?
ABSOLUTELY.
I'M JUST GLAD...GLAD I WAS ABLE TO HELP OUT.
BUT RIGHT NOW, MY JOB IS TO GET THIS MAN TO A HOSPITAL.
GO, WE'VE GOT OUR RIDE.
I JUST CALLED IN THE CHOPPERS FROM THE 10-MILE PERIMETER.
SO LONG, ***CAPTAIN ATOM.***
IT'S BEEN REAL!

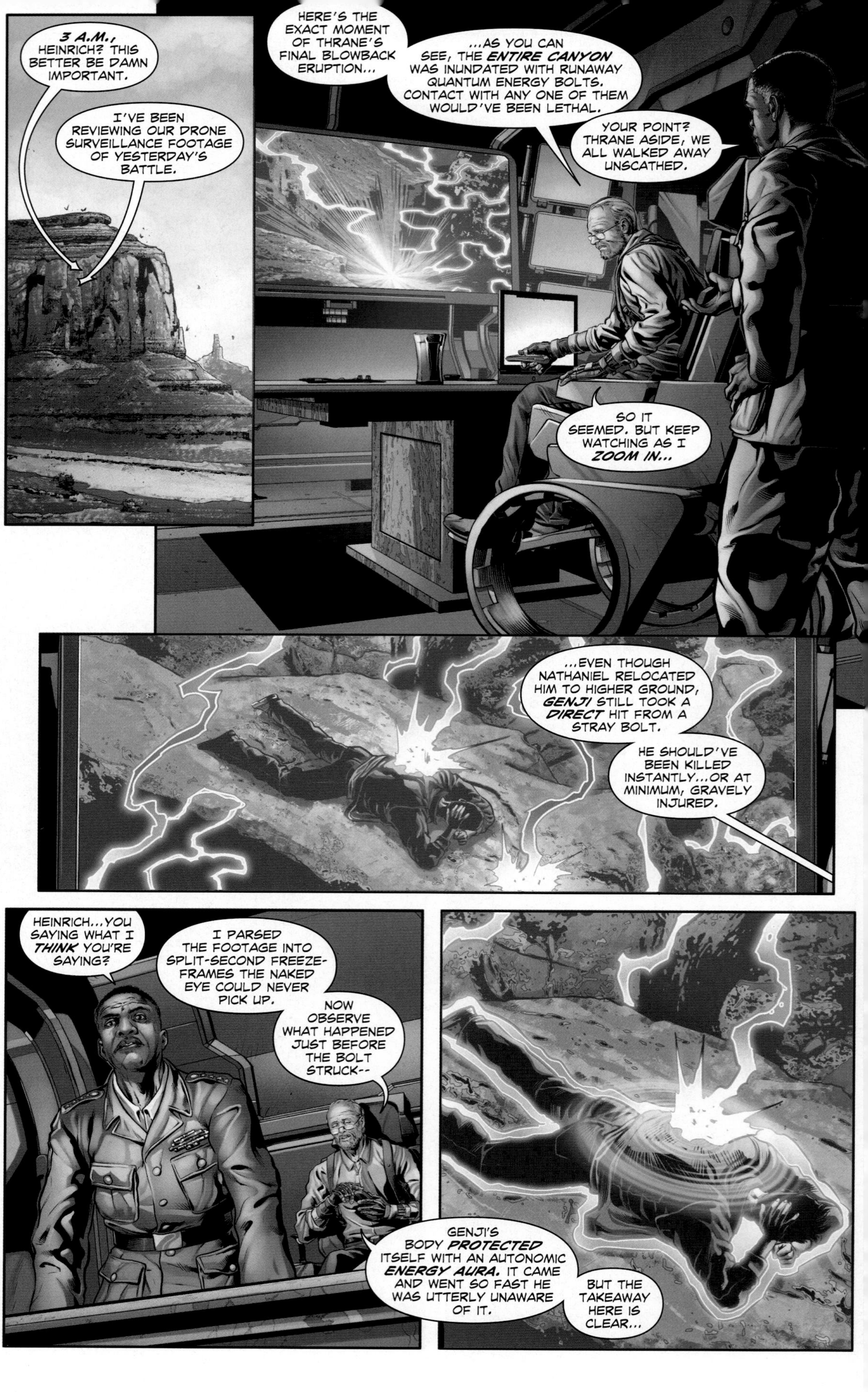
3 A.M., HEINRICH? THIS BETTER BE DAMN IMPORTANT.
I'VE BEEN REVIEWING OUR DRONE SURVEILLANCE FOOTAGE OF YESTERDAY'S BATTLE.
HERE'S THE EXACT MOMENT OF THRANE'S FINAL BLOWBACK ERUPTION...
...AS YOU CAN SEE, THE ENTIRE CANYON WAS INUNDATED WITH RUNAWAY QUANTUM ENERGY BOLTS. CONTACT WITH ANY ONE OF THEM WOULD'VE BEEN LETHAL.
YOUR POINT? THRANE ASIDE, WE ALL WALKED AWAY UNSCATHED.
SO IT SEEMED. BUT KEEP WATCHING AS I ZOOM IN...
...EVEN THOUGH NATHANIEL RELOCATED HIM TO HIGHER GROUND, GENJI STILL TOOK A DIRECT HIT FROM A STRAY BOLT.
HE SHOULD'VE BEEN KILLED INSTANTLY...OR AT MINIMUM, GRAVELY INJURED.
HEINRICH...YOU SAYING WHAT I THINK YOU'RE SAYING?
I PARSED THE FOOTAGE INTO SPLIT-SECOND FREEZE-FRAMES THE NAKED EYE COULD NEVER PICK UP.
NOW OBSERVE WHAT HAPPENED JUST BEFORE THE BOLT STRUCK--
GENJI'S BODY PROTECTED ITSELF WITH AN AUTONOMIC ENERGY AURA. IT CAME AND WENT SO FAST HE WAS UTTERLY UNAWARE OF IT.
BUT THE TAKEAWAY HERE IS CLEAR...

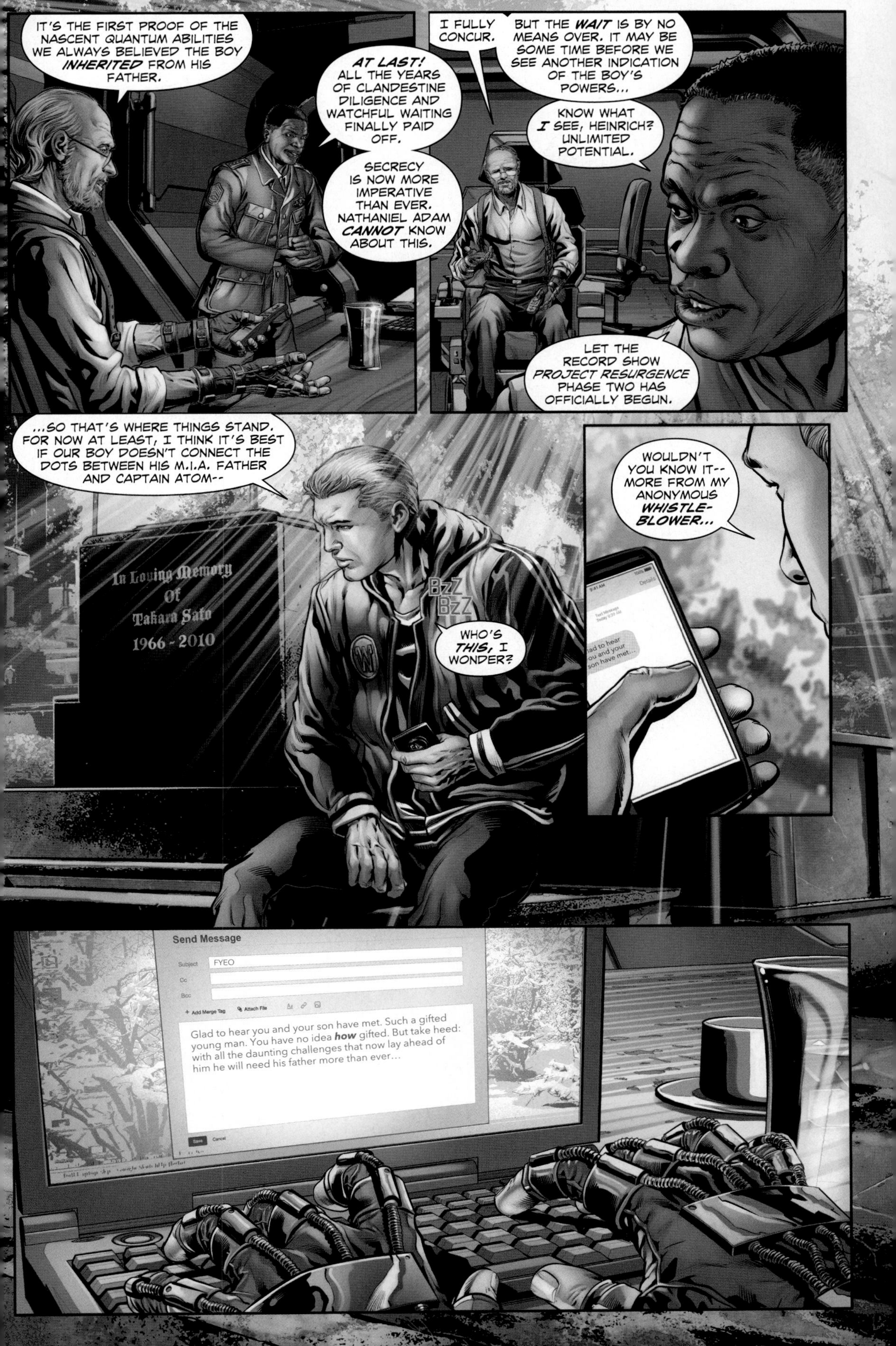
IT'S THE FIRST PROOF OF THE NASCENT QUANTUM ABILITIES WE ALWAYS BELIEVED THE BOY *INHERITED* FROM HIS FATHER.
AT LAST! ALL THE YEARS OF CLANDESTINE DILIGENCE AND WATCHFUL WAITING FINALLY PAID OFF.
SECRECY IS NOW MORE IMPERATIVE THAN EVER. NATHANIEL ADAM *CANNOT* KNOW ABOUT THIS.
I FULLY CONCUR.
BUT THE *WAIT* IS BY NO MEANS OVER. IT MAY BE SOME TIME BEFORE WE SEE ANOTHER INDICATION OF THE BOY'S POWERS...
KNOW WHAT *I* SEE, HEINRICH? UNLIMITED POTENTIAL.
LET THE RECORD SHOW *PROJECT RESURGENCE* PHASE TWO HAS OFFICIALLY BEGUN.
...SO THAT'S WHERE THINGS STAND. FOR NOW AT LEAST, I THINK IT'S BEST IF OUR BOY DOESN'T CONNECT THE DOTS BETWEEN HIS M.I.A. FATHER AND CAPTAIN ATOM--
In Loving Memory Of Takara Sato 1966 - 2010
BZZ BZZ
WHO'S *THIS,* I WONDER?
WOULDN'T YOU KNOW IT-- MORE FROM MY ANONYMOUS *WHISTLE-BLOWER...*
9:41 AM
100%
Details
lad to hear ou and your son have met...
Send Message
Subject
FYEO
Cc
Bcc
+ Add Merge Tag
Attach File
Glad to hear you and your son have met. Such a gifted young man. You have no idea **how** gifted. But take heed: with all the daunting challenges that now lay ahead of him he will need his father more than ever...
Cancel

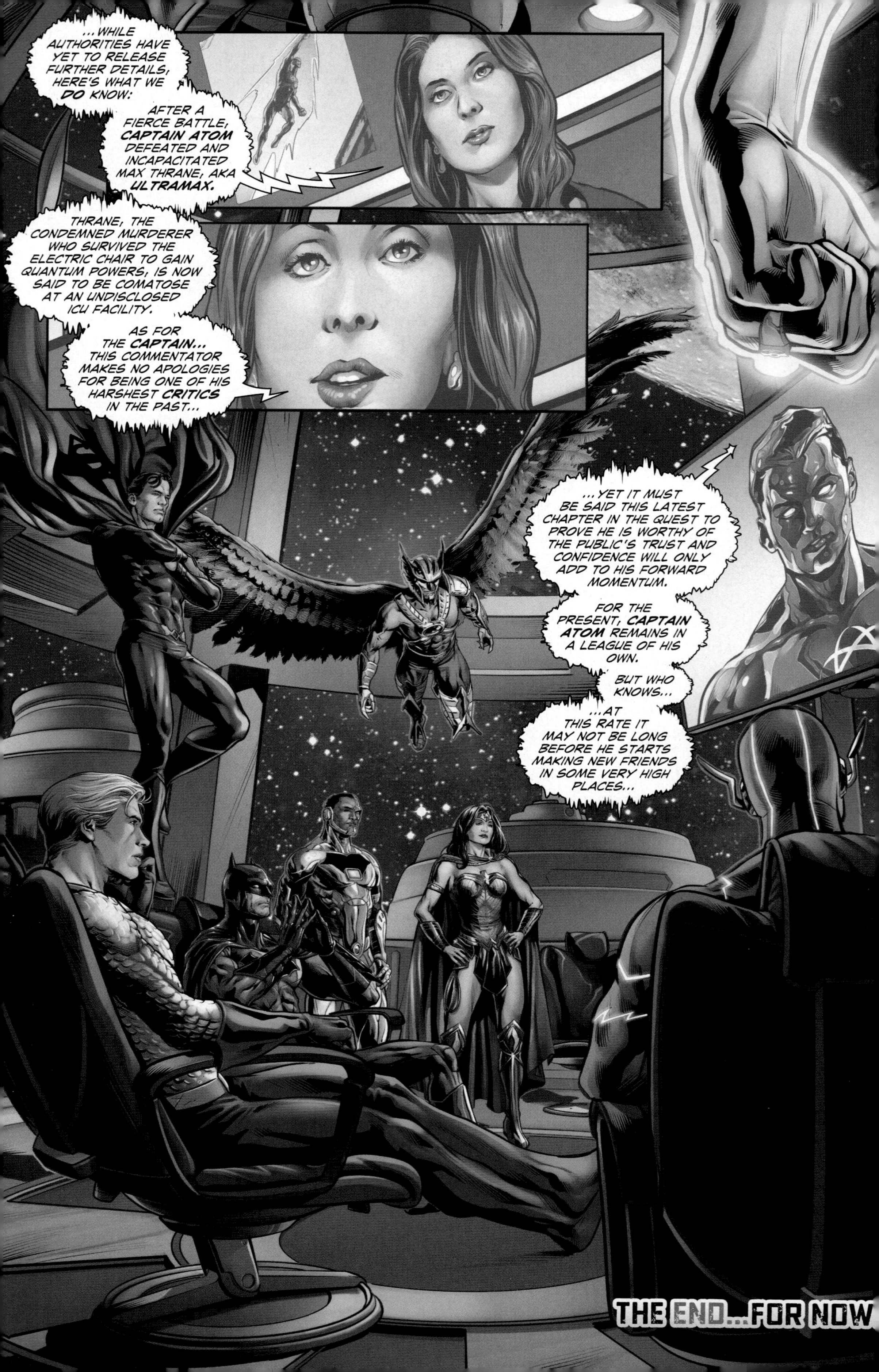
...WHILE AUTHORITIES HAVE YET TO RELEASE FURTHER DETAILS, HERE'S WHAT WE DO KNOW:
AFTER A FIERCE BATTLE, CAPTAIN ATOM DEFEATED AND INCAPACITATED MAX THRANE, AKA ULTRAMAX.
THRANE, THE CONDEMNED MURDERER WHO SURVIVED THE ELECTRIC CHAIR TO GAIN QUANTUM POWERS, IS NOW SAID TO BE COMATOSE AT AN UNDISCLOSED ICU FACILITY.
AS FOR THE CAPTAIN... THIS COMMENTATOR MAKES NO APOLOGIES FOR BEING ONE OF HIS HARSHEST CRITICS IN THE PAST...
...YET IT MUST BE SAID THIS LATEST CHAPTER IN THE QUEST TO PROVE HE IS WORTHY OF THE PUBLIC'S TRUST AND CONFIDENCE WILL ONLY ADD TO HIS FORWARD MOMENTUM.
FOR THE PRESENT, CAPTAIN ATOM REMAINS IN A LEAGUE OF HIS OWN.
BUT WHO KNOWS...
...AT THIS RATE IT MAY NOT BE LONG BEFORE HE STARTS MAKING NEW FRIENDS IN SOME VERY HIGH PLACES...
THE END...FOR NOW

THE FALL AND RISE OF CAPTAIN ATOM

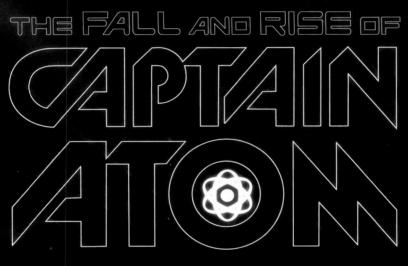

SKETCHBOOK

BOOK CAPT. ATOM ISSUE# 5 DATE 1-10-2017

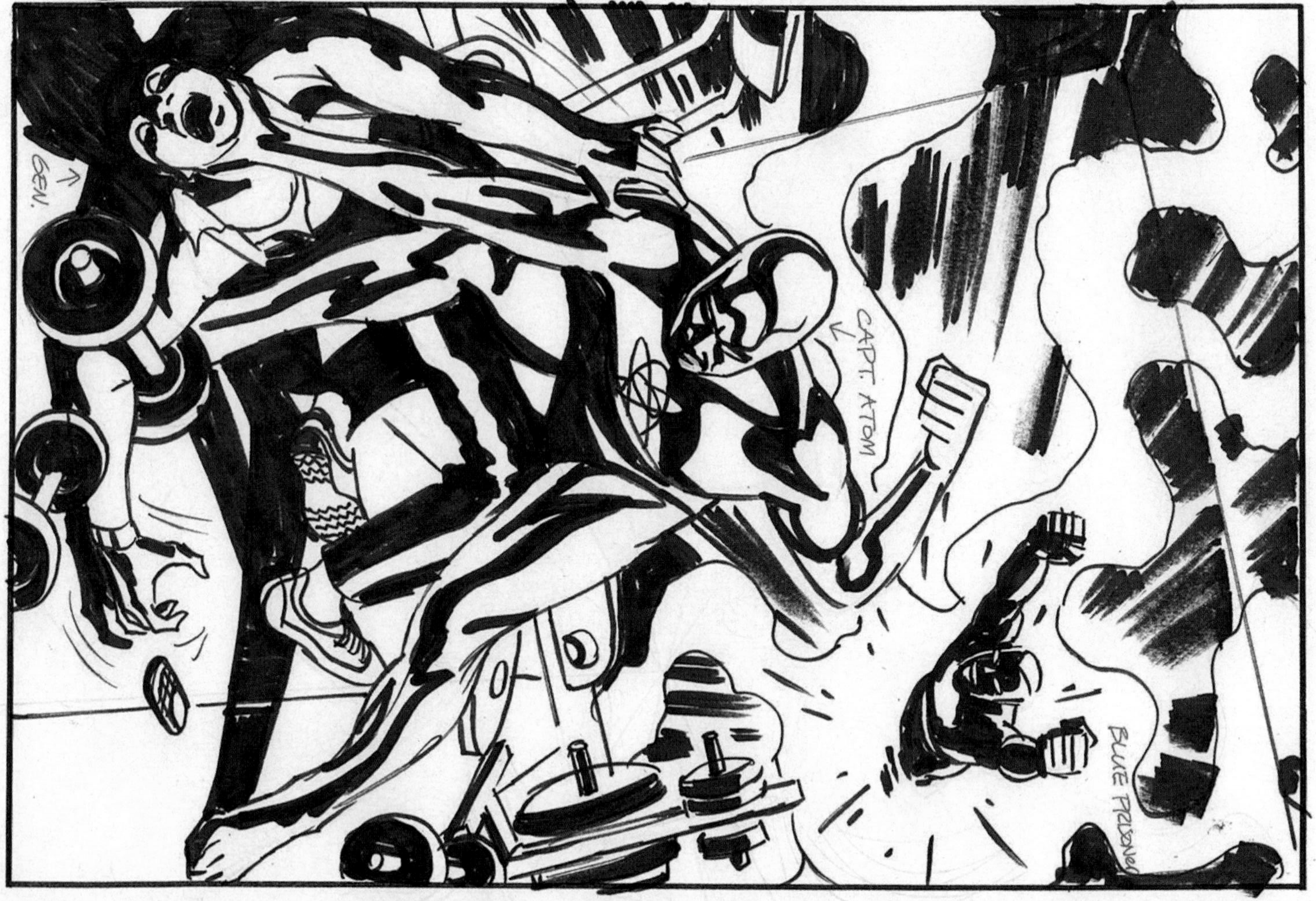
GEN.
CAPT. ATOM
BLUE PRISONER

ALTERNATIVE POSING COVER

BOOK CAPTAIN ATOM ISSUE# 5 DATE Jan. 10 2017

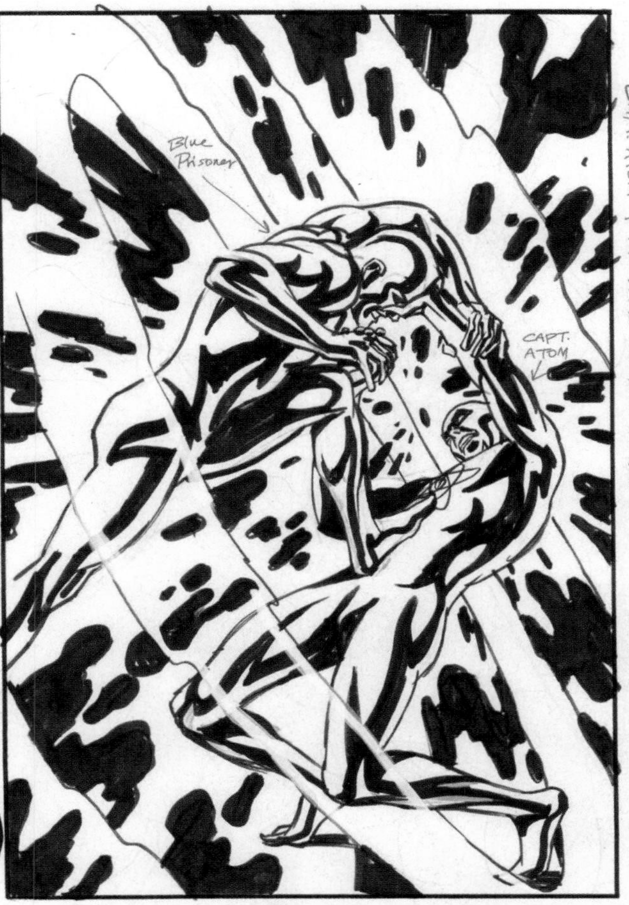
Blue Prisoner
CAPT. ATOM

"CAPT. ATOM & HIS BLUE NEMESIS BATTLE WITHIN AN ALTERNATE DIMENSION."

BOOK CAPTAIN ATOM ISSUE# 5 DATE Jan 10, 2017

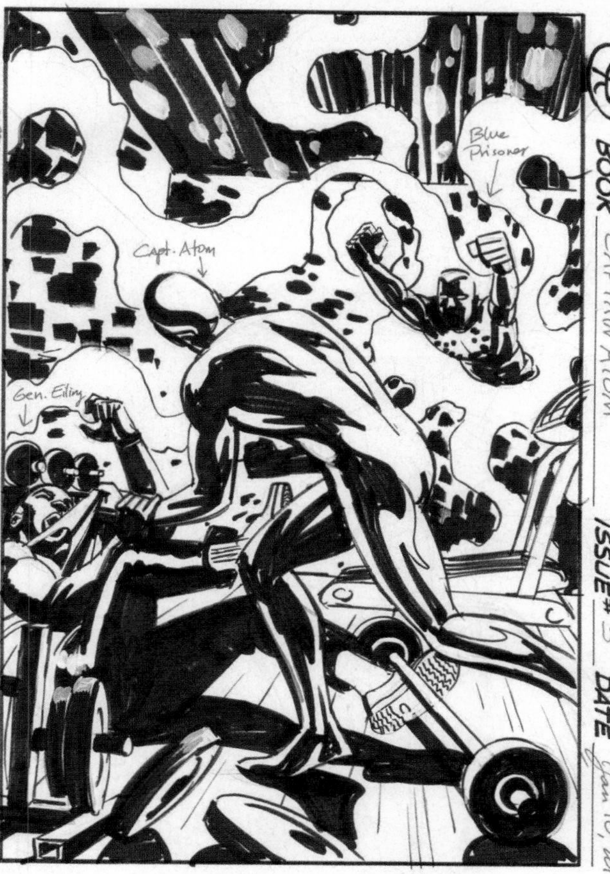
Blue Prisoner
Capt. Atom
Gen. Eiling

"Blue Prisoner breaches wall of General Eiling's workout space, as Atom interrogates him about his son."

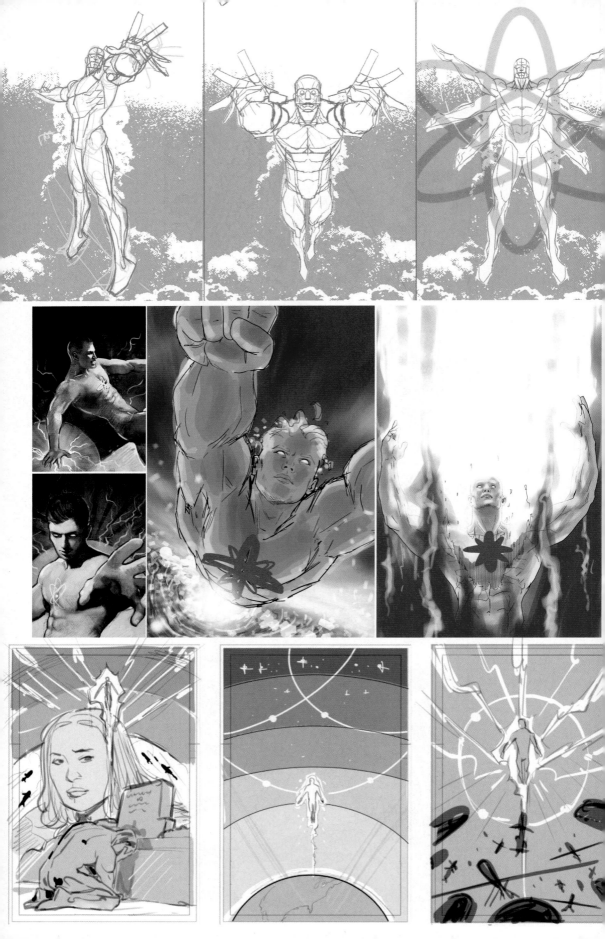

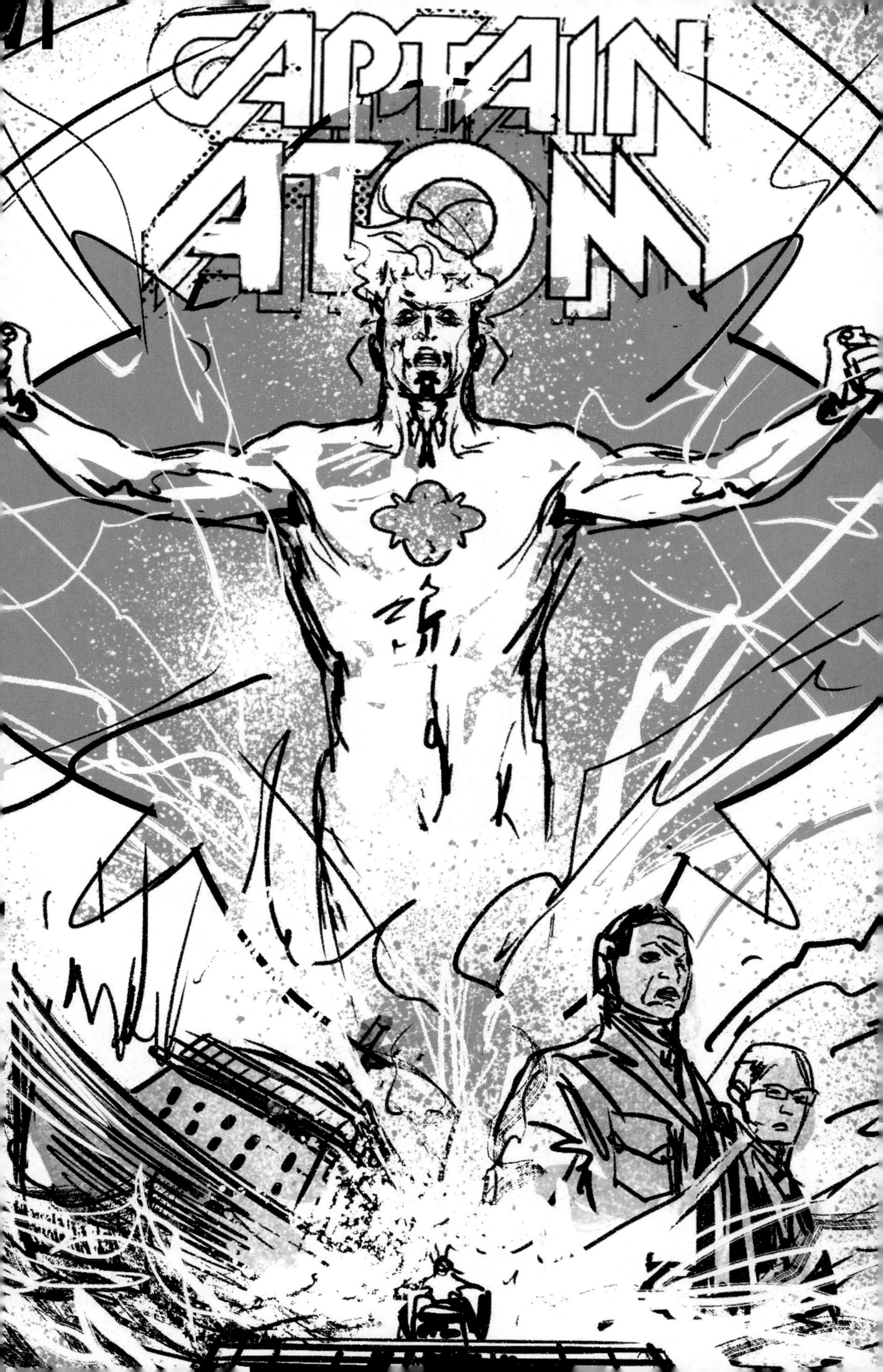
CAPTAIN
ATOM

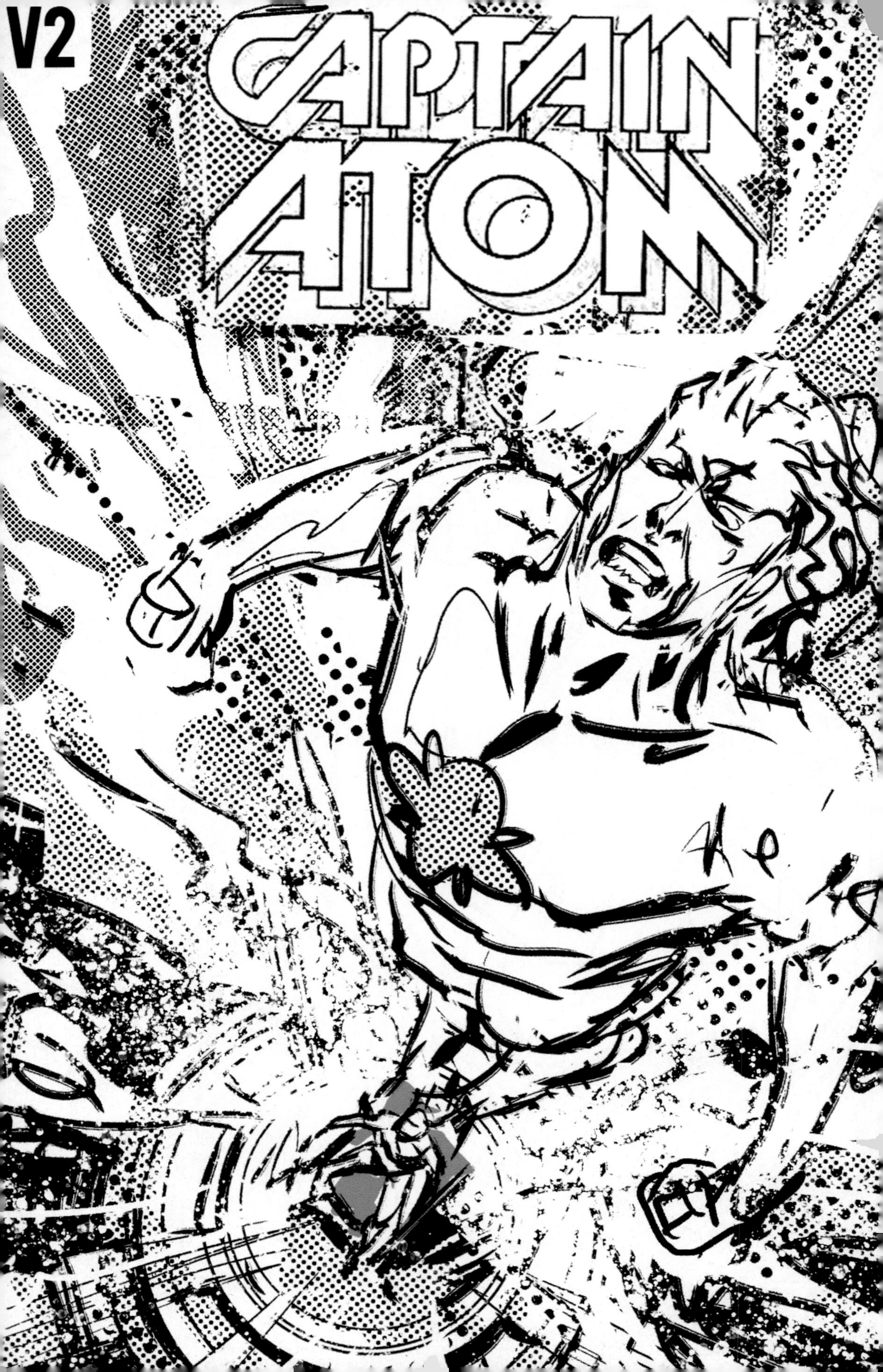
V2
CAPTAIN
ATOM